This is an analysis of the fiction of Nathaniel Hawthorne and his perception of history. In his study, Charles Swann ranges over the whole of Hawthorne's literary career and gives proper weight to the unfinished work. Hawthorne saw history as a struggle between the authoritative claims of tradition on the one hand and the conflicting but equally valid claims of the desires for revolutionary transformation on the other. To evaluate Hawthorne's view of history, Swann provides close readings of such key shorter works as "Alice Doane's Appeal" and "Main Street," as well as the most detailed analysis to date of the unfinished works *The American Claimant Manuscripts* and *The Elixir of Life Manuscripts*. This study asks us to explore how Hawthorne presents and interprets history through his fiction: for example, the history of crucial sins of the past (and the contemporary placing of such sins) in "Alice Doane's Appeal", the problematic nature of the American Revolution in *The Elixir of Life Manuscripts* and the role of society in *The Scarlet Letter*.

Cambridge Studies in American Literature and Culture 52

# Nathaniel Hawthorne

Cambridge Studies in American Literature and Culture

Editor: Albert Gelpi, *Stanford University*

*Series list continues on p. 283*

# Nathaniel Hawthorne
## Tradition and revolution

*CHARLES SWANN*

*University of Keele*

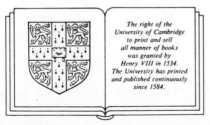

The right of the
University of Cambridge
to print and sell
all manner of books
was granted by
Henry VIII in 1534.
The University has printed
and published continuously
since 1584.

*CAMBRIDGE UNIVERSITY PRESS*

*CAMBRIDGE*
*NEW YORK   PORT CHESTER*
*MELBOURNE   SYDNEY*

Published by the Press Syndicate of the University of Cambridge
The Pitt Building, Trumpington Street, Cambridge CB2 1RP
40 West 20th Street, New York, NY 10011–4211, USA
10 Stamford Road, Oakleigh, Melbourne 3166, Australia

© Cambridge University Press 1991

First published 1991

Printed in Great Britain at the University Press, Cambridge

*British Library cataloguing in publication data*

Swann, Charles
  Nathaniel Hawthorne: tradition and revolution. –
  (Cambridge studies in American literature and culture).
  1. Fiction in English. American writers. Hawthorne,
  Nathaniel, 1804–1864
  1. Title
  813.3

*Library of Congress cataloguing in publication data*

Swann, Charles.
    Nathaniel Hawthorne, tradition and revolution / Charles Swann.
        p.    cm. – (Cambridge studies in American literature and
    culture)
    Includes bibliographical references (pp. 260–279) and index.
    ISBN 0-521-36552-X (hardback)
      1. Hawthorne, Nathaniel, 1804–1864 Knowledge–History.
    2. Hawthorne, Nathaniel, 1804–1864–Criticism and interpretation.
    3. Historical fiction, American.–History and criticism.    1. Title
    11. Series.
    PS1892.HS9    1991
813'.3—dc20    90-2688    CIP

ISBN 0 521 36552 X hardback

SE

# Contents

# Acknowledgements

My first and greatest debt is to Raymond Williams – to whom this book is dedicated. My next is to Keele University and to the staff and students of its American Studies Department – particularly to Karen Harrison and Martin Crawford but especially to Richard Godden. I am also very grateful to Arnold Goldman, Richard Gray and George Dekker – as I am to the *Journal of American Studies, Literature and History* and *The Modern Language Review* for first allowing parts of this to see the light of day. In common with many another Cambridge University Press author I owe a lot to Andrew Brown.

# Note on the texts

Where possible I have used the Library of America editions of Hawthorne (and anyone in the UK interested in American literature owes Cambridge University Press a large debt for making those editions available here) – *The Novels* and *The Tales and Sketches* (that second including *A Wonder Book for Girls and Boys* and *Tanglewood Tales*). The first is edited by Millicent Bell and the second by Roy Harvey Pearce. These volumes have the advantage of the texts established by the editors of the Centenary Edition of Hawthorne's works (Ohio State University Press, 1962–   ) with the considerable additional advantage that they are portable, even pocketable. When the Library of America has failed me, I have retreated to the Centenary Edition. And it has to be said that it is thanks to Edward H. Davidson, Claude M. Simpson and L. Neal Smith, the editors of the volumes containing the unfinished works now known as *The American Claimant* and *The Elixir of Life Manuscripts*, that any real reading (let alone criticism) of those wonderful fictions can be done. However, the Centenary Edition is still an unfinished project, and this means that I have had to go to George Parson Lathrop's Riverside Edition (Boston and New York; Houghton, Mifflin and Company, 1883) for the life of Franklin Pierce and "Chiefly About War Matters." The works contained by the Library of America volumes are referred to respectively as N and T&S if there is any doubt about which volume is being referred to; those in the Ohio edition by Roman numerals; and for the life of Pierce and "War Matters," I have used the Arabic numeral: 12.

# 1

## Tradition and revolution

The seeds of this book were sown some years ago when I was lucky enough to acquire an incomplete set of Lathrop's Riverside Edition of Hawthorne's works. That edition has very properly come under attack for such matters as bad texts, but it did at least make available many of Hawthorne's writings which were – and to an extent still are – not easily to be found elsewhere. Incomplete though the set was, it contained volumes 11 and 12. In the first I discovered *Septimius Felton*, one of the unfinished fictions of Hawthorne's last phase; in the second, "Alice Doane's Appeal" (published in 1835 though existing in some form as early as 1829, before Hawthorne had published anything but *Fanshawe*), and "Chiefly About War Matters" (1862) – as well as the campaign biography of Franklin Pierce (1852). The Pierce work is, of course, scarcely a masterpiece even in the not exactly competitive field of presidential campaign biographies, but it served as a forcible reminder of the sheer range of Hawthorne's literary enterprises. However, the first three works seemed to me – not only startlingly brilliant works in their own right but also key works for any understanding of Hawthorne's literary career, and not only because they so conveniently come so near the beginning and ending of that career.

When I turned to the critics for help in appreciating these splendid works, I was largely disappointed – much as I had been bemused to find that great and profoundly historical fiction, *The Scarlet Letter*, a key item of evidence in the a-historical Romance theory of American literature as propounded by Richard Chase *et al.*[1] There was remarkably little on *Septimius*, "Alice Doane" or "War Matters" in the early 1970s – and that little was, almost without exception, notably unenthusiastic. Things have improved on *The Scarlet Letter* front as far as Romance theory is concerned, and "Alice Doane's Appeal" has, to an extent, emerged from the shadows. Yet it still tends to be damned with faint praise even by such a critic as Michael Colacurcio whose admirable if sometimes overpowering commitment to Hawthorne as moral historian should, it might be thought, predispose him to celebrate such a tale. However, Colacurcio judges that "For all that critical patience can do to answer the charge of incoherence or lack of control, it remains that the admixture of argumentation is scarcely a beauty; historical critics may find it a godsend, but ordinary readers can hardly learn to love it." This is, from such a source, a hard judgement indeed, for here is a man who thinks that "The Minister's Black Veil" is a story which "actually enjoins its readers to acquaint himself with certain election sermons preached 'during Belcher's administration.'" Nor is this a hostile criticism. In his celebratory seventy-one page chapter on the story, Colacurcio returns to the point: "the story obviously suggests that the responsible reader [of "The Minister's Black Veil"] ought" to read all twelve sermons delivered before Belcher. Now this is historicism running riot. How else is his judgement on "The Maypole of Merrymount" to be placed – that, unless all the available sources have been read closely, "the story itself is virtually insignificant"?[2] One doesn't have to be a structuralist or a New Critic to find this worrying. What, I wonder does Colacurcio make of all the praise that has come from critics who cannot claim any informed knowledge of the sources? But, if Colacurcio expects this degree of sophisticated historical knowledge to be acquired by any fair-minded reader, then "Alice Doane's Appeal" would seem to make almost impossible demands on *any* reader. Yet this was not my experience. When I first read the story, all I knew about the Salem witchcraft cases of 1692 were vague memories of Arthur Miller's *The Crucible* (which, it may be felt, meant that I knew less than nothing) and yet I found it fascinating. While historical knowledge certainly is crucial for a full understanding of the tale, even on a first reading it should be clear that Hawthorne is overtly concerned with what sort of a writer he should be, discussing how he should use history when faced by an audience who know little of and care less for the past.

But whatever the critical fate of that early story, when we turn to the end of Hawthorne's career, we find that things have remained much the same. Despite the monumental work that went into the Centenary editions of *The American Claimant Manuscripts* and *The Elixir of Life Manuscripts*, commentators have in general seemed willing to see those volumes as books better left closed. There is very little on these works at all, and what there is still very largely takes its tone from E.H. Davidson's unenthusiastic descriptions.[3] Profoundly grateful though I am to his pioneering critical and editorial work, I cannot share his evaluation. What he sees as practically unredeemed failures seem to me (as I try to argue in the relevant chapters) to be extremely ambitious and consistently fascinating attempts by Hawthorne to develop a new kind of fiction which would go beyond his achievements of the 1850s. "Chiefly About War Matters" is in still worse case. The Centenary edition has yet to include it and, indeed, I am not aware that there has been any recent reprinting of this witty and tough-minded piece of (un)civil-war reporting. Yet even a cursory reading of this poised and perceptive piece should make it impossible for anyone to believe that Hawthorne's failure to complete the unfinished novels was due in any way to failing intellectual powers, showing as it does a remarkable power to deal with materials at once contemporary and deeply disturbing – even threatening.

The three works share in their different ways a recognition of the centrality of history for an understanding of the world. The historical sense is central to almost all of Hawthorne's greatest achievements, whether it is the ancient history of the colonies in "Alice Doane's Appeal," or the modern history of the American Revolution in *Septimius Felton*, or the absolutely contemporary history of "War Matters" which may be the end of the history of the Union. And at the same time this is connected with the question of writing. The subtitle of "Alice Doane" could be "How and How Not to Tell a Story," Septimius struggles to interpret an alchemical text, and much of the ironic subtlety of "War Matters" comes from Hawthorne's mimicking in his footnotes the tone of a very respectable editor who has far too much deference for the powers that be. To have read "Alice Doane" and *Septimius Felton* in juxtaposition was forcibly to see Hawthorne's profound and developing concern with history – history as composed of the conflicting claims of tradition and revolution, history as continuity and attempted rupture, history as a struggle for new beginnings or as a series of returns of that which it had too optimistically been hoped had been escaped from or transcended. There is a constant emphasis on the need to recognize that the past is not dead, while at the same time Hawthorne is equally aware that history is something that can be made, which can, or at least should, take new directions.

Hawthorne's is a profoundly complex position which can in some formulations be made to look like a contradictory or paradoxical one. Perhaps the best known of such judgements is Matthiessen's: "A peculiar kind of social understanding made Hawthorne hold to both the contrasting terms of this paradox of being at once a democrat and a conservative."[4] More relevant for nineteenth century America might be Cooper's comment in *A Letter to His Countrymen*: "Here the democrat is the conservative, and, thank God, he has something worth preserving."[5] But a nineteenth century critic had pointed quite brilliantly to the dialectical nature of Hawthorne's work – and that critic is (of all people) George Parsons Lathrop: "Hawthorne's repose is the acme of motion; and though turning on an axis of conservatism, the radicalism of his mind is irresistible; he is one of the most powerful because unsuspected revolutionists of the world."[6] Hawthorne recognizes the power of tradition. Yet he resists any simplistic celebration of its authority, making it clear that, while it may be perceived as a natural inheritance, it is only too often a selective and highly ideological construct. At the same time he is fascinated by the idea of a (justifiable) desire for a revolutionary break with the past and its values, whether that past be personal or cultural. That fascination is accompanied by a sad, a tragic, recognition on his part that such a break too often cannot be achieved at all or cannot be made without such suffering that the cost may be too high – so high that the original ethical impulse for revolutionary change is or may be subverted, corrupted, thwarted or destroyed. Hester's story, Holgrave's career, and the Blithedale enterprise provide, I shall be arguing, variant examples of this tragic problem, while the most direct statement of his ambivalent fascination with revolution appears in *The Elixir of Life Manuscripts*. Not that the revolutionary impulse is always presented as morally compromised, defeated or destroyed. Though it is rebellion rather than revolution or rehearsal for revolution that is most immediately at issue, it seems to me unquestionable that Hawthorne, while certainly intending his readers to see the past as something that demands complex moral evaluation, means those readers to read the conclusions to such stories as "The Gray Champion," "Endicott and the Red Cross," and – the most complex but perhaps the most revealing case – "My Kinsman, Major Molineux" as exemplifying positive values.

In other words, I have to differ radically from what appears as a recent consensus which, with varying degrees of emphasis, stresses Hawthorne's axis of conservatism and would, I think, regard the description of him as a revolutionist as positively libellous. We are offered a subversive and ironic Hawthorne – one whose subversion turns out to be on behalf of a straightforward conservatism and whose irony is based on or leads to passivity. Thus, Frederick Newberry, for example, claiming Colacurcio in support, argues that "Hawthorne's historiography adamantly resists a patriotic reading in any way commensurate with the democratic ideology of his time" and states that his "was the familiar problem of the classical conservative," going so far as to say that "were we to align him with any political thinker, Edmund Burke would likely come closer than anyone to representing Hawthorne's moral and cultural politics." Sacvan Bercovitch pushes the point further: "Process (for Hawthorne) is a form of partiality that accepts limitation, acknowledges its own incompleteness, and so tends toward tolerance, accommodation, pluralism, acquiescence, inaction." Jonathan Arac speaks of Hawthorne attempting "to separate the artwork from pragmatic concerns" and achieving "of the programmatically willed alienation of the artist." He also contrasts *Uncle Tom's Cabin* as art and propaganda to change your life with *The Scarlet Letter* – art, of course, but also propaganda "*not* to change your life."[7] I fail to recognize this quietist neo-conservative wolf in the sheep's clothing of a (Jacksonian) democrat. A refusal to sentimentalize the past, to see it as unitary in a golden nostalgic haze, is not a commitment to Burkean conservatism – rather the opposite, indeed, if Burke's language about Marie Antoinette is remembered. Nor does such a refusal mean that he does not give a positive valuation not only to the American Revolution but also to earlier episodes in the long revolution of American history such as are dramatized in "The Gray Champion," "Endicott and the Red Cross" and "My Kinsman, Major Molineux." It is not that he saw the American Revolution as an unqualified good but rather as a necessary, even inevitable, tragic action, but not the end of evil, the end of a fallen history that some crude Democratic ideologues may have presented it as. The Revolution is, for him, one crucial act in a still continuing *sequence* of struggling for better things. I certainly do not want to deny that there is a pervasive strain of ironic scepticism in Hawthorne, but I would argue that, for example, the Blithedale enterprise is among other things at once a recognition that, to use Melville's phrase, the Declaration of Independence makes a difference and at the same time a recognition that it has not (yet) made enough of a difference for Americans to escape or transcend the tragedy that, too often, is history.

Arac is anything but alone in using *Uncle Tom's Cabin* to hit Hawthorne over the head – yet we should not be too quick to use this tactic. Is Harriet Beecher Stowe really the figure that modern enlightened opinion should celebrate? I have some sympathy with the views of two of her not illiberal contemporaries, George Eliot and Thomas Wentworth Higginson. Eliot, while praising *Dred*, was worried: "If the negroes are really so very good, slavery has answered as a moral discipline." And she goes on to say that such a view deprives Mrs. Stowe of "the most terribly tragic element in the relation of the two races – the Nemesis lurking in the vices of the oppressed." Higginson hits the same note: "If it is the normal tendency of bondage to produce saints like Uncle Tom, let us offer ourselves at auction immediately."[8] Higginson's statement has particular authority as that of a man who bought a dozen handaxes to break a slave imprisoned in Boston because of the Fugitive Slave Law – asking for, and getting a five per cent discount for cash. God bless Boston! I would, however, agree that *The Scarlet Letter* may well not be propaganda for changing one individual life. Hawthorne shows throughout his work remarkably little interest in individual conversion experiences, an attitude which can appear rather odd if one has placed him in one kind of seemingly tempting Protestant tradition – such as one that might start from or draw upon Bunyan. Indeed, the only approximation to such an experience I can think of is found in the decidedly a-typical "conversion" experience of Donatello (see chapter 19 of *The Marble Faun*: "The Faun's Transformation"). As I argue more fully in my chapter on *The Scarlet Letter*, the ending of the novel invites us to consider that *society* rather than any individual may need a radical transformation, that, indeed, isolated individual transformation is virtually impossible. Is this not what Hester clearly hopes for at the end of the fiction?

> She assured them . . . of her firm belief, that, at some brighter period, when the world should have grown ripe for it, in Heaven's own time, a new truth would be revealed, in order to establish the whole relation between man and woman on a surer ground of mutual happiness.                    (N, 344)

Hester's position is open to criticism – but not the criticism that is often mounted.[9] By its very radicalism it may pre-empt all attempts at piece-meal reform, at building a long revolution. And, if I am right in thinking that Hester is asking for the Second Coming of Christ – only this time as a woman ("The angel and apostle of the coming revelation must be a woman" [N, 344–5]) – then this *may* encourage passivity on society's part as we wait for God to get round to doing the decent and necessary thing. Here, a kind of conservatism can enter by the back door, but it can only do so because the social transformation demanded is so radical, so political, so revolutionary. The passivity, of course, is not inevitable – if society is to *make* way for the Second Coming – and Hester seems to be casting herself as a female John the Baptist. And the clear implication of Hester's statement is that she rejects the Pauline admonition: "Wives, submit yourselves unto your own husbands, as unto the Lord." (Ephesians, v, 22) She is, though, closer to an earlier statement in the same epistle: "We are members one of another." (iv, 25)

It may be said that Hawthorne's attitude to slavery marks him out as at best a culpable quietist. I deplore as much as anyone his attitude as expressed in the life of Pierce – but that single issue does not exhaust his political views, nor can one infer from that the remainder of his views on democracy. Such a study as the excellent *"Agrarians" and "Aristocrats:" Party Political Ideology in the United States 1837–1846* demonstrates in absorbing detail that a genuinely radical commitment to egalitarian democracy by sections of the Democratic party could, alas, almost necessarily co-exist with the less than liberal ideas on the race and slavery issue.[10] It is no doubt to our credit that we have such enlightened views on the race issue – but we have one or two advantages including the fact that we do not have to decide how slavery should be abolished. We have to be careful not to be guilty of presentism. There is another problem, as well. Just what were Hawthorne's views on the issue? The notorious passage from the life of Pierce may seem clear enough – but is it representative or merely tactical?

> Those northern men . . . who deem the great cause of human welfare as [is?] represented and involved in this present hostility against southern institutions, and who conceive that the world stands still except so far as that goes forward, – these, it may be allowed, can scarcely give their sympathy or their confidence to the subject of this memoir. But there is still another view, and probably as wise a one. It looks upon slavery as one of those evils which divine Providence does not leave to be remedied by human contrivances, but which, in its own good time, by some means impossible to be anticipated, but of the simplest and easiest operation, when all its uses have been fulfilled, it causes to vanish like a dream. There is no instance, in all history, of the human will and intellectual having perfected any great moral reform by methods which it adapted to that end; but the progress of the world, at every step, leaves some evil or wrong on the path behind it, which the wisest of mankind, of their own set purpose, could never have found the way to rectify. Whatever contributes to the great cause of good, contributes to all its subdivisions and varieties; and, on this score, the lover of his race, the enthusiast, the philanthropist of whatever theory, might lend his aid to put a man, like the one before us, into the leadership of the world's affairs. (12, 416–17)

Obviously there is here a regrettably large element of – if we close our eyes tight enough, perhaps the problem will go away, though it should be remembered that Melville in the free space of his semi-allegorical fiction, *Mardi*, could come up with nothing better.[11] Presumably the emphasis on will and intellect leaves it open for Hawthorne to remember if not overtly appeal to that great conservative, the heart. There is also an intriguing, if undeveloped, suggestion that the historical changes that actually occur and human plans for change may rarely be identical. But even if this version of "Man's accidents, God's purposes" is being tentatively promoted, Hawthorne cannot – least of all in a piece of writing designed to persuade the reader to act, to vote for Pierce – suggest that it does not matter what we do. And Hawthorne himself had not always chosen a wise passivity on the issue. There is an 1851 letter to his friend of the Custom-House, Zachariah Burchmore: "I have not, as you suggest, the slightest sympathy for the slaves; or, at least, not half as much as for the laboring whites, who, I believe, as a general thing, are ten times worse off than the Southern negros." So far, so much regrettably predictable commonplace, it may be felt. But it gets more interesting: "Still, whenever I am absolutely cornered, I shall go for New England rather than the South; – and this Fugitive Law cornered me. Of course, I knew what I was doing when I signed that Free-Soil document, and bade farewell to all ideas of foreign consulships, or other official stations" (xvi, 456). It is not known what this document was, but it sounds as though Hawthorne (who does not strike me as one of nature's signers of contentious documents) had put his name to a petition which he was convinced would spoil his chances of Democratic patronage. If so, given his appalling financial position at the time, the fact he was a father, and his political visibility after the row about his dismissal from the Custom-House, this would not be without courage.

What much recent criticism seems to have missed is Hawthorne's sheer tough-mindedness, his willingness to accept that the past (to say nothing of the present) is rarely pure, that historical change is not only inevitable but also bound to be marked by moral complexities and ambiguities, yet to take the position that this does not mean that the artist should retreat from history and politics, and indifferent, sit there paring his fingernails à la Stephen Daedalus. I rejoice to concur with George Dekker when he argues that the principal issue in Hawthorne's historical fiction of frontier New England is "national survival and its human cost," that Hawthorne does not "seriously question that his . . . ancestors acted as they sincerely believed necessary or that their epic struggle for survival as a people standing at once together and apart was, in the end, historically justified." He suggests that those historical tales of the seventeenth century make it clear that, whatever the moral inadequacies of that world, from a nineteenth-century perspective no patriotic American reader could wish the course of events in which the Revolution is centrally important to be essentially otherwise.[12] I would have thought that *Liberty Tree*, the final section of Hawthorne's children's history of America, *The Whole History of Grandfather's Chair* (1840), would have shown that Dekker was right. But, given that there have been attempts to incorporate even that into the argument that Hawthorne intends us to regard any positive valuation of the American Revolution with sceptical irony, I offer a gloss on *Grandfather's Chair* from one of Hawthorne's letters to his beloved Sophia. Whatever one's valuation of those letters (I find them too syrupy), they are very obviously sincere:

> Now for Liberty-tree – there is an engraving of that famous vegetable in Snow's History of Boston; but thou wilt draw a better one out of thine own head. If thou dost represent it, I see not what scene can be beneath it, save poor Mr. Oliver taking the oath. Thou must represent him with a bag wig, ruffled sleeves, embroidered coat, and all such ornaments, because he is *the representative of aristocracy and artificial system*. The people may be as rough and wild as thy sweetest fancy can make them; – nevertheless, there must be one or

two grave, puritanical figures in the midst. Such a one might sit in the great chair, and be *an emblem of that stern, considerate spirit*, which brought about the revolution.                                                    (xv, 570–1, my emphases)

No wonder Hawthorne went on to say "But thou wilt find this a hard subject."

Dekker bases his argument at least in part on a passage that Hawthorne deleted from "The Gentle Boy" when he prepared it for publication in *Twice-Told Tales*. I too think it significant, but want to use it to differ from another of Dekker's judgements. He argues that the "Olympian foreknowledge we bring to Hawthorne's historical tales" is knowledge of "an essentially comic plot in which" the Puritan spirit "lives on in New England and eventually wins the long war against British monarchical 'tyranny.'"[13] I would argue that, as the passage from Hawthorne's letter sufficiently shows, Dekker identifies the right narrative structure – but that Hawthorne sees that narrative as a tragedy rather than as a comedy. If we come to Hawthorne with any idea that (American) history has a comic plot, what we should take away is knowledge of the tragic plots of history, however desirable a comic, a utopian narrative might be. The end of "Alice Doane's Appeal" is, it seems to me, one clear example of this in terms of American history, whereas, as I shall be arguing, *The Marble Faun* provides a tragic version of a much larger narrative usually told as a comedy: the Fortunate Fall. But more immediately I find it impossible to assimilate the passage from "The Gentle Boy" (to be quoted later) to any version of a comic plot. I rather see it as evidence of what I have called Hawthorne's tough-mindedness which can incorporate a view of history as full of tragic errors without retreating to a paralyzed scepticism – especially when a passage from "Mrs. Hutchinson" is put in evidence – and "My Kinsman, Major Molineux" remembered.

First, "Mrs. Hutchinson" – and note that it is unity, not freedom of worship, that Hawthorne sees as the identifying mark of the new society:

> These proceedings of Mrs. Hutchinson could not long be endured by the provincial government. The present was a most remarkable case, in which religious freedom was wholly inconsistent with public safety, and where the principles of an illiberal age indicates the very course which must have been pursued by worldly policy and enlightened wisdom. Unity of faith was the star that had guided these people over the deep, and a diversity of sects would either have scattered them from the land to which they had as yet so few attachments, or perhaps have excited a diminutive civil war among those who had come so far to worship together.                       (T&S, 21)

Now, I would certainly agree that irony comes into the sentence that follows this: "Mr. Cotton began to have that light in regard to his errors, which will sometimes break in upon the wisest and most pious men, when their opinions are unhappily discordant with those of the Powers that be." However, it is clear that the irony plays on Cotton rather than on the verdict of society or its rulers. The more interesting, tougher, irony is that the Puritans may be doing the right thing (if only in terms of sheer survival) for what may be, from a nineteenth-century liberal democratic perspective, the wrongest of reasons. And, earlier, Hawthorne has made it quite clear just how dangerous Mrs. Hutchinson might be: "the young men lean forward . . fit instruments for whatever rash deed may be suggested . . . The woman tells them, (and cites texts from the Holy Book to prove her words,) that they have put their trust in unregenerated and uncommissioned men, and have followed them into the wilderness for naught." Whatever our good liberal feelings, however strong our feminism, our proper resentment of patriarchy, Hawthorne has surely made it clear that the infant community is, from his historical perspective, not strong enough, not mature enough, not rich enough culturally to be able to afford the disruptive dissent of a Mrs. Hutchinson: "Therefore their hearts are turning from those whom they have chosen to lead them to Heaven, and they feel like children who have been enticed far from home, and see the features of their guides change all at once, assuming a fiendish shape in some frightful solitude" (T&S, 21). It is admittedly a hard position that Hawthorne has taken, a tragic choice not entirely dissimilar to that of *Antigone* in the Hegelian formulation (a conflict of ethical substance), only Hawthorne is making a version of Creon's argument: either the survival of the community or a necessarily short-lived tolerance.

This should help to explain why, whatever our proper nineteenth- or twentieth-century respect for a Mrs. Hutchinson or a Hester Prynne, the seventeenth-century Puritans could legitimately, if not likeably, take a different view of some types of dissent. Surely, Hawthorne here shows himself as possessing a genuine historical consciousness, and attempting to train his readers to acquire just such a consciousness. Yet he manages to try to inculcate that historical sensibility without ending up in that radical historicism where it is felt impossible to make any (moral) judgement about the past. One way of escaping this trap is to show how the past is not, as it so easily can appear, a seamless tradition carrying only one meaning, but that it is to be seen as fraught with tensions, internal contradictions in its ideologies, and external conflicts. Another, if related way, is to note the past's judgement on itself, a product if not a cause of historical change. This is one reason for finding the 1692 Salem witchcraft trials *and* their aftermath so significant. For there, repentance for (unconscious?) sin did take place; there one can find not only conflict (see, for example, Calef's baiting of Cotton Mather, discussed more fully in the next chapter), but also a general if not universal recognition that a tragic mistake had been made – and one that was not only mortally fatal for the poor victims but possibly even worse for those who were in any way responsible for those fatal sentences. Repeatedly in the statements of repentance the fear can be found that innocent blood may have been shed, a statement that carries a lot of weight both for seventeenth-century Puritan America and for a biblically informed nineteenth-century audience. As the statement of twelve of the jurymen involved in the Salem trials makes clear, the shedding of innocent blood is, in a phrase which resonates for any reader of Hawthorne, an unpardonable sin:

> We confess that we our selves were not capable to understand, nor able to withstand the mysterious delusions of the Powers of Darkness, and Prince of the Air; but were for want of Knowledge in our selves, and better Information from others, prevailed with to take up with such Evidence against the Accused, as on further consideration and better Information from others, we justly fear was insufficient for the touching of the Lives of any, Deut. 17.6, whereby we fear we have been instrumental with others, tho Ignorantly and unwittingly, to bring upon ourselves, and this people of the Lord, *the Guilt of Innocent Blood*; which sin the Lord saith in Scripture, *he would not pardon*, 2 Kings 24.4, that is we suppose in regard of his temporal Judgments. We do therefore signifie to all in general (and to the surviving Sufferers in especial) our deep sense of, and sorrow for our Errors, in acting on such Evidence to the condemning of any person.[14]

This is a fascinating passage which deserves more attention than it gets here, if only for the way in which the jurymen, clearly and rightly terrified of eternal damnation, while attempting to qualify and spread the guilt, admit what it is difficult for most of us to admit: that they were wrong.

I may seem to have strayed far from Dekker and his argument about Hawthorne's offering of American history as comic plot. But the deleted passage from "The Gentle Boy" seems to need contextualization both in terms of history and in terms of Hawthorne's attitude as expressed elsewhere before anything like its full meaning can be recognized. Even if this kind of contextualization is provided, the whole of the deleted passage needs to be quoted. Dekker begins with the second sentence:

> That those who were active in, or consenting to, this measure [the persecution of the Quakers], made themselves responsible for *innocent blood*, is not to be denied: yet the extenuating circumstances of their conduct are more numerous than can generally be pleaded by persecutors.          (My emphasis)

The parallels with the passage from "Mrs. Hutchinson" become clearer still:

> For the peaceful exercise of their own mode of worship, an object, the very reverse of universal liberty of conscience, they had hewn themselves a home in the wilderness; they had made vast sacrifices of whatever is dear to man; they had exposed themselves to the peril of death, and to a life which rendered the accomplishment of that peril almost a blessing. They had found no city of refuge prepared for them, but, with Heaven's assistance, they had created one; and it would be hard to say whether justice did not authorize their determination, to guard its gate against all who were destitute of the prescribed title to admittance. The principle of their foundation was such, that to destroy the unity of religion, might have been to subvert the government, and break up the colony, especially at the period when the state of affairs in England had stopped the tide of emigration, and drawn back many of the pilgrims to their native homes.

Here, Dekker stops, but it is worth remembering that Hawthorne, having said what can be said for the colony, ends with a clear judgement: "after all allowances, it is to be feared that the death of the Quakers was principally owing to the polemic fierceness, that distinct passion of human nature, which has so often produced frightful guilt in the most sincere and zealous advocates of religion and virtue." (T&S, 1483–84) It is difficult to decide why Hawthorne decided to cut this for *Twice-Told Tales*. Dekker offers three possibilities: either "because he decided it was mistaken in principle," or because it was "socially dangerous for his own times," or because it was "rhetorically premature."[15] If it were the first, that would need justification in terms of a radical change in Hawthorne's attitudes; if the second, it would need to be justified in terms of his perception of the political situation in the late 1830s; the third seems to ask for a change in his attitudes to language. My own feeling is that he wanted to promote the blue-eyed Nathaniel, in Lawrentian phrase. But, as Dekker says, whatever the reason, the passage should hold a place in the Hawthorne canon "as an unusually explicit, albeit partial statement of the main issues in historical fiction of New England."[16] The closeness of much of this to the relevant passage from "Mrs. Hutchinson" does not, as I have suggested, need stressing. Like that, this is a tough-minded recognition of the claims for survival. But here the statement is bracketed by two kinds of moral judgement and it is clear that a tragic error has occurred. The Puritans of the past cannot get off with a slap on the wrist – however much the Quakers threatened their world, however much they may have invited persecution. That reference to the (shedding of) innocent blood means that there is a strong probability that those persecutors have been, are being, and will be punished – if 2 Kings xxiv.4 is remembered: "he filled Jerusalem with innocent blood; which the Lord would not pardon." And the conclusion points to a lesson learnt from history – a trans-historical lesson.

"My Kinsman, Major Molineux" often appears the most complex, the most problematic of the stories dealing with the anticipations of the American Revolution, given the overwhelming sympathy that so many readers understandably feel for poor Major Molineux in his tar and feathers. But it seems to me to exemplify Hawthorne's tragic (not negative) view of Revolution. Raymond Williams in *Modern Tragedy* (a book that I have drawn on very heavily in what follows) identifies a nineteenth-century tradition in which tragedy and history were consciously connected. It is precisely that tradition to which Hawthorne belongs – one which enables him to situate revolution in history. As Williams points out, there is a tendency for heirs of revolutions to deny the tragic elements in the action or series of actions that transformed their society:

> A time of revolution is so evidently a time of violence, dislocation and extended suffering that it is natural to feel it as tragedy, in the everyday sense. Yet, as the event becomes history, it is often quite differently regarded. Very many nations look back to the revolutions of their own history as to the era of creation of the life which is now most precious. The successful revolution, we might say, becomes not tragedy but epic: it is the origin of a people, and of its valued way of life. When the suffering is remembered, it is at once either honoured or justified. That particular revolution, we say, was a necessary condition of life.[17]

Hawthorne is writing from and for a society that is in no danger of undervaluing its revolution, which, very much in Williams' terms, reads its history as epic rather than tragedy – and he firmly resists that reading. See, for example, the celebrations of 1826, or Webster's speech at the laying of the corner stone of the Bunker Hill monument. His achievement is to hold to the recognition both that the American Revolution was almost inevitable, a necessary condition for American life, and that it necessarily involved tragic suffering. The first paragraph of "My Kinsman" recognizes the long series of struggles that is the pre-history of the American Revolution – a history that, as set down by Hawthorne here and elsewhere, is so long and complex that it is a naive reader indeed who can see 1776 as an ending or an origin rather than a crucial node in a still developing history. For example, there is *The House of the Seven Gables*. I shall be arguing that this is to be read as Hawthorne's novel of that year of revolutions, 1848. But what is clear in that book is that the American Revolution played no part in resolving the social struggles, the class differences between the Pyncheons and the Maules – and it is also clear that Hawthorne had considerable problems – problems that he acknowledges – when he tried to find a comic plot for this strand of American history.[18]

"My Kinsman" offers a direct recognition of the tragic cost of revolutionary struggle. As Q.D. Leavis pointed out long ago, Robin feels before he joins in anarchic laughter in Aristotelian phrase "a mixture of pity and terror" (T&S, 85). I would argue that the revolutionary mob is right to rebel against Molineux as far as his *public* role is concerned. It is not a point that Hawthorne needs to stress when writing for an American audience in the late 1820s or early 1830s. And, very unusually for a nineteenth-century middle-class writer, Hawthorne had no fear of the populace. As he wrote in *The French and Italian Notebooks*, "I remember, in America, I had an innate antipathy to constables, and always sided with the mob" (xiv, 330). It has to be remembered that Molineux is a Major, taking that title, that status, that identity because of the *King's* commission – and here is a military man in a civil office. As public official, the Major can embody the institutional violence of the British state. Raymond Williams makes the point that, until a revolutionary transformation has taken place, the institutions of the state can seem natural and innocent so that the revolt of those oppressed can appear the very origin of violence.[19] But what happens in the story is that justifiable revolutionary activity against the representative of the British imperialist state tragically involves the humiliating suffering of a private man. The consequence is a *private* agony: "On they went, in counterfeited pomp [note how the rebels parody the authority they resist], in senseless uproar, in frenzied merriment, trampling all on an old man's heart" (T&S, 86). The injured and oppressed indeed seem the source of disturbance and violence. It is only those outside history, like the Man in the Moon, who can read this tragedy as comedy: "'Oho,' quoth he, 'the old Earth is frolicsome to-night!'" (T&S, 86). Those who remain in history cannot and should not reach for that Olympian detachment – and the story remains open to history. We are told that Robin is only one of the protagonist's names. That should remind us that one of his other names is certainly Molineux and that another may well be William – the William Molineux who, according to Roy Harvey Pearce in his notes for the Library of America edition of Hawthorne's tales and sketches, was associated by Hawthorne's contemporaries with the name of a "well-to-do trader, an organizer and leader of anti-Loyalist mobs, member of the Boston Committee of Correspondence, one of those who are said to have been at the Boston Tea Party" (T&S, 1,483). The real conclusion to the story may be in history – and the anonymous gentleman who befriends Robin may be right when he says to him, "you may rise in the world, without the help of your kinsman" (T&S, 87).

One of Hawthorne's successes in this remarkable story is his repudiation of what Williams calls revolutionary romanticism. Williams argues that revolution is not only tragic in its origins but in its action since the struggle is against other men rather than gods or things – something he claims that has too often been an area of silence: "what is properly called utopianism, or revolutionary romanticism, is the suppression or dilution of this quite inevitable fact."[20] This is directly applicable to Hawthorne's achievement in "My Kinsman." And, as so often, Hawthorne's subtle intelligence adds a further turn of the screw to this tragedy of revolution (tragic in its inevitability as well as in the suffering of a man). The Major's most acute pain is caused not by feeling himself an object of pity but by being the object of an anarchic laughter which demystifies and destroys his authority, and which is perhaps to be placed by what Hawthorne had to say of it in "Ethan Brand": "Laughter, when . . . bursting from a disordered state of feeling, may be the most terrible modulation of the human voice" (T&S, 1,054–55). Perhaps it is the experience of seeing Britain lose an Empire to the valid demands of other nations without those nations immediately becoming utopias which makes me sympathize with Hawthorne's version of the long struggle which includes the Revolution – and perhaps it has been Americans' experience of American imperialism that has made some so reluctant to join with Hawthorne in celebrating, however ambivalently, the long history of the American Revolution.

It was, I think, Gore Vidal who said that America's second name should be Amnesia. From Hawthorne's perspective it is not only total but partial amnesia which is to be feared. The celebration of half a history, the presentation of half a history as if it were a whole, may be as dangerous as the positive repudiation of all the past (or, perhaps worse, simply ignoring it). Thus, his versions of the Puritan heritage which stress the sour as well as the sweet, the demands of necessity, as against the purely sweet version offered by Bancroft and others of that ilk. Tradition is necessary, then, if only as a way of countering the amnesiac tendencies of American culture; yet what Hawthorne has apprehended in his uses, his re-creations, of tradition is not only a recognition of the claims and powers of conservatism but also a recognition of the ways in which tradition is a (necessary) construct. Yet again I appeal to Raymond Williams. He points out that a tradition is not natural, not "the past" but an evaluative interpretation, a construction: "And if this is so, the present, at any time, is a factor in the selection and valuation [of the past]. It is not the contrast but the relationship between modern and traditional that concerns the cultural historian."[21] In this sense, Hawthorne is an exemplary cultural historian. As he wrote in "Old News" – and the idea informs almost all his work – "All philosophy, that would abstract man from the present, is no more than words" (T&S, 252).

A continuous concern with the problematic relationships between those children of an historical view of experience, tradition and revolution, is absolutely central to Hawthorne's whole career – and his achievements. And those three major works I first encountered thanks to Lathrop's edition illuminate that achievement. Very near the beginning of Hawthorne's career stands "Alice Doane's Appeal." There, Hawthorne ends his tale with the tensions between the belief that a new and virtuous beginning has been made which permits an amnesiac repudiation of history (symbolized by a reference to the Bunker Hill monument) and the continuities of social division and conflict exemplified by the witchcraft terror of 1692 – but not, crucially, exhausted by that experience as Hawthorne makes clear throughout his work. "War Matters" meditates on the only too immediately real battle about two versions of America – versions appealing to, and built on, two very different traditions of what American had been. And Hawthorne builds his argument on a striking difference: that the Mayflower may have carried the Pilgrim Fathers on one voyage – but slaves on another. That story, if true, makes for a striking irony if only in that it opens up the questions of the origins of the United States of America in a way that problematizes not so much "origin" as "United."

The unfinished fictions explore the claims and temptations of both tradition and revolution. *The American Claimant Manuscripts* take a long, hard and sympathetic look at the extraordinarily attractive powers of tradition, principally in the form of what the country-house can be made to stand for: "a device for giving length, fullness, body, substance to this thin and frail matter of human life" (XII, 86). And *The Elixir of Life Manuscripts* look at the ruptures of revolution. Even if the argument is confined to the alchemical theme, it can be seen that alchemy is being used (to steal the words of a recent newspaper critic of Jonson's *Alchemist*) to signify the deep, imaginative desire in human beings for sudden, radical transformations and liberation. Yet at the same time, Hawthorne points out not only that there is a long tradition of alchemical endeavour but also that long, patient hard work both scientific and moral is precisely what the would-be alchemist must submit himself to. In other words, the means and the end may radically contradict each other. The result in this potential masterpiece is not a paralyzing stasis but rather a brilliant exploration of the ironies of such a situation.

Emerson, writing in 1846 and perhaps thinking of "The Old Manse," complained that Hawthorne "invites his readers too much into his study, opens the process before them. As if the confectioner should say to his customers now let us make the cake." This seems to me rather a matter for praise than blame, allowing us to see that a work of art is made rather than dropping from the heavens, that the reader too has a part to play – to say nothing of the criticism seeming slightly surprising, coming as it does from a man who also thought "In reading there is a sort of half & half mixture. The book must be good, but the reader must also be active.";[22] But the sentiment behind Emerson's criticism may partly account for the neglect of "Alice Doane's Appeal." There, Hawthorne invites us not so much into the kitchen as into the workshop where he dismantles one piece of work, shows us why it does not and should not work, and experiments with putting another construction in its place.

# 2

## An experimental fiction: "Alice Doane's Appeal" or, how (not) to tell a story

I

About "Alice Doane" I should be more doubtful as to the public approbation.
(S.G. Goodrich to Hawthorne, January 19, 1830.     (xv, 200))

Goodrich was, almost certainly, writing about the original "Alice
Doane" which would have made one of the *Seven Tales of My Native
Land* – Hawthorne's first attempt to get a coherent collection of his tales
into print. But whether it was that lost story or its reconstruction/
deconstruction ("Alice Doane's Appeal") that was at issue, Goodrich
seems to have set the tone for subsequent criticism. In the last half century
or so the story has not had what could be called a good press. Indeed,
compared to tales of equal quality, it has had scarcely any attention at all
– something helped along by the fact that it reposed in the decent (very
decent) obscurity of the 1835 *Token* until it was dug up by Lathrop for
his 1883 edition of Hawthorne's work – not that there is much evidence
that this resurrection caused a great flurry of excitement. Modern critics
are spared an editor's concern about public reception but they have
rarely been more enthusiastic than was the hard-nosed, commercially
minded editor, Mr. Goodrich. Formalist and psychological critics have
tended to write as though a subtitle should read "How Not to Write a
Story" – or else have proclaimed with varying degrees of pleasure,
"Incest Theme Here! Dig for Further Clues!" S.L. Gross, for example,
discovered how "the incestuous and sexual portions of the narrative
were toned down" for publication. H.H. Waggoner, in a preface to one
of his editions of Hawthorne's stories, spends a fairly lengthy paragraph
discussing the tale but ends by deciding that its symbols "invite
psychological rather than structural criticism." With his verdict in mind,
one turns to F.C. Crews's *The Sins of the Fathers* with a sinking feeling of

18

what is to come. And, of course, how right one is – except that it is not only fathers but brothers and sisters who preoccupied him.[1] It is strange (though, perhaps, in a way, to their credit) how often Freudian critics seem to be happier with works they consider to be bad art than they are with masterpieces. But in this case, as far as evaluation goes, Crews was wrong. While "Alice Doane's Appeal" may not be a flawless work of art it is certainly not the ruin, the halting work that Crews suggested. His concentration on the incest theme to the exclusion of any serious consideration of the way in which the Alice Doane section is presented and situated in the text guarantees a misreading and a misevaluation. Crews has, of course, repented of his Freudian days – and it is tempting to use that repentance to dismiss his comments on "Alice Doane's Appeal." But he was undoubtedly right to note that the incest theme is a crucial element in the story – even if he refused to consider that it makes most sense when seen not in terms of Hawthorne's life-history but rather in the context of literary and cultural history.

When we turn to the historical critics, however, not all the problems are solved, though it is true that more promising approaches are offered by, for example, R.H. Pearce and Harry Henderson III. Both see the tale's significance as being in some way connected with an understanding of the historical past – an interpretation which it is hardly necessary to say Crews regarded with distaste.[2] Pearce is persuasive:

> Hawthorne tells the story of telling a story in order to draw us directly into the struggle to relate ourselves to our history and to assume the moral responsibilities, the guilt and righteousness, stemming from it.

But he, like Crews, sees the story as a whole as a failure: "Sad to say, he cannot make the story work; and we must read only an unsuccessful trial." The story must be judged in this way because

> We can interpret it as an experiment in the direct communication of the sense of the past. Hawthorne, in this interpretation, [the *right* one Pearce implies – but is too polite to substitute "should" for "can"] would confront his readers with the past out of which have come their character and their fortune.

But we should not confine the story's meanings within such narrow limits. Pearce leaves the Alice Doane section unexplained or, rather, too easily explained away: "unimportant, an incidental means to a large end." Henderson, impressed by the "fine Freudian analysis" of Crews, makes a serious attempt to reconcile the Alice Doane section with the narrator's evocation of the witchcraft trials:

> The narrator fails in his first, subtle attempt imaginatively to recreate the past for the present. His method was nothing less than persuading his audience to assume the imaginative positions of the "afflicted," of momentarily adopting

the psychology of those who believed in and so persecuted the witches . . .
Where fictional evocation of the inner psychology of the time had failed, the
impassioned narration of the outer, or conventionally "true" history
succeeds.[3]

This still leaves us with problems. Henderson does not consider why – if
the Alice Doane section is to be seen as an historical mini-novel – the
attempt at "psychological" history fails nor why Hawthorne should
choose to present his readers with an acknowledged failure.

One reason for misinterpretation is the recurring desire to make part
of the tale stand for the whole, to see thematic repetitions rather than
differences within the story as a whole. Another is the related temptation
to see the tale as displaying, in Henderson's words, "the device of the
story within a story." But "Alice Doane's Appeal" is made up of two
stories within a story – or, more accurately, a dismantled story and an
unfinished sketch within a story – and no interpretation can be right
which does not take full account of all three parts and the intricate and
subtle relationships between them. Hawthorne is constantly drawing
attention to the problems involved in writing or telling a story. Pearce
does mention that Hawthorne "tells the story . . . regularly breaking off
to remark to the readers on the effect he is striving to create,"[4] but he
does not pause to consider that this self-consciousness about means and
ends might be central to the effect that Hawthorne is trying to create.
Nor does he draw attention to the important fact that the way the story is
told to the reader and the way it is told to the auditors differ. The listeners
get the full works while the reader only gets edited and recorded Gothic
highlights accompanied by, as it were, a post-match commentary.

It is here that I want to begin my disagreement with the most recent
substantial treatment of the story, that of Colacurcio in his massive
*Province of Piety*. I have already referred to his evaluation of the story in
my first chapter. It is, perhaps, not surprising that he does not rate the
story more highly as his interpretation is not so very far from those of
Pearce and Henderson. He does recognize that there are two stories
within the story but insists that they are to be seen as essentially the same
story:

> The first thing we need to observe about the narrator's two efforts is their
> ideological identity: both concern the Puritan problem of "specter evidence."
>
> Ultimately, therefore, the function of the narrator's second effort is not simply
> to move to tears some clearly inadequate audience; it is, rather, to suggest the
> extent to which his original story was itself already adequate – in spite of its
> rather wild indulgences – to the essential history of Salem Witchcraft.
>
> Once the identical historicity of the two experiments is understood, other
> nagging problems of interpretation tend to solve themselves. The narrator is

not so much substituting a true story for a wild romance as he is merely literalizing psychohistory for an audience which obviously lacks the literary sophistication to discern the historical truth of a metaphorical fiction – an audience which insists on regarding all fantasy as *mere* fantasy.[5]

I am unable to share his confidence that the audience can so easily be blamed. And I wonder why, if the narrator is not substituting a true story for a wild romance, he says this: "I . . . made a trial whether truth were more powerful than fiction" (T&S, 215). I agree that the question of spectre evidence does appear, at least in the Alice Doane section, but it is raised, as I will show, as something deeply problematic for the meaning of Alice's story. Colacurcio fails to consider why the Alice Doane story is presented in such a peculiarly dismantled fashion – and this refusal to examine such an obvious formal point weakens his argument beyond repair. I shall be arguing that Hawthorne has taken that story to pieces precisely because he recognizes its ideological incoherence.

Given the problematic structure of "Alice Doane's Appeal," one has to attempt to set it in a context provided by some of Hawthorne's recurrent concerns and by his particular strategies in the early 1830s. It is hardly necessary to do more than remind ourselves that Hawthorne not infrequently showed signs of suspicion about the values of art in general and his own in particular. At times it can look as though the artist comes close to committing a version of the unpardonable sin – and this should prevent a reader from too quickly blaming the female audience in "Alice Doane's Appeal." While the narrator certainly thinks that his New England audience is morally diminished by its shocking lack of historical knowledge, this does not mean that the artist is necessarily presented as fault free. Rather than doubting the audience, the reader needs to question the motives of the writer. Why, for example, in the Alice Doane section of the tale, does the narrator want to frighten his audience? Their laughter is, I shall argue, a proper criticism of at least the (improvised) ending of the tale – and the narrator seems to have learnt this lesson for, in his second attempt on his audience's feelings, he no longer tries to frighten his audience but to move them by suggesting that man's inhumanity to man should make countless thousands mourn.

Two other recurrent and related concerns should also be remembered: first, Hawthorne's confessed need for a relationship with his audience, and, second, his interest in getting the frame into the picture. Probably the best-known expression of the first is in "The Custom-House": "thoughts are frozen and utterance benumbed, unless the speaker stand in some true relation with his audience" (N, 121). The preface to the 1851 edition of *Twice-Told Tales* develops this position further, though not entirely seriously. The author "is by no means certain that some of his subsequent productions have not been influenced by a natural desire

... to act in consonance with the character assigned to him" (T&S, 1153). As I have suggested, "Alice Doane's Appeal" is concerned with the problem of the audience – or audiences. The narrator shows himself self-consciously aware of both his listeners *and* of his readers – and part of his problem is to find a way of telling the readers how and why he told the girls a story, and to differentiate between not only the two versions of the Alice story but between that narrative and the sketch of Salem witchcraft. One solution is to exploit the relationship between frame and picture. The concern with getting the frame into the picture, the felt need to situate the work in social, historical and psychological contexts is, of course, brilliantly done in "The Custom-House." However, this had been a long-standing preoccupation. Shortly before the publication of "Alice Doane's Appeal," Hawthorne had made his most ambitious and, alas, his last doomed attempt to do just this as he attempted to get a coherent collection of his stories into print: *The Story Teller*. This was sent to Goodrich in early 1834, who, according to Turner, kept a couple of pieces for the *Token*, and passed the rest of the manuscript on to the *New England Magazine*.[6] "The Story Teller Number I" and "The Story Teller Number II" appeared in that magazine's November and December issue, "Number II" containing not only the framing device but the story teller's first tale, "Mr. Higginbotham's Catastrophe." But that was as much as appeared – at least, in the form Hawthorne intended. Early in 1835, Park Benjamin took over as editor and we have Hawthorne's word for it that it was Benjamin who broke up *The Story Teller* (to use stories from it as the decade wore on). When it came to book publication, Hawthorne severed "Mr. Higginbotham's Catastrophe" from its context and put it in *Twice-Told Tales* (1837). The introductory framing material was rescued for the 1854 edition of *Mosses from an Old Manse* under the sad title of "Passages from a Relinquished Work."

The plan was to have had an oral storyteller on his travels accompanied by a young man with religious tendencies who would sermonize while the teller told his tales. Even the fragments we have are profoundly interesting, and it is infuriating that Hawthorne was not allowed to develop the oppositions and relations between religion and art, between sermons and fiction – to say nothing of the question of the audiences for both genres. By dramatizing them, Hawthorne had potentially found a way of dealing with problems that were to plague him as artist and moralist. Such a form would not only have allowed him to display the full range of his powers but also to escape from (or at least explore) the guilt that troubled him when he felt that he was not writing about what he should be writing about:

> It was a folly, with the materiality of this daily life pressing so intrusively upon me . . . to insist on creating the semblance of a world out of airy matter, when, at every moment, the impalpable beauty of my soap-bubble was broken by the rude contact of some actual circumstance . . . The fault was mine. The page of life that was spread out before me seemed dull and commonplace, only because I had not fathomed its deeper import. A better book than I shall ever write was there.                                    (N, 151)

The soap-bubble of fiction would not, in *The Story Teller*, have been incompatible with the material world – indeed, quite the opposite. The interaction with an audience would have allowed the story teller to respond to their responses. He tells us that "even when I stepped upon the stage" it was not "decided whether Mr. Higginbotham would live or die" (T&S, 184). The title allows the narrator to go either way – for, while we tend to think of "catastrophe" as meaning disaster, Johnson's *Dictionary* reminds us of its technical meaning: "The change or revolution which produces the conclusion or final event of a dramatic piece." Since for reasons not entirely due to the teller's style (unknown to him, a fun-loving character had attached "a stiff queue of horse-hair" to his collar which made "the queerest gestures of its own, in correspondence with mine" [T&S, 186]), the audience find the tale hysterically funny – and so we get a comic ending to the plot. More importantly, the tensions between fiction and reportage, between romance and realism – tensions that also appear for examination in "Alice Doane's Appeal" – would have been further extended and explored in *The Story Teller*:

> The following pages will contain a picture of my vagrant life, intermixed with specimens, generally brief and slight, of that great mass of fiction to which I gave existence . . . With each specimen will be given a sketch of the circumstances in which the story was told. Thus my airdrawn pictures will be set in frames perhaps more valuable than the pictures themselves, since they will be embossed with groups of characteristic figures, amid the lake and mountain scenery, the villages and fertile fields, of our native land.
>
> (T&S, 176–6)

I am not going to join in the absorbing debate as to which pieces we have may have been constituent parts of *The Story Teller*, but it is clear that, though "Alice Doane's Appeal" may only focus on one hill and one village, it was sent to a publisher at much the same time as *The Story Teller* – and it patently shares with that aborted work some similar emphases and similar structures designed to expose or control problems common to both. Obviously I do not mean to suggest that these strategies are only shared by these two projects – for example, Hawthorne's interest in using one part of a tale to criticize another, in dialectical forms, frequently recurs – but rather that the work we now encounter as "Passages from a Relinquished Work" is particularly helpful in enabling us to avoid and reject some misreadings of "Alice Doane's Appeal." Both works share a preoccupation with (possibly fragmentary) improvisation, both enact some of their most important meanings by exploiting the relationships – and the gaps – between the frame and the picture. Even though *The Story Teller* now only exists as a lost possibility, our knowledge that it could have been should make it clear that "Alice Doane's Appeal" can only be understood by paying attention to the question of the type of tale with which the narrator is concerned, and that it is impossible – or at least improper – to rest happy with content analysis alone.

## II

> Incest is like many other incorrect things a very poetical circumstance. It may be the excess of love or hate. It may be the defiance of everything for the sake of another which clothes itself in the glory of the highest heroism, or it may be that cynical rage which, confounding the good and the bad in existing opinions, breaks through them for the purpose of rioting in selfishness and antipathy.        (P.B. Shelley, letter to Maria Gisborne, November 16, 1819)

"Alice Doane's Appeal" can be formally divided into four sections: (a) an introduction which establishes a context for what follows; (b) the edited version of Alice's story; (c) the narrator's version of the execution of the Salem "witches"; and (d) a conclusion and a moral. This spatial organization of the tale exists in a tension with what the story tells us must be stages of composition – the story's production seen temporally. (This is apparent even if a reader does not have access to the evidence which suggests that another version of the story may once have existed.) Archaeologically speaking, the lowest layer is the story of Alice and incestuous desires which had been written before the narrator encountered his female audience and which we, the readers, get in a version edited at some time after the story has been told. Then we have the improvised sketch of the "witches" on their way to execution, and finally we have the narrator's report on the whole experience. For all this complex layering, though, the story begins in an apparently highly conventional way. On a pleasant June afternoon, the story teller takes two young ladies for a walk. The only unconventionality would seem to be his choice of destination: Gallows Hill. But as it turns out, he just happens to have a "wondrous tale" in his pocket which he intends to inflict on his captive audience. Before telling his tale, however, he tells the reader about Gallows Hill in terms of its nature and its history, something about himself, and about the prosperity of the community and its lack of historical consciousness. The hill is covered with apparently fertile greenery except when the plant flowers, when "to a distant spectator, the hill appears absolutely overlaid with gold, or covered with a glory of sunshine." The appearance of fertility and beauty is, it turns out, deceptive: the woodwax has destroyed "all the grass, and everything that should nourish man or beast." The consequent image is pretty well irresistible – especially as it allows the narrator to make the transition to what really interests him about Gallows Hill:

> its tufted roots . . . permit nothing else to vegetate among them; so that a physical curse may be said to have blasted the spot, where guilt and phrenzy consummated the most execrable scene that our history blushes to record. For this was the field where superstition won her darkest triumph; the high place where our fathers set up their shame, to the mournful gaze of generations far remote. The dust of martyrs was beneath our feet. (T&S, 205)

But that reference to "the mournful gaze" turns out to be largely wishful thinking. Too few know about this blushing history. The narrator defines himself as the possessor of an historical consciousness which differentiates him from his fellow citizens. They are not a "people of legend or tradition" but rather "a people of the present" who "have no heartfelt interest in the olden time."[7] The history they do celebrate they are ignorant of – and it is, in essence, irrelevant to them, a meaningless ritual:

> Every fifth of November, in commemoration of they know not what, or rather without an idea beyond the momentary blaze, the young men scare the town with bonfires on this haunted height, but never dream of paying funeral honours to those who died so wrongfully, and without a coffin or a prayer, were buried here. (T&S, 206)

A Catholic threat was hardly a serious one for New England, and to celebrate the defeat of a Papist conspiracy on the site of one of Puritanism's most frightful mistakes is, however unconsciously, an act in the worst of bad taste.

After a short and somewhat perfunctory attempt to recreate the Salem of 1692, the narrator "began the tale, which opened darkly with the discovery of a murder" (T&S, 208). Briefly, the tale is something like this: Leonard Doane has killed Walter Brome, believing that Walter has seduced Alice Doane, his sister. Leonard subsequently discovers that Walter is his twin brother – having always thought they were surprisingly similar. The tragedy has been set up by a wizard – and the denoucment, such as it is, takes place when the wizard who, "on certain conditions" (we are not told what these are) "had no power to withhold his aid in unravelling the mystery" (T&S, 211), leads – or seems to lead – Alice and Leonard to the graveyard. Everyone rises from his or her grave – or seems to – and

> The story concluded with the Appeal of Alice to the spectre of Walter Brome;
> his reply absolving her from every stain; and the trembling awe with which
> ghost and devil fled, as from the sinless presence of an angel.    (T&S, 214)

I have no intention of denying or playing down the incest theme which has been found in the story. Indeed, I insist on its presence – it would take an entirely improper ingenuity to do otherwise especially when faced by a passage like this which tells of Leonard "shuddering with a deeper sense of some unutterable crime, perpetrated, as he imagined, in madness or a dream" (T&S, 211) – but I also insist on Hawthorne's consciousness, his very careful choice of this theme. For the story is a deliberate example of what must be called pseudo-history. The narrator may have imagined it to be an historical mini-novel, but (and this is Hawthorne's point) it is initially a Gothic "Tale of Terror," a romance closer to "The Fall of the House of Usher" than to *The House of the Seven Gables* – though the narrator is unable to sustain the pure Gothic (perhaps because, for Hawthorne, the pure Gothic is unsustainable) throughout the whole story. It is not necessary at this late date to prove the attraction that *doppelgangers*, alter egos, brother and sister relationships, incest and the supernatural had for the Gothic novelists and the Romantics. Nor is it necessary to go into detail to show that Hawthorne knew the appropriate sources well.[8] And Shelley's letter, the epigraph to this section, provides a nice example of why incest was so useful for Romantic literature. Rather than looking towards Freudian or any other psychology to provide an explanation of the Alice story, it might be wiser to look at least initially to history and particularly to literary history.

Hawthorne fragments his narrator's story because he sees that it does not, cannot and should not work as a whole because of the context in which it exists and because the history it claims to be based on gradually creeps into the tale and subverts the Gothic elements. The story teller on retelling his narrative for readers has (as well he might) partially lost confidence in it. It is this loss of confidence which goes some way towards accounting for the very odd way the Alice Doane section is presented – a mixture of summary, indirect reporting, direct speech, direct narrative – brought before the reader in isolated units:

> he had sought the interview with the wizard, who, on certain conditions, had
> no power to withhold his aid in unravelling the mystery. The tale drew near its
> close.

> The moon was bright on high; the blue firmament appeared to glow with an
> inherent brightness; the greater stars were burning in their spheres; the
> northern lights threw their mysterious glare far over the horizon; the few small
> clouds aloft were burdened with radiance; but the sky with all its variety of

light was scarcely so brilliant as the earth. The rain of the preceding night had frozen as it fell, and by that simple magic had wrought wonders. The trees were hung with diamonds and many-colored gems; the houses were overlaid with silver, and the streets paved with slippery brightness; a frigid glory was flung over all familiar things, from the cottage chimney to the steeple of the meeting house, that gleamed upward to the sky. This living world, where we sit by our firesides, or go forth to meet beings like ourselves, seemed rather the creation of wizard power, with so much of resemblance to known objects, that a man might shudder at the ghostly shape of his old beloved dwelling, and the shadow of a ghostly tree before his door. One looked to behold inhabitants suited to such a town, glittering in icy garments, with motionless features, cold, sparkling eyes, and just sensation enough in their frozen hearts to shiver at each other's presence.

By this fantastic piece of description, and more in the same style, I intended to throw a ghostly glimmer round the reader, so that his imagination might view the town through a medium that should take off its every day aspect, and make it a proper theatre for so wild a scene as the present one. (T&S, 211–12)

The form in which the story is presented guarantees that the reader never becomes involved: it constantly cools us off – which is the very opposite of what the narrator originally tried for (as he tells us). Take the example above. Hawthorne offers us a set-piece of descriptive and highly atmospheric writing, designed (apparently) precisely to involve the reader and to prepare him or her for the final scene – then he carefully destroys any effect it might have had by drawing attention to its status and purpose. Hawthorne tells the reader: "This is how it was done, this is why it was done – but does it work? Is this what should be done? Is this the right subject?" And, of course, he answers his questions. The writing is not allowed to become invisible: there is no way to avoid a consideration of the stylistic strategies employed. It is insisted upon that this is a twice-told tale. We can, up to a point, reconstruct the first version of the tale from the narrator's deconstruction of it. It was longer, and it was more detailed. It was more realistic: "The story described, at some length, the excitement caused by the murder, the unavailing quest after the perpetrator, the funeral ceremonies, and other common places matters" (T&S, 208). And it was more horrific: "I dare not give the remainder of the scene, except in a very brief epitome" (T&S, 214). It is irrelevant for my purposes whether the story did ever exist in an earlier form. My point is that this mode of presentation is at once creation and criticism of that creation – criticism of content, theme, and style. I do not want to suggest that the criticism is wholly evaluative or that the part which is evaluation is wholly hostile, though at the last it must be, for the sake of the whole narrative of "Alice Doane's Appeal."

Hawthorne uses the Alice Doane section of the story to identify the

essence of the Gothic tale – particularly in two speeches allowed
Leonard, which Hawthorne allows us to see do contain a certain power.
But at the same time that we are shown the temptations of the Gothic,
Hawthorne offers those speeches as examples of analysis and identifica-
tion by selective quotation, as examples which offer hints about how we
read a story, how we can anticipate the plot with the help of the author:
"I began the tale, which opened darkly with the discovery of a murder"
(T&S, 208). "Darkly" is nicely chosen, suggesting both a deliberate
obscurity of meaning and plotting and menace. The narrator prefaces
Leonard's first speech by telling us we should expect to find a clue: "In
the following passage, I threw a glimmering light on the mystery of the
tale" (T&S, 209). "Mystery" also carries a double meaning. Of course it
refers to Leonard's feelings towards Alice (which are something of a
mystery to him if not to us), but it also hints at the mystery of the
similarity between Leonard and Walter: "There was a resemblance from
which I shrank with sickness, and loathing, and horror, as if my own
features had come and stared upon me in a solitary place, or had met me
in struggling through a crowd" (T&S, 209). And it is this point that is
reinforced by Leonard's second speech where he describes his feelings
after having killed Walter. A Freudian critic cannot have anything to do
with such a simple-minded explanation:

> Leonard shows us in this moment of vision that by killing Walter he is
> symbolically reliving the murder of a prior "dead enemy," his father. To be
> sure, it was an Indian raiding party that performed the first crime; but
> Leonard's fantasy ambiguously casts himself in the Indians' place. The open
> murder of Walter becomes horrible to him by virtue of Walter's resemblance
> to his father, and we may surmise that this resemblance had something to do
> with the urge to kill him. Leonard has seen in Walter a reincarnation of the
> dead parent toward whom, we perceive, he has continued to harbor both
> hostility and penitence – tears that are inappropriate to the despicable Walter
> but not to the dimly remembered father for whom he stands.
>
> No one who is acquainted with psychoanalytic theory will be astonished by
> these inferences.[9]

No, indeed – though whether that is to the credit of psychoanalytic
theory is something that Crews has himself pronounced on. In any case,
Leonard "shows" us nothing of the sort. But the very nakedness of this
argument is helpful in enabling us to see that it is Romantic psychology
that informs the tale – indeed, that overloads it – and not a twentieth-
century theory nor, for that matter, a seventeenth-century notion. The
"open" murder does not become horrible because Walter looks like
their father – nor is it open: Leonard intended to conceal the body.
Hawthorne is quite clear about Leonard's emotional shifts and shows this
by the repetitive pattern of the speech, statements followed by

qualifications. First, Leonard feels exhilaration at seeing his enemy dead before him – understandably given that "the similarity of their dispositions made them like joint possessors of an individual nature, which could not become wholly the property of one, unless by the extinction of the other" (T&S, 210). Straight Romantic egoism. "But the burst of exulting certainty soon fled" (T&S, 210). So he tries to make his soul "glad with the thought, that" Walter "lay dead before me" (T&S, 210). Regret at the death of Walter precedes the discovery of resemblance between father and son – it rather initiates it. The first speech emphasizes the emotional similarity between Walter and Leonard; the second stresses the physical resemblance between Walter and Leonard's father – the fact that he is also Walter's father being unknown to Leonard at this point. The inference is so clear as to allow for a rather crude dramatic irony: "But the delusion was not wholly gone; that face still wore a likeness to my father" (T&S, 211). There is not the slightest evidence that it was Walter's resemblance to the father that caused Leonard to kill his brother, nor is there any need to guess that that might be a reason as the motives for the murder are made perfectly clear – and they are to do with perverted sexual feelings within one generation. (Indeed, it sounds as though the narrator had been reading rather too much Byron – and too much about Byron and Augusta.) These motives include the straightforward "I kill the man who dishonours my sister;" the unconsciously incestuous feeling, "I cannot bear that *anyone else* should possess my sister – especially someone so like me;" and a distaste for sex: "that impure passion that alone engrosses all the heart" (T&S, 209–10). The point that *is* made in Leonard's second speech is the Romantic idea of the innocent child as opposed to the experienced and therefore guilty adult: "I stood again in the lonesome road, no more a sinless child, but a man of blood" (T&S, 211). This is as far from a twentieth-century Freudian idea of childhood as it is from a seventeenth-century Puritan notion. Indeed, knowledge of what happened at Salem makes it very difficult to believe in the innocence of childhood – as the narrator knows perfectly well, and shows in his second attempt on his audience: "a mother . . . groaned inwardly . . . for there was her little son among the accusers" (T&S, 215).[10] And to have the father slain by the Indians is to remove that death as far as possible from a son's feeling that he may, somehow, be responsible for the father's death. It is contrast, not identity, that Hawthorne is working for here as elsewhere in his story: before the body of his father Leonard felt innocent, while before the body of his (unknown) twin-brother he felt guilty. His father's face was "fierce with the strife and distorted with the pain" while Walter's face had a "look of evil and scornful triumph" (T&S, 211, 208). The contrast could hardly be clearer.

One of Hawthorne's intentions is to educate a reader into seeing how a story is told and structured. The description of Walter's face is another hint about the story's future: its appearance made "death so life-like" that an anonymous beholder thought "the stiffened corpse" might "rise up" (T&S, 208). The "resurrection" which is to end the tale is prepared for at the beginning. The Alice Doane section is a mystery which invites the reader to be detective and critic; that it can be too easily "solved" makes it a poor mystery but an excellent way for writer and reader to explore narrative technique, allowing us to see how parallelism and contrast work as structural devices so that we can see how we follow a story and how we can have a (possibly confused) presentiment about what is to come. *Why* the story is told is another question, and is much more suspicious. The narrator wants to shock his audience — so we have murder, incest, a mysterious wizard, evil spirits and devils. One at least of these should work and it may indeed do so — just so long as the story does not come to an end and make the audience come to a conclusion about what they have just heard.

Crews is right when he says that "Every reader must feel cheated when he is told that the wizard has prearranged the greater part of the plot; with one blow Hawthorne thus cancels all the personal motivation he has so carefully established." And he is right too when he says that "this strikes me as exactly why the wizard is useful." But he is wrong in the conclusion that he draws, in his attempt to make him represent the unconscious mind: "He acts as a *deus ex machina* who relieves the other characters of responsibility for their compulsions." Colacurcio has offered one reason why this will not do: "When has it ever closed the moral case to say that 'the devil made me do it?'"[11] But I would rather argue that Hawthorne intends the readers to feel cheated — and also expects them to be not too surprised for we have already been told that "While Leonard spoke, the wizard sat listening to what he already knew" (T&S, 210). If, feeling cheated, we take a more careful look at the wizard, we can see that Hawthorne has so designed the Alice Doane section that no coherent interpretation of her tale is possible. This is not so much a self-consuming artefact as one which self-destructs on close examination. Hawthorne refuses to allow that part of his story to exist as a whole, and it is clear that this is his intention when his predilection (amounting almost to obsession at times) for alternative explanations is remembered. Here, there is no attempt to provide a rational explanation for the wizard. The supernatural is accepted apparently without question — we must either take the wizard or leave him — and this is very rare indeed in Hawthorne's fiction.[12] However, the final rejection of the Gothic strain in the tale comes with the narrator's final flourish: "I added that the wizard's grave was close beside us, and that the wood-wax had sprouted originally from his unhallowed bones" (T&S, 214). It is an ending that does not make sense in terms of Alice's story. Before that began, we were told that the graves close to the narrator and his lady friends were those of the innocent "witches," and that the site chosen for telling the tale is close to where they choose to believe the gallows stood. So the ending cannot be taken seriously, not only because historical fact is being opposed to Gothic fantasy, but because of the moral reversal: the graves of the persecuted good – "martyrs" even (T&S, 205) – have been converted into the grave of the evil persecutor by merely authorial *fiat*. It does, however, make a kind of sense in terms of the somewhat confused associations in the narrator's mind. The wood-wax was initially presented as an unnatural part of nature: incest too is unnaturally natural. The narrator, under the pressure of the need to provide a satisfactory end for his tale, forgets the first connection he has made between one kind of evil and the wood-wax and substitutes another.[13] He is in an impossible position – if one of his own making. He is at one and the same time trying to restore the purely Gothic element in the story *and* trying to connect the story to history and real life. Yet, as Hawthorne knows, these are irreconcilable aims. He implies that "the tale of Terror" is intended principally to shock and appal and that it works while the story continues and disbelief is suspended: "Their bright eyes were fixed on me; their lips apart" (T&S, 212). This is fine for just as long as the story is going on, but how is it to be ended? For Hawthorne, such a tale should not, cannot survive the encounter with reality that an ending almost inevitably involves – and this is especially true or, at the least, obvious, when the tale is spoken. The narrator's attempt to restore the story to the world by making a connection to a knowable landscape while at the same time trying to top all previous efforts is bound to be absurd.

### III

> And yet I must most humbly beg you that in the management of the affair in your most worthy hands, you do not lay more stress upon pure spectre testimony than it will bear.[14]

I suggested that the reference to the wizard's grave was an attempt to re-establish the Gothic element in the tale, and the implication that something else, some kind of history had entered the Alice Doane section is what I now want to draw attention to. Until the graveyard scene is reached there is really no evidence as to when the story is taking place – apart from the narrator's flat assertion that it is 1692. Leonard and Walter, for example, are young Romantics, only too clearly closer to Byron and "Monk" Lewis than to Goodman Proctor or Cotton Mather. But when we in company with the Doanes reach the graveyard, we are pulled into history. I do not mean simply that the whole past population of Salem appears – or rather seems to appear, for as we shall see that is a pseudo-past. It is more that a different set of references come into play, and these do have direct reference to the seventeenth century and more particularly to the witchcraft trials which are to be the subject of the narrator's second attempt. The early part of the Alice Doane section deals with the irrational. There is no need to ask too many reasonable questions about the relationships between the Doanes, Walter Brome and the wizard – the Gothic gets its strength precisely because of its exploitation of the irrational, the forbidden and the very immoral, and it would be extremely silly to start worrying about how Walter got separated from his brother and sister and why he had a different surname.

Yet there are some serious unanswered questions left at the end of Alice's story even if we remain strictly within that story. Alice may be absolved, but whether any moral blame remains from Leonard's killing of Walter is a question left unanswered. Can and should the reader rest happy with "the Appeal of Alice to the spectre of Walter Brome" and his reply "absolving her from every stain" – especially when it is remembered that, according to Leonard, Walter has offered "indubitable proofs of the shame of Alice"? (T&S, 214, 210) The normal use of "absolve" has to do with the remission of sins. If it is accepted that Walter is evil, what right has he to remit sins, and which sins is he remitting? Even if the less common usage of "acquittal" is meant, what makes him a judge? This, of course, may be nit-picking, though at the very least it seems to me to suggest some ambiguity in Walter's verdict. But the choice of the word "spectre" is incontrovertibly crucial. Whether we choose to interpret it as a Gothic term or as a technical term directly relevant to the Salem witchcraft trials is a decision that radically affects the meaning we take from the story. The word was undoubtedly common enough in Gothic and Romantic fiction. "Monk" Lewis, for example, was also the author of *Alonzo and Imogen: Or, The Bridal Spectre* and *The Castle Spectre: A Drama*. *The Monthly Review* as early as 1795 comments on recent fiction in a way that shows that much of the matter of the Alice Doane tale was, at least in part, commonplace:

> The Platonic idea of influencing demons or disembodied spirits by human rites and adjurations, of learning secret phenomena from their revelation, and of accomplishing by their intervention, important purposes of this world, had scarcely been mentioned, much less credited, since the time of the old Alchemists and Rosicrucians, until some modern novelists chose once more to familiarize their superstition; partly in order to expose it, and partly in order to extract from it new sources of the terrible.[15]

And Carlyle refers to the appearance of spectres as almost a defining element in German Gothic. But the word has another and more specialized meaning to which no one who has read anything at all about the Salem trials could fail to respond.

The significance of Walter's spectre can only be approached by recognizing what is going on in the graveyard scene. Careless readers have in the past thought that all the former inhabitants of Salem rise from their graves and are recognized as damned. But Hawthorne very carefully repeatedly distinguishes between two categories – the genuinely damned and those that seem to be damned: "none but souls accursed were there, and fiends counterfeiting the likeness of departed saints;" "both sinful souls and false spectres of good men;" "This company of devils and condemned souls had come on a holiday" (T&S, 213, 213–14, 214). To understand the importance of this distinction that Hawthorne so hammers home it is necessary that the reader should have at least a limited historical knowledge. It is well known that spectre evidence was a key issue in the Salem trials: "This was evidence that a spectre, or shape, or apparition, representing Goodman Proctor, for instance, had tormented the witness or had been present at a witches' meeting." The question was, could the spectre only appear with the permission of the person impersonated – he or she having made a pact with the Devil – or could the Devil trap the community into persecuting the virtuous by acting entirely without the individual's co-operation?

> Hawthorne knew that there had been a debate about whether the Devil could ... "take the shape of an angel of light." ... He was well aware that Cotton Mather had warned against putting too much confidence in this form of evidence; he also knew that after the Mathers and Thomas Brattle had opposed even the admission of spectre evidence (the Mathers on the ground that it was the Devil's testimony), the court had convicted almost no one and not a single convict had been executed.[16]

Given this information, it seems to me that something very odd happens to the ending of Alice's story – if, like Colacurcio, we think that the "original story was ... adequate ... to the essential history of Salem Witchcraft."

If no trust is to be placed in spectre evidence, where does this leave Alice? And even if a reader tries to imagine himself as belonging to those who did believe in spectre evidence, he still has problems. If, as Colacurcio assures us, we should read the story as true to the spirit of 1692, what should be done with this – straight from New England, August 9, 1692? "It is utterly unlawful to inquire of the dead or to be informed of them (Isaiah viii.19). It was an act of the Witch of Endor to raise the dead, and of a reprobate Saul to inquire of him (1 Samuel xxviii.8; Deuteronomy xviii.11)."[17] Increase Mather some ten years earlier had been equally confident (and also referred to the case of the Witch of Endor): "good angels never appear in the shape of dead men;

but evil and wicked spirits have oftentimes done so" – and therefore little confidence can be put in what they say:

> Chrysostom . . . saith that daemons would oftentimes appear, falsely pretending themselves to be the souls of some lately dead. He saith . . . that the spirits in them would feign the voices of men lately killed, and would discover the secrets of such persons, professing they were the souls of those very men. But those were no other then [sic] devilish lies. Upon which account men had need be exceeding wary what credit they give unto, or how they entertain communion with such spectres. I do not say that all such apparitions are diabolical; only that many of them are so.[18]

If spectre evidence cannot be trusted and if evidence from the dead is (to put it at its weakest) highly unreliable, then what credibility can be given to Walter's "spectre"? Alice may very well be guilty and the wizard's plot may have succeeded. After all, it has certainly partly succeeded:

> the wizard . . . had cunningly devised that Walter Brome should tempt his unknown sister to guilt and shame, and himself perish by the hand of his twin-brother.    (T&S, 214)

And what is one to make of the "look of evil and scornful triumph" on dead Walter's face? (T&S, 208) More: there is the virtual certainty that Alice is herself sinning – from the seventeenth-century point of view – merely by making her Appeal. To read "spectre" historically as a term with a very precise seventeenth-century meaning may be to subvert the Gothic interpretation, but, in subverting that narrative, the story falls apart. Hawthorne seems to have intended to allow a reading which would deny the surface moral of the tale, but which would only be noticed by those readers who possess the historical knowledge that he knows most of his audience lack, and as such it is a bitter joke on his unhistorical audience. Those who have knowledge of Gothic fiction can read the story one way, and those who know Salem's history can interpret in another. Both must, finally, define the tale as a failure. Only those who read it carelessly can be satisfied with it: they can see a tale with a reasonably happy ending – female purity seems to have been preserved and the villain has been killed.

For Hawthorne the joke is not simply on the audience – or audiences – but also on the narrator with his attempts to discover a style and a subject to move his audience. The vision of the past that confronts Leonard and Alice is so evil that there is no reason at all to value it. Yet the narrator wants his audience, his society, to have a sense of the past, to respect history. His feeling of pique that "a narrative which had good authority in our ancient superstitions, and would have brought even a church deacon to Gallows Hill, in old witch times, should now be considered too grotesque and extravagant, for timid maids to tremble at" shows that on one level his tale is too subjectively historical. The girls are not invited to tremble at the fact that people did once believe such superstitions: they can only be frightened if they become, in effect, paid-up members of the seventeenth century. If they did get seriously frightened by the witchcraft element in the tale, if they regarded it as, in some sense, true, they would necessarily still believe in witches, they would believe in spectre evidence, and witchcraft trials would logically have to resume in Salem (with the narrator as, no doubt, the first victim denounced by his female audience). Hawthorne here demonstrates his own profound historical sense. He allows the reader to see not only how and why seventeenth-century and Romantic frames of reference cannot co-exist, but also that the form the narrator's attempt at historical penetration cannot and should not work because there is no way back from his seventeenth century to the nineteenth century, to the present. For the sake of wholeness, relevance and coherent meaning the narrator must abandon his previous attempt, with its mixture of genres and its internal contradictions, and turn instead towards a real understanding of history and its significance. This is, very literally, an experimental work: "I . . . made a trial whether truth were more powerful than fiction" (T&S, 215).

The second experiment is set up in a similar way to the first as another attempt is made to imagine what old Salem looked like, but, while the scene-settings are similar, they are not identical. In the first case, the past is patronized (the buildings of the past are merely "quaint") and possession of that pseudo-past is taken far too easily (T&S, 207). In the second, the narrator recognizes the "obscurity" of the past and reinforces the contrast as he moves on and into the past – it is a populated landscape that comes into view (T&S, 215). These differences need stressing as those critics who have tried to discuss the story as a whole have only too often given themselves insoluble problems by trying to discover similar structures and intentions in the Alice Doane section and the historical picture. The problem has often been concentrated on a discussion of Cotton Mather's role in the narrator's sketch rather than of his historical role:

> In the rear of the procession rode a figure on horseback, so darkly conspicuous, so sternly triumphant, that my hearers mistook him for the visible presence of the fiend himself; but it was only his good friend, Cotton Mather, proud of his well won dignity, as the representative of all the hateful features of his time; the one blood-thirsty man, in whom were concentrated those vices of spirit and errors of opinion, that sufficed to madden the whole surrounding multitude.
>
> (T&S, 216)

"Surely," says Crews, "the bitterness of this paragraph was not inspired by an objective study of Cotton Mather's peripheral role in the Salem trials." For Bell, this is a "Gothic picture of Cotton Mather as superstitious villain." For Colacurcio, this is a hint that the narrator is to be read as more than a trifle untrustworthy and unbalanced: "Unless we wish to concede that Hawthorne's tone really is, for once, entirely out of control, or unless we are willing to suppose that Hawthorne's view of the matter greatly changed between "Alice Doane's Appeal" and *Grandfather's Chair*, it seems necessary to conclude that the final vision of Cotton Mather is strategically overwrought."[19] We have to be careful as to how we appeal to Grandfather – whether we are psychoanalytic or historical critics – as his history is a tale for children. And in "Time's Portraiture" (1838), Hawthorne had shown himself still anti-Mather: "Some would look for him [Time] on the ridge of Gallows-Hill, where, in one of his darkest moods, he and Cotton Mather hung the witches" (T&S, 587). This is not the place to debate at length what part Cotton Mather did play in the trials as a whole, but there is one point at which he does move pretty close to the centre of the stage and that is at the execution of George Burroughs, and that is clearly what Hawthorne is referring to here:

> I watched the face of an ordained pastor, . . . his lips moved in prayer, no narrow petition for himself alone, but embracing all, his fellow sufferers and the frenzied multitude; he looked to heaven and trod lightly up the hill.
>
> (T&S, 215–16)

As Colacurcio points out, it is clear that Hawthorne had read and believed Calef's account – the emphasis on Burroughs being an ordained minister makes that clear – and, if one believes Calef (and Cotton Mather never denied this part of Calef's narrative even in his own copy), it is hard to feel forgiving about Cotton Mather's role:

> Mr. Burroughs was carried in a Cart with the others, through the streets of Salem to Execution; when he was upon the Ladder, he made a Speech for the clearing of his Innocency, with such Solemn and Serious Expressions, as were to the Admiration of all present; his Prayer (which he concluded by repeating the Lord's Prayer,) was so well worded, and uttered with such composedness, and such (at least seeming) fervency of Spirit, as was very affecting, and drew Tears from many (so that it seemed to some, that the Spectators would hinder the Execution), The accusers said the black Man stood and dictated to him; as soon as he was turned off, Mr. Cotton Mather, being mounted upon a Horse, addressed himself to the People, partly to declare, that he was no ordained Minister, and partly to possess the People of his guilt; saying, That the Devil has often been transformed into an Angel of Light; and this did somewhat appease the People, and the Executions went on . . .[20]

And the executions went on. I wonder whether John Proctor, John Willard, George Jacobs, and Martha Carrier (defined posthumously by

Mather as a "rampant hag") felt that Mather's role was "peripheral." Such behaviour as Mather's surely justifies some bitterness on Hawthorne's part. In any case, Hawthorne very carefully does not do what many nineteenth-century historians did – make him the villain (Gothic or otherwise) or scapegoat for the community as a whole. Mather is offered as a more complex moral case composed of "vices of spirit" *and* "errors of opinion," who is "the *representative*" of those vices and errors "that sufficed to madden the *whole surrounding community*." All my emphases, of course, are to make the point that Cotton Mather is not presented as the originator of these terrible happenings but as the "representative" of the community – a word that carries, however problematically, a lot of weight in a democracy. Hawthorne emphasizes the importance of the whole community in this, referring to the "multitude," "the universal heart," "the whole crowd," the "people," and "the whole surrounding multitude" (T&S, 215, 216). As the whole community stream up the hill, Cotton Mather, their representative at the bar of history, is merely at the tail-end of the procession. And here Hawthorne differs from the liberal establishment of his own time – not only from a writer such as Upham but also Bancroft who attempted to save his version of democratic history by differentiating between the basically decent common mind of New England, "more wise" than that representative of the clerical aristocracy, Cotton Mather: "The responsibility of the tragedy, far from attaching to the people of the colony, rests with the very few, hardly five or six, in whose hands the transition state of the government left, for a season, unlimited influence."[21] The problems (if there are problems) are not centred on questions as to whether the narrator is out of control – his sketch is very carefully structured – nor the related question whether the narrator assesses Mather's historical significance correctly, but whether he is justified in asking the reader to read carefully enough to see how he has presented Mather and, possibly, whether he is justified in being so allusive. Can the reader be expected to have read Calef? And if he has, how will he react to the historical inaccuracy of the narrator's list of victims? To an extent, of course, the two problems cancel each other out – but I still have to explain why Hawthorne does not get the victims right – if Hawthorne is, as I have claimed, appealing to history.

This is only troubling, however, if it is thought that "Alice Doane's Appeal" is patterned round a simple straightforward opposition of fiction to literal historical fact. While those elements can be found in the story, Hawthorne never allows them to be separated out into neat isolated units: they always remain in a complex interrelationship. We have already seen that history enters into Alice's tale. And Hawthorne has left us a very useful explanation of how he approached the historical world in his early work ("Sir William Phips," 1830):

> The knowledge, communicated by the historian and biographer, is analogous to that which we acquire of a country by the map, – minute, perhaps, and accurate, and available for all necessary purposes, – but cold and naked, and wholly destitute of the mimic charm produced by landscape painting. These defects are partly remediable, and even without an absolute violation of literal truth, although by methods rightfully interdicted to professors of biographical exactness. A license must be assumed in brightening the materials which time has rusted, and in tracing out the half-obliterated inscriptions on the columns of antiquity; fancy must throw her reviving light on the faded incidents that indicate character, whence a ray will be reflected, more or less vividly, on the person to be described.                                                        (T&S, 12)

Imaginative possession of the past must be taken. This passage is helpful in understanding the changes Hawthorne makes to the historical record. He clearly has August 19, 1692 in mind – the references to Burroughs and Mather are proof enough of that. But while historical equivalents for the victims he mentions can be named with a fair degree of confidence, they were not all executed on the same day. The victims here are three women and two men: in actuality, four men and one woman died that day. What we are being offered is a representative range of the victimisation – from someone so senile that she does not even understand what is happening, to a woman so brain-washed that "feverish dreams were remembered as realities, and she almost believed her guilt," to a woman denounced by her young son – and ending with the pastor who attempts to return good for evil, his prayer "embracing all, his fellow sufferers and the frenzied multitude" (T&S, 215, 216). Horrific details (such as those of torture) are excluded, and a dramatic incident (such as Burroughs' flawless recitation of the Lord's Prayer just before execution – thought to be something of a hurdle for witches) is transformed into a privately spoken prayer to which only the novelist/historian has access. One of the most striking features of the trials is not mentioned: it was those who denied they were witches, or who, in Burroughs' case at least (plagiarizing, unfortunately), denied the existence of witchcraft as usually understood, who died. As Calef says, "though the confessing Witches were many; yet not one of them that confessed their own guilt and abode by their Confession, were put to Death."[22] It is the sort of bitter irony that I would have thought would have appealed to Hawthorne – yet his restraint is such that it only appears here in the form of his conviction that the victims were innocent. The details of history have been filtered through the mind of the artist to produce a representative description which will have the strength of typicality. For it is only through typicality that the writer can make his moral, artistic, and historical points – points centrally concerned with ideas of process, and which are in contrast with the static world of the Alice Doane section. What I mean here by typicality is best shown by Raymond Williams' discussion of realism in *The Long Revolution*:

> Tipichnost . . . radically affects the whole question of realism. For the "typical", Soviet theorists tell us, "must not be confused with that which is frequently encountered" . . . We can see that the concept of *tipichnost* alters "realist" from its sense of the direct reproduction of observed reality: "realism" becomes, instead, a principled and organized selection.[23]

Hawthorne's narrator has, of course, moved the other way from that Williams is tracing. He has moved from semi-fantasy to history – while Williams was examining a movement away from photographic naturalism towards an historically minded realism. Still, the narrator's sketch offers the reader "a principled and organized selection" of the historical world.

To claim that it is the Alice story which is static may seem to be the opposite of the apparent structure of the tale. The historical sketch appears, at first sight, to be static, a moment snatched out of history, out of time, which does not even have a proper ending – while the Alice Doane section seems to have, if anything, too much story. Yet it is here that Hawthorne has played most subtly on his seeming parallels and actual contrasts. It is, partly, these apparent similarities that emphasize the contrasts. We have already seen how alike the respective scene-setting attempts are – and how and why they differ. The few repetitions of language share much the same purpose. Take the use of the phrase "loathing and horror." In the first case, it occurs as Leonard compares himself with Walter:

> There was a resemblance from which I shrunk with sickness, and loathing, and horror, as if my own features had come and stared upon me in a solitary place, or had met me in struggling through a crowd. (T&S, 209)

In the second, it comes as the crowd attempts to define itself as totally other than the "witches:"

> I strove to realize and faintly communicate the deep, unutterable loathing and horror, the indignation, the affrighted wonder, that wrinkled on every brow, and filled the universal heart. See! the whole crowd turns pale and shrinks within itself, as the virtuous emerge from yonder street. (T&S, 215)

In the first case, loathing and horror stem from an appalled recognition of identity: in the second, they come from the insistence on difference. These minor points indicate the radical difference between the two sections. For all the events that crowd the Alice Doane section, its moral structure is essentially static – and not only because its various elements fight each other to a standstill. Finally it relies for its effect on an acceptance of the supernatural which itself implies an acceptance of an

irresponsibly deterministic view of moral life. It is, then, *outside* history –
and thus outside society too. The inhabitants of Salem might as well not
exist as far as the Doanes (and the reader) are concerned – or rather the
Salem community that does appear to exist is a vision of a perverted
resurrection composed of damned souls and devils, which both gives a
false picture of the moral status of the past and implies a denial of any
possibility of change. Everything that takes place can be blamed on the
wizard: it is his vision of the past that we see in the graveyard and it is he
who is responsible for the plot. And because he is responsible, all that the
reader is left with is the temporary frisson to be gained from a shocking
story. The only problems the story raises *as a paraphrasable unit* (i.e. one
where the word "spectre" can be replaced by – say – ghost or spirit) – as
opposed to the invitation to consider the ways in which we make sense of
stories which the *form* insists on – are comparatively trivial such as, how
conscious is Leonard of his incestuous feelings towards Alice and is Alice
innocent or not?

The historical section, in deliberate and careful contrast, dramatizes a
social world, a world of process, a moment in history which genuinely
belongs to history, which just because of this historicity is relevant to the
present. The victims are witches only in terms of their society. It is an act
of definition by society which leads them to the scaffold – that, and their
own quite remarkable courage. For the accused are not merely innocent:
they are "virtuous" (T&S, 215).[24] In the Alice Doane section, the lost
souls and the devils are frozen into the static moral category of the
irredeemable. Here, there is a more complex moral structure –
beginning from the irony that the guilty crowd define themselves as
innocent while they define the virtuous as guilty, and from the
distinction between the way they see themselves and the way they are
seen by the narrator. There is no point in asking why the wizard acted as
he did. Wizards just do things like that. But here, in the human world of
history the question can be asked and, perhaps, answered. Because
motive is introduced, because the crowd is not *simply* evil, we must
speculate about why such a thing happened and reflect on its
significances – among which is the possibility that something analogous
might occur even in our brave new world. We are returned to a world of
human responsibility – a world where judgement is necessary:

> Behind their victims came the afflicted, a guilty and miserable band; villains
> who had thus avenged themselves on their enemies, and viler wretches, whose
> cowardice had destroyed their friends; lunatics, whose ravings had chimed in
> with the madness of the land; and children, who had played a game that the
> imps of darkness might have envied them, since it disgraced an age, and dipped
> a people's hand in blood.                                          (T&S, 216)

If these motives alone were considered to provide a satisfactory explanation, the story would hardly belong to history for these are, alas, commonplaces of human behaviour. But it is not simply "vices of spirit" but "errors of opinion" that we are invited to recognize and repudiate, and those errors clearly refer to the culturally conditioned belief in witchcraft – yet another blow at Alice's tale. (While villainy, cowardice and lunacy may be the commonplaces of behaviour, they do not always result in such appalling consequences – or so one would like to think).

The moral structure of the witchcraft section is specifically historical – allowing for change and development and again stressing human responsibility. One moral dimension is notably lacking from the Alice section – repentance. It has, of course, no real place there. But here it does, and *must*, if the contrast is to work: "thus I marshalled them onward, the innocent who were to die, and the guilty who were to grow old in long remorse" (T&S, 216). It is not just a question of patterning but of historical accuracy: it is notable and considerably to New England's credit that, as I pointed out in my introduction, that long remorse did take place. Pattern is important, though. The "remorse" that Leonard briefly feels is only one feeling among many that flash across his confused mind. Here remorse is the conclusion to the moral movement of the evocation of the past. (And it may be worth remembering that Hawthorne says this of Hester's return to Boston: "Here had been her sin; here her sorrow; and here was yet to be her penitence" [N, 344].) The deterministic moral structure of the Alice Doane section can be recognized simply from a reading of it – but the reasons for repudiating that come from the historical section. The narrator refuses to permit the possible dignity of sin or even the rigidity of evil to his historical characters. Even Cotton Mather is only allowed "vices." There is no Devil, no wizard to take the blame away from the community.

The historical sketch has been so constructed that it cannot be dismissed as only a unique event which might be open to patronage by a "superior" present which thinks that change means progress means improvement, which thinks that it has transcended its history. The allusion to the Bunker Hill monument and thus to the American Revolution is not there by accident. It is only a single sentence but it is the penultimate one of the story: "We build the memorial column on the height which our fathers made sacred with their blood, poured out in a holy cause" (T&S, 216). At the beginning of the story, the narrator criticized his society for its ignorance of its history and for its symbolic celebration of a history at once unknown and irrelevant to it. Here it is the uncritical celebration of half a history that he warns against: the

Revolution did not redeem Americans from the tragic realm of history – that redemption must come from confronting the past as a whole, by escaping from false because partial versions of the past. The prose emphasizes the separation and the connection between the two events – the triumph and the tragedy – as the narrator continues and concludes: "And here in dark, funereal stone, should rise another monument, sadly commemorative of the errors of an earlier race, and not to be cast down, while the human heart has one infirmity that may result in crime" (T&S, 216).

"And now the past had done all it could." (T&S, 216) That is not simply to reduce the listeners to tears. If that was all the narrator would merely be a rapist of the emotions on very much the same moral level as the wizard – a possibility Hawthorne draws attention to in order to repudiate. It is an acknowledgement that a transition to the modern world must be made if the understanding of history just gained is to mean anything – a point also made by the conclusion to *The Scarlet Letter*. The account of Alice's adventures ends with incredulous laughter: the historical section ends with tears. For while Alice's adventures had been designed to horrify the audience, for his second attempt the narrator "plunged into" his "imagination," for "horror" admittedly, but more importantly for "a deeper woe" (T&S, 216). The story teller began by criticizing his audience, his society, for its lack of an historical sense: he ends by attempting to create that sense. His first tale exploits, plays with that lack – and fails in the attempt. For the published version he dismantles the story so that writer and reader can see what went wrong and why, and in doing this a critique of a particular type of literary endeavour is enacted – the art which reveals art. The second attempt no longer exploits or condescends to the audience. The narrator has been educated by the audience into accepting his role of educator.

One of the problems with Alice Doane's tale was that the narrator could not provide a proper ending yet, of necessity, had to make the attempt. It has two endings neither of which can make sense of the story and neither of which can successfully return the story to reality. In direct contrast, the account of the Salem executions does not need an ending because there is no single, no correct, ending to such an enterprise. We do not need to be told anything more about what will have happened because we either know or can predict what will follow from what we have been told. The girls weep because they *anticipate* what is to come. We perceive a pattern – a dynamic structure – which the artist does not need to fill in. More importantly, the significance, the meaning, of the historical sketch is precisely that what it represents has not got an ending and cannot have one until society changes enough to recognize the need to build a public monument "to assist the imagination in appealing to the heart" (T&S, 216). Such a monument would be a positive symbol of the society that would build it — its recognition of human needs and deficiencies. Art and social change become inextricably linked. It is no longer merely a question of what the past can do for the present but of what the present should do for the past: a dialectical relationship where the hoped for synthesis is attempted by the story as a whole — yet which lies outside the tale in history, in a desired and desirable future. The narrator has discovered a way to connect art and life — and it is that connection which is the final success of a brilliant story: "Alice Doane's Appeal" by the Author of "The Gentle Boy."

# 3

## Sketches experimental and ideal: "Main-Street" and "Ethan Brand"

> I send you, at last, the manuscript portion of my volume; not quite all of
> it, however, for there are three chapters still to be written of "The Scarlet
> Letter." . . .
> I shall call the book Old-Time Legends; together with *sketches, experimental
> and ideal.* I believe we must consider the book christened as above.
> (Hawthorne to Fields, Jan. 15, 1850. XVI, 305, 306)

Here, Hawthorne yet again announces another title which was to join
*Seven Tales of My Native Land, Provincial Tales, The Story Teller,* and
(possibly) *Allegories of the Heart* in the realm of the might-have-been.[1]
The loss is hardly to be regretted in this case for Hawthorne's intention
seems to have been largely tactical as can be seen from a letter written
only five days after Hawthorne had apparently committed himself:

> Is it safe . . . to stake the fate of the book entirely on this one chance? [ *The Scarlet
> Letter*] A hunter loads his gun with a bullet and several buck-shot; and,
> following his sagacious example, it was my purpose to conjoin the one long
> story with half a dozen shorter ones; so that, failing to kill the public outright
> with my biggest and heaviest lump of lead, I might have other chances with
> the smaller bits, individually and in the aggregate. (XVI, 307)

And Fields' advice to publish *The Scarlet Letter* as a separate work must
have seemed the more persuasive as it allowed Hawthorne to achieve an
ambition of the Old Manse period – a "novel that could stand
unsupported, on its edges" (T&S, 1,148). However, even though the
book never materialized, the terms which Hawthorne saw as suitable for
categorizing his work are intriguing. "Old-Time Legends" is not
particularly problematic as it, of course, recalls "Legends of the
Province-House" which contains Hawthorne's sustained meditation on

the eighteenth century. But what did he precisely mean by "experimental" and "ideal"? We can perhaps only hypothesize about those meanings by considering what would have been included in the volume. *The Scarlet Letter* obviously would have had pride of place – presumably as an old-time legend. No doubt the remainder would have included some of the material that was later included in *The Snow-Image* – though just how much must be a matter for debate.[2] "Main-Street" would have definitely been there and almost certainly "Ethan Brand." And I would suggest that "Main Street" should be read as coming under the experimental label – while "Ethan Brand" would most probably come under the heading of the ideal considering the reference on its first page to "that portentous night when the IDEA was first developed" though there is a way in which it too could be read as an experiment as I suggest below, p. 59 (T&S, 1,051).

Colacurcio has argued that "the matter of 'Main-Street' reads like a table of contents of Hawthorne's Puritan tales of the 1830s, and it actually serves him as a sort of finger exercise in preparation for the symphonic form of *The Scarlet Letter*." I share his admiration for this brilliant sketch and agree that it does read as a return to and an attempt at a summation of his views of the seventeenth century – an attempt at a remarkably ambitious and complex narrative which incorporates and reflects on much of the materials and many of the concerns of those tales – as well as a fascinating exploration of the formal problems inherent in presenting these issues. But I would suggest that, rather than seeing it alone as "an 'Introduction' to *The Scarlet Letter* almost as essential as 'The Custom-House' itself," it should be taken with "Ethan Brand" which is equally crucial as a rehearsal of one thematic element in *The Scarlet Letter*.[3] The shift from the Esther of "Ethan Brand" to Hester Prynne can be dismissed as coincidence, but there is a very clear relationship between Ethan and Chillingworth. Ethan "with . . . cold and remorseless purpose . . . had . . . wasted, absorbed, and perhaps annihilated" Esther's "soul" (T&S, 1,060). Chillingworth, according to Dimmesdale, had "violated, in cold blood, the sanctity of a human heart" (N, 286). And "Ethan Brand" as much as "Main-Street" is also to be read as a summation of another strand in Hawthorne's short fiction, looking back to and developing on (for example) the concerns of such a tale as "The Man of Adamant" (1837), but, more importantly, continuing some of the themes of the Manse period – an allegory of the heart, it might be said, to end all allegories of the heart. To pick up on Emerson's culinary metaphor quoted at the end of my introduction, I would argue that the ingredients that go to make up "Main-Street" and "Ethan Brand" have been stirred together and brewed to produce *The Scarlet Letter*. Whether or not this convinces, the two pieces seem to have been composed one after the other. "Ethan Brand," if the evidence of Hawthorne's letters can be trusted, was completed very shortly before December 14, 1848. "Main-Street" was published in Elizabeth Peabody's *Aesthetic Papers* in May, 1849. Hawthorne took Felt's *Annals of Salem* from the Salem Athenaeum on January 2, 1849 for the first time since 1834, and since Felt undoubtedly lies behind much of the detailed information retailed in "Main-Street," it does not seem illegitimate to infer that the sketch was almost certainly composed or, at the least, revised for publication in the first months of 1849.[4] In any case, it must have been completed at some date after November 1848, given the reference to Zachary Taylor's election triumph.

The two pieces, however, share something much more important than historical propinquity: both present themselves as works which might – indeed, should – be other than they are. "Brand" is overtly offered as part of a longer work. It was first titled "The Unpardonable Sin. From an Unpublished Work" and subsequently appeared in *The Snow-Image* with the subtitle "A Chapter from an Abortive Romance." "Main-Street" ends with the break-down of the showman/narrator's equipment and its historical narrative remains stuck in 1717. One, then, insists on being read as a fragment and the other as an unfinished work, and no interpretation can hope to be adequate which does not confront the question of form. This kind of formal concern is the more important as it is not unrepresentative of an element of Hawthorne's practice throughout his career. I discuss the way in which *The Marble Faun* offers itself as an unfinished work – one which contains reflections on the fragment – in chapter VIII. "Alice Doane's Appeal," as we have seen, includes an incomplete story and an unfinished sketch. "Passages from a Relinquished Work" and "Fragments from the Journal of a Solitary Man" speak for themselves – if they may also indicate a resentment at the blindness of editors and publishers (as I suspect that "From the Unpublished Allegories of the Heart" was offered in the hope that such a subtitle would attract the attention of an intelligent publisher). That subtitle to "Ethan Brand" means that we cannot focus only on achievement but must also consider frustrated possibilities. And – given Hawthorne's continued fascination with the fragmentary and the unfinished so exemplified in these pieces – it is virtually impossible to evade considering (however briefly and inadequately) Hawthorne's relation to Romantic literary practice.

That question of Hawthorne's relation to Romanticism is profoundly difficult – and not only because of the difficulties involved in any definition of Romanticism. At times it is tempting to see Hawthorne as self-consciously post-Romantic. "P.'s Correspondence" (1845), for example, I would argue, should be read as Hawthorne's ironic reflections

on the English Romantics and *The Marble Faun* as a critical examination
of certain Romantic tropes. But at least in relation to one Romantic
concern – the fascination with the unfinished – Hawthorne's position is
fairly clear and fairly consistent throughout his career. "Ethan Brand"
and "Main-Street," for example, are analogous to if not identical with
such famous examples of the fragment as "Kubla Khan" and "Christabel." It is significant that at least twice Hawthorne referred to
"Christabel" in terms that recall the Romantic theory which, it has been
argued, "suggests . . . the necessity for a fragmentary poetry." Shelley is
quoted in support of this view: "when composition begins, inspiration is
already on decline, and the most glorious poetry that has ever been
communicated to the world is probably a feeble shadow of the original
conception of the Poet."[5] The most relevant of Hawthorne's references
to Coleridge appears in "A Select Party," published the year before "P.'s
Correspondence:"

> In the alcoves of another vast apartment was arranged a splendid library, the
> volumes of which were inestimable, because they consisted not of actual
> performances, but of the works which the authors only planned, without ever
> finding the happy season to achieve them. To take familiar instances, here were
> the untold tales of Chaucer's Canterbury Pilgrims; the unwritten Cantos of the
> Fairy Queen; the conclusion of Coleridge's Christabel; and the whole of
> Dryden's projected Epic on the subject of King Arthur. The shelves were
> crowded; for it would not be too much to affirm that every author has
> imagined, and shaped out in his thought, more and far better works than those
> which actually proceeded from his pen.                          (T&S, 955)

The connections between the idea of the unfinished work and the
statement that the best works remain unwritten, the closeness of the last
sentence to the passage from Shelley, are points that hardly need spelling
out. This invites the consideration that the confessed fragment merely
declares what is, from this Romantic perspective, true of all art-works –
all are necessarily incomplete, inadequate, radically imperfect. In which
case, from this point of view, the (deliberate?) fragment might well seem
to be the most typical art-work. As Friedrich Schlegel put it (in
Athenaeum fragment no. 24), "Many works of the ancients have
become fragments. Many works of the moderns are fragments from
their inception."

The case is, however, too complex to be entirely subsumed under
Schlegel's rubric. Even if it is accepted that a certain type of fragment
may be one defining characteristic of the Romantic work of art, does it
follow that the writer should *plan* to produce a fragmentary work? One
contemporary critic rapped Byron firmly over the knuckles for
producing what he saw as the poetic equivalent to an artificial ruin in
"The Giaour: A Fragment of a Turkish Tale." Byron

has so extravagantly accommodated himself to the perpetual hurry of the days we live in, as utterly to omit all those parts of the poem which he conceives would be least interesting; to build a fabric of picturesque fragments . . . We cannot bring ourselves to think the shattered skeleton of a regiment quite as fine a spectacle as a complete regiment. Nor should we, independently of the associations which ruins may bring along with them, be disposed to lavish the same praise upon the fragments of the Pantheon as upon the Pantheon itself . . . [I]f this be true, that the beauty of ruins is to be sought in the associations which they create, then the man who *erects* a ruin wholly mistakes the real source of the gratification they afford.[6]

Byron was not without defenders of the form and I shall return to him, but first I want to look briefly at Coleridge's best-known unfinished works. In his headnotes to "Kubla Khan" and "Christabel" he is notably regretful. These pieces are as they are very much *faute de mieux*, and for both he claims that there was a whole to which he had somehow lost access but that he hopes (at some date) to complete the work – or at least to offer a more complete version: "from the still surviving recollections in his mind the author has frequently purposed to finish for himself what had been originally, as it were, given him."[7] These examples may seem clear enough – but even here there are further difficulties. Would readers know that "Kubla Khan" was a fragment if the title did not insist on this – and if the person from Porlock had not become such a legendary figure? I ask the question because I am not at all sure of the answer as the headnote is so much of my experience of the poem and also because of its bearing on "Ethan Brand." It would have been very easy for Hawthorne to have presented that as a conventional autonomous short story. All he needed to do was to suppress the sub-title and delete or rewrite half a dozen sentences or so – an hour's work at most. Both Coleridge and Hawthorne (in these works at least) want to insist that what we are reading is not only a fragment but a failure – if for different reasons.

Byron's strategy is very different in the case of "The Giaour." According to a note in my edition, "the fragmentary style of composition was suggested by the then new and popular 'Columbus' of Samuel Rogers" (to whom the piece is dedicated).[8] Here are two works which are designed to be fragmentary. Rogers offers an "explanation" for this form: "The Vision of Columbus" is yet another of those works that claims (with a wink to the reader) to be based on an ancient manuscript itself incomplete and hard to decipher, which enables the author, having offered "The Argument" of the poem, to turn into poetry the bits he fancies. Of course, one thinks of *The Scarlet Letter* in this context – but there Hawthorne's statement about his practice is, while also claiming to be based on a (fictional) ancient manuscript, quite the opposite to Rogers:

> I must not be understood as affirming, that, in the dressing up of the tale, and imagining the motives and modes of passion that influenced the characters who figure in it, I have invariably confined myself within the limits of the old Surveyor's half a dozen sheets of foolscap. On the contrary; I have allowed myself, as to such points, nearly or altogether as much license as if the facts had been entirely of my own invention. What I contend for is the authenticity of the outline.                                              (N, 147)

Hawthorne denies his fake manuscript any real authority – and claims imagination for himself. Rogers seemingly claims for himself only the authority of "the Translator" – and his preface begins by telling the reader how the poetic fragments are to be taken: "The following Poem (or, to speak more properly, what remains of it) has here and there a lyrical turn of thought and expression. It is sudden in its transitions, and full of historical allusions; leaving much to be imagined by the reader." This leaving of a space for the reader is taken, however unseriously, remarkably far:

> "Yet, tho' we fled yon firmament of fire,
> Still shall we fly, all hope of rule resigned?"
>
> \*   \*   \*   \*   \*   \*   \*
> \*   \*   \*   \*   \*   \*   \*
>
> He spoke; and all was silence, all was night!
> Each had already winged his formidable flight.

These undistinguished lines have an intriguing note appended to them, inviting the reader to do what is conventionally the poet's task: "These scattered fragments may be compared to shreds of old arras, or reflections from a river broken and confused by the oar; and now and then perhaps the imagination of the reader may supply more than is lost."[9] Even the most ardent enthusiast for reader–response theory might be surprised by that.

Byron was understandably tempted by this tactic. His preface begins by insisting that the poem is composed of "disjointed fragments" but he gives enough of the story to enable a reader to situate the fragments in their places in the narrative. His explanation for the form differs from that of Rogers. His was, he claims, originally an oral tale:

> The story in the text is one told of a young Venetian many years ago, and now nearly forgotten. I heard it by accident recited by one of the coffee-house story-tellers who abound in the Levant, and sing or recite their narratives. The additions and interpolations by the translator will easily be distinguished from the rest, by the want of Eastern imagery; and I regret that my memory has retained so few fragments of the original.[10]

It is interesting that he claims that the story is "in" the text and not, say, behind it. However, given what he did to the poem, this account of origins gives him some problems – as it gives the reader for "The Giaour" raises yet another problem for the question of the fragment and the unfinished work. What are we to do with a poem which, while continuing to announce itself as a fragment, grows from the original manuscript to its seventh edition by accretion as passages are inserted into the narrative? "The Giaour" grew from 407 lines to 1,334 lines, the first 6 and the last 16 remaining the same. The problem for Byron is clear enough on one level. As McGann asked, "Were his readers to assume, as each new and augmented edition of his 'snake of a poem' came out, that he periodically recalled additional snatches of the original lay?"[11] Presumably the logical conclusion to such a process should be that the work would end up as a conventional totality which had simply been written over a longish period – that is, supposing that the author could maintain the tone and continue to improve his memory or, if we do not go along with his story of its origin, remember his original intentions. If we do accept his story, then it would be much like a jigsaw: the frame is easy enough to establish – the bits in the middle can be filled in at our leisure. That, however, may be all right in theory: judgement of Byron's practice may be different. "The Giaour" may have ended up with more fragments than in its first appearance but it is an open question whether that makes it more or less fragmentary. And at least one critic has argued that the last state is not better than the first: the accretions "do not constitute a whole that can be pieced together . . . Whatever were his intentions, he badly weakened the poem."[12] It may be, of course, that the demands for organic coherence implied by this critic's terms of judgement are mistaken but his suggestion that this may be almost a different work are worth considering. But a discussion of the formal implications of such a strategy would need a study to itself – though accretion and revision/restructuring through accretion are clearly practices that have their relevance for the varying versions of *The American Claimant Manuscripts* and for the two versions of the Septimius story about his search for the elixir of life.

Not everybody, however, was troubled by Byron's strategy. Even in 1813 with the first edition of "The Giaour" – when a reader could hardly be expected to know that the poem would be added to – there was a remarkable justification of its form from (of all people) Jeffrey:

> This, we think, is very beautiful – or, at all events, full of spirit, character, and originality; nor can we think that we have any reason to envy the Turkish auditors of the entire tale, while we have its fragments thus served up by a *restaurateur* of such taste as Lord Byron. Since the increasing levity of the present age, indeed, has rendered it impatient of the long stories that used to delight our ancestors, the taste for fragments, we suspect, has become very general; and the greater part of polite readers would no more think of sitting

down to a whole Epic, than to a whole ox: – And truly, when we consider how few long poems there are out of which we should not wish very long passages to have been omitted, we will confess, that it is a taste which we are rather inclined to patronize – notwithstanding the obscurity it may occasionally produce, and the havoc it must necessarily make, among the proportions, developments, and *callidae juncturae* of the critics. The truth is, we suspect, that after we once know what it contains, no long poem is ever read, but in fragments; – and that the connecting passages, which are always skipped after the first reading, are often so tedious as to deter us from thinking of a second; – and in very many cases so awkwardly and imperfectly brought out, that it is infinitely less laborious to *guess at* the author's principle of combination, than to follow out his full explanation of it.[13]

Marjorie Levinson says of this that Jeffrey "registers the extent and the nature of 'The Giaour's' irresolution and . . . this quality becomes for him the preeminent textual feature."[14] Despite my indebtedness to her, I must quarrel slightly with this. Jeffrey goes on to say that, while he is not afraid of irresolution, the narrative here is so clear that a reader should have no trouble in situating any one fragment in its proper place in the story: "the story . . . certainly appears to us to be as free from obscurity as any *poetical* narrative with which we are acquainted."[15] I agree, however, that it is a significant passage – despite its slight touch of *The Readers' Digest* condensed book – and not just because Jeffrey is shrewd enough to pick up on the point that Byron's *alibi* for the fragmentary form is that the story was an oral one. Perhaps the most intriguing point is his suggestion that Byron's form is not strange to contemporary reading practices – a point further sophisticated by his implication that the experience of reading "The Giaour" is analogous to that of rereading a text if only because we encounter the poetry after Byron has outlined the story-line.

I am, however, entirely convinced by Levinson's well documented argument that passages like that from Jeffrey show that there were strategies available to both writers and readers which enabled them to produce and receive the fragment (though perhaps "receive" should read "consume" given Jeffrey's image of Byron as *restaurateur*). It is in the context of such literary practices that Hawthorne's own practice (and particularly "Ethan Brand" and "Main-Street") should be situated. And here I want to draw on Levinson's brilliant attempts to theorize about the Romantic fragment poem. It is an attempt at categorization which seems designed to improve reading by provoking debate. Levinson distinguishes between four main types of fragment. The first is "the true fragment . . . a form that suggests both an antecedent and subsequent context of events and description." The reader's strategy here should be to "extrapolate from the given text the before-and-after from which it appears to have been excerpted." Examples of this are Wordsworth's "Nutting" and Coleridge's "Christabel." The second is the "completed fragment" which gives the impression of being the result of "the poet's effort to finish his fragment some time after it was first written and from an antithetical and remedial position." Here the reader's task is to interpret "the discrepancy between the two moments and positions," and effectively to cancel that discrepancy, "healing the breach, as it were, with his own hermeneutic resources and activities." Here, her examples are "Kubla Khan" and "The Giaour." The third is "the deliberate fragment, a form which presents its imperfections as a semantic determination — roughly, a theme." The reader "must read" such fragments "as instances of imitative form." The test cases here are Byron's twelve-line fragment ("When, to their airy hall"), Shelley's *Posthumous Fragments of Margaret Nicholson* and his "Julian and Maddalo." And finally Levinson offers us "the dependent fragment" which "presents itself as an episode in the poet's career." For Levinson, Keats' "Hyperion" and "The Fall of Hyperion" exemplify this category. I have most difficulty with this. Levinson argues that, as with the true fragment, "the incompletion displayed by this fragment form appears to be (and often truly is) fortuitous." But she claims that "whereas the true fragment invites the reader to tease out of the truncated form an essentially autonomous or text-specific context, the dependent fragment at hand performs some particular function." She goes on to argue that "The perceived form of the fragment depends upon the perceived function of the exercise in advancing the poet's thought and improving his craft."[16] What worries me about this is that the definition here seems, so to speak, to be text led rather than dependent on what the reader — quite validly — chooses to do to the text. Take the case of "Ethan Brand." From one point of view this can be very adequately read as an example of the true fragment. From another it would seem equally valid to interpret it as a dependent fragment — where much of its significance comes from it being seen as a work which enables *The Scarlet Letter* (much as Colacurcio wants to read "Main-Street") — if only in the way in which Ethan is a forerunner of the much more important figure of Chillingworth. Nor do these seem to be mutually exclusive ways of reading the piece — at least, I hope not — as I have been and will be taking it more-or-less for granted that it needs to be read both ways — though it is thanks to Levinson's discriminations that I realize that this is what I am doing.

There is a further case where, useful though her categories are, they do not seem fully to cover what I would argue, in the light of Hawthorne's practice, to be a crucial distinction: that between the work which is *designed* to be unfinished, incomplete, that is, in terms of conventional demands for formal completion. In other words, not "The Giaour" but "Main-Street" and *The Marble Faun*. Thus, in "Main-Street" the "failure" to provide a conclusion is prepared for at the beginning and internalized so that it becomes a crucial part of the narrative as the paraphrasable content is fused with the form of the work. Levinson's deliberate fragment comes close to this but the examples she gives indicate the gap between the kind of form I am trying to point to and her definition. In my chapter on *The Marble Faun* I try to discuss this not so much in the light of literary theory but rather in that provided by the art-historian's category of the *non finito*. Coincidentally, Levinson, when considering towards the end of her book developments in the idea of the fragment also turns to sculpture – or rather to literary comments on sculpture as she quotes Rilke on Rodin:

> Completeness is conveyed in all the armless statues of Rodin: nothing necessary is lacking. One stands before them as before something whole. The feeling of incompleteness does not rise from the mere aspect of a thing, but from the assumption of a narrow-minded pedantry, which says that arms are a necessary part of the body and that a body without arms cannot be perfect . . .
> There are among the works of Rodin hands, single, small hands which, without belonging to a body, are alive . . . There is a history of hands; they have their own culture, their particular beauty; one concedes to them the right of their own development . . . Rodin, knowing . . . that the entire body consists of scenes of life, of a life that may become in every detail individual and great, has the power to give to any part of this vibrating surface the independence of a whole.[17]

Such a statement should further force us to keep in mind the distinction between the work that is unfinished because, for whatever reason, it is abandoned and one where the lack of conventional finish is always a deliberate intention. The implications of such a position are, as I have said, more fully explored later but here one can note the difference – and the relation – between Kenyon's abandoned marble bust of Donatello (which puzzles spectators) and the form of the novel as a whole (which left readers with conventional ideas of fictional form so dissatisfied). Of course one has to be careful not to elide the radical differences between spatial and narrative forms – especially in the case of "Main-Street" where the subject is so centrally the presentation of history. And Rilke on Rodin is hardly relevant to "Ethan Brand" which is, in Levinson's terms, indeed a Romantic fragment – though it too has its dismembered hands – one in the Jew of Nuremberg's "show-box" which "might have been mistaken for the Hand of Destiny . . . pointing its forefinger to various scenes of conflict while its owner gave historical illustrations" (T&S, 1,061).

II

> At last, by main strength, I have wrenched and torn an idea out of my
> miserable brain; or rather, the fragment of an idea, like a tooth ill-drawn, and
> leaving the roots to torture me. (NH on "Ethan Brand," Dec. 14, 1848, XVI,
> 251)
>     *Objection.* Alas! man, I am afraid that I have sinned the unpardonable sin, and
> therefore there is no hope for me.
>     *Answer.* Dost thou know what the unpardonable sin, the sin against the
> Holy Ghost, is? and when it is committed?
>     *Reply.* It is a sin against light.
>     *Answer.* That is true; yet every sin against light is not the sin against the Holy
> Ghost.
>     *Reply.* Say you so?[18]

One question that immediately presents itself on looking at "Ethan
Brand" in the perspective provided by Romanticism's obsession with
the fragment is this: if the story by its very insistence on its fragmentary
form claims a relationship (however indirect) with Romantic concerns
then do its contents or themes also overtly further continue those
concerns – or are they to be read as another of Hawthorne's meditations
on Puritanism, to be read beside (say) "Young Goodman Brown" and
"The Minister's Black Veil"? The second option has a long history
behind it, going back at least to Paul Elmer More's insistence on "the
central significance of . . . 'Ethan Brand' in the circle of Hawthorne's
works," and his claim that "manifestly . . . the doctrines of Cotton
Mather stalk through that tale under the transparent mask of fiction."
Among the passages from the *Magnalia* that More cites is this:

> There are many men, who in the very constitution of their *bodies*, do afford a
> *bed*, wherein busy and bloody *devils*, have a sort of lodging provided for them
> . . . 'Tis well if *self-murder* be not the sad end, into which these hurried people
> are thus precipitated. *New England*, a country where *splenetic* maladies are
> prevailing and pernicious, perhaps above any other, hath afforded numberless
> instances, of even *pious people*, who have contracted those *melancholy
> indispositions*, which have unhinged them from all service or comfort; yea not a
> few persons have been hurried thereby to lay *violent hands* upon themselves at
> the last. These are among the *unsearchable judgments* of God![19]

More's is an attractive argument – particularly as it is not hard to find a
Puritan fascination with the Unpardonable Sin, that intriguing and
mysterious sin against the Holy Ghost. Winthrop reports two cases
which bear on this terrible matter. Here is the first:

> A woman of Boston congregation, having been in much trouble of mind
> about her spiritual estate, at length grew into utter desperation, and could not

endure to hear of any comfort, etc., so as one day she took her little infant and threw it into a well, and then came into the house and said, now she was sure she should be damned, for she had drowned her child; but some, stepping presently forth, saved the child.

I am indebted to Colacurcio for drawing attention to this passage and for the way in which, paraphrasing Crews, he makes the point that in such a society a guilty identity can seem better than none. The second case also involves a woman attempting to drown her child: "She would give no other reason for it, but that she did it to save it from misery, and withal that she was assured, she had sinned against the Holy Ghost, and that she could not repent of any sin."[20]

This concern with the Unpardonable Sin was not only an American or even an English concern. There is the case of Francis Spira, an Italian who converted to Protestantism and then was tried for heresy by the Catholics in 1548. He publicly recanted but shortly afterwards bitterly regretted that recantation — so bitterly that he repeatedly tried to commit suicide and died, it was thought, in and of despair:

> that he was all ready in hel, in continual torment, that he was voide & destitute of all hope and fauoure of God, that he ought not to loke for the mercy of god, for that he had sinned against ye holy ghost and that his faulte was unpardonable, that the merites of chryst did auayle hym nothynge, that he had no maner faithe or hope lefte, wysshynge too be in the place of Iudas or Cayne, that he loked for nothynge else daylye, but the horrible sentence of the iuste God, and that the mercy of God, dyd farre surmount all the synnes of the world; but yet could not auayle hym any thynge, for that he was reprobate from the begynnynge: neither wrytten at anye tyme, in ye boke of lyfe, that Christ neither suffered nor praied for him: but for the elect onely, that the iudgement of God was declared and his iustice fulfylled in hym onely. Finally, that within short space, hys horryble ende should come: that he might geue an example to all the electe, of his abiuration.[21]

The case was widely reported. A Latin account with a preface by Calvin (among others) was translated into English in 1550 (the passage above comes from this), and was made the subject of a sixteenth-century morality play, *The Conflict of Conscience* by Nathaniel Woodes. Among the many accounts of this exemplary sinner was a seventeenth-century version by Nathaniel Bacon which was repeatedly reprinted — the last edition appearing as late as 1845.

One important thing about Bacon's biography is that it was almost certainly the source for Bunyan's use of Spira. Bunyan refers to him explicitly in *Grace Abounding to the Chief of Sinners* when he was recounting his worries as to whether he had committed the Unpardonable Sin and Spira most probably lies behind the Man in the Iron Cage: "I am now a man of despair, and am shut up in it, as in this iron cage. I cannot get out. O now I cannot! I have so hardened my heart, that I cannot repent."[22] Hawthorne makes it quite clear that Bunyan lies behind "Ethan Brand" – for early on in the story he compares the lime-burner's furnace to "the private entrance to the infernal regions, which the shepherds of the Delectable Mountains were accustomed to show to pilgrims" (T&S, 1,042). Given that Hawthorne, unlike Melville, for example, makes very little use of intertextuality, this overt reference should be taken seriously. What else has Ethan done but taken a private entrance to a (secularized) hell? And this becomes clearer if we look at the passage from *The Pilgrim's Progress* where the shepherds tell Christian that "This is a by-way to hell . . . namely, such as sell their birthright, with Esau; such as sell their master, with Judas; such as blaspheme the gospel, with Alexander." What makes this so relevant to "Ethan Brand" is that the cases the shepherds cite are, Bunyan tells us, particularly significant in that they are all pilgrims who went wrong after having gone far on the proper path – much as Ethan's quest was initially admirable. One point where Ethan and Bunyan come close is in the shared insistence that to commit the Unpardonable Sin is often, though not always, damned hard work – though their motives differ much as the nineteenth differs from the seventeenth century. Bunyan wants to reassure the pardonable sinner: Ethan is making a Romantic, a Faustian claim that he is special – and, unlike Bunyan, the Bible, the authority of a text, plays little part in his quest:

> For a man after he hath made some profession of salvation to come alone by the blood of Jesus, together with some light and power of the same upon his spirit; I say, for him after this knowingly, wilfully, and despitefully to trample upon the blood of Christ shed on the cross, and to count it an unholy thing, or no better than the blood of another man, and rather to venture his soul any other way than to be saved by this precious blood. And this must be done, I say, after some light, He.vi.4,5, despitefully, He.x.29, knowingly, 2 Pe.ii.21, an wilfully, He.x.26, compared with ver.29, and that not in a hurry or sudden fit, as Peter's was, but with some time beforehand to pause upon it first, with Judas; and also with a continued resolution never to turn or be converted again; "for *it is* impossible to renew such again to repentance," they are so resolved and so desperate. He.vi.[23]

Bunyan puts no emphasis on the notion of election but otherwise the parallels with Spira are clear enough. What is particularly noticeable – given Hawthorne's stress on the hardening of Ethan's heart – is Bunyan's stress on the way in which the Unpardonable Sin is linked to the wilful hardening of the sinner's heart – as in this passage from *The Barren Fig-Tree Or The Doom and Downfall of the Fruitless Professor*:

> *A . . . sign* that such a professor is quite past grace is, when his heart is grown so hard, so stony, and impenetrable, that nothing will pierce it . . .

Now, to have the heart so hardened, so judicially hardened, this is as a bar put in by the Lord God against the salvation of this sinner. This was the burden of Spira's complaint, "I cannot do it! O! now I cannot do it . . .!

Barren fig-tree, hearken, judicial hardening is dreadful! There is a difference betwixt that hardness of heart that is incident to all men, and that which comes upon some as a signal or special judgment of God . . .

1. It is a hardness that comes after some great light received, because of some great sin committed against that light, and the grace that gave it . . .

2. It is the greatest kind of hardness; and hence they are said to be harder than a rock, or than an adamant, that is, harder than flint: so hard, that nothing can enter . . .

3. It is a hardness given in much anger, and that to bind the soul up in an impossibility of repentance.

4. It is a hardness, therefore, which is incurable, of which a man must die and be damned.[24]

It would certainly be possible to compare the effect of Ethan's misuse of his intellect ("the heart . . . had withered – had contracted – had hardened") with Bunyan's stress on the hardness of heart consequent on the great sin against the Holy Ghost (T&S, 1,064). But the significant relationship is rather, I'd suggest, one of historical sequence rather than parallelism. It is clear that it is principally the failure to be able to have a relationship with one member of the Trinity or another that obsesses these suffering souls. However acute the psychological suffering, it is expressed almost without exception in theological terms. Thus, Philologus (the character based on Spira in *The Conflict of Conscience*) can say the Lord's Prayer – but cannot *mean* it. His is a fascinating case of what must be called a divided self – where the character deeply desires to repent yet feels that, despite the intensity of the desire, that repentance is impossible for the heart has been so hardened. The obsessional Brand is not so much a divided self as a man who has destroyed one part of himself – as much a psychological and moral cripple as Lawyer Giles is "a fragment of a human being" – indeed, more of one for although Giles' "corporeal hand was gone, a spiritual member remained" (T&S, 1,058). And not only is his sin a sin against humanity and society rather than the Almighty but he has to work hard to commit it, while the point that recurs in the seventeenth-century cases is that the Unpardonable Sin is, oddly, sometimes presented as something one has done more-or-less without noticing, almost by accident.

Whether "Ethan Brand" is compared to these Puritan cases or to Hawthorne's own practices in such stories as "The Man of Adamant," it is remarkably empty of a theological vocabulary. Apart from a throwaway reference to "atonement," the only other real possibility (apart, of course, from the Unpardonable Sin itself) is when Ethan asserts that his sin was the result of his free choice – and "Freely, were it to do again, would I incur the guilt" (T&S, 1,057). Indeed, Ethan seems to have no need of the conventional theological villain: "what need have I of the devil?" (T&S, 1,056) Romantic egotist that he is, he has to assert that it is all his own work. I cannot be persuaded that Mather's *Brand Pluckt out of the Burning* or Thomas Hooker's *Firebrand* are relevant despite Colacurcio's insistence that they "clearly *do* apply" – apart, that is, from Hawthorne's black joke that there is a Brand that insists on the burning (and this is a story full of black jokes).[25] Despite the attractiveness of More's thesis, "Ethan Brand" cannot be glossed in any simple way by an appeal to the theological and moral landscape of a Mather or a Bunyan. And that is part of the story's point. Where Mather *et al. are* profoundly relevant is the way in which they are the necessary starting-point of a tradition that is no longer really alive for Ethan in the nineteenth century. It is an obvious point, of course, but Hawthorne makes it quite clear that the action takes place in the nineteenth century: whatever else the function of the Jew of Nuremberg, his diorama dates the action with its ancient pictures of Napoleon's battles and Nelson's sea-fights. It is here, however, that the fragment form is a weakness: there is no way of internalizing this tradition in the text as we have it and thus the reader has to do a little research to provide the fragment with a history that situates its meaning.

There is also a need to look at the contemporary scene. It is well known that much of "Ethan Brand" is a reworking of Hawthorne's account of a trip in the summer and early autumn of 1838 to Western Massachusetts. I must confess that I would like to think that Hawthorne had set the story then – if only so that his account of Brand's heretical perversion of a Puritan preoccupation could be parallelled with Emerson's equally though differently heretical speech of July 15, 1838: "An Address delivered before the Senior Class in Divinity College, Cambridge." Emerson and Ethan would have found each other mutually incomprehensible – given Emerson's attitude to evil: "Good is positive. Evil is merely privative, not absolute: it is like cold, which is the privation of heat. All evil is so much death or nonentity."[26] Nor would Brand have found much sympathy from moderate Calvinism – if a sermon, *Concio ad Clerum*, preached in Yale chapel on September 10, 1828, by Nathaniel W. Taylor, can be taken as representative. His text came from Ephesians ii, 3: "And were by nature the children of wrath." Parts of this sermon can sound as though it could be assimilated both to the tradition *and* to Ethan. For example: "The question still recurs, what is the moral depravity for which man deserves the wrath of God? I answer – *it is man's own act, consisting in a free choice of some object rather than God*, as his chief good."[27] But, while the tradition has been liberalized, Ethan's project – at least in terms of his own intentions – cannot come under this indictment. Man's depravity may be the result of free choice but it is "by nature" since it is consistent with man's nature so to choose – and, while Ethan's choice may well be free, it is explicitly unnatural and that both in terms of this theology *and* in terms of Emersonian appeals to the authority of Nature.

Of course it may be said that the historical material which I have been trying to argue is crucial as the necessary source of the tradition to which Ethan however heretically belongs is largely redundant, since a passage from *The American Notebooks* provides an entirely adequate source for "Ethan Brand" – that it is an "experimental" work in that it offers a narrative which is an attempt (however flawed) to test an hypothesis put forward in the note:

> The Unpardonable Sin might consist in a want of love and reverence for the Human Soul; in consequence of which, the investigator pried into its dark depths, not with a hope or purpose of making it better, but from a cold philosophical curiosity, – content that it should be wicked in whatever kind or degree, and only desiring to study it out. Would this, in other words, be the separation of the intellect from the heart? (VIII, 251)

The closeness of this to a passage from "Ethan Brand" is unquestionable:

> He was no longer a brother-man, opening the chambers or the dungeons of our common nature by the key of holy sympathy, which gave him a right to share in all its secrets; he was now a cold observer, looking on mankind as the subject of his experiment, and, at length, converting man and woman to be his puppets, and pulling the wires that moved them to such degrees of crime as were demanded for his study. (T&S, 1,064)

The parallel is clear but it hardly solves all – or any – of the problems. Most obviously, to appeal to the passage from *The American Notebooks* is to evade asking why Hawthorne came up with the very idea of an – or rather *the* – Unpardonable Sin. It is not a self-evidently obvious moral category and the concept does seem to be almost exclusively a Protestant/Puritan obsession. A place – however problematical – in the Puritan tradition even though it may be at the fag-end of that tradition is necessarily claimed by Hawthorne by his choice of the term. But, given that Hawthorne phrases the problem of the separation between the head and the heart as a question, given the fragmentary form with its consequent openness, is the reader not invited to speculate about what constitutes the Unpardonable Sin, to wonder, indeed, if Ethan is right about the Unpardonable Sin he thinks he has committed? There is the possibility that the sinner cannot forgive himself (*cf.* Spira/Philologus) – and transfers that inability to a more powerful punisher such as God. It is open too for the reader to consider that the Unpardonable Sin may be merely the human arrogance of thinking that one has committed – or even that one *can* commit – it for (depending on the liberalism of our Christianity) is not God's mercy infinite? And there may be a further black joke involved – and that is that Brand only commits the Unpardonable Sin when he acts on the belief that he has committed it – when, in short, he commits suicide. Such a point of view can claim the support of Augustine: "Judas' act was worthily detestable, and yet the Truth saith, that by hanging himself, he did rather augment than expiate the guilt of his wicked treachery because his despair of God's mercy . . . left no place in his soul for saving repentance" (*The City of God*, Book I, ch.xvi).

While the form of the story, however, insists that readers consider such questions, there is another perspective that demands consideration – that of Brand himself. If he has committed the Unpardonable Sin, who is it that he thinks cannot or will not forgive him? Four options would seem to present themselves: God, himself, Nature and the community. God hardly appears to matter to him. He seems to feel (if anything) pride in his achievement. While he has undoubtedly offended against Nature, she is hardly shown in a position to be condemnatory – though she apparently celebrates his death in what may be a version of the pathetic fallacy. As little Joe says, "that strange man is gone, and the sky and the mountains all seem glad of it!" (T&S, 1,066) That leaves the community – who flee him on hearing his appalling laughter. The four principal figures who come up the hill-side to see Brand represent society however obliquely and however unsaintly they are. The stage-agent's connections with a communications system are obvious enough – and, when natural harmony is restored after the death of Ethan, the stage-coach fits almost too neatly into the system:

> To supply that charm of the familiar and homely, which Nature so readily adopts into a scene like this, the stage-coach was rattling down the mountain-road, and the driver sounded his horn; while echo caught up the notes and intertwined them into a rich, and varied, and elaborate harmony, of which the original performer could lay claim to little share.          (T&S, 1,066)

Drunken sot though the village Doctor may be and even though the community may think that his pipe is metaphorically "alight with hell-fire," "there was supposed to be in him such wonderful skill . . . that society caught hold of him, and would not let him sink out of its reach" (T&S, 1,059, 1,058). Nor does the Doctor reject its claims: "swaying to and from upon his horse, and grumbling thick accents at the bedside, he visited all the sick chambers for miles about the mountain towns" (T&S, 1,058–9). Lawyer Giles may have sunk through drink to the level of "a soap-boiler, in a small way," but, though a "maimed and miserable wretch," society "could not trample on" nor could "scorn" him "since he had still kept up the courage and spirit of a man, asked nothing in charity, and, with his one hand – and that the left one – fought a stern battle against want and hostile circumstances" (T&S, 1,058). And the one point at which Ethan "quailed" is when old Humphrey asks about the fate of his daughter who has left the valley for the life of a circus-performer (T&S, 1,060). But even then there is a certain if perverse comfort for Ethan in this encounter. Contacts with the stage-agent, the Doctor and the Lawyer caused him "to doubt – and, strange to say, it was a painful doubt – whether he had indeed found the Unpardonable Sin, and found it within himself" (T&S, 1,059). The fear that this search "on which he had exhausted life" might be "a delusion" is destroyed by his memory of Humphrey's daughter – "the very girl whom, with such cold and remorseless purpose, Ethan Brand had made the subject of a psychological experiment, and wasted, absorbed, and perhaps annihilated her soul, in the process" (T&S, 1,059, 1,060). Reminded of her, he can say that "it is no delusion. There is an Unpardonable Sin" (T&S, 1,060).

As the examples of especially Lawyer Giles and the Doctor make clear, society's claims on the individual are not so easily repudiated as Brand imagines. And nature – in the admittedly eccentric form of the dog chasing its tail – also puts in its criticism. Hawthorne tells readers that Ethan may have "a perception of some remote analogy" between his own case and that of this "self-pursuing cur." But it may well be that the analogy is not so remote as Ethan would like to think. The dog begins his futile chase "of his own mere motion" and never "was seen such headlong eagerness in pursuit of an object that could not possibly be attained" – an indirect but not irrelevant criticism of Ethan's very project. And even Ethan's idea of the coherence of his own identity may be equally indirectly exposed for examination for it is "as if one end of the ridiculous brute's body were at deadly and most unforgivable enmity with the other." Hammering home the querying of Brand's project, Hawthorne tells us that "the foolish old dog" ended "as far from the goal as ever" (T&S, 1,062).

Ethan's final speech before he commits his body to the flames of the lime-kiln is addressed not to God the Father, nor God the Son, nor to God the Holy Ghost but to pagan Mother Earth, to the community and to the light of the stars. The man who has denied the authority of Nature, repudiated "brotherhood" and sinned against the light has – he thinks – committed himself to the destructive element of fire. But Hawthorne's irony comes into full play here. For all of Ethan's attempts to evade or repudiate the claims of society, he has enriched Bartram's lime-kiln with an extra half bushel of good lime – and, through Bartram, the community which he has despised. Here, in another of Hawthorne's black jokes, is a man who has undergone a secular – indeed, a material – conversion experience: "on its [the lime-kiln's] surface in the midst of the circle – thoroughly converted into lime – lay a human skeleton, in the attitude of a person, who, after long toil, lies down to long repose" (T&S, 1,067). Long repose is precisely what the skeleton does not get – and if, as is most probable, the lime is to be used as fertilizer, Brand has not managed to escape the embrace of Mother Earth and, indeed, will enrich her. Brand's attempted rejection of Mother Earth is not to be taken lightly. Hawthorne is far from conventional praises of Nature, but in "The Hall of Fantasy" (1843) he celebrates the sheer materiality of the world: "The poor old Earth! . . . What I should chiefly regret in her destruction would be that very earthliness which no other sphere or state of existence can renew or compensate . . . [O]ur Mother Earth! . . . I want her great, round, solid self to endure interminably" (T&S, 743, 744).

The lime-kiln may symbolize the mouth of Hell for Ethan but it is a human construct which transforms a fragmented Nature to satisfy social needs. For all the ambition of Brand's attempt to transform himself into pure mind ("an intellect" which has, he announces proudly, "sacrificed everything to its own mighty claims"), his ambition to become – literally – meta-physical, the claims of society and the material world (reality, in short) are not so easily denied – and the very form of the story is emblematic of his failure (T&S, 1,057). Not only is the piece a fragment and not only does the word "fragment" repeatedly recur throughout the narrative, but, as I have suggested, Ethan is himself morally a fragment of a man (as anyone who separates himself from society must be for Hawthorne – remember "Wakefield," "the Outcast of the Universe") – and the fate of his body mimics the fate of what Ethan would have to call his soul (T&S, 298). The story ends "the rude lime-burner lifted his pole, and letting it fall upon the skeleton, the relics of Ethan Brand were crumbled into fragments" (T&S, 1,067).

### III

I have contrived a certain pictorial exhibition, somewhat in the nature of a puppet-show, by means of which I propose to call up the multiform and many-colored Past before the spectator, and show him the ghosts of his forefathers, amid a succession of historic incidents, with no greater trouble than the turning of a crank.                                    (T&S, 1,023)

In New England the Lyceum, as we call it, is already a great institution . . . The topics are as miscellaneous as heart can wish . . . I see not why this is not the most flexible of all organs of opinion, from its popularity and from its newness permitting you to say what you think, without any shackles of prescription. The pulpit in our age certainly gives forth an obstructed and uncertain sound, and the faith of those in it, if men of genius, may differ so much from that of those under it, as to embarrass the conscience of the speaker, because so much is attributed to him from the fact of standing there. In the Lyceum nothing is presupposed. The orator is only responsible for what his lips articulate. Then what scope it allows! You may handle every member and relation of humanity. What could Homer, Socrates, or St. Paul say that could not be said here?                                    (Emerson to Carlyle, April 8, 1836)

If, as seems almost certain, "Ethan Brand" was completed in late 1848 and "Main-Street" written in early 1849, then "Main-Street" can be read as a deliberate correction of an inadequacy in "Ethan Brand" as well as a further experiment with the form of the unfinished. That inadequacy, I have suggested, is the absence from "Ethan Brand" of a history of the Unpardonable Sin which would enable the reader more easily to situate Brand as the heir to a Puritan tradition which has become so attenuated that it is necessarily exposed to Hawthorne's irony. In "Main-Street" the matter of history and the problem of its representation become the principal subject. It is a remarkable feat of economy to get the salient outlines of the best part of a century into less than thirty pages and at the same time to include a self-conscious examination of the way in which that history is to be presented – and received. The old Dutchman (and his diorama with its historical pictures) is merely a side-show in "Ethan Brand." In "Main-Street" the showman moves to a centre stage to generate a narrative, to represent the story of the history of Salem.

It is, on the face of it, a perverse way of writing a sketch to base it on a showman's commentary on images which are entirely unavailable to the reader except in so far as they can be imagined. But what such a process does is force the reader to realize that history is not a given but a construct – and one that demands imaginative re-creation. It is a way of foregrounding the whole problem of representation. The showman begins from a discussion of his intentions and his means. His initial statement of his intention is my first epigraph to this section. His means is a time-machine which is a combination of technology with its "little wheels and springs" and art (of however low a grade) aiming at mimesis with his "puppets dressed in character" and his lamps which mimic the sun and the moon "as the nature of the scene may require" (T&S, 1,023). Everything that is to come, it is made clear, is mediated by artifice and culture.

The showman's own role is complex – a considerable advance on the narrator of "Alice Doane's Appeal" where we have a portrait of the artist as a young man educated by his audience into producing a genuinely historical art. Here the narrator is presumably mature and is certainly "respectable" (T&S, 1,023). He is at once entertainer, historian, educator and would-be sermonizer/moralist – belonging in the tradition of the

Lyceum lecturer so optimistically described by Emerson in the second epigraph to this section. (And it is worth remembering that in the autumn of 1848 Hawthorne became corresponding secretary of the Salem Lyceum and arranged for lectures by Emerson and Thoreau among others). However ambivalent his valuation of the Puritan heritage, the showman sees himself and his audience as – problematically – in that tradition. This shows up in his usage of one term in his vocabulary, where the referent has changed over time and the term has thus been transvalued. That crucial word is – as it was in "Alice Doane's Appeal" – spectre. When he comes to discuss the witchcraft trials he shows that he knows about the problem of spectre evidence: "Proctor and his wife . . . or their spectral appearances, have stuck pins into the Afflicted Ones" (T&S, 1,044). But readers only encounter this technical application of the word after four other usages of the term where the showman has explicitly compared his images to spectres and thus, it might seem, has conditioned his audience to think about the word in terms of questions of representation. For example: "Among those who came to Naumkeag were men of history and legend . . . You shall behold their life-like images, – their spectres, if you choose so to call them" (T&S, 1,032). And, describing Governor Winthrop's authoritative respectability, he invites his audience to recognize that quality in his puppet: "Is not this characteristic wonderfully perceptible in our spectral representative of his person?" (T&S, 1,033). This is a question which the mere reader simply cannot answer and thus is forced into speculation. It is as if the showman is claiming that his art is a kind of modern secular witchcraft – "so perfectly is the action represented in this life-like, this almost magic picture!" – where it looks as though mimesis equals magic, though this is to smooth over the problem as to how we know that the picture is an accurate image of a lost historical actuality. The first quotation, however, raises a rather more intriguing question: why *should* the audience choose to call the images spectres? It would seem that there are two alternative possibilities – both of which need to be kept in mind. Either the showman thinks that his audience share a Puritan suspicion of (mimetic) art – or he invites them to consider his art as a kind of spectre evidence, inviting them to learn to read as useful fictions what the past insisted on reading as a kind of reality – in other words, to persuade them that the art of history has taken over from the theological realm. If the first option is emphasized, the hostile critic can be see as a debased heir to the Puritan tradition – which is to raise the question of the relationship between the past and present – a relationship explored in one part of the showman's strategy towards his audience.

The showman twice invites his audience to identify with a section of the past rather than merely being spectators. These occur when two perceived threats to the New England way appear: the coming of the Quakers and the witches. "You can discern" in the Quakers "the gift of a new idea," and this is potentially a revolutionary moment since "the very existence" of a new idea "seems to threaten the overthrow of whatever else the toilsome ages have thrown up, . . . as if an earthquake rumbled through the town . . . causing the spire of the meeting-house to totter." "Our" traditions and institutions are radically threatened by this challenge. "We are in peril!" – and our answer is persecution (T&S, 1,039). Much the same strategy is followed in the case of the witches: the audience is invited into the past to identify with the crowd watching the witches on the way to the scaffold. In both cases "we" are invited into the past to become part of the establishment – and both are instances of those bits of history that an "enlightened" present feels that it can smugly and safely feel superior to. There is a nice ambiguity here. On the one hand, "we" are invited to acquire a genuine historical understanding by imagining how those who, from a nineteenth-century perspective, we can safely despise, could legitimately act as they did. On the other, there is an indirect criticism of at least some of his audience as latter-day Puritans who may be (at least potentially) as intolerant persecutors as the figures from the past – in which case the showman's warning at the end of the witchcraft episode should be taken very seriously: "Never, never again, whether in this or any other shape, may Universal Madness riot in the Main-street" (T&S, 1,047).

In so far as the narrator is showman rather than educator, he is bound with his "tropic love of sunshine" to be unsympathetic to part of the Puritan project – and the hostile critic, the latter-day Puritan, is equally bound to criticize his secular art on the grounds of a narrow aesthetics which has replaced a narrow theology. The narrator in describing the shift in consciousness from the first to the second Puritan generation, makes an historical and a moral judgement:

> nor, it may be, have we even yet thrown off all the unfavorable influences which, among many good ones, were bequeathed to us by our Puritan forefathers. Let us thank God for having us such ancestors; and let each successive generation thank him, not less fervently, for being one step further from them in the march of ages.                                    (T&S, 1,039)

The acidulous-looking critic complains that this is too close to a sermon. Since sermons are necessarily usually directed at the present generation, it can hardly be the narrator's mature and measured verdict on the Puritan heritage that the critic wants to repudiate but rather the implication that the bad part of the Puritan tradition still may too largely determine present day consciousness – accompanied by his unwilling-ness to allow the artist/historian the right to exercise any moral authority. The show has not worked on him in that he fails to realize that he is a product (however decadent) of the very tradition that the narrator is trying to re-create. Despite the fact that his principal criticism is aesthetic, his aesthetics leaves something to be desired. His main objection is to a lack of photographic naturalistic detail – and the form that objection takes largely misses the point. He makes "it a point to see things precisely as they are" but this formulation ignores problems of representation – problems of which Hawthorne was perfectly well aware, as the showman's vocabulary sufficiently evidences when he tries to persuade his critic to adopt a different perspective. One purpose of the pictures is to show not how things are but how things were and, since we cannot have direct access to the past, the question of mimetic accuracy will always be problematic. The simplistic critic fails to consider such hardly esoteric questions and refuses even to test the narrator's suggestion that – if only the recalcitrant spectator would have the decency to move – "the proper light and shadow will transform the spectacle into quite another thing" and "the bedaubed canvas become an airy and changeable reflex of what it purports to represent" (T&S, 1,029, 1,035).

The Puritan of the seventeenth century might have equally denied the values of the showman's art – and certainly the narrator's description of the original meeting-house stresses the way its makers ignored or repudiated the conventional aesthetic qualities of an English parish church or cathedral: "How could they dispense with the carved altar-work? – how, with the pictured windows, where the light of common day was hallowed by being transmitted through the glorified figures of saints?" But the spirit of the original settlers conferred values and qualities on that building which, while not purely aesthetic, are clearly associated in the narrator's mind with aesthetic values:

> the zeal of a recovered faith burned like a lamp within their hearts, enriching every thing around them with its radiance; making of these new walls, and this narrow compass, its own cathedral; and being in itself, that spiritual mystery and experience, of which sacred architecture, pictured windows, and the organ's grand solemnity, are remote and imperfect symbols.    (T&S, 1,030)

For the first Puritans in their first flush of enthusiasm the arts of and in the church are unnecessary. But this (religious) "aesthetics" is too subjective and internalized to be sustainable through history – according to our historian:

> All was well, so long as their lamps were freshly kindled at the heavenly flame. After a while, however, whether in their time or their children's, these lamps began to burn more dimly, or with a less genuine lustre; and then it might be seen, how hard, cold, and confined, was their system, – how like an iron cage was that which they called Liberty!    (T&S, 1,031)

The clear implication is that the purity of the Puritan project may have partially been enabled by their repudiation of the aesthetic realm but that it was the absence of this dimension which goes some way in accounting for the decline in the second generation. The critic belongs in that tradition. He may seem merely to deny the mimetic accuracy of the puppets and their back-cloth but that insistence on the validity of his point of view (however accidentally arrived at) is the image of a self-righteous conservatism. Despite the narrator's invitation to sit beside a nice young woman so that he may see a transformation of the spectacle ("take my word for it, the slips of pasteboard shall assume spiritual life"), the critic stands smug and firm: "I know better," he says, "with sullen but self-complacent immoveableness" (T&S, 1,035). With that statement the parallel is clear between his situation and the provincialism of the second generation of the Puritans, who, among their other defects, lack historical consciousness: "Their fathers and grandsires tell them, how, within a few years past, the forest stood here with but a lonely track beneath its tangled shade. Vain legend! They cannot make it true and real to their conceptions." History is merely myth to them: "Nothing impresses them, except their own experience" (T&S, 1,031, 1,032). His conservatism is equally evident: "as for my own pleasure, I shall best consult it by remaining precisely where I am" (T&S, 1,035). Hawthorne undercuts the critic from his first appearance. This is a man who cannot be trusted to debate about problems of representation since he has a visual defect. Spectacles may correct that deficiency in part – but, since his have blue-tinted lenses, he can hardly be trusted to comment on images of "the many-colored Past" with any authority – a serio-comic version of the problem of perception that the Minister with his black veil refuses to recognize as a problem.

I do not mean to suggest that the showman's production is offered as invulnerable to criticism. The other less hostile critic picks up the narrator on points of historical detail. On one level, the validity of such criticism obviously cannot be questioned – that is, if the showman's project is defined as conventional illustrated historiography. But this does not explain why Hawthorne should include deliberate errors in his sketch. Several options present themselves. For example, perhaps it is to test the knowledge of his audience, or to make the audience sceptical of the authority claims of showmen and authors. But the most convincing reason is, I think, that Hawthorne is drawing attention to the fictive element which is necessarily involved in such a dramatic presentation of history – that here we have a sophisticated exemplification of the point Hawthorne had made long ago in "Sir William Phips:" "without an absolute violation of literal truth" a "license must be assumed in brightening the materials which time has rusted" in order to re-create the past (T&S, 12). The gentlemanly critic makes two points both of which depend on interpreting the lecturer's words very, very literally. First: Anna Gower had no children and "consequently, we cannot be indebted to that honorable lady for any specimens of feminine loveliness, now extant among us" (T&S, 1,030). Second: the lecturer shows on his stage a variety of well-known historical characters at the same time – yet they "might, and probably did, all visit our old town, at one time or another, but not simultaneously and you have fallen into anachronisms that I positively shudder to think of!" (T&S, 1,034). But if the showman's words are read sympathetically, his first account can be interpreted as a metaphorical way of saying that Anna Gower was a type of female beauty and that there are still pretty girls around, while his second can be read as a shorthand way of indicating the range of historical characters who had ties with Salem in its earliest years. Hawthorne can have his cake and eat it with this tactic: he draws attention to what technically may be an inaccuracy, but at the same time he has found a way of getting a range of characters into his text (who cannot without a worse distortion be omitted) without tiresome and lengthy detailing. But it is more than shrewd laziness. His narrator has got very close to "an absolute violation of literal truth" and may, in the second instance, even have crossed over the divide – yet there is a defence: that he is aiming to re-create the past of Salem not so much by offering a narrative of particulars but by presenting typical, representative moments of that history. And, if that is so, he has not betrayed his original intention – to offer a view of "the vicissitude of *characteristic* scenes" (T&S, 1,023, my emphasis).

To raise the question of typicality, and thus of the relations between representation and the representative, is necessarily to raise the question of the structure of the sketch. The very way in which the narrative ends with a break in the machine foregrounds the question of form. From inside the fiction it is an accident. From the reader's point of view it is a deliberate choice by the author to begin the ending with a rupture which has analogies with a revolutionary break in history and which has been prepared for at the beginning when the showman speaks of "the casualties to which such a complicated piece of mechanism is liable" (T&S, 1,023). The period covered (*c*. 1630–1717 – and 1717 is the only date in the piece) is to an extent a coherent one – that of one man's life and his a significant life: "the first town-born child" (T&S, 1,027, 1,037, 1,041, 1,049). He has been "the index-figure whereby to note the age of his coeval town" (T&S, 1,048). But this is not the form the showman had in mind: he had planned to continue up to the present and, indeed, into the future and in that aim it can be seen that he intended a political art – if Rahv's definition is accepted: "the subject of political art is *history* . . . A political art would succeed in lifting experience to the level of history if its perception of life . . . were organized around a perspective relating the artist's sense of the *society* of the dead to his sense of the *society* of the living and the as yet unborn."[28] While the "random" nature of the ending of the showman's narrative invites the reader to speculate as to how far the time covered constitutes what historians might call a period, it is clear that Hawthorne does want to present certain structural changes in Salem society. I have touched on a couple of these – the growing provincialism of Salem and the related matter of the decadence of second generation Puritanism. Another historical shift – which might be called the irruption of history and to which attention has frequently been drawn – is that from Indian matriarchy (with the evocation of the "majestic and queenly . . . Squaw Sachem") to Puritan patriarchy (T&S, 1,024). Given the way in which the Indians are identified with Nature ("Of all the wild life that used to throng there, only the Indians still do"), the Puritans represent both patriarchy and culture (alias history) – a patriarchy that is very clear about the place of women: "Dorothy Talby is chained to a post . . . with the hot sun blazing on her matronly face, for no other offence than lifting her hand against her husband" (T&S, 1,031, 1,037).[29]

The possibility – even the desirability – of matriarchy haunts Hawthorne's fiction and is nearly always defined as natural or Utopian. Nor is that attitude sentimental. He has recently been frequently criticized for his attack in a letter of 1855 on "a d——d mob of scribbling women" but his very next letter to Fields more than makes amends (if amends are really necessary for attacking such a piece of hokum as *The Lamplighter*):

> In my last, I recollect, I bestowed some vituperation on female authors. I have since been reading "Ruth Hall"; and I must say I enjoyed it a good deal. The woman writes as if the devil was in her; and that is the only condition under which a woman ever writes anything worth reading. Generally, women write like emasculated men, and are only to be distinguished from male authors by greater feebleness and folly; but when they throw off the restraints of decency, and come before the public stark naked, as it were – then their books are sure to possess character and value. (XVII, 304, 308)

Feminist critics who say nasty things about Hawthorne should have this statement tattooed on their hearts. Hawthorne has endorsed a claim for a special place for good woman writers – and it is a radically subversive one, not one where the female writer demurely and weakly echoes the authoritative tones of a man. When he turns to woman as angel rather than devil, he is equally radical. I shall be arguing in the next chapter that Hester ends by prophesying the second coming of Christ – only this time as a woman. Coverdale, in *The Blithedale Romance*, attacks Hollingsworth for "the intensity" of his "masculine egotism" and claims a woman ruler for his Utopia: "I should love dearly – for the next thousand years at least – to have all government devolve into the hands of women . . . Oh, in the better order of things, Heaven grant that the ministry of souls may be left in charge of women!" (N, 740, 738). But most relevant for "Main-Street" is "The New Adam and Eve" – a story which begins from the problem of the dominance of culture – a dominance so pervasive that culture can be mistaken for nature:

> We, who are born into the world's artificial system, can never adequately know how little in our state and circumstances is natural, and how much is merely the interpolation of the perverted mind and heart of man. Art has become a second and stronger Nature; she is a step-mother, whose crafty tenderness has taught us to despise the bountiful and wholesome ministrations of our true parent. It is only through the medium of the imagination that we can loosen those iron fetters, which we call truth and reality, and make ourselves even partially sensible what prisoners we are.          (T&S, 746)

It is only through art as experimental fiction that it can be seen how art as culture and politics has imprisoned us:

> our wanderers next visit a Hall of Legislature, where Adam places Eve in the Speaker's chair, unconscious of the moral which he thus exemplifies. Man's intellect, moderated by Woman's tenderness and moral sense! Were such the legislation of the world, there would be no need of State Houses, Capitols, Halls of Parliament, nor even of those little assemblages of patriarchs beneath the shadowy trees, by whom freedom was first interpreted to mankind on our native shores.          (T&S, 751)

If the second sentence here was taken in isolation, then this would merely be a conventional cliché about the (domestic) role of woman *à la* Coventry Patmore and his tiresome *Angel in the House* – but Hawthorne insists on thrusting Eve into the public realm and giving her an authoritative voice.

Just how far liberty was interpreted by the patriarchy of New England is problematic. Even the showman (who, I have suggested, is not necessarily a friendly witness on this issue) does not condemn Puritanism out of hand. While he may say "how like an iron cage was that which they called Liberty!" he also celebrates the Thursday Lecture – perhaps because he sees an analogy between it and his own enterprise (T&S, 1,031). It was "an institution . . . which it would have been better to retain, as bearing relations to both the spiritual and ordinary life, and bringing each acquainted with the other" (T&S, 1,037). The patterns the narrator detects in his history are not only the rigidifying of a once great theological world-view nor the accompanying narrowing of intellectual horizons leading to provincialism but also a ruthless expansionism which has direct links with the present. The area that has been "a wilderness from the creation" and looks as though it should remain one for ever is transformed for "Anglo-Saxon energy – as the phrase now goes" has been at work with terrible consequences: "The pavements of the Main-street *must* be laid over the red man's grave" (T&S, 1,025, 1,030, 1,028, my emphasis). Without denying the possibility of progress, the narrator ironically questions the celebratory rhetoric of contemporary Demo-crats. As Levin makes clear, the Romantic historians and especially Bancroft had indentified the Anglo-Saxons with liberty. Nor did Bancroft confine this Anglo-Saxon virtue to New England:

> Shall the Virginians be described in a word? They were Anglo-Saxons in the woods again, with the inherited culture and intelligence of the seventeenth century . . . The Anglo-Saxon mind, in its serenest nationality, neither distorted by fanaticism, nor subdued by superstition, nor wounded by persecution, nor excited by new ideas, but fondly cherishing the active instinct for personal freedom, secure possession, and legislative power, such as belonged to it before the reformation, and existed independent of the reformation, had made its dwelling place in the empire of Powhatan.[30]

Hawthorne subversively if demurely questions that identification for the reference to the iron cage called liberty is neatly bracketed by his two references to Anglo-Saxon energy.

Nor was the praise of the Anglo-Saxon confined to stories of the origins of liberty and America – and the need to question that valuation appears even more clearly in its application to contemporary issues. McWilliams draws attention to an 1846 essay by Una Hawthorne's godfather, O'Sullivan, with the title "Annexation:"

> Without even a phrase acknowledging the existence of Mexicans or Indians, O'Sullivan exclaimed: "The Anglo-Saxon foot is already on its [California's] borders. Already the advance of the irresistible army of Anglo-Saxon emigration has begun to pour down upon it, armed with the plough and the rifle . . . Their [the Anglo-Saxons'] right to independence will be the natural right of self-government belonging to any community strong enough to maintain it."[31]

The showman implies that a certain scepticism should greet such claims. Though unsentimental about the fate of the Indians, he offers a chilling image of that fate. While their incantations and shrieking in the woods may have terrified the first settlers, the whites of both the seventeenth and nineteenth centuries take in their varying ways a terrible revenge – the more terrible in that it is largely unconscious. Those of the mid seventeenth century have chosen in effect to forget the history that lies behind them: "It seems all a fable . . . that the Squaw Sachem, and the Sagamore her son, once ruled over this region, and treated as sovereign potentates with the English settlers" (T&S, 1,042). They may have found amnesia convenient: the nineteenth century offers the Indians the cruel tribute of a museum. While the Indians terrified the original settlers, "greater would be the affright of the Indian necromancer, . . . if he could be aware" that a "future edifice will contain a noble Museum, where, among countless curiosities of earth and sea, a few Indian arrow-heads shall be treasured up as memorials of a vanished race!" (T&S, 1,024). The Indian heritage is reduced to the level of "curiosities" – a fate from which the showman tries to redeem them by conferring dignity on them. The Squaw Sachem is "majestic and queenly" and she and her husband hold "high talk on matters of state and religion" – though at the same time the narrator cannot resist taking advantage of the easy irony of historical aftersight: they "imagine . . . that their own system of affairs will endure for ever" (T&S, 1,024, 1,025).

Where Hawthorne does radically differ from O'Sullivan is not in the degree of their commitment to a Democratic polity but rather in their ideas on the nature of American history. In 1839, O'Sullivan wrote an essay for the *Democratic Review* titled "The great Nation of Futurity:" "Our national birth was the beginning of a new history, the formation and progress of an untried political system, which separates us from the past and connects us with the future only."[32] The very existence of "Main-Street" is a repudiation of this future-orientated history – not necessarily of its desirability but of its possibility. The revolutionary break that does exist is that between the natural world and the beginning of a main-street. The showman's narrative begins from an evocation of the natural world – a world untouched by the irreversible sequence that is history: "this is the ancient and primitive wood, – the ever-youthful and venerably old, – verdant with new twigs, yet hoary, as it were, with the snowfall of innumerable years, that have accumulated upon its intermingled branches. The white man's axe has never smitten a single tree" (T&S, 1,024). The story ends with a return of the dominance of nature – the Great Snow of 1717 – which the showman deliberately parallels with the opening scene: "It would seem as if the street . . . were all at once obliterated, and resolved into a drearier pathlessness than when the forest covered it" (T&S, 1,049). But that dominance is only apparent for not only has the Great Snow been assimilated into history – 1717 is, as I have said, significantly the only date in the sketch – but also it is used as a metaphor for, as analogous to a revolutionary moment. The vocabulary of a secular historiography penetrates everything and has even taken over the language of the Bible. The showman introduces what is to be his final scene thus: "Behold here a change, wrought in the twinkling of an eye, like an incident in a tale of magic" (T&S, 1,049). No student of the Puritans, those people of the book, could write this without intending to recall to a reader's memory I Corinthians, chapter xv, verses 51 and 52: "Behold, I shew you a mystery . . . we shall all be changed, In a moment, in the twinkling of an eye, at the last trump . . . the dead shall be raised incorruptible, and we shall be changed." While St. Paul shows his readers the supernatural mystery of the resurrection on judgement day, the showman/historian presents his viewers with an historically placed natural scene – which is not quite his last judgement on the Salem community and which allows for the consideration of the possibility of radical political change. In the view of this historian, the Bible would appear to be little more than a mere "tale of magic."

It is not that the showman simplistically celebrates revolution as a secular equivalent to resurrection for even when he interprets the Great Snow as offering the Salemites a blank sheet on which they can rewrite their enterprise, he seems to feel profoundly ambivalent about that apparent cancellation of historical process, undecided as to whether it is better read as new beginning or as ending:

> The gigantic swells and billows of the snow have swept over each man's metes and bounds, and annihilated all the visible distinctions of human property. So that now, the traces of former times and hitherto accomplished deeds being done away, mankind should be at liberty to enter on new paths, and guide themselves by other laws than heretofore; if, indeed, the race be not extinct, and it be worth our while to go on with the march of life, over the cold and desolate expanse that lies before us. (T&S, 1,049)

It is left open whether the early eighteenth century did see any radical change in the New England way. Perry Miller and Colacurcio would probably argue that this is a significant date for the machinery to break down. But the indications from any revolutionary or utopian perspective are not encouraging. Given the propinquity of "property" and "deeds" no doubt there is a pun on "deeds" – as (historic) acts and title-deeds. In any case, the narrator points to the way in which the Puritans have inscribed and thus enforced their ideas about the nature of property on the page of the natural world. If property titles could only be expunged, "mankind" (not just Salem) "*should* be at liberty" to redeem and remake history. But the conservative powers of property are not so easily written off as Hawthorne frequently bitterly noted – perhaps most forcefully in *The American Claimant Manuscripts* when brooding over a plot problem: "It must be related to property; because nothing else survives in this world. Love grows cold and dies; hatred is pacified by annihilation" (XII, 287).

The artist/showman not without apparent reason claims an even greater control over his images of Nature than ever the Salem community have done over their land. Perhaps the finest irony of the sketch – and even a prescient one – comes in his realm of art where he thinks he can claim a God-like mastery: "Here, at least, I may claim to be ruler of the seasons" (T&S, 1,049–50). But he is the victim of his own technology: "The scene will not move. A wire is broken. The street continues buried beneath the snow" (T&S, 1,050). Rather as Hawthorne claims in "The Custom-House" to have failed to write the contemporary realistic fiction he should have done ("A better book than I shall ever write was there; leaf after leaf presenting itself to me, just as it was written out by the reality of the flitting hour"), so, as a result of the break-down, the narrator cannot offer his audience "a reflex of the very life that is flitting past us" (N, 1,51; T&S, 1,050). All he can do is end by offering his audience his vision of the/a future – one which entirely lacks the redemptive optimism of Hester Prynne's prophecy about the Second Coming and which is totally secular in that there is no suggestion of resurrection: "Lastly, I should have given the crank one other turn, and have brought out the future, showing you who shall walk the Main-street tomorrow, and, perchance, whose funeral shall pass through it!" (T&S, 1,050). But since he cannot show his audience this because his own technology has let him down, he is reduced to a modern artist/ entertainer's confession of failure – to admit that the relationship between artist and audience is best indicated by the cash-nexus. He has failed to give his pictures of the present or the future so even though these "like most other human purposes, lie unaccomplished" he can only offer to return the money – an offer (of course) taken up by his Philistine critic: "I said that your exhibition would prove to be a humbug, and so it has turned out. So hand over my quarter!" (T&S, 1,050). How wrong can a critic be?

# 4

## The Scarlet Letter *and the language of history: past imperfect, present imperfect, future perfect?*

> But the object that most drew my attention, in the mysterious package, was a certain affair of fine red cloth, much worn and faded ... It had been intended, there could be no doubt, as an ornamental article of dress; but how it was to be worn, or what rank, honor, and dignity, in by-past times, were signified by it, was a riddle which (so evanescent are the fashions of the world in these particulars) I saw little hope of solving. And yet it strangely interested me. My eyes fastened themselves upon the old scarlet letter, and would not be turned aside. Certainly, there was some deep meaning in it, most worthy of interpretation, and which, as it were, streamed forth from the mystic symbol, subtly communicating itself to my sensibilities, but evading the analysis of my mind. (145–6)

The first appearance of the scarlet letter is particularly striking in that everything about the artefact is remarkably obscure – except for its ambiguous historicity: "time, and wear, and a sacrilegious moth, had reduced it to little other than a rag." Initially it is not even recognizable – merely "a certain affair of fine red cloth," an object stripped of its glamour, its "glitter." Its history is doubly one of loss for not only is it "defaced" but, even in its decayed state, it "gives evidence of a now forgotten art." Its very form has to be recovered: only careful examination allows it to assume "the shape of a letter" (145). However, although its shape may have been established, form does not confer meaning, but only the strong possibility that the letter has significance: "there was *some* deep meaning in it, most worthy of interpretation." For that interpretation to be possible, story is needed – Mr. Surveyor Pue's narrative which reveals the meaning (which is to say the social function) of the letter. Hawthorne makes it clear that his central symbol belongs to, is the product of history and therefore can only be understood in terms provided by narrative, by a (fictional) historiography. And, as "The Custom-House" further indicates, history is not only a crucial subject of the fiction as a whole, but the very existence of *The Scarlet Letter* is the product of history – as Hawthorne's personal history intersects with a wider public history.

If the Democrats had won the Presidential election of 1848 and if we are to believe Hawthorne, *The Scarlet Letter* would most likely not have been written. It is then as Hawthorne tells us, the product of contemporary political history, of "the period of hardly accomplished revolution, and still seething turmoil, in which the story shaped itself" (156). The period between Hawthorne losing his job in the Salem custom-house in June, 1849 and his departure for England in July, 1853 (when he had acquired, largely thanks to his campaign biography of Pierce, the best paid job of his life as consul in Liverpool) is the most remarkable in his life for sustained and successful literary production – productions all strikingly marked by a concern with history, politics, and the problematic nature of the contemporary. Most important, of course, are the three full-length fictions. *The Scarlet Letter* (1850) starts from an autobiographical meditation on the present before turning back to the seventeenth century, to end with Hester's prophecy of an utopian future of sexual equality – a prophecy which has conspicuously not been fulfilled in the America of 1850 (nor in that of 1990). *The House of the Seven Gables* (1851) begins from an act of expropriation in the 1690s and goes right up to the autumn of 1848, ending with an apparent (but only apparent) reconciliation of class tensions in New England history. *The Blithedale Romance* (1852), though set some ten years in the past, takes as its subject an attempt radically to transform the present state of things in the name of a desired Utopian future, an attempt which belongs crucially to American history in that it is overtly analogous both to the Puritan project of the Pilgrim Fathers and to 1776.

Though these were the major works of those remarkably productive years, the other literary enterprises also bear on the history/politics/modernity nexus. Thus, the campaign biography – Hawthorne's most rewarding work in the financial sense and probably the most widely read in his life-time – is, however modestly, an attempt to make history through writing. Even the two volumes of Greek myths retold for children – *A Wonder-Book for Girls and Boys* (1851) and *Tanglewood Tales* (1853) – are offered as ways of making modern ("Gothic or romantic") those pre-historic stories: "an attempt to render the fables of classical antiquity into the idiom of modern fancy and feeling" (T&S, 1,163, 1,235). Here with *A Wonder-Book* we have at last a version of that dream of the 1830s, *The Story Teller* – a framed set of stories, as the story-teller (the college student, Eustace Bright) with his audience of children provide a context in which the myths are told and set — and Hawthorne insists that the reader should be conscious of the fictitiousness of that context with a sophistication surely aimed at adults rather than children:

> "Hush, Primrose, hush!" exclaimed Eustace . . .
>
> "Our neighbor [Hawthorne] in the red house is a harmless sort of person enough, for aught I know, as concerns the rest of the world; but something whispers me that he has a terrible power over ourselves, extending to nothing short of annihilation."                                           (T&S, 1,301)

Hawthorne ends *A Wonder-Book* with a jokey reminder that what we are reading is a fiction, that whatever the origin of these myths, their interpreter has the power not only to create or transmit, but to destroy.

It is no longer necessary to argue that "The Custom-House" is to be considered as an intrinsic part of *The Scarlet Letter* — that, in other words, it is a variant on the strategy of *The Story Teller*. It is in "The Custom-House" that Hawthorne offers a semi-fictive genetic account of the origin of his fiction of the scarlet letter, beginning from a reminder of the previous production of his pen ("The Old Manse") before foregrounding the question of the writer/reader relationship. Hawthorne repudiates the romantic ambition "to find out the divided segment of the writer's own nature and complete his circle of existence" but insists that "thoughts are frozen and utterance benumbed, unless the speaker stand in some true relation with his audience" (121). Readers quickly understand the running pun on "custom" — once they realize they have entered the Interpreter's House through which they must pass before encountering the main structure of the story of the letter. The story proper is carefully situated in its social, historical and psychological contexts — for the work of art is not allowed to appear to float free, but is rooted in the concrete historical situation of its genesis and production. It is in "The Custom-House" that Hawthorne launches an investigation of the relationships of fiction to the real world and indicates a subtle and complex inter-relationship between the two worlds. By describing his surroundings in the custom-house he goes a long way towards justifying his historical fiction by suggesting the inadequacies of that way of life. To be a custom-house officer is to be excluded from the ethical world of men in a way which ironically parallels Hester's situation: "the very nature of his business . . . is of such a sort that he does not share in the united effort of mankind" (151). Punning on "custom," Hawthorne argues that the experience which is dependent on habit destroys the historical imagination on which a true recognition of reality must be based. The elderly members of the Custom-House are condemned for their inability to have made anything useful or valuable from their pasts. And — given that the stars and stripes flies over the Custom-House, given the explicit references to the patriarchs of the Custom-House – Hawthorne surely intends to suggest a wider placing: is *this* what the seventeenth century patriarchy even with its admitted faults and inadequacies has come to, with its "fortitude . . . self-reliance" and "natural authority" (323)?

Seeing Salem as a dust-heap of history, Hawthorne creates the impression that his tale has an authentic base, and obliquely suggests its nature and the nature of his fictional developments, as he famously describes the conditions where his imagination works best: "the floor of our familiar room has become a neutral territory, somewhere between the real world and fairy-land, where the Actual and the Imaginary may meet, and each imbue itself with the nature of the other" (149). But the historical imagination is necessary to perceive the reality of anything but the world of pure objects, as Hawthorne makes clear when discussing the old General. He can be described as he appears, but this is to miss the true, the important realities. The General has a public, an historic identity, but, if that is to be recovered, Hawthorne has to become, so to speak, an archaeologist:

> To observe and define his character, however . . . was as difficult a task as to trace out and build up anew, in imagination, an old fortress, like Ticonderoga, from a view of its gray and broken ruins. Here and there, perchance, the walls may remain almost complete; but elsewhere may be only a shapeless mound, cumbrous with its very strength, and overgrown, through long years of peace and neglect, with grass and alien weeds. (136)

The General's identity can be recreated, as Hawthorne shows when he looks at him "affectionately." And he suggests that the true reality for the General himself lies within his own consciousness as he recreates and inhabits his past. As the scarlet letter initiates Hawthorne's desire to retell Hester's story and come to terms with old New England, so it is one item from the General's past that makes it possible for Hawthorne to understand him:

> There was one thing that much aided me in *renewing and recreating* the stalwart soldier of the Niagara frontier, – the man of true and simple energy. It was the recollection of those memorable words of his, – "I'll try, sir!" – . . . breathing the soul and spirit of New England hardihood, comprehending all perils, and encountering all. (138–9, my emphasis)

It is the (historical) imagination that makes it possible for Hawthorne to comprehend what the General was – which is at least as important as what he is.

One purpose of "The Custom-House" is, then, to demonstrate that the past can be reconstructed through the sympathetic and informed imagination – an imagination whose other name should be the historical

sense. Hawthorne stresses that he has a double past, and with that
emphasis he prepares us for his concern with the different but ideally
united realms of the public and private sides of human identity which is
so crucial in the main story. One of Hawthorne's pasts is his immediate
personal past when he defined himself as a writer (but, of course, that is
not totally private in that he is also publicly known as a writer – that,
after all, is largely why he got the Custom-House job). He emphasizes
that the "discovery" of the letter re-awoke his literary feelings and made
him realize that neither his own past as writer nor the public, historical
past was dead. That fictive fragment from history is presented as having a
wider function than re-awakening his old artistic impulses for it also
brings into focus a concern with a wider history, with Hawthorne's
evocation of the past of Salem and his serio-comic account of his
relationship with his ancestors. And, as I began by implying, it is with the
way that Hawthorne introduces the letter and the question of its original
meaning that it can be seen that, while Hawthorne is profoundly
concerned with the functions and powers of symbols, his fiction is really
a criticism of symbolic modes of perception and definition – a criticism
made in the name of historical, of narrative modes of knowing the
world. The fact that the discovery of the only too clearly symbolic A is so
obviously at the centre of "The Custom-House" might seem to
contradict this. But, as I have tried to suggest, while the reader is told that
the letter is an artefact containing considerable power, as long as its
meaning remains unknown, which is to say as long as its historical
context is unknown, as long as it lacks a placing narrative, it can only
communicate itself to Hawthorne's "sensibilities" while "evading the
analysis of" his "mind." However "worthy of interpretation" the sign
in isolation may be, it cannot be decoded until the accompanying text is
read, when it can take its meaning from its place in a story. Until then,
what it "signified" is an insoluble "riddle" because of the way in which
meanings can be lost from history, "so evanescent are the fashions of the
world" (145–6).

   Not that Pue's narrative is unproblematic: the discovery of the letter
and the text is, of course, a fictional origin for Hawthorne's fiction – an
origin that, however, does not significantly contradict the known facts
and thus claims the authority of history – or demands, at the least, a
willing suspension of disbelief on the part of his audience: "the reader
may smile, but must not doubt my word" (146). Yet, however much
Hawthorne may claim Pue's story as an authentic authorization for his
tale, he almost immediately undercuts that authority in a way that has
understandably bothered many readers: "I have allowed . . . myself
nearly or altogether as much license as if the fact had been entirely of my
own invention." Something of a solution to this difficulty lies in the fact

that the wearing of an A was a New England punishment for adultery – and in Hawthorne's next paragraph, where he seems to have done his homework in taking an appropriate metaphor from needlework: "There seemed to be here the groundwork of a tale" (147). "Ground-work" is nicely chosen given an OED definition: "The body or foundation on which parts are overlaid, as in embroidery work, painting and the like." The dictionary gives a seventeenth-century (1655) illustration: "In needlework, the sad groundwork is laid before the beautiful colours." The production of the text of *The Scarlet Letter* is, then, presented as analogous to Hester's elaboration of the letter. Hawthorne transforms the sad groundwork of a simple fact about a way that seventeenth-century New England punished adultery into a complex narrative meditation on signs and meanings in history: Hester transfigures a simple sign of society's condemnation of her transgression of its rules into a work of art. And that subversion of the sign of society's intention to define (to limit) the transgressor, to reduce Hester's very self to a sign reading "Thou shalt not . . ." problematizes the symbolic definition to which that society is committed and by which the society had intended to limit the transgressor. Society's intention – or, rather, the intention of those in power who claim to represent the society – had been to contain Hester in, so to speak, an eternal present so that her life would largely be constituted by a sense of history as repetition and she would be stripped of the social relationships that make so much of our identity:

> To-morrow would bring its own trial with it; so would the next day, and so would the next; each its own trial, and *yet the very same* that was now so unutterably grievous to be borne . . . Throughout them all, *giving up her individuality*, she would become *the general symbol* at which the preacher and moralist might point . . . Thus the young and pure would be taught to look at her . . . as the figure, the body, the reality of sin.    (185–6, my emphases)

But that intention to reduce Hester to a government moral health warning would involve the impossible – the elimination of process – whether that process takes the form of the history of a community, of a self, or the interactions between the two.

If the main narrative argues that history will vanquish symbolism's attempt to freeze time and meaning, "The Custom-House" suggests that the present is in any case both a fragile and a problematic concept. There Hawthorne makes a confession of failure yet the very fact of making the confession invites us to consider whether the question of (social) reality in the present is not always dependent on history. His fiction of contemporary life, *The House of the Seven Gables*, is overtly built on history, connecting as the Preface tells us "a by-gone time with the very

present that is flitting away from us" – and it is that historical narrative
which enables Hawthorne to offer a picture of the modern world (351).
One crucial problem in producing or, rather, reproducing the realistic
text that Hawthorne might have written instead of *The Scarlet Letter* is
the way in which contemporary reality is always vanishing – not so
much into history as into limbo because Hawthorne lacks the proper
perspective to deal with the experience even though contemporary
reality appears to him as an already written text:

> A better book than I shall ever write was there; leaf after leaf presenting itself to
> me, just as it was written out by the reality of the flitting hour, and vanishing as
> fast as written, only because my brain wanted the insight and my hand the
> cunning to transcribe it.                                                   (151)

Hawthorne fails to write his full-length book about contemporary life
partially at least because he could not stop time, because memory is not
enough on its own – yet, and surely it is a deliberate irony, one point
about "The Custom-House" is that he has shown ways that such a work
might be constructed with its necessary roots in private and public
history. Another related point is that the difference between Hawthorne's historical romance and a realistic fiction of contemporary life is
one of degree, not kind. The rupture with the Custom-House means that
the immediate past is in danger of being lost to history even if it is history
as autobiography – were it not for "The Custom-House":

> The life of the Custom-House lies like a dream behind me. The old
> Inspector . . . and all those other venerable personages who sat with him at the
> receipt of custom, are but shadows in my view; white-headed and wrinkled
> images, which my fancy used to sport with, and has now flung aside for ever.
> The merchants . . . – these men of traffic, who seemed to occupy so important a
> position in the world, – how little time has it required to disconnect me from
> them all, not merely in act, but recollection! It is with an effort that I recall the
> figures and appellations of these few. Soon, likewise, my old native town will
> loom upon me through the haze of memory, a mist brooding over and around
> it; as if it were no portion of the real earth, but an overgrown village in cloud-
> land, with only imaginary inhabitants to people its wooden houses . . .
> Henceforth, it ceases to be a reality of my life.                          (157)

Dream, shadows, images, fancy, haze of memory, mist cloud-land,
imaginary: these are the words that Hawthorne uses to describe his sense
of his very recent past. This is analogous to the equally radical break with
the past evidenced by Hester's reflections in the first scaffold scene where
her memories of her European past take the shape of "phantasmagoric
forms" under the pressures of the "weight and hardness of the reality"
(167). After those phantasmagoric memories have flashed across the
screen of Hester's mind, Hawthorne returns to that key term which

resonates throughout the novel: reality. The letter, "the infant and the shame were real. Yes! – these were her realities, – all else had vanished!" (168) Hester, having lost her past through her sin and society's punishment of it, has to construct a new history, a new identity for herself which will go beyond the limitations of symbolic definition until, by the end of the novel, there is "a more real life" for her in New England (344). For Hawthorne, all fiction should necessarily be historical fiction – and the worlds both of nineteenth-century Salem and seventeenth-century Boston are not so much to be read as inventions or creations but as re-creations.

II

> One thing that quickned [sic] his Resolution to do what might be in this Matter expected from him, was a Passage which he heard from a Minister Preaching on the Title of the *Fifty-first* Psalm: *To make a publick and an open Profession of Repentance, is a thing not mis-becoming the greatest Man alive.*

> Every disease is the penalty for what the Salteaux call "bad conduct." . . .
> The illness can be combated in only one way – by confession. But it is a different idea of confession from what we are used to. We assume that any confession made to a priest, psychoanalyst, friend, or lawyer will be held in strictest confidence; it is a private matter. But among the Salteaux, the whole point of confession is that it must be public; the transgressor must suffer all the shame of self-exposure. By confessing his guilt and telling the members of the band exactly what he did wrong, the sinner deters others from making the same mistake in the future.[1]

Here, both Mather the minister and Farb the anthropologist discuss social contexts in which public confession is valued, and their very different perspectives help to illuminate Hawthorne's concern with what he sees as the necessary relationship between the public and private sides of man's being – necessary for full humanity. The minister speaks from the structure of feeling of the society that Hawthorne is re-creating – and (up to a point – the point perhaps where symbolic definition of a person negates social relationships) respecting if only for the seriousness with which it responds to experience, its refusal to trivialize as (and this is surely Hawthorne's implication) is the tendency of the modern world:

> The scene was not without a mixture of awe, such as must always invest the spectacle of guilt and shame in a fellow-creature, before society shall have grown corrupt enough to smile, instead of shuddering, at it. The witnesses of Hester Prynne's disgrace . . . were stern enough to look upon her death, had that been the sentence, without a murmur at its severity, but had none of the heartlessness of another social state, which would find only a theme for jest in an exhibition like the present. (166)

The anthropologist contrasts the world view of the primitive Indian to that of modern liberalism – a world view which not so much accepts as endorses a split between the public and private sides of man's being and which, I would argue, does not necessarily see adultery as wrong because an anti-social act as Hawthorne most certainly does. Hawthorne's emphasis that meaning must be socially negotiated to be valid, that morality is above all social morality, means that, however palliated, Hester's and Dimmesdale's adultery must be seen as wrong. Adultery destroys the possibility of the fulfilment of private relationships and of wider public relationships. For Hawthorne it is only when the two are brought together that there is the possibility of sustained authentic life. It is to take the diseased Dimmesdale seven years to learn the lesson that public confession is necessary to heal the split not only between the way he sees himself and the way he is seen but also to heal the relationship between father and daughter, and, indeed, to enable Pearl to escape from the solitary confinement of symbolic definition imposed by her mother.

It is crucially important to realize the value that Hawthorne places in living in right relationship in society, in living a life of open and spontaneous reciprocity, because it is only by remembering this that we can adequately recognize the way symbolism is presented and judged in the fiction. It cannot be emphasized too strongly that Hawthorne is writing a fiction critical of symbolic definition rather than a symbolist work. Thus, Pearl is forced to exercise the function of a symbol not by the reader but by Hester as she replicates what the authorities had done to her. Pearl's whole appearance

> was the scarlet letter in another form; the scarlet letter endowed with life! The mother herself – as if the red ignominy were so deeply scorched into her brain, that all her conceptions assumed its form – had carefully wrought out the similitude; lavishing many hours of morbid ingenuity, to create an analogy between the object of her affection, and the emblem of her guilt and torture. But in truth, Pearl was the one, as well as the other; and only in consequence of that identity had Hester contrived so perfectly to represent the scarlet letter in her appearance. (204–5)

Hester makes Pearl into "the living hieroglyphic . . . the symbol" of her sin, a sign that she can redeem herself, and by doing so she depersonalizes, dehumanizes Pearl. It is only with Dimmesdale's public confession that Pearl can become fully human and escape from the narrowness and distortion inherent in symbolic identity (296). If Pearl is Hester's victim, so is Chillingworth (*né* Prynne) – only his symbolic self-definition is self-imposed. He takes up a symbolic function, defining and limiting himself by the new name he has chosen, until he becomes fully "unhumanized" (342). By his allegorical/symbolical way of viewing the world, he abnegates human responsibility for actions. He tells Hester

> "It is not granted me to pardon . . . By thy first step awry, thou didst plant the
> germ of evil; but, since that moment, it has all been a dark necessity. Ye that
> have wronged me are not sinful, save in a kind of typical illusion; neither am I
> fiend-like, who have snatched a fiend's office from his hands. It is our fate. Let
> the black flower blossom as it may!"                                    (268)

Since Hawthorne tells us elsewhere explicitly that Chillingworth is to be seen as a self-made fiend, we know how to place this abnegation of responsibility. But in this way of seeing experience symbolically, as "a kind of typical illusion," it can be seen that he shares the way of seeing of the "highly respectable" but mistaken Calvinist witnesses who wish to deny the particular historical meaning of Dimmesdale's confession on the scaffold: "After exhausting life in his efforts for mankind's spiritual good, he had made the manner of his death a parable, in order to impress on his admirers the mighty and mournful lesson, that, in the view of Infinite Purity, we are sinners all alike" (341).

Those witnesses have failed to comprehend the change in Dimmesdale's scaffold confession from his earlier pulpit rhetoric where his confession of his specific sin is interpreted as sublime humility, as he predicted, "subtle, but remorseless hypocrite" that he is (242). But despite the self-hatred that his double-dealing induces, paradoxically his very consciousness of his sinfulness moves him towards comprehension of his congregation: "this very burden it was that gave him sympathies so intimate with the sinful brotherhood of mankind" (240). One effect of the sin on Hester has been to make her doubt the virtues of others. One effect on Dimmesdale has been to make him doubt the very nature of reality itself. Hester has the advantage of being a confessed and known sinner – and it is a very real advantage for Hawthorne. But Dimmesdale cannot dare to communicate in any sincerity with his fellow-men:

> It is the unspeakable misery of a life so false as his, that it steals the pith and
> substance out of whatever realities there are around us, and which were meant
> by Heaven to be the spirit's joy and nutriment. To the untrue man, the whole
> universe is false, it is impalpable, – it shrinks to nothing with his grasp. And he
> himself, in so far as he shows himself in a false light, becomes a shadow, or,
> indeed, ceases to exist.                                              (243)

Reality is a social construct: it comes from sharing experience and emotion. To live privately is to live immorally and to destroy one's identity. For Hawthorne, social being is at the core of all identity and of all virtue. The only "truth" that gave Dimmesdale "a real existence" was "the strength in his inmost soul, and *the undissembled expression of it in his aspect.* Had he once found power to smile and wear a face of gayety, *there would have been no such man!*" (243–4, my emphases)

Dimmesdale, in his search for "a moment's peace" ascends the scaffold at night but as carefully dressed "as if it had been for public worship" as if in unconscious rehearsal of his final confession (244). When Hester and Pearl join him on their return from Governor Winthrop's death-bed, there is a temporary escape from isolation in this social contact. As the minister takes Pearl's hand:

> there came what seemed like a tumultuous rush of new life, other life than his own, pouring like a torrent into his heart, and hurrying through all his veins, as if the mother and the child were communicating their vital warmth to his half torpid system. The three formed an electric chain.                      (250)

But the minister still lacks the courage to stand with them in the public light of noontide, as Pearl asks him to do, and says that he will stand with them only on one other day – the judgement day (which tells the reader how to place the community and the occasion when Dimmesdale does make his open confession). At this point, however, only a symbolic and therefore inadequate harmony can be achieved. The position is unreal because it is private. Dimmesdale can only gain subjective meaning from it rather as he imposes meaning on the meteor. And here Hawthorne seems to distinguish between the communal interpretation of a natural phenomenon as they read the meteor as a sign welcoming Winthrop to Heaven, which he respects if he does not endorse, over against Dimmesdale's private reading which he unequivocally condemns, imputing it "solely to the disease in his own eye and heart," his "egotism" (252).

If the significance of the first meeting lies in the stress on the inadequacy of symbolic definition and the impossibility for the guilty sinner to escape from this straitjacket, the meeting in the forest deals with the impossibility of escape from one's personal history and the inadequacy of the appeal to nature. Seven years have passed since the birth of Pearl. Hester and Dimmesdale have acquired new histories since the break caused by the discovery of their sin, though these new histories have pushed them in different ways. (Pearl has not changed: her symbolic status prevents significant human development.) Hester no longer measures her idea of right and wrong by any standard external to herself: "The scarlet letter had not done its office" (261). The symbol has had the effect of creating a split between her public appearance and her private thoughts. Dimmesdale similarly suffers from the division between private and public identity: "No man, for any considerable period, can wear one face to himself, and another to the multitude, without finally getting bewildered as to which may be the true" (304). In the forest, Hester can make a bid for life in her appeal to Dimmesdale to escape into the wilderness or to the old world. In spite of the fact that the minister, with his fixed place in the social system, "was only the more trammelled by its regulations, its principles, and even its prejudices," he feels the attraction of Hester's plea: "there appeared a glimpse of human affection and sympathy, a new life, and a true one" (290, 291). Hester explicitly attempts to deny the past any validity: "Let us not look back ... The past is gone! See! With this symbol, I undo it all, and make it as it had never been!" (292) "Make it new" with a vengeance! But her attempt to escape from her past by identifying herself with a Nature "never subjugated by human law" is doomed (and rightly doomed) to failure, for Hawthorne sees a romantic assertion of the value of passion based on the appeal to nature as immoral and unworkable. Ironically, at the very moment that Hester attempts to repudiate the authority of the past, her abandonment of the symbol shows how the past can erupt into the present: "Her sex, her youth, and the whole richness of her beauty, came back from what men call the irrevocable past" (293). Pearl, at once their past and their future, shows that they cannot escape from time or society by her insistence that Hester must wear the letter.

Dimmesdale returns from the forest full of an amoral energy produced by his dislocation from his previous history and by the feeling that he can now have hopes for the future. When he returns to his house, this vitality needs to be channelled, and, as Male puts it, "nourished by a communion with the tomb-fed faith and the tome-fed wisdom of the past":[2]

> Here he had studied and written; here, gone through fast and vigil, and come forth half alive; here, striven to pray; here, borne a hundred thousand agonies! There was the Bible, in its rich old Hebrew, with Moses and the Prophets speaking to him, and God's voice through all! (310)

Here the private and the public selves can begin to be reintegrated. The minister is greatly relieved that the ship in which he and Hester intend to escape to Europe will not be sailing until after the day appointed for the Election Sermon which is to prove his salvation. Hawthorne apparently criticizes him for this, describing his desire to "leave no public duty unperformed, nor ill performed!" as "pitiably weak," as evidence of "a subtle disease" (304). But it is the public duty of the Election Sermon which is to prove his salvation. It is because he has to preach that he returns to his study. It is because of his awareness of his public duty that he can bring himself to confess: it is the sermon and its effects which enables him to decide which is his real self. The sermon does not have an effect on Dimmesdale alone. It enables him to open a reciprocal intercourse with the world (and here we look back to Hawthorne's suggestion that "thoughts are frozen and utterance benumbed, unless the speaker stand in some true relation to his audience" [121]). The sermon inspires both audience and speaker, and by inspiring his audience the minister can no longer evade his responsibility to them and to Hester and Pearl. He has been *both* "so etherealized by spirit" *and* "so apotheosized by worshipping admirers" (334). The sermon, given before the whole known community, has two levels of meaning: first, the prophecy about the political future of New England, expressed by conventional language; and second, the private cry, expressed by his tone of voice – the universal language of the heart. It is "The complaint of a human heart, sorrow-laden, perchance guilty, telling its secret, whether of guilt or sorrow, to the great heart of mankind; beseeching its sympathy or forgiveness, . . . and never in vain" (328).

For such a short fiction, *The Scarlet Letter* covers a remarkable length of time – and a period which has a considerable historical resonance: seven years – 1642–49. Whatever the reason for choosing the period of England's Civil War for the main action of the novel, a substantial length of time is necessary for Hester to build a new identity after her old European self had been destroyed by her sin and its punishment on the scaffold: "It was as if a new birth, with stronger assimilations than the first, had converted the forest-land . . . into Hester Prynne's . . . life-long home" (186). And not only Hester's construction of a new self but also the related matter of the mutual relationships between herself and the community have to be given time to develop so that a long revolution in the community's interpretation of the letter and Hester can take place. That relationship is not only long but complex – and not without its ironies. One irony is that her subversion by decoration of the letter not only enables Hester to find a place in the community's economy but also that art of needlework, that labour of the outsider, in large part reinforces the power structure of the society – even though her own thoughts radically question that structure:

> Public ceremonies, such as ordinations, the installation of magistrates, and all that could give majesty to the forms in which a new government manifested itself to the people, were, as a matter of policy, marked by a stately and well-conducted ceremonial, and a sombre but yet a studied magnificence. Deep ruffs, painfully wrought bands, and gorgeously embroidered gloves, were all deemed necessary to the official state of men assuming the reins of power; and were readily allowed to individuals dignified by rank or wealth, even while sumptuary laws forbade these and similar extravagances to the plebeian order.
>
> (188)

There is much that could be said about this passage – but one obvious point is that Hawthorne is drawing attention to the class structure of the infant democracy. In so far as her identity is constituted by the letter signifying one meaning along with her labour for the establishment, the patriarchy could hardly ask for a more useful "citizen" than Hester – at once a strong warning against hiding the father who has broken the rules and a figure who enables the patriarchy (both fathers in Christ and fathers in the law) symbolically to declare their command over "painfully wrought" labour – a labour which in its products signifies their power, their difference from "the plebeian order." But the simplicity of symbolic labelling cannot, over time, survive the necessary multiplicity of Hester's relationships with the society as a whole. For example, not all Hester's labour (if all her paid work) goes towards making the symbols of power: she uses the profit ("all her superfluous means") to make "coarse garments for the poor" (189). Though that activity certainly reflects and by reflecting may endorse class difference within the society, it is also a response to need – and in that response a beginning to her social work as well as private penance (remorse for past sins, in its technical meaning – but not, significantly, yet penitence – technically the resolve to sin no more).

The original interpretation of the letter can survive over a limited period of time especially when it is confined to the class that imposed the definition. Pearl is three when she and Hester go to the Governor's Hall and Hester, notoriously, sees an image of herself in the breast-plate of his armour. As Hawthorne forcibly suggests, authority's definition has to be seen as a distortion: "owing to the peculiar effect of this convex mirror, the scarlet letter was represented in exaggerated and gigantic proportions, so as to be greatly the most prominent feature of [Hester's] appearance" (208). But one point to make about that representation is that the breast-plate may embody as well as reflect a truth – that the sign on Hester's breast may not only distort other's perceptions of her but may also be a protective device behind which her (possibly irresponsible) subversive ideas can shelter, grow, and flourish. More obviously, that breast-plate definition of Hester is not stable: under the pressure of historical experience, the sign's meaning has shifted. Hester's new social role, after seven long years, is not so much a production intended by either Hester or the society as something that the history of the interaction between the two parties has rendered up:

> She was self-ordained a Sister of Mercy; or so we may rather say, the world's heavy hand had so ordained her, when neither the world nor she looked forward to this result. The letter was the symbol of her calling. Such helpfulness was found in her, – so much power to do, and power to sympathize, – that many people refused to interpret this scarlet A by its original signification. They said it meant Able; so strong was Hester with a woman's strength. (257)

Authority had once, we have to infer, defined Hester as Adulteress: now the people define her not by the static reductiveness of a noun, but by an adjective – an attribute, not an identity. Notably, it is "the men of rank," conscious of their role as guardians "of the public morals" who are slow to accept any redefinition of the sign, while it is "the people" and those "in private life" (significant terms) who, having redefined the sign, incorporate *Hester*, a person not a symbol, into the community: "our Hester, – the town's own Hester" (258). Of course, their Hester may not be Hester's Hester – and Hester may not accept, may not deserve this incorporation – as Hawthorne subtly indicates. And, following from her secret resistance to incorporation into the town's ideology, society's redefinition of the sign is not enough to heal the split between the way society sees Hester and the way she sees not only this society but, it would appear, all societies in which men dominate women – a view of the world about which at this stage Hawthorne seems profoundly ambivalent. If this split is to be healed – and, from Hester's point of view, it may matter little whether she is labelled as Adulteress or Able – then the story has to go beyond the moment of Dimmesdale's confession and death which, though convenient for him, Pearl and, no doubt, the author, leaves Hester still at the centre of the stage. For her, neither death, nor escape are real options.

I have already argued that one consequence of Dimmesdale's public acknowledgement of his connection with Pearl and Hester is that Pearl can escape from her limiting status as symbol and become fully human, a woman in the world. It is this that explains her movement to Europe. Pearl is not a Jamesian heroine who has somehow strayed into the wrong book, as is occasionally suggested. She can go to Europe because she has no historical ties with New England. Her only identity there has been as symbol, used by others but without independent existence: when that is destroyed, she is free. Hester must return, because it is New England and her sin that has given some sort of organizing principle to her life. After her first appearance on the scaffold, "Her sin, her ignominy, were the roots which she had struck into the soil . . . The chain that bound her here was of iron links . . . but never could be broken." (186) During Dimmesdale's sermon, Hester stands at the foot of the scaffold "whence she dated the first hour of her life of ignominy . . . There was a sense within her, . . . that her whole orb of life, both before and after, was connected with this spot, as with the one point that gave it unity." (328) To be true, as Hawthorne admonishes us, is freely to declare ourselves to the world, to recognize that we cannot reject or deny the personal history that defines us. We must choose reality over symbol, as Hester chooses to return to New England to live the ethical life: "But there was a more real life for Hester Prynne, here, in New England, than in that unknown region where Pearl had found a home. Here had been her sin; here her sorrow; and here was yet to be her penitence" (344). That last sentence is a more economical version with authorial approval of a feeling that Hester had experienced at the beginning of her life of isolation:

> Here, she said to herself, had been the scene of her guilt, and here should be the scene of her earthly punishment; and so, perchance, the torture of her daily shame would at length purge her soul, and work out another purity than that which she had lost; more saint-like, because the result of martyrdom.    (187)

### III

"Frailty, thy name is WOMAN."
"The Earth waits for her Queen."
The connection between these quotations may not be obvious, but it is strict.

The connection may not be obvious, but I want to argue that this, the opening of Margaret Fuller's *Woman in the Nineteenth Century* provides the right perspective in which to see the following crucial passage from *The Scarlet Letter* – crucial, that is, for the sexual politics of the novel – right, in that Fuller's epigraphs link a present definition (if not condition) with a desired Utopian future, very much as the narrative of Hester does:

> Women . . . – in the continually recurring trials of wounded, wasted, wronged, misplaced, or erring and sinful passion, – or with the dreary burden of a heart unyielded, because unvalued and unsought, – came to Hester's cottage demanding why they were so wretched, and what the remedy! . . . She assured them . . . of her firm belief, that, at some brighter period, when the world should have grown ripe for it, in Heaven's own time, a new truth would be revealed, in order to establish the whole relation between man and woman on a surer ground of mutual happiness. Earlier in life, Hester had vainly imagined that she herself might be the destined prophetess, but had long since recognized the impossibility that any mission of divine and mysterious truth should be confided to a woman stained with sin, bowed down with shame, or even burdened with a life-long sorrow. The angel and apostle of the coming revelation must be a woman, indeed, but lofty, pure, and beautiful; and wise, moreover, not through dusky grief, but the ethereal medium of joy; and showing how sacred love should make us happy, by the truest test of a life successful to such an end!    (344–5)

With this passage as evidence, I want to argue that Hester finishes as rather more than a social worker specializing in female clients whom "she counselled as best she might," more than just an early representative of the caring professions – and doing more than running a seventeenth-century counselling group. She is genuinely subversive in that she desires and prophesies a radical subversion of the patriarchal structures of the society and, most significantly, of the religion that legitimates that patriarchy. Such a view, however, seems to run counter to the comparatively few recent critics who have found the passage worthy of notice.

Michael Colacurcio in an important and learned article has argued convincingly for the relevance of Ann Hutchinson's moral and intellectual structure of feeling for the world inhabited by Hester Prynne and Dimmesdale. But he does not go further when describing Hester's final position than to say that it is "in Hawthorne's mental universe, just about half way between Ann Hutchinson and Margaret Fuller." This could mean almost anything, but Colacurcio has made it clear that he does not want to see Hester as making a radical critique: "What Hester's experience came to finally – in an epilogue, and after a painful and complicated development forced upon her by others – is some insight about the double standard, or perhaps about the new morality."[3] Is that *all*? It hardly seems an adequate commentary on a statement asking for a total restructuring of the relations between man and woman – one which rewords and makes public Hester's private feelings about male/female relations in chapter XIII. However, he does realize that the passage matters. One of the few other critics to have paid serious attention to these words of Hester's is Austin Warren in an excellent piece, though I cannot go along with his gloss on the passage ("falsetto" strikes me as a peculiarly unfortunate and tasteless epithet):

> Whether applied to Hester specifically or to the mysterious revelation to come – reminiscent of Ann Hutchinson, Margaret Fuller, or Mother Ann Lee, the pronouncement seems falsetto. Hawthorne's "new revelation," which seems (so far as I can understand it) not very new, is certainly not feminist but feminine and familial.[4]

Here he falters. He introduces the right names – but fails to notice that Hester does not exactly replicate any of their positions and may indeed be new – and feminist. Ann Hutchinson's antinomianism and her insistence on exercising a powerful and intelligent female voice are, as Colacurcio shows, clearly relevant. And Margaret Fuller's "great lawsuit" of Man *versus* Men, Woman *versus* Women equally clearly bears on Hester's case: "Those who would reform the world must show that they do not speak in the heat of wild impulse; their lives must be unstained by passionate error; they must be severe lawgivers to themselves."[5] Even more to the point is Mother Ann, foundress of the Shakers. It seems to be their insistence on celibacy that is remembered, while the theology behind that insistence is usually forgotten. The immediately relevant points are these: God is a dual person, male *and* female. Adam likewise necessarily had in himself both sexes, being created in the image of God. Christ appeared first in the person of Jesus, embodying the male order, and then in the person of Ann Lee, representing the female element. The day of judgement has begun with the establishment of the Shaker church, and will be completed with that church's full development.

If I understand Hester's coded statement correctly, she is going beyond any of these three prophetesses. (Mother Ann never claimed to be Christ come again: she merely represented the female element in God.)[6] Hester has come to believe that what is needed is a second Revelation of God to man – and woman. In other words, she looks forward to the Second Coming of Christ – only this time as a woman. Angel and Apostle indeed of a coming Revelation! Perhaps capitalizing Angel and Apostle is cheating slightly – but the choice of the two words, given their significant first letter and accompanied by the phrase "the destined prophetess" suggests that Hester has more in mind than just a very good female person. Cruden, in his *Concordance*, gives these definitions:

> ANGEL signifies, A messenger or bringer of tidings, and is applied (1) To those intellectual and immaterial beings, whom God makes use of as his ministers to execute orders of providence . . . (2) To Christ, who is the mediator and head of the church . . . (3) To ministers of the gospel, who are ambassadors for Christ . . . (4) To such as are employed by God as instruments for executing his judgments.

> APOSTLE signifies, A messenger sent upon any special errand . . . It is applied (1) to Christ Jesus who was sent from heaven to assume our nature, with authority to exercise prophetical and all his offices, and to send forth his apostles to publish the gospel . . . (2) To a minister immediately sent from Christ to preach the gospel.

The coupling of these words with "revelation" – a term that needs no theological gloss – makes the millenarian nature of Hester's prophecy quite clear.

Whether Hawthorne approves or disapproves of this prophecy is not an open question – if one is Austin Warren, who claims that the author wrote the conclusion "in the voice of Hawthorne, the commentator, the husband of Sophia." But even if one shares this confidence that the voice of Sophia's husband was always a conservative and conventional one, the announcement can hardly be dismissed as "not very new" and (by implication) therefore not very important. There were plenty of claims to be the especial Bride of Christ in both the seventeenth and nineteenth centuries – as a reading of Christopher Hill's *The World Turned Upside Down* shows for the seventeenth century, and J.F.C. Harrison's *The Second Coming* shows for the late eighteenth and early nineteenth centuries. But there were few (if any) who waited for the Second

Coming expecting Christ to be a woman – and such an expectation would make for a radical (but reasonable) re-ordering of theological language.[7] (Incidentally, Mother Ann said that "we are the people who turn the world upside down." "The world turned upside down" was an old English song which she probably knew, though she is, no doubt, principally thinking of Acts xvii, 6, where this is the accusation levelled against the primitive church. Ironically it was the tune played by the English army when Cornwallis surrendered at Yorktown – unintentionally playing into the hands of those who would claim that America is indeed the Redeemer Nation.)

If my interpretation of Hester's claim is accepted, it may at least help Warren with another of his problems – the question of the paraphrasable content of Dimmesdale's Election Sermon:

> That the preacher, about to declare himself an avowed sinner, cannot (like Cotton Mather) denounce his New England's sins, I can see; but why need he celebrate its high destiny? It would appear that Hawthorne, to whom the "subject matter" of the sermon does not seem to matter, has inserted and asserted, his own strong regional loyalties. (42)

It may be that we should feel – with the New England world described in "The Custom-House" in mind – that this forecast of the region's "high and glorious destiny" is one of Hawthorne's fiercest ironies – or, at best, his own very patient prophecy. These glories *may* lie in New England's future – just as there *may* be a future revelation of a new truth which will make the relation between the sexes mutually happy. But these prophesied futures can hardly be said to have arrived by 1850 – unless one has the optimism of a George Bancroft. (On the spine of my edition of his *History of the United States* are these words circling an eagle sitting on top of the world: "Westward the Star of Empire Takes its Way".) But, however these prophecies are to be evaluated, what is clear is that they are to be paralleled and compared as secular and religious prophecies – and it is a nice irony that the clergyman makes a secular prophecy while the laywoman makes a religious one.

What Hester had only thought privately in chapter xiii, she can now speak (though not practice) – and what she desires, if it were to take place, surely would be to overthrow and rearrange "the whole system of ancient prejudice," "to undermine the foundations of the Puritan establishment" (259, 260). Nina Baym writes about Hester's return in a particularly disappointing, even surprising, way:

> Hester has in fact brought about a modest social change. Society expands to accept her with the letter – the private life carves out a small place for itself in the community's awareness. This is a small, but real, triumph for the heroine . . . [H]er return to Boston and the consequent loosening of the community to

accommodate her lighten the conclusion. A painfully slow process of social relaxation may, perhaps, be hoped for.[8]

Perhaps. But this liberalist gradualism is clearly not what Hester looks for or desires. It is (perhaps) the most that Hawthorne thinks can be achieved, but even if we define Hawthorne as a liberal gradualist, that doesn't answer the obvious problem that the small advances may only be generated by great expectations and demands. And – even if she can only cast herself as Jane the Baptist – it looks as though Hester expects a lot: the Second Coming. To be without sin, shame and sorrow is to be more than human. Hester prophesies a world when there will be no more marrying and giving in marriage, when the apostle/angel will transcend or at least radically define the sexual relationship. Perhaps celibacy is meant by "the truest test" – as might be indicated by the emphasis on "ethereal." Perhaps Hester has read Revelations – in company with other sexual radicals in a radical Protestant tradition such as William Blake – and particularly chapter XII like him, and awaits "the woman clothed with the sun."

But even the new historicist Sacvan Bercovitch will have none of this. He calls Hester's prophesies a "moment of reconciliation," tells us that Hester "*must* now make compromise the work of culture," suggests that Hawthorne "absorbs the radical energies of history into the polar oppositions of symbolic interpretation," and worries that a potential confrontation in the novel "endangers both symbolic process and narrative closure."[9] I fail to see how a desire for – expressed as a prediction of – a transformation of the relationship between men and women can be called "reconciliation" or "compromise." I have argued that Hawthorne has criticized symbolic interpretation in the name of "the radical energies of history." And I would further suggest that here, as in all of Hawthorne's longer fictions, his narrative forms resist closure. In this case, it remains deliberately open – open to the future. To argue that Hawthorne speaks from and celebrates an ideology of liberal consensus seems entirely wrong. A man recently fired for his political views is hardly likely to think that political consensus exists in his own political culture – and, as he quite gratuitously chooses to identify himself in "The Custom-House" however ironically as the Loco-foco Surveyor, that is, as a radical, an egalitarian Democrat, he is hardly trying to assimilate himself to a consensus position.[10]

Hawthorne, by giving Dimmesdale and Hester the role of prophet, brings the future into the sphere of the novel, so that readers are not (or at least should not be) trapped into conservatively dwelling in and on the past. With both characters, the reciprocal relationships between the public and the private spheres are stressed and developed throughout the course of the novel. (One reason for the inadequacy of the appeal to nature is that it can only speak to the private side of man's being.) The symbolic sign is, at the last, stripped of its various imposed meanings, and becomes simply the letter A, a dead letter. The true significance of the novel can be seen to lie in its creation of a structure based on the personal histories of the central characters interacting with the historical life of the new community of New England. Both in turn interact with the double history of the artist and with an imagined better future. *The Scarlet Letter* is an historical novel – one which takes past, present and future into consideration – and is at the same time political in that the future is presented as something that we have to struggle to make – a making based on desire corrected by our perspectives on the past.

# 5

## The House of the Seven Gables:
### *Hawthorne's modern novel of 1848*

Towards the end of "The Custom-House" it will be remembered that Hawthorne blames himself for writing about the past rather than the present. *The House of the Seven Gables* seems to be written with that concern for contemporaneity in mind.[1] Certainly, Melville saw it as centrally concerned with modernity. In the famous letter of April, 1851 to Hawthorne about the novel, he praised the book for its "visible truth," by which he meant "the apprehension of the absolute condition of present things." Hawthorne in his preface at once admitted and denied a connection between his fiction and the modern situation. The novel is, he says, an "attempt to connect a by-gone time with the very Present that is flitting away from us" but goes on to deplore any attempt to give the action a local habitation and a name – even though Salem in the County of Essex is, very clearly, the "actual locality" (351, 352). He has to admit that there is an "essential" historical connection but he seems to be trying to distance his story from that connection as much as possible:

> Not to speak of other objections, it [the historical connection] exposes the Romance to an inflexible and exceedingly dangerous species of criticism, by bringing his fancy-pictures amost into positive contact with the realities of the moment.
>
> (352)

Yet, as so often with Hawthorne's introductions, the preface is a mixture of revelation and mystification, for Hawthorne has exposed the text to the criticisms he claims to fear by giving himself at least some of the problems that confront one kind of realist; repeatedly virtually insisting on risking the "positive contact" he says he wishes to avoid. He writes at the least very close to history. In the "Governor Pyncheon" chapter (XVIII) that enables us – indeed, invites us – to date the action, he brings the Judge very close to a knowable public history. Indeed, it could be said

96

that Pyncheon *has* to die if survival would make him Governor of Massachusetts in the elections of 1848. The action may not explicitly take place in Salem but Hawthorne does say that it takes place in Massachusetts – and 1848 is too recent a date to deploy the decent vagueness of "once upon a time." The real Governor is bound to be remembered a mere three years laters – if not still in office.

The action of the novel is carefully set in a single summer – with the exception of two chapters. The first chapter looks back to the 1690s; and chapter XIII, "Alice Pyncheon," the story that Holgrave/Maule tells Phoebe Pyncheon, is set thirty-seven years after that. (It is an open question whether we are to read that story as a fiction or as a traditional tale passed down in the Maule family). Chapter II begins by telling us that it is the day following midsummer night, and the last chapter refers to a September gale. But it is the year rather than the season which is important. The reference to the "fall campaign" in the "Governor Pyncheon" chapter taken with the statement that "the fate of the country is staked on the November election" shows that this is a presidential election year – and given the mention of the Free-Soilers who came into prominence only in 1847 this means that it must be 1848 (585). This, of course, was the year that saw the election of Zachary Taylor to the Presidency and therefore the subsequent dismissal of Hawthorne from the Salem Customs (as he ruefully tells us in "The Custom-House"). Hawthorne is therefore writing about a time which coincides with his last summer as Surveyor of Customs, a recognizable historical moment that had some considerable personal meaning for him. There can, then, be no question that the year is 1848, and the insistent references to the paraphernalia of a distinctively modern world (such as mesmerism, telegraphy, photography and the railroad) reinforce the sense that an historical world, a distinctively modern environment is being documented and commented on.

These technological signs of the times are accompanied by a modern view of politics, for it would be only too possible to see it as a novel that Marx might have read (with some head-shaking) in between scribbling the *Communist Manifesto* and the *18th Brumaire*. It starts, after all, from the expropriation by that incipient bourgeois, Colonel Pyncheon, of the land won by the labour of Matthew Maule – and there is a clear suggestion that Maule's witchcraft trial shows religion used as a convenient mystification for Pyncheon's economic motives. The only property of Maule's son is his labour of hand and brain – to be employed to Pyncheon's advantage as young Maule is both architect and builder of the house of seven gables. The shift from a society based on status to one based on contract, from military to legal power is neatly enough signalled by the difference implied by the move from Colonel to Judge.

Marx might shake his head over the woolly utopianism of Holgrave and see his initial radicalism as that of the "critical-utopian" socialist – to borrow a phrase from the *Communist Manifesto*. Hepzibah may not be the most informed or reliable witness – but this is how she describes Holgrave to Phoebe:

> He had the strangest companions imaginable; – men with long beards, and dressed in linen blouses, and other such new-fangled and ill-fitting garments; – reformers, temperance-lecturers, and all manner of cross-looking philanthropists; community-men and come-outers . . . As for the Daguerreotypist, she had read a paragraph in a penny-paper . . . accusing him of making a speech, full of wild and disorganizing matter, at a meeting of his banditti-like associates. (424)

At the same time that we get this picture of the modern American radical, we get Hawthorne's explicit criticisms of the mystifications of a so-called representative democracy:

> They are practiced politicians, every man of them, and skilled to adjust those preliminary measures which steal from the people, without its knowledge, the power of choosing its own rulers. The popular voice, at the next gubernatorial election, though as loud as thunder, will be really but an echo of what these gentlemen shall speak, under their breath . . . They meet to decide upon their candidate. This little knot of subtle schemers will control the convention, and, through it, dictate to the party.[2] (587)

America has come a long way since Dimmesdale preached an Election Day sermon foretelling "a high and glorious destiny for the newly gathered people of the Lord" and Hester told Pearl about the significance of the day:

> "The children have come from their schools, and the grown people from their workshops and their fields, on purpose to be happy. For, today, a new man is beginning to rule over them; and so – as has been the custom of mankind ever since a nation was first gathered – they make merry and rejoice; as if a good and golden year were at length to pass over the poor old world!" (322–3, 316)

The "happy" ending which reinforces a bourgeois version of the extended family (complete with the parody of the old family retainer in the person of Uncle Venner) under the guise of a marriage which merely symbolizes the transcendence of class barriers seems only too suitable when read as an example of the predictable defeat of the revolutionary dreams of 1848. Thus, even the chorus of working men (recognized as such because of their "rough voices") speculating over the profits and losses to be got by keeping a cent shop takes its place as the ironized commentary of the mystified working class from whom, presumably, Holgrave came. His desire that "once in every half-century, at longest, a family should be merged into the great, obscure mass of humanity, and forget all about its ancestors" (511) may be sentimentally optimistic but not without its significance as a confused recognition that history is based on class conflict.

This is not to imply that Hawthorne necessarily endorses Holgrave's radicalism. His attitude appears ambivalent. On the one hand he approves of Holgrave's hope that "in this age" the "lifeless instititutions" are to be "thrust out of the way" and everything is "to begin anew" (506). On the other, he rebukes the daguerreotypist for his lack of realism, for "supposing that this age . . . is destined to see the tattered garments of Antiquity exchanged for a new suit instead of renewing themselves by patchwork" – and expresses scepticism about the value of radical political action (507). Holgrave, then, is in a double bind situation – if he was in a position to know Hawthorne's placing of him. He is damned if he abandons

> that . . . inward prophecy – which a young man had better never have been
> born, than not to have, and a mature man had better die at once than utterly to
> relinquish – that we are not doomed to creep on forever in the old, bad way,
> but that, this very now, there are the harbingers abroad of a golden era, to be
> accomplished in his own lifetime.                                         (506)

But Hawthorne contradicts himself. Holgrave is equally damned if he believes that he can achieve the golden age, in "fancying that it mattered anything to the great end in view, whether he himself should contend for or against it." Yet Hawthorne himself confesses "Yet it was well for him to think so." Hawthorne has trapped himself, and attempts to resolve this paralyzing ambivalence by distancing himself in what is very close to a distasteful aestheticizing of his perspective. The question of the future of this "representative" modern young man is "delightfully uncertain" (508).

However, Hawthorne is certain that Holgrave is "representative" – representatively modern. And modernity seems to thrust itself in. At one point in chapter XII, Holgrave, criticizing the desire of a man to build a house for his posterity, says that "he might just as reasonably order a durable suit of clothes – leather or gutta percha" and expect that to be worn by and to fit his descendants (510). No doubt a leather suit is suggested to a bright young radical like Holgrave by his reading about the Quaker George Fox in that text for English and American young radicals – Carlyle's *Sartor Resartus*. It is, I would speculate, a book that must have impressed Hawthorne – given his use of clothes imagery as he discusses the differences between reformism and revolution. (The first book publication of Carlyle's great work was in Boston in 1836 – thanks to help from Emerson.) In *Sartor* Teufelsdrockh calls Fox's tailoring of a leather suit "the most remarkable incident in modern history" – while his editor speculates as to why "in a discussion on the Perfectability of Society" Teufelsdrockh should "reproduce" it – even if we are aware of his "deep Sansculottism."

There can be, however, no literary heritage for gutta percha. According to the OED, its first use in England was in 1845. It did not make the Webster's of 1852 though it does appear in Worcester's Dictionary of 1859. According to the ninth edition of the *Encyclopædia Britannica*, the material (which comes from the inspissated juice of various plants of the natural order *Sapotaceae*) did not come into general use in Europe until the middle of the 1840s (though Dr. Montgomerie who introduced it into England had used it out East for making splints and "other surgical apparatus"). Its real importance and fame, though, was as insulation for telegraph wires. As Emerson noted in "Works and Days" (1870), "No sooner is the electric telegraph devised than gutta percha – the very material it requires – is found." Holgrave, it would appear, is presented as thinking of the most up to date material he can imagine, if one hardly suitable for clothing (except perhaps for rainwear but even the catalogue of the Great Exhibition [1851] does not record this use for gutta percha). Would most contemporary readers of *The House of the Seven Gables* even have recognized the word? Hawthorne seems to have playfully speculated that what could insulate the telegraph wire could (dangerously) insulate humanity.

Emerson was right to note the ways in which technological changes were interdependent. The telegraph, for example, by making an efficient signalling system possible, greatly facilitated the advance of a speedy and reliable railway system. And American could claim something very like priority in the invention and development of the electric telegraph – a technological development emblematized by the fascinating figure of S.F.B. Morse, painter, photographer, inventor of the telegraph (according to him) and certainly inventor of that crucial means of communication, the Morse code. In May 1844, the first line was opened between Washington and Baltimore. (The first official message was "What hath God wrought!") By 1846, Newark was linked to Philadephia, Philadelphia to Boston, and New York to Boston. "In 1848 the network of wires joined Albany, Utica, Buffalo and Pittsburgh, and three rival lines were racing towards New Orleans."[3] There could hardly be a more suitable place than a train for Clifford to discuss modern communications. To talk about these matters as he does in "The Flight of Two Owls" (ch. XVII) in "1848" or 1851 was to be very close to the forefront of the impact of modern technology on everyman. Indeed, his enthusiastic radicalism is surprising given his "innate" conservatism and his fear of the "terrible energy" of the "steam-devil" in "The Arched

Window" (490) – striking evidence of the liberation caused by the strange death of Judge Pyncheon. Clifford in "The Flight of Two Owls" shares many of the positions of Holgrave – especially the dislike of the ideology of the old home. Both have a utopian dimension to their radicalism. Holgrave hopes for a "golden era." Clifford is less extreme: he anticipates a "better era." Oddly, the daguerreotypist/artist suggests a (rather vague) political solution to get rid of the weight of the old home – while Clifford the aesthete seems to imagine that technology will transform social consciousness. Both, however, would regard "of no fixed abode" as a title of honour – at least until the conclusion of the novel (or the journey in the case of Clifford).

The train, according to Clifford, liberates the traveller from the clumsiness and suffering that travel had previously involved, liberates man from being "a prisoner for life in brick, and stone, and old worm-eaten timber": "Transition being so facile, what can be any man's inducement to tarry in one spot?" (575). For Clifford in this moment of transport the fixed abode, the ideology of the old home ("real estate . . . the broad foundation on which nearly all the guilt of this world rests"), is once more an unattractive idea politically, morally and hedonistically, now that the spiral of history has enabled a modern improved nomadism. Clifford moves "naturally," as it were, through mesmerism to rapping spirits to electricity and the telegraph – all for him harbingers of a better era. "Naturally" because they are all trendy ideas of 1848, all to do with communication and all are somehow connected with ideas of a universal electro-magnetic fluid:

> "Then there is electricity – the demon, the angel, the mighty physical power, the all-pervading intelligence" exclaimed Clifford . . . "Is it a fact – or have I dreamt it – that, by means of electricity, the world of matter has become a great nerve, vibrating thousands of miles in a breathless point of time? Rather, the round globe is a vast head, a brain, instinct with intelligence! Or, shall we say, it is itself a thought, nothing but thought, and no longer the substance which we deemed it!"                                                           (578)

We will shortly see that the concepts here expressed were those not only of the unstable rhapsodic Clifford but of more respectable figures in the culture. And Hawthorne's attention to the details of his modern history come out even in Clifford's reference to spiritualism:

> "These rapping spirits that little Phoebe told us of the other day," said Clifford. "What are these but the messengers of the spiritual world, knocking at the door of substance? And it shall be flung wide open!"            (578)

We do not have to share Clifford's confidence and may prefer to agree with his interlocutor, "the old gentleman" who saw this as a "humbug" – but it is evidence of Hawthorne's precise historical accuracy. Howard

Kerr begins *Mediums, and Spirit-Rappers, and Roaring Radicals* by telling the reader that "Spiritualism began in America in 1848." He justifies this by arguing (as, incidentally, did that true believer, Conan Doyle) that spiritualism "had its obscure birth in Hydesville, in upstate New York" on the night of March 31, 1848, when the rappings of the Fox sisters launched them on their unedifying career. And Kerr provides evidence to show that the connections Clifford makes are not merely the result of an overstrained imagination when he refers his readers to Nathaniel Parker Willis's report of a "Post-Mortuum Soiree" (1850). Willis joked (after having felt rappings jar the furniture) that a Fulton or a Morse might put "ghost power into harness."[4]

The anonymous old gent whom Clifford engages in conversation looks at the telegraph in a more sober manner. His materialism confronts Clifford's idealism:

> "If you mean the telegraph," said the old gentleman, glancing his eye toward its wire, alongside the rail track, "it is an excellent thing – that is, of course, if the speculators in cotton and politics don't get possession of it. A great thing, indeed, sir, particularly as regards the detection of bank robbers and murderers!"
> (578–9)

He was too late to exclude financial and political speculations but he could have provided evidence for his hopes for the telegraph's aid in arresting the criminal. On January 1, 1845, for example, the telegraph was used in England to bring about the arrest of the murderer Tawell, "and this circumstance had the effect of attracting attention to the telegraph, which up to that time had been little used."[5] A little later an embezzler from Hartford was intercepted at New Haven – and examples could be multiplied.

Yet Clifford, when he imagines a world of telegrams and love, in which an "almost spiritual medium like the telegraph" is "consecrated to high, deep, joyful, and holy missions", isn't being uniquely airy-fairy. William F. Channing may have come from transcendentalist stock but he was also a serious scientist/technologist with an interest in photography and an expertise in electric fire alarms – and he called the telegraph the nervous system of the nation. He was not alone in seeing the world (or at least the nation) as transformed by the electric telegraph into a body. Morse himself wrote

> it is not visionary to suppose that it would not be long ere the whole surface of this country would be channelled for those *nerves* which are diffuse, with the speed of thought, a knowledge of all that is occurring throughout in the land, making, in fact, one *neighbourhood* of the whole country.[6]

A figure like Edward Hitchcock, however, is more representative and relevant for Hawthorne's apprehension of the present condition of things – as he is at the centre of culturally respectable New England.[7] In his *Religion of Geology* (1851), he collected together lectures he had been giving over the past decade so there is no sense that what he has to say is eccentric. (Incidentally, he was no great friend to the views of Agassiz which he seems to find potentially radical and atheistic.) As president of Amherst he was a well known and respectable figure. Yet he doesn't scruple at seeing mesmerism as "a glimpse of the manner in which the soul will act in the future spiritual body." He does allow himself an escape route if confronted by a sceptic but goes on to suggest that mesmerism is "best explained by supposing the soul to act independently of the bodily organs, and through the same medium which we have supposed to constitute the future spiritual body." In this view, mesmerism forms "a link between the present and the future world." How very close this is to Clifford, who thinks that "when a good man has departed, his distant friend should be conscious of an electric thrill, as from the world of happy spirits, telling him – 'Your dear friend is in bliss!'" (579).

In Hitchcock's following chapter, "The Telegraphic System of the Universe," he takes his communications theory still further:

> The principle which I advance in its naked form is this: *Our words, our actions, and even our thoughts, make an indelible impression on the universe.* Thrown into a poetic form, this principle converts creation
>> Into a vast sounding gallery;
>> Into a vast picture gallery;
>> And into a universal telegraph.

The recording angel, it seems, has been placed by recording mechanisms. After several excited pages (drawing in part on Babbage of calculating engine fame) Hitchcock sums up almost hymning the body electric:

> If is as if each man had his foot upon the point where ten thousand telegraphic wires meet from every part of the universe, and he were able, with each volition, to send abroad an influence along these wires, so as to reach every created being in heaven and in earth. [L]et the suggestions to which our reasonings have conducted us prove true, let our sensorium be so modified and spiritualized that every thought, word, and action . . . shall come to us through pulsations falling upon the organ of vision, or by an electric current through the nerve of sensation, or by some transmitted chemical change, and on what vantage ground should we be placed!

Clifford's speculations (such as his ideas about the proper use of an "almost spiritual medium, like the electric telegraph") sound positively modest when set beside the rhapsodies of the orthodox divine and educator. If Babbage is right in claiming that matter cannot be destroyed and in theory can be traced through all its transmutations, then, claims Hitchcock, we can make a moral application of this mechanical proposition of Babbage's: "the air is one vast library on whose pages are for ever written all that man has ever said or woman whispered."[8] The whole universe, then, for Babbage and Hitchcock is a volume in which we write our histories whether we will or no: "the sentence I am now uttering shall alter the whole atmosphere through all future time." Oliver Wendell Holmes, who wrote three important and intriguing essays on photography, also uses this image of the book but develops it so that the image of writing is replaced by that of the photograph as he reflects on a photograph of a city scene:

> What a fearfully suggestive picture! It is a leaf torn from the book of God's recording angel. What if the sky is one great concave mirror, which reflects the picture of all our doings, and photographs every act on which it looks upon dead and living surfaces, so that to celestial eyes the stones on which we tread are written with our deeds, and the leaves of the forest are but undeveloped negatives where our summers stand self-recorded for transfer into the imperishable record?[9]

Whether the metaphor of script and text can be so easily replaced by that of the photographic image and what the implications of such a change might be are points to which I shall return. But one can note the Promethean implications of Holmes' claim that we can make the equivalent of a page from the recording angel's book – and thus see why the figure of a daguerreotypist can seem a natural radical hero in Hawthorne's fiction. Of course Holgrave is not troubled by the problems of the negative and of the multiplicity of images – but this, in one sense, means that his pictures are, so to speak, purer, more natural records of reality – a reality which may go behind or beneath a world of appearances.

However, the description of Holgrave's career suggests that Hawthorne is as interested in documentary "photographic" realism as in the symbolic implications and meanings of photography. Holgrave, though not yet twenty-two, has been a country school-master, a salesman in a country store, the politial editor of a country newspaper, a pedlar selling cologne water and other essences, a dentist (especially in factory towns), an official aboard a packet ship, a member of a community of Fourierists, and a lecturer on Mesmerism. (It sounds a bit like the career of another young would-be intellectual: Herman Melville). Robert Taft in his very useful book quotes Ryder, a well known Cleveland photographer, on the situation in the 1840s:

> It was no uncommon thing to find watch repairers, dentists and other styles of business folk to carry on daguerreotyping "on the side!" I have known blacksmiths and cobblers to double up with it, so it was possible to have a horse shod, your boots tapped, a tooth pulled, or a likeness taken; verily a man – daguerreotype man – in his time played many parts.

And Taft, drawing on Ryder, suggests that the "professors" of this artistic science (or scientific art) were frequently connected with other not always respectable sciences (or pseudo-sciences) such as phrenology (and, no doubt, mesmerism). Gouraud, for example, who claimed to be a friend and pupil of Daguerre, "attempted to capitalize on his reputation by selling drugs, nostrums, and toilet preparations."[10] The parallels with Holgrave's multiplicity of jobs right down to the selling of cologne water doesn't need stressing. But it is also worth noting that part-time daguerreotypists are not middle-class professionals: they are either working-class or socially marginal figures who can exploit the social fluidity of mid-century America. Hawthorne notes of Hepzibah that "we have stolen upon" her, "too irreverently, at the instant of time when the patrician lady is to be transformed into the plebeian woman." He goes on to note that in "this republican country, amid the fluctuating waves of our social life, somebody is always at the drowning-point" (382–3). That chapter is called "The Little Shop-Window" – and if someone is always at drowning-point, by the same token someone else may have so displayed his or her wares as to be economically buoyed up – Holgrave after all can afford to lodge with a lady. He uses the contemporary cliché to describe the productions by which he makes his living: "pictures made out of sunshine." It may have been a profession that depended upon sunlight – it certainly had some shady types.

Holgrave's, however, is as he sees it an ethical artistic science – and in his declaration of the morality of the daguerreotype he echoes contemporary commentary:

> "There is a wonderful insight in heaven's broad and simple sunshine. While we give it credit only for depicting the merest surface, it actually brings out the secret character with a truth that no painter would ever venture upon, even could he detect it. There is, at least no flattery in my humble line of art." (430)

That proud declaration of the humbleness of his art emphasizes Holgrave's democratic commitment (and his commitment to the democracy of nature). As early as 1841, Emerson claimed the daguerreotype for democracy – and the puritan heritage:

> 'Tis certain that the Daguerreotype is the true Republican style of painting. The Artist stands aside & lets you paint yourself. If you make an ill head, not he but yourself are responsible and so people who go Daguerreotyping have a pretty solemn time. They come home confessing & lamenting their sins. A Daguerreotype Institute is as good as a national Fast.[11]

In 1846, a writer in a popular Boston journal wrote

> Daguerreotypes, properly regarded, are the indices of human character. Lavater judged of men by their physiognomies and in a voluminous treatise has developed the principles by which he was guided. The photograph one

> considers to be the grand climacteric of that science . . . hence posture, attitudes
> and expression of countenance are so many exponential signs of dispositions,
> design, character.

This is to give considerable authority to the photograph – at once the recorder *and* interpreter of appearances. The daguerreotype was accomplishing "a great revolution in the morals" of portrait painting:

> The flattery of the countenance delineators is notorious . . . Everybody who
> pays, must look handsome, intellectual or interesting at least – on canvas. The
> abuses of the brush photographic art is happily designed to correct.[12]

Daguerreotypy is a democratic art not only because everyone can have their image taken cheaply or take an image themselves. It is also democratic, Holgrave suggests, because the daguerreotype does not allow the operator deferentially to flatter the patron – even if he would. It is a point reinforced by Emerson and the journalist: here cash cannot buy an image that lyingly reinforces a self-loving self-image. (This of course was only true for a brief moment in the history of photography. With the coming of the negative the skills of the toucher-up, that cosmetician of the image, were introduced).

Holgrave also suggests not merely that the camera cannot lie but that the daguerreotype has an advantage over the painting in telling truths the painter could not tell even if he would. But Hawthorne (being Hawthorne) problematizes this apparently straightforward comparison between flattering portrait and truthful daguerreotype. Holgrave makes two claims – that the daguerreotype reveals the truth about Judge Pyncheon *and* that the daguerreotype is like the Colonel. There is no real problem with the first – as long as one accepts that physiognomy can act as a reliable guide. Holgrave tells Phoebe

> "Now, the remarkable point is, that the original wears, to the world's eye . . .
> an exceedingly pleasant countenance . . . The sun . . . tells quite another story,
> and will not be coaxed out of it, after half a dozen patient attempts on my part.
> Here we have the man, sly, subtle, hard, imperious, and, withal, cold as ice.
> Look at that eye! Would you like to be at its mercy? At that mouth!" (431)

Here is a truth which the narrative will confirm for any sceptical reader. But while Holgrave may know about the Colonel from Maule family tradition, he can only know about his appearance from the portrait. He cannot make the point that the Judge physically as well as morally resembles the Colonel without allowing that portraiture does have a certain validity as a record of more than physical resemblance – even if history is necessary to enable interpretation. This is also a problem for Hawthorne – as he realizes – and he has to argue that the passage of time may reveal that the painter possesses a kind of "deep" (unconscious?)

knowledge which has little or nothing to do with conscious intention or even recognition. Hepzibah looks at the Colonel's seventeenth century portrait — and Hawthorne moves from her perceptions to his more generalized reflections, endorsing what might otherwise appear merely as her "fancy":

> In one sense, this picture had almost faded into the canvass, and hidden itself behind the duskiness of age; in another, she could not but fancy that it had been growing more prominent, and strikingly expressive, ever since her earliest familiarity with it as a child. For, while the physical outline and substance were darkening away from the beholder's eye, the bold, hard, and, at the same time, indirect character of the man seemed to be brought out in a kind of spiritual relief. Such an effect may occasionally be observed in pictures of antique date. They acquire a look which an artist (if he have anything like the complaisancy of artists now-a-days) would never dream of presenting to a patron as his own characteristic expression, but which, nevertheless, we at once recognize as reflecting the unlovely truth of a human soul. In such cases, the painter's deep conception of his subject's inward traits has wrought itself into the essence of the picture, after the superficial coloring has been rubbed off by time. (402)

It is a somewhat odd position — if one that Hawthorne virtually had to adopt — and its implications for his aesthetics are not entirely reassuring. It is as though the exposure of the portrait to history is a peculiar equivalent of the exposure of the photographic plate to light — only while light writes the true image on to the plate, time rubs out the decorative untruths from the painting (though how long this exposure needs to be and how pleased the painter would be are difficult questions to answer).

It does, however, seem that line and form are more important than color which is not surprising when Hawthorne's fascination with the defamiliarizing effects of moonlight is remembered — and, of course, the daguerreotype is not a colour picture. Perhaps Hawthorne would agree with Holmes in his view that "color is, after all, a very secondary quality as compared with form." He defends this by arguing thus:

> The color of a landscape varies perpetually, with the season, with the hour of the day, with the weather, and as seen by sunlight or moonlight; yet our home stirs us with its old associations, seen in any and every light.[13]

This, clearly, is potentially highly sentimental about home values in the best (or worst) high Victorian fashion — and Holmes had already made a point about the significant personal meaning of a natural detail that an artist would ignore but which that good and faithful servant, the photograph, automatically records:

> The very point which the artist omits, in his effort to produce a general effect, may be exactly the one that individualizes the place most strongly to our

memory. There, for instance is a photographic view of our own birthplace, and with it of a part of our good old neighbor's dwelling. An artist would hardly have noticed a slender, dry, leafless stalk which traces a faint line, as you may see, along the front of our neighbor's house next the corner. That would be nothing to him – but to us it marks the stem of the *honey-suckle vine*, which we remember . . . as long as we remember the stars in heaven.[14]

The seasons are irrelevant, colour is irrelevant. Nature's significance resides in its historical meaning – be that history ever so personal.

The instability of Holgrave's radicalism is connected to his highly ambivalent attitude towards the past – and much of his sense of the past is a product of his sense of his (family) past. He is at once self-consciously and privately a Maule (and thus necessarily defined by the narrative of the Maules and the Pyncheons) *and* someone who desires to be the type of modern man – one who repudiates the signs and claims of the past. It is, surely, no accident that the most extended and explicit statement of his radicalism occurs in chapter XII: "The Daguerreotypist."

I would like to speculate that his daguerreotypy is connected to the form his radicalism takes – using a point made by Oliver Wendell Holmes in the first of his three articles on photography. Holgrave does not only want to destroy the class-based idea of the "family" but also to see the "public edifices," such as "capitols, state-houses, court-houses, city-halls, and churches," (which support and embody the institutions of the conservative state) build out of temporary materials as a reminder of the need for criticism and innovation: "they should crumble to ruin once in twenty years, or thereabouts, as a hint to the people to examine into and reform the institutions which they symbolize" (510). It is too easy to see this (as Bewley does) as "basically . . . the purest and extremest Jeffersonianism." Jefferson as the University of Virginia and Monticello, as well as his profound respect for the Maison quarrée at Nismes, bear witness, was deeply committed to the forms of a past architecture and by implication to the permanent values that such an architecture embodies.[15] And Holgrave's appeal to "the people" is more in the spirit of 1848 than a Jeffersonian 1776. Stronger still than his hostility to state powers – and more understandable *when* we know of his Maule identity – is his desire to destroy the home his family might have had and which has been designed and built by a Maule – the house with the seven gables which "ought to be purified with fire – purified until only its ashes remain!" (510).

This is, of course, principally a matter of moral and political revulsion caused by what those "immortal" objects embody and symbolize but it is, arguably, a revulsion that can more easily be felt and acted on when a "perfect" mode of representing those objects is available. Holmes saw photography revolutionizing man's relationship to the material world:

*Form is henceforth divorced from matter*. In fact, matter as a visible object is of no great use any longer, except as the mould on which the form is shaped. Give us a few negatives of a thing worth seeing, taken from different points of view, and that is all we want of it. *Pull it down or burn it up*, if you please . . . We have got the fruit of creation now, and need not trouble ourselves with the core.

We should be led on too far, if we developed our belief as to the transformation to be wrought by this greatest of human triumphs over earthly conditions, the divorce of form and substance . . . We are . . . wondering over the photograph as a charming novelty; but before another generation has passed away, it will be recognized that a new epoch in the history of human progress dates from the time when He who

    – never but in uncreated light

    Dwelt from eternity

took a pencil of fire from the hand of the "angel standing in the sun," and placed it in the hands of a mortal.[16]

Holmes is deliberately extreme in his account of the revolution to be wrought in the history of human perception but he was not alone. Ruskin, for example, gives (somewhat surprisingly) what is admittedly a less excited and less radical version of much the same idea. In *Practerita*, he reflects on his first encounters with daguerreotypy:

at Venice I found a French artist producing exquisitely small plates . . . which contained, under a lens, the Grand Canal or St. Mark's Place as if a magician had reduced the reality to be carried away into an enchanted land . . . [W]ith two hundred francs I bought the Grand Canal . . . and packed it away.

Interestingly he does not think of himself as purchasing an image of the Grand Canal but, apparently, virtually the thing itself. This is not merely the advantage of hindsight. In 1845, Ruskin wrote to his parents that a daguerreotype "is very nearly the same thing as carrying off the palace itself" and returned to the subject in another letter:

It's a most blessed invention, that's what it is. I've been walking all over St. Mark's place today, and found a lot of things in the Daguerreotype that I never had noticed in the place itself. It is such a happy thing to be able to depend on *every*thing – to be sure not only that the painter is perfectly honest, but that he *can't* make a mistake. I have got the Palazzo Foscari to its last brick, and booked St. Mark's up, down, and round about.[17]

As the context of the letter makes clear (it is addressed from Padua), Ruskin does not mean that he sees St. Mark's Place differently after having looked at the photograph but rather that the reality of the daguerreotype is such that it is "visitable" with advantages for the perceiver over the real thing – and possession of the image means that he has "got" the Palazzo. In the light of these statements – and especially the inverse Prometheanism of Holmes' striking statement – it seems more than possible that Holgrave's repudiation of the materiality of the history that surrounds him and his desire to reduce the old house to ashes are connected to his role as daguerreotypist. The images make the actuality redundant. Phoebe need not see Judge Pyncheon's body. Holgrave breaks the news to her by showing her two photographs – before and after, as it were. *Of course* Holgrave takes a picture of the corpse of the Judge: that is the only "memorial valuable to" him that he thinks he needs.

Yet matter is not so easily repudiated nor death so easily placed. Holgrave notoriously goes into the fall of 1848 as a conservative engaged to an heiress and moving to the country house of the deceased Judge – regretting that Pyncheon had not seen fit to build his house out of more permanent materials. In so far as Holgrave's identity is indicated by his daguerreotypy and in so far as that is connected to his radicalism, this is (at the least) surprising. But Holgrave is also a writer. Among his other gifts and trades, he writes for the genteel female market of magazines and gift books – the very audience that Hawthorne knew so well. And when we see a sample of Holgrave's work, he tells a story of the past – a story of his and Phoebe's ancestors. The story has two related functions. It fills in a portion of the eighteenth century and thus problematically extends our knowledge of the Maule/Pyncheon narrative – problematically because it is never made entirely clear whether this is Holgrave's re-creation of a Maule family story or whether it is his invention of a fantasy past in which a Maule dominates a Pyncheon. Also his refusal to exploit his hypnotized auditress is evidence that he has advanced further up the moral ladder than his ancestor. Whether that was a real ancestor or Holgrave/Maule's fantasy of what a past Maule would have done scarcely matters for this point. Whether fictionalized history or historicized fiction, Holgrave's writing claims an intimate relationship with the past and implies the possibility of evolutionary improvement. Neither his art nor his morals here suggest the possibility or desirability of the revolutionary rupture with the past that he felt he wanted in "The Daguerreotypist" (ch. XII) – a rupture based on his resentment of the authoritarian power of the dead:

> "Shall we never, never get rid of this Past! . . . It lies upon the Present like a giant's dead body! In fact, the case is just as if a young giant were compelled to waste all his strength in carrying about the corpse of the old giant, his grandfather, who died a long while ago, and only needs to be decently buried."
> (509)

At this moment, Holgrave feels that the acceptance of the conservative power of the dead limits and constricts the self: "Whatever we seek to do, of our own free motion, a Dead Man's icy hand obstructs us." Yet it

is the death of the Judge which, strangely, helps to bring Phoebe and
Holgrave together and to generate the possibility of a new beginning
which builds on the past:

> all the circumstances of their situation seemed to draw them together . . . The
> image of awful Death, which filled the house, held them united by his stiffened
> grasp.
>     These influences hastened the development of emotions, that might not
> otherwise have flowered so soon. Possibly, indeed, it had been Holgrave's
> purpose to let them die in their undeveloped germs.                    (614)

"The image of awful Death" cannot be confined within the miniature
image of the daguerreotype that Holgrave showed Phoebe. This leads on
to the strange Edenic moment when Holgrave and Phoebe confess their
love for each other – surely one of the oddest love scenes in fiction:
"They transfigured the earth, and made it Eden again, and themselves
the first two dwellers in it." Hawthorne may claim that the "dead man so
close beside them was forgotten," and may assert that "at such a crisis,
there is no Death; for Immortality is revealed anew" – but he has already
unforgettably suggested that it is the corpse of the Judge which has made
the "germs" of Holgrave's love flower (616). There is no death in the
biblical Eden except the death of innocence – but "The Flower of Eden"
(as ch.xx is entitled), the love of Phoebe and Holgrave, grows from a
death.

   Strange though the scene is, it has, however, been prepared for. The
effect of reading "Alice Pyncheon", that story about a dead Maule and a
dead Pyncheon to a Pyncheon at a particular time of day is to initiate
Holgrave's conservatism. It is the light of the moon that reveals his moral
superiority to his ancestor; it is by the light of the moon that Holgrave
prophesies his incipient abandonment of his radicalism: "Moonlight,
and the sentiment in man's heart responsive to it, are the greatest of
renovators and reformers. And all other reform and renovation, I
suppose, will prove to be no better than moonshine!" This is principally
an internal "reform," a merely subjective feeling – and Holgrave
recognizes this:

> "this garden, where the black mould always clings to my spade, as if I were a
> sexton, delving in a grave-yard! Could I keep the feeling that now possesses
> me, the garden would every day be virgin soil . . . and the house! – it would be
> like a bower in Eden."                                                  (536)

Hawthorne had prepared for Holgrave's outburst with a couple of
paragraphs somewhat ambiguously describing the moonlight. The odd
and unsettling simile about the moon and demagoguery prevents the
passage from being simplistically celebratory (while also anticipating the

"Governor Pyncheon" chapter — another night-time scene and a deliberate *tour de force* of word painting and atmosphere):

> The moon . . . which had long been climbing overhead, and unobtrusively melting its disk into the azure — like an ambitious demagogue, who hides his aspiring purpose by assuming the prevalent hue of popular sentiment — now began to shine out, broad and oval, in its middle pathway . . . With the lapse of every moment, the garden grew more picturesque . . . The commonplace characteristics — which, at noontide, it seemed to have taken a century of sordid life to accumulate — were now transfigured by a charm of romance. A hundred mysterious years were whispering among the leaves.                (535–6)

Oddly, history is banished in one sentence only to reappear "whispering among the leaves" in the next. It is hard to read this without remembering the famous passage in "The Custom-House" where it is the moonlight which stimulates the "imaginative faculty": "Moonlight . . . falling so white upon the carpet, . . . making every object so minutely visible, yet so unlike a morning or a noontide visibility, — is a medium the most suited for a romance writer" (149). If this is the light for an imaginative writer, it is certainly not the light for a daguerreotypist.

Hawthorne seems to be suggesting that the new technology is less liberating (at least so far) than it at first appears, that the narrative power of literature still maintains its authority. What, after all, had daguerreotypy told the characters within the novel? Is it, finally, any more than a shorthand way of making the point that there are parallels between the Colonel and the Judge? It emphasizes identity and repetition — yet this is a perception that Hepzibah has — and she is unaided by the magic of modern technology but rather helped by history's exposure of the truth of the Colonel's portrait. Her "hereditary reverence" makes her reluctant to judge the Colonel as harshly as "a perception of the truth compelled her to do." Such inhibitions, however, do not apply to her verdict on the Judge:

> still she gazed, because the face of the picture enabled her . . . to read more accurately, and to a greater depth, the face which she had just seen in the street.
> "This is the very man!" murmured she to herself. "Let Jaffrey Pyncheon smile as he will, there is that look beneath . . . [N]obody would doubt that it was the old Pyncheon come again! He has proved himself the very man to build up a new house! Perhaps, too, to draw down a new curse!"    (402–3)

Hawthorne goes on to undercut this judgement — suggesting that her perception might be a fantasy resulting from too much solitude — but, of course, the narrative confirms her recognition, product of dangerous isolation though it may be. And the narrative goes on to confirm the truth of another painting in which Hepzibah puts great faith: Malbone's miniature of Clifford in which he is portrayed as an innocent. Both these paintings and the interpretations of them (subsequently to be proved true by the story) significantly precede Clifford's appearance and Holgrave's invitation to Phoebe to interpret his daguerreotype of the Judge. Both historically and in the ordering of this narrative, painting has priority over the daguerreotype – and tells in both cases a true story.

The emblem of modern transportation, that modern magic carpet, the train, delivers Hepzibah and Clifford to the vision of a past that (however lifelessly) relentlessly exists:

> They gazed drearily about them. At a little distance stood a wooden church, black with age, and in a dismal state of ruin and decay, with broken windows, a great rift through the main-body of the office, and a rafter dangling from the top of the square tower. Farther off was a farm-house in the old style, as venerably black as the church . . . It seemed uninhabited. (580)

Clifford's dreams of the bliss of modern nomadic life are confronted and undercut by the sight of these bleak houses of God and man. At this moment all that is left for the "two owls" to do is to pray – even though the "dull, gray weight of the clouds" makes the sky invisible. Again, this is no light for a daguerreotypist but this is not the time for radical doubts and questions: "no juncture this, to question that there was a sky above, and an Almighty Father looking down from it!" (581). After Hepzibah's prayer, all that remains for Hepzibah and Clifford to do is to use their return tickets, and (thanks to the death of the Judge and his son) to drive out of the narrative in a more traditional form of transport – a green barouche. *That* church, *that* farm may no longer possess social relevance owing to the coming of the railroad but that does not mean that agriculture and religion are redundant – as Hepzibah's prayer indicates. And Clifford's transports about the nomadic life ignore the necessary stasis of agriculture: it is indeed hard to conceive of Clifford as a hunter/gatherer. It is difficult to read the conclusion of "The Flight of Two Owls" without considering the social costs which have inevitably been incurred in making those particular symbols of necessary social institutions redundant.

The telegraph is similarly exposed to anti-utopian criticism. It should, Clifford suggests, exemplify a way of communicating which would eliminate misunderstanding and spiritualize communications, enabling love to transcend the obstructions of distance. But Clifford's ideal ideas are undercut by the "old gentleman." He sees it as a useful tool for catching transgressors, helping to cut out any space between crime and punishment. Even his fear that the telegraph will be useful to speculators and politicians in its recognition of economic and political power is more perceptive than Clifford's dreams of love, of personal and private communications. At best, for the old gentleman the telegraph is a tool for social control.

Hawthorne's novel, I would argue, suggests that the dominant mode of representation is still (historical) writing – and the history of the naming of new ways of communication supports the notion that this was, at some level, recognized as the master code. (It is no accident that the tele*graph*, and the pho*tograph*, even the daguerreo*type*, are so named). If that is so, then however much the radical ruptures with the past are (temporarily) desired by Hawthorne's hero of the summer of 1848, they remain subordinated to the syntax and grammar of a particular kind of historical sentence and narrative – one which emphasizes continuity and development (as Holgrave's "Alice Pyncheon" does) rather than discontinuity and new beginnings – while at the same time recognizing the tragedy of the irredeemable losses of the past, as, for example, in the fact that Clifford's life-story cannot have a fully happy ending. The three modern technologies that principally appear in the novel (the railroad, the telegraph, and the daguerreotype) all attempt to annihilate distance rather than time. The daguerreotype is perhaps less obviously concerned with the problems of distance – but we need to think here of Holmes' point (which is that of many others) that the daguerreotype could be felt to make travel for at least some purposes more or less redundant: Jules Janin, for example, wrote that the daguerreotype "is not a picture . . . You will write to Rome: send me by post the dome of St. Peter's; and the dome of St. Peter's will come to you by return of mail."[18] But even such claims do not escape from Hawthorne's implied criticism that the failure of modern technology is that it cannot abolish or redeem history – however much it may attempt to destroy the difficulties of distance.

Temporality remains problematic. Oliver Wendell Holmes was struck by a paradox suggested by close examination of a photograph:

> And what a metaphysical puzzle have we here in this simple-looking paradox! Is motion but a succession of rests? All is still in this picture of universal movement. Take ten thousand instantaneous photographers of the great thoroughfare in a day; every one of them will be as still as the *tableau* in the "Enchanted Beauty." Yet the hurried day's life of Broadway will have been made up of just such stillnesses. Motion is as rigid as marble, if you take only a wink's worth at a time.[19]

Clive Bush points out that Holmes describes the photograph as a mirror with a memory, "a kind of philosophical rebuff to religious and metaphysical use of the mirror as an image of transient vision." (Hawthorne's "Monsieur du Miroir" would be relevant here.) Bush goes on to argue that the

> old Parmenides and Zeno paradox that, if movement is a succession of still moments, how do we tell one moment from another, is here given a new twist. The photograph seems to lend authority to a view of time as a succession of still moments. For Holmes this moment is more real than the flux and

change of human intercourse. The simile "rigid as marble" is an exact one, for in this view, the photograph is a monument of time, an icon of memory as a guide to human consciousness.[20]

The quotation here from Holmes follows directly on from the passage about the sky as a concave recording – and I am unconvinced that Bush's is an entirely accurate gloss. Even if he is right about Parmenides and Zeno, if he is also correct about the photograph as an icon of memory, then past and present, then and now, a firm idea of sequence have all necessarily entered Holmes' theory.

What Holmes has realized is that change and movement (even history) inevitably lie behind the photograph – as he confesses he does in his discussion of the use of photographs in his lectures on the physiology of walking. The daguerreotype's recording of movement as a blur may – oddly – be truer to experience. The paradox that he enjoys playing with takes place within a larger apparent paradox in cultural history as Barthes points out:

> A paradox: the same century invented History and Photography. But History is a memory fabricated according to positive formulas, a pure intellectual discourse which abolishes mythic Time . . . [T]he age of the Photograph is also the age of revolutions, contestations, assassinations, explosions, in short, of impatiences, of everything that denies ripening.[21]

Is not this evocation of the qualities of the "age of the Photograph" very precisely applicable to Holgrave in his phase as radical and daguerreotypist, making speeches "full of wild and disorganizing matter", with his "impatiences", his hatred of "ripening," his mistrust of the idea of a slow-growing maturity? (424). Doesn't Hawthorne abolish mythic versions of the past – in, for example, the insistence on a naturalistic, physiological explanation for the deaths of the Colonel and the Judge?

Holgrave may be captured by love and a conservative view of history so that his vision of reform becomes limited to interior decoration of the social fabric rather than a restructuring of the whole social edifice. He himself confesses (with an understandable "half-melancholy laugh") that he has become a "conservative":

> "I wonder that the late Judge – being so opulent, and with a reasonable prospect of transmitting his wealth to descendants of his own – should not have felt the propriety of embodying so excellent a piece of domestic architecture in stone, rather than in wood. Then, every generation of the family might have altered the interior, to suit its own taste and convenience; while the exterior, through the lapse of years, might have been adding venerableness to its original beauty, and thus giving that impression of permanence, which I consider essential to the happiness of any one moment." (621)

But this does not mean that Hawthorne's historical narrative is itself conservative: rather it places Holgrave by interrogating the convention of the "happy ending." That ending is only happy if the clichés of one kind of narrative are uncritically accepted. A marriage which seems to symbolize a reconciliation of a struggle between two classes that has lasted for over 150 years accompanied by a shower of gold certainly looks as though it should be a happy ending – but it can only be read as such if the moral of the preface is ignored, and if the working-men's doubts are suppressed even though they come so close to the ending (to say nothing of the problem of the Judge's son).

Hawthorne tells us in the preface that he would

> feel it a singular gratification, if this Romance might effectually convince mankind (or, indeed, any one man) of the folly of tumbling down an avalanche of ill-gotten gold, or real estate, on the heads of an unfortunate posterity, thereby to maim and crush them, until the accumulated mass shall be scattered abroad in its original atoms.          (352)

It is hard not to recall this entirely unambiguous authorial voice when we read in "The Daguerreotypist" of Holgrave's condemnation of the desire to "plant a family" – a desire necessarily accompanied by the fertilizing qualities of gold. Hepzibah, Clifford and Phoebe (plus Holgrave by proxy) all inherit gold and real estate – and there is a clear implication that this wealth has been ill-gotten. Hawthorne's ambition to convince "mankind" has its own radical – even revolutionary – egalitarian implications. His gratuitous gift of a son to the Judge and his equally gratuitous killing of that shadowy figure so that the surviving Pyncheons can inherit surely should make even the reader who skipped the preface ask questions about the ending. No doubt Judge Pyncheon did not intend to leave his money and estate to Hepzibah, Clifford and Phoebe – but, even so, it is to misread to argue that Death accidentally enforces a kind of justice. Rather it plays into the hands of Holgrave-as-radical as he appears in "The Daguerreotypist": "a Dead Man, if he happens to have made a will, disposes of wealth no longer his own; or, if he die intestate, it is distributed in accordance with the notions of men much longer dead than he" (509).

Such questions should be reinforced by the last piece of dialogue in the novel – spoken by "laboring men", recognized as such (it is worth remembering) because of their "rough" voices as they see the barouche drive off:

> "Well, Dixey, . . . what do you think of this? My wife kept a cent-shop, three months, and lost five dollars on her outlay. Old Maid Pyncheon has been in trade just about as long, and rides off in her carriage with a couple of hundred thousand – reckoning her share, and Clifford's and Phoebe's – and some say

twice as much! If you choose to call it luck, it is all very well; but if we are to take it as the will of Providence, why, I can't exactly fathom it!"

"Pretty good business!" quoth the sagacious Dixey. "Pretty good business!!'

(393, 626)

If the conclusion is called "luck" – either part of the loaded roulette wheel of the inheriting classes or sheer chance – then it may be "all very well" but if it is to be considered as embodying "the will of Providence" with whatever implications of justice, significant meaning, or even the aesthetic shaping of a plot might accompany such a portentous phrase then the anonymous working-man is surely right to confess that he is mystified, that he cannot "fathom it." Nor is the reader in a much better situation: Maule's well throws up a series of "kaleidoscopic pictures, in which a gifted eye *might* (my emphasis) have seen foreshadowed" the futures of Hepzibah, Clifford, Phoebe and Holgrave. But since the Pyncheon elm whispered "unintelligible prophecies," the reader is deliberately discouraged from imagining futures for the characters (626).

That speech of Dixey's friend is one of Hawthorne's rare jokes about the novelist as God and the difficulty his creations have in understanding his plan (if plan there be) and the problem the author/Creator has in bringing his narrative to a meaningful conclusion. As he was writing the story, he noted that it darkened damnably towards the close and said that he wanted to pour some sunlight over the conclusion. Sunlight (or treacle) there may be if one ignores the logic of the narrative and clings to the convention of the "happy ending" without considering how it was arrived at and the price that has been paid not only by Holgrave but also by poor Clifford:

> It is a truth . . . that no great mistake, whether acted or endured, in our mortal
> sphere, is ever really set right. Time, the continual vicissitude of circumstances,
> and the invariable inopportunity of death, render it impossible.          (621)

A reader is left having to examine the choice between the two options offered by the working-man: luck – or a creator's inscrutable purposes? The idea if not the reality of social tension (even class-conflict) remains residually but unavoidably present – once one has heard and listened to the working-men's voices. A new script, a new theatre for human endeavour are needed, but as *The Blithedale Romance* was shortly to show, that script, that theatre (however much desired, and however desirable) are hard to find and to sustain. Coverdale, that frustrated lyric poet, has to take to narrative in an attempt to define and explain the problems that face the Utopians who aim to rewrite history, to add (in Coverdale's words) "a leaf of some mysterious volume, interpolated into . . . current history" (759).

# 6

## The Blithedale Romance – *translation and transformation: mime and mimesis*

> . . . I could not help interpreting.
>
> (Miles Coverdale, *The Blithedale Romance*, 844)

*The Blithedale Romance* may usefully be approached by looking at the ways it foregrounds the question of the difficulties of description and the related problems of interpretation – by beginning from the juxtaposition of two names (Coverdale and Fauntleroy) and a recognition of what those names so contrastingly and problematically signify: translation and forgery. Among the dictionary definitions given for "to translate" are: to interpret, to explain, to change, to transform. Among those for "to forge" are: to pretend something to have happened, to make something in fraudulent imitation of something else, to make or devise something spurious. The relevance of these definitions for any narrative dealing with the relationships between "reality," descriptive explanations and the authority to be given to such explanations is clear though complex: the particular significance for *The Blithedale Romance* is signalled by Hawthorne naming his narrator after a translator and including a character named after a famous forger. The historical Miles Coverdale was a sixteenth-century translator of the Bible. The historical Fauntleroy (the name given old Moodie by Coverdale in ch. 22) was the "prototypal forger for his contemporaries."[1] Hawthorne does not deploy the terms in a crudely literal way. For example, the metaphor of translator is never made directly available to Coverdale even though the reader is constantly aware that Coverdale has to interpret the unstable and incomplete text before him. It is rather that the concepts provide a way of speculating about the problems that *The Blithedale Romance* is so concerned with. In the juxtaposition of the two names, and in the connections and oppositions of meanings that they symbolize, narrative, authority, authenticity, interpretation, mimesis, politics and tragedy can

118

be seen to come together in a brilliantly structured dialectical fiction – a fiction which is sceptical of its own authority and of the terms on which such authority is based.

The most successful sceptical examination of the authority of the author and his narrative is *The Blithedale Romance*. Here the novelist as God is *Deus Absconditus* – or rather he bows out after Hawthorne's ambiguous and ambivalent preface. Authority to tell the tale is transferred to Coverdale (a minor poet whose poems we never see) who, despite repeated invitations to turn the whole affair into a ballad, reconstructs as best he can a narrative – an interpretation. His attempts at historiography, at authoritative narrative, are inevitably incomplete.[2] Not only does he fail to overhear important conversations, not only does Zenobia deny him the right to be her witness, but Hawthorne makes him an accidental but crucial half an hour late for the big scene between Hollingsworth, Zenobia and Priscilla that takes place at the Apostle's Rock.[3] Coverdale is forced to recover and re-create his narrative without knowing what the origins, the genesis of the actions he observes really are. What, for example, is Westervelt's real relation to Zenobia? He never knows. And he confesses that Fauntleroy's story is shaped by him, that (as it were) the lacunae in the text are filled in by him. Coverdale sees himself as at once "small poet" *and* "grave biographer" as he reconstructs the story of "Fauntleroy":

> having once got the clue, my subsequent researches acquainted me with the main facts of the following narrative; although in writing it out, my pen has perhaps allowed itself a trifle of romantic and legendary license.     (790)

The very name is, of course, Coverdale's fictive clue: "Five-and-twenty years ago . . . there dwelt . . . a man whom we shall *call* Fauntleroy" (791, my emphasis). Hawthorne suggests the narrative is inevitable – yet necessarily a fiction.

To call the narrator of the fiction after a translator of the Bible is a brilliant stroke, raising as it does so directly the problems of authority and writing. The Bible is *the* authoritative text for Western civilization – yet just because of its authority the connections and disjunctions between translation and interpretation are foregrounded. Walter Benjamin may announce in "The Task of the Translator" that the interlinear version of the Scriptures is the prototype or ideal of all translation, but this is in many ways to beg the question. For example, it gives (perhaps justifiably but the point is not argued) primacy to writing over speech. And what parts of the Scriptures are authoritative and why? I think it is more than pedantry to note both that Coverdale was the first Englishman to include the Apocryphal books in his translation – and that his is not the Authorized Version. Can a translation of a sacred (or any other) text have the authority of the original? How can one trust the translator? And if these questions are asked, they have to followed by another: how authentic, how original is the original text?

R.R. Male and Joan Magretta are the two critics who have most usefully drawn attention to the importance of Coverdale's name.[4] Yet valuable though their comments are, they are seriously inadequate. Male writes that the fictional Coverdale ought to be a translator, "but one of the book's recurrent ironies is that during the empty religious experience" of Blithedale "no translation – moral or artistic – occurs." This is to ignore the large number of more-or-less successful kinds of art that inhabit the book and the fact that Coverdale's text exists – and that it, metaphorically, is a type of translation (as are the various kinds of art). Male's refusal to consider most of the implications of the meanings of the word presumably is the result of his desire to interpret Hawthorne as a religious artist. His real interest is in translation as a metaphor for religious and moral conversion. Joan Magretta sees the inadequacies of Male's approach, but because of her willingness to see Zenobia's legend and the story of Fauntleroy as "parables" and because of her insistence that Fauntleroy's crime is "never specified" – is, indeed, a rather vague "primal transgression" (when it is explicitly stated in the book that the crime is both a product of society and an offence against it) – she too fails to see anything like the full significance of the translation metaphor.

That metaphor operates as an illuminating analogy for the concern with the shifting relationships between various "arts" and "reality" that characterize so much of *The Blithedale Romance* because of *historical* reasons: because two theories of art had been (and still were) available as dominant similes for translation. T.R. Steiner, in his excellently documented study of translation theory, points to the two dominant traditions historically available to the mid-nineteenth-century writer. The first is the neo-classical image of the translator as painter – where painting is defined primarily though not simplistically as a mimetic art. The second, related to the beginnings of Romanticism, which gradually though not entirely superseded the first, was that of the translator as poet. The contrast between mimesis and creative art, even as analogies for translation, is less absolute than it may at first appear and not only because it is probably more accurate to speak of mimetic theories rather than mimetic theory, but also because, as Steiner shows, the two ideas, however notionally separate, often overlap in practice and even in theory.[5]

The difficult and problematic connections between mimesis and creativity as models for translation (and theories of art) still remain, though later Romantic theory attempted to solve or transcend the problems. Well before *The Blithedale Romance* was written, translation had, for some, become a metaphor for all communication in ways relevant to the concerns of that fiction. As Susan Basnet-McGuire points out, "the hermeneutic approach of the great English and German Romantic translators connects with changing concepts of the role of the individual in the social context." And in further extending her historical analysis of the Romantic debate about translation she reports A.W. Schlegel's assertion that "all acts of speaking and writing are acts of translation because the nature of communication is to decode and interpret messages received." She also suggests that Friedrich Schlegel "conceived of translation as a category of thought rather than as an activity connected only with language and literature."[6]

American Romanticism (at least as represented by Emerson in his essay "Books") had seen little worrying in translation:

> The respectable and sometimes excellent translations of Bohn's Library have done for literature what railroads have done for internal intercourse. I do not hesitate to read . . . all good books in translations. What is really best in any book is translatable – any real insight or broad human sentiment. Nay, I observe that in our Bible, and other books of lofty moral tone, it seems inevitable to render the rhythm and music of the original into phrases of equal melody. The Italians have a fling at translators – *i traditori tradittori*; but I thank them. I rarely read any Latin, Greek, German, Italian, sometimes not a French book, in the original, which I can procure in a good version.[7]

Perhaps the most interesting thing about this comment is Emerson's emphasis on the metaphor of mechanical communication to which he returns a page later when discussing Gibbon: "his book is one of the conveniences of civilization, like a new railroad from ocean to ocean." This is a statement which would have irritated Gibbon with his insistence that some of his footnotes were in the decent obscurity of a learned language. It should have given an Emerson some pause – for anyone who stresses the importance of metaphor for language as he does should surely at least have hesitated when he discussed translation. How could he know, for example, that what he reads is a "good version"? And even if one plays down the cultural rankings implied by Emerson's references to languages ancient and modern, it is still clear that the transcendentalist democrat is a linguistic and cultural snob.

It is worth recalling the number of art forms either embodied, described or referred to in *The Blithedale Romance*. Among them are (romantic) poetry, drama, tragedy, story-telling, masque and painting. The ways in which they are presented make a not inadequate anthology of the mirror and the lamp theories of art. But when the crime of forgery is also incorporated it can be seen that all these re-presentations of reality are held together not so much by an explicitly aesthetic theory but rather by the metaphor of the translator or interpreter figure. In other words, ethics as well as aesthetics are involved. Susan Basnett-McGuire's comments obviously can be related to Coverdale's role – as well as to many of the social and political implications of the text.[8] Translation above all other literary modes is dependent on the writer's idea of his audience, whether it be the appreciative sharer of the parent-language or the grateful single-language recipient. The metaphor of translator, of course, is available only to the reader not to the characters, but even without the historical clue the first-person mode of narration fore-grounds the question of how the story is told – and what is represented.

An exemplary instance of Hawthorne's sophistication about the complexities of mimetic theory and practice comes in chapter 21, where Coverdale is waiting in a bar for Moodie (who, when he appears, is described as "very faintly shadowed on the canvas of reality"). In it, Coverdale describes the paintings in the saloon. At first reading the passage may seem to be merely padding, or all the paintings may appear to be on the same uninteresting, merely decorative, aesthetic level. The passage is usually ignored; or if it is mentioned, is used as an example of how easily and how often Hawthorne used his notebooks. The notebook reference *is* simply descriptive. But when he reworks this memory in his fiction, representation is seen as difficult to interpret and in that difficulty interesting:

> The saloon was fitted up with a good deal of taste. There were pictures on the walls, and among them an oil-painting of a beef-steak, with such an admirable show of juicy tenderness, that the beholder sighed to think it merely visionary, and incapable of being put upon a gridiron. Another work of high art was the lifelike representation of a noble sirloin; another, the hind-quarters of a deer, retaining the hoofs and tawny fur; another, the head and shoulders of a salmon; and, still more exquisitely finished, a brace of canvass-back ducks, in which the mottled feathers were depicted with the accuracy of a daguerreotype. Some very hungry painter, I suppose, had wrought these subjects of still life, heightening his imagination with his appetite, and earning, it is to be hoped, the privilege of a daily dinner off whichever of his pictorial viands he liked best. Then there was a fine old cheese, in which you could almost discern the mites; and some sardines on a small plate, very richly done, and looking as if oozy with the oil in which they had been smothered. All these things were so perfectly imitated, that you seemed to have the genuine article before you, and yet with an indescribable, ideal charm; it took away the grossness from what was fleshiest and fattest, and thus helped the life of man, even in its earthliest relations, to appear rich and noble, as well as warm, cheerful, and substantial. There were pictures, too, of gallant revellers, those of the old time, Flemish, apparently, with doublets and slashed sleeves, drinking their wine out of fantastic long-stemmed glasses; quaffing joyously, quaffing forever, with inaudible laughter and song; while the champagne bubbled immortally

against their moustaches, or the purple tide of Burgundy ran inexhaustibly down their throats.

But, in an obscure corner of the saloon, there was a little picture – excellently done, moreover – of a ragged, bloated, New England toper, stretched out on a bench, in the heavy, apoplectic sleep of drunkenness. The death-in-life was too well portrayed. Your only comfort lay in the forced reflection, that, real as he looked, the poor caitiff was but imaginary, a bit of painted canvass, whom no delirium tremens, nor so much as a retributive headache, awaited, on the morrow.                                                                  (785–6)

The paintings do not all have identical relationships to the real. They fall into three classes: the first is the group of paintings of objects which are meant to be eaten, the second is the historical paintings and the third is the portrait of the drunk. The first group might seem to be simplistically mimetic – after all do not these still-lifes have "the accuracy of a daguerreotype"? But those apparently photographic pictures are, it is suggested, the product of economic need and physical desire. Yet even though they may have been produced by a "very hungry" painter whose imagination is intensified by his need, that first set of paintings manages to celebrate the life of man in a way which is at once spiritual and secular.

The historical paintings also emphasize stasis (and offer images of inexhaustible abundance) – forcibly reminding us that all paintings are, in an important sense, still lives however much and in whichever ways they may contain or refer to narrative. We are not told whether these pictures are the products of their time or of historical imagination and recreation, but either way they are to be seen as further from reality than the (technical) "still-lives."

But, of course, all this description is dependent on the interpreter. It has to be the act of the interpreting imagination which defines the painter of some dead ducks as hungry, which leaves it open whether there was a model for the painter or whether the works were produced by a combination of memory and hope. This point is brought home forcibly in the description of the drunk. This picture certainly lacks "ideal charm": it is "too well portrayed" to give its audience comfort not only because of the subject but because of the treatment. It is "too well portrayed" – too real. Here the stasis inevitable in a painting becomes a comfort even though it has to be the result of "forced reflection." The comfort comes not only from the thought that this is a moment snatched from time, from narrative, but from the fact that the painting is only a painting, an imaginary fiction. It may – it does – refer to a known social reality, but it only refers.

The painters translate the objects of their paintings on to canvas, and Coverdale interprets their translations. Hawthorne deploys and extends his translator metaphor with sophistication in this passage: first there are the varying relationships between the objects to be imitated (some real, some probably invented); second, the modes of imitation and/or interpretation employed by the artists and the question of their motives for so doing; and third, the audience (initially Coverdale) decoding the art-objects before him. The interpretation of the "gallant revellers," say, would be different if it was given by a teetotaller. There is an irony in having the still-life paintings in a saloon: the aesthetic bliss they generate is analogous to the effect of strong drink on the poor who frequent the place, "whose only glimpse of a better state is through the muddied medium" of their liquor, whose (Utopian?) "true purpose" for drinking is to gain a brief "brisk, cheerful sense of things present and to come." Indeed, perhaps there is a further analogy between this state and the Blithedale enterprise.

It should not be surprising that Coverdale's most extended passage on the problems of mimesis precedes his history of the fate of a forger. This passage and its relationship to the whole of the chapter in which it appears makes it clear not only that there is a crucial social dimension to interpretation (one necessarily related to narrative) but also that connections should be made between the questions involved in the imitation of reality and politico-moral issues. Drinkers, teetotallers and vegetarians would all have to agree that these pictures are paintings – "works of art." The "perfect" imitation of reality might, at least in theory, be indistinguishable from an item in the real world (except for an ardent Platonist or neo-Platonist). Forgery is a kind of bastard realism, which claims to be "the real thing" – unlike mimetic art, which can claim to illuminate reality by being *like* reality whether by analogy or simile or whatever. Forgery shows how dangerous mimesis can be for and in a particular kind of society when mimesis is not explicitly or implicitly announced (and recognized as fictive). In Boswell's words, discussing the notorious forgery of the Reverend Dr. William Dodd (and he is not referring to that famous forger's death sentence), it is "the most dangerous crime in a commercial country," while Coverdale writes "it is just the sort of crime growing out of its artificial state, which society neither could nor ought to pardon. More safely might it pardon murder" (791).[9] Any force this point may have of course hangs by one thread: that the fictional Fauntleroy, like his historical namesake, is a forger. I have already given some of my reasons for arguing this in my second footnote. But it is not illegitimate when discussing a text which so strongly demands that the reader be an interpreter to ask what other crime could be more grievous for an "artificial" society – one in which identity can be defined through "show" backed up by the shining deceptive light that gold gives. Mere theft would not be so serious, since it in so many ways confirms the institution of property: if property is theft, then theft reinforces the institution of property. It is only forgery that fits the bill, which is understandable when Fauntleroy's fragile identity is considered: "superficial . . . an optical delusion, created by the sunshine of prosperity" (792).

Blithedale claims to be natural – however artificial that claim may turn out to be. The references to commercial society and artificial states are forcible reminders of the ambiguous economic position of the Blithedale community and the connections between the aims of that community and its views about personal identity. It is a Utopian community, which whatever we are *not* told about its aims and organization (a considerable amount) has at least this aim in view – to abolish and transcend the division of labour – and one way of maintaining itself: by acting as *market*-garden to the city of Boston, by producing crops for *cash*. The question of the division of labour was only too clearly part of the spirit of the age (as anything discussed by such disparate figures as Marx, Thoreau, Fourier and Hawthorne had to be). Here fact and fiction overlap, for these points stand whether it is Brook Farm or Blithedale that is being discussed. Richard Francis, writing about the ideology of Brook Farm but drawing heavily on Hawthorne's fictional accounts, makes the point that there are "interesting connections between the assumptions underlying masquerade" and those related to the intention to transcend the division of labour:

> From the very beginning, the Farmers were conscious that the individual's identity, or rather his sense of it, was unduly restricted by the rigidity of the social role that was forced on him in "civilization." . . . This desire to run the gamut of occupations and identities, to be everything from Diana to a schoolmarm, from a woodsman to an intellectual, is the Brook Farmers' most noticeable characteristic.[10]

The suggestion that part of the Utopian adventure involved a break between the conventional distinctions between work and play allows the customary accusation that the Brook Farmers/Blithedalers were having, in Emerson's words, a perpetual picnic, were playing at revolution: *homo ludens* indeed. If this point is accepted, it raises, in rather different terms from those usually deployed, the question of what is the real self. To "be" (say, to mime) Diana in a masque, may seem no more or less real or revealing than to "be" a farmer or a milkmaid. This celebration of the fluidity of identity in terms of a defence of masks and mime is, however, criticized by the narrative of *The Blithedale Romance*. While revolutionary changes in self and society may well be desirable, they are presented as impossible because (among other reasons) of the irreconcilable contrast between the fluidity of personality and the evasive fixity of the mask. To identify by occupation, because of the historical consequences of the development of the division of labour, may be seriously inadequate. But the Blithedalers' happy hope that definitions of identity can reside elsewhere ignores both the powerful complexities of historical development and Marx's (among others) perception that the division of labour may have its genesis in biological difference.

"A Village-Hall" (ch. 23) does not so much advance the story; rather it operates as a critical parody (often indirect) of the Blithedalers' attempt, generated as it is by the same historical forces that produce Blithedale. There is "the ventriloquist with all his mysterious tongues," the thaumaturgist with his "miraculous transformations" and the "museum of wax figures" which exhibit "the catholicism of earthly renown . . . mixing up . . . every sort of person" except authors (802–3). There are stories of the man in blue spectacles:

> Human character was but soft wax in his hands; and guilt, or virtue, only the
> forms into which he should see fit to mould it . . . If these things were to be
> believed . . . the idea of man's eternal responsibility was made ridiculous. (804)

Westervelt's act with the Veiled Lady (and he is *all* mask) extends that parody; he claims that she has through his power transcended history, and he speaks of "a new era that was dawning upon the world – an era that would link soul to soul" with "a delusive show of spirituality . . . imbued . . . with a cold and dead materialism" (806). But Zenobia and Hollingsworth really provide the tragic examples of why the Blithedalers' dreams will not work. Hollingsworth is, in Zenobia's words, "a better masquerader than the witches and gypsies yonder: for your disguise is a self-deception." She speaks as one "awake, disenchanted" and "disenthralled" (822). Zenobia's attempt to transcend the limitations imposed by social definitions is defeated by her past and by her in the final resort too conservative view of her femininity – while both Zenobia and Hollingsworth are also the prisoners of the definitions imposed by economic need and desire.

In Hawthorne's work people cannot easily evade their histories. Nor can they facilely escape from the related issues of economic reality even at Blithedale, for economics has its history in this fiction. (How much even in plot terms, to take a minor example, depends upon Fauntleroy's brother dying intestate.) I suggested earlier that there is a tragically destructive contradiction between Blithedale's economic means and ends. The characters make much of the contrast between innocent country and sinister city, but that contrast is more apparent than real. The Blithedalers – as all market-gardeners must – depend on and profit from the city they claim to have repudiated. The easy movement between Blithedale and the city that Zenobia and Coverdale enjoy is not so much a criticism of those characters as it is an emblem of the complicity between country and city that the Blithedalers all tacitly or unconsciously exploit.

Yet this relationship to the city, ironically, contains the seeds of more than Blithedale's fatal contradictions: it might have been a way of transcending or at least of revising the middle-class sexist division of labour. As Silas Foster says, "We shall never make any hand at market-gardening unless the women-folk will undertake to do all the weeding" (649). He thus effectively repudiates Zenobia's response to a question from an anonymous member of this amateur dramatic society: "Have we our various parts assigned?" Zenobia, the self-appointed spokesperson of the women's cause, answers surprisingly conventionally: "We women . . . will take the domestic and indoor part of the business as a matter of course" (645).

However, Blithedale has to fail: given its relationships to the larger economic structure, it has, quite literally, to deliver the goods. But at once farcically and tragically, the price of that delivery is the good life at which they aim. That aim becomes even more unstable as there is a traitor within the gates. Hollingsworth's whole purpose is in no way a repudiation of society as it is – however he may define that purpose. It is not enough to confine criticism of Hollingsworth to his unscrupulous methods. His aims are even more seriously antagonistic to Blithedale's best hopes. His project involves no real criticism of the existing social organization. He merely aims to re-form the criminal and never considers analysing what constitutes a crime. In that failure he is at least as conservative as the bankers of Boston (and could be remarkably serviceable to them and the institutions they support).

It is tempting to describe the tragedy of *The Blithedale Romance* as when the miming had to stop, but to consider tensions in mimetic theories and practices is to provide a way of examining what defines and generates that tragedy. There may well be, as Frederic Jameson has argued, an implicit contract between describing the world as it is and an (unconscious?) desire to keep it that way.[11] On the other hand, critical realism (as defined by Lukacs, for example) certainly has radical implications. *The Blithedale Romance* may be called a romance by Hawthorne, but this does not mean that reality and realism can be ignored. When Coverdale comments on the ways in which the Blithedale project is related to reality (and thus to history) he significantly uses the image of the text:

> True; if you look at it one way, it had been only a summer in the country. But, considered in a profounder relation, it was part of another age, a different state of society, a segment of an existence peculiar in its aims and methods, a leaf of some mysterious volume, interpolated into the current history which Time was writing off. (759)

That tipped-in page of utopianism disrupts the narrative of main-stream history. It is a fiction. On one level Blithedale is obviously real enough, but on another its utopianism is radically a-historical. That a-historicism allows the potential for tragedy while at the same time it may liberate human energies and imagination:

> I was beginning to lose the sense of what kind of a world it was, among innumerable schemes of what it might or ought to be. It was possible, situated as we were, not to imbibe the idea that everything in nature and human existence was fluid, or fast becoming so; that the crust of the Earth, in many places, was broken, and its whole surface portentously upheaving; and it was a day of crisis, and that we ourselves were in the critical vortex.        (755)

Coverdale's return to the city of course does not enable him to evade the critical vortex and its tragic implications. Indeed, the city itself contains a more modest, but perhaps at least as important a tragedy as repetition and duplication replaces the self-conscious miming of the Blithedalers:

> I could only conceive of the inhabitants as cut out on one identical pattern, like little wooden toy-people of German manufacture . . . After the distinctness of separate characters, to which I had recently become accustomed, it perplexed and annoyed me not to be able to resolve this combination of human interests into well-defined elements. It seemed hardly worth while for more than one of those families to be in existence.        (763)

The relations to liberal ideas of personality are clear enough.

A.W. Schlegel, whose emphasis on the crucial significance of translation as a metaphor for communication has already been noted, makes a point in his discussion of Greek tragedy which casts a light on Coverdale's role in this tragedy (and the reasons for his self-criticism):

> publicity . . . according to the republican notion of the Greeks, was essential to all grave and important transactions. This was signified by the presence of the chorus, whose presence during many secret transactions has been judged of according to rules of propriety inapplicable to the country, and so most undeservedly censured . . . In a word, the chorus is the ideal spectator.[12]

Behind this statement lies a repudiation of simplistic liberalism and the related issue of "realism." Coverdale is, whether despite of or because of his own doubts about his role, the best advocate for Blithedale, its best voice, its best critic and analyst. He is not only the voice of an agonized modern self-consciousness trapped in a liberal dilemma, nor is he merely the anatomist – though there may be an element of guilty though suffering complicity in the part Coverdale feels he plays in the tragedy:

> I began to long for a catastrophe . . . Let it all come! As for me, I would look on, as it seemed my part to do, understandingly, if my intellect could fathom the meaning and the moral, and, at all events, reverently and sadly. The curtain fallen, I would pass onward with my poor individual life, which was now

attenuated of much of its proper substance, and diffused among many alien interests.                                                                          (769–70)

Even here the interest lies not so much in Coverdale's sense of his guilt as in the way in which he expresses his desire for an ending to the narrative (remembering the fact that "catastrophe" is a word that Coverdale frequently uses and the definition that Johnson's dictionary gives the word: "the change or revolution which produces the conclusion or final event of a dramatic piece"). Coverdale is, centrally, the interpreter, the chorus:

> My own part, in these transactions . . . resembled that of the Chorus in a classic play, which seems to be set aloof from the possibility of personal concernment, and bestows the whole measure of its hope or fear, its exultation or sorrow, on the fortunes of others, between whom and itself this sympathy is the only bond. Destiny it may be – the most skilful of stage-managers – seldom chooses to arrange its scenes, and carry forward its drama, without securing the presence of at least one calm observer. It is his office to give applause, when due, and sometimes an inevitable tear, to detect the final fitness of incident to character, and distil, in his long-brooding thought, the whole morality of the performance.                                                                          (716–17)

In recognition of his role and his stress on sympathy (a term used over and over again in the text, especially towards the end) Coverdale points to the modern tragic element in the book. That modernity lies not only in the "mixed" form, but also in that so much of the tragedy is generated by a liberal insistence on privacy, by a refusal publicly to acknowledge the past, and by the denial of the need for a witness.

One element in the mixture is farce – Coverdale's modern ironic perception which actually intensifies the tragedy. His comments on Zenobia's death provide an example of this perception – that death which is a triumph for reality, just as her funeral is a victory for tradition:

> A reflection occurs to me, that will show ludicrously, I doubt not, on my page, but must come in, for its sterling truth. Being the woman she was, could Zenobia have foreseen all these ugly circumstances of death . . . she would no more have committed the dreadful act, than have exhibited herself to a public assembly in a badly-fitting garment! Zenobia, I have often thought, was not quite simple in her death. She had seen pictures, I suppose, of drowned persons, in lithe and graceful attitudes . . . But in Zenobia's case, there was some tint of the Arcadian affectation that had been visible enough in all our lives, for a few months past.
>
>    This, however, to my conception, takes nothing from the tragedy. For, has not the world come to an awfully sophisticated pass, when, after a certain degree of acquaintance with it, we cannot even put ourselves to death in whole-hearted simplicity?                                                                          (838)

Whether Zenobia is meant to be seen as entirely unaware of at least some of the ironies in her position is an open question. When Coverdale is agonizing over her predicament in chapter 26, she, notoriously, invites him to turn the whole affair into a ballad, to "turn his sympathy to good account" as she comments on her own experience: "'It is genuine tragedy, is it not?' rejoined Zenobia, with a sharp, light laugh" (827). That laugh coupled with her invitation to convert her experience into a work of art, suggests some ironic perception, even though Coverdale refuses that ironic invitation – refuses the harmony implied by a ballad's metrical form – and instead produces a different kind of interpretation in his translation of the Blithedale experience, a product of his "long-brooding thought" which attempts to discover coherence and conclusions by connecting "the final fitness of incident to character."

Emerson, looking back on life and letters in New England, described Brook Farm as "a French Revolution in small." That sense that history may be treated parodically and be repeated helps place *The Blithedale Romance*, and this point becomes even clearer when a much more famous text than Emerson's is set beside Coverdale's account. It is a nice coincidence that *The Eighteenth Brumaire of Louis Bonaparte* was published in the same year as *The Blithedale Romance*, for its famous opening eerily parallels many of the central concerns of that fiction – in the ways, for example, in which tragedy and farce are connected, in the references to the uses of historical/mythical mime, and in the appearance of text and translation as important metaphors:

> Hegel remarks somewhere that all the great events and characters of world history occur, so to speak, twice. He forgot to add the first time as tragedy, the second as farce . . . And we can perceive the same caricature in the circumstances surrounding the second edition of the eighteenth Brumaire!
>
> Men make their own history, but not of their own free will; not under circumstances they themselves have chosen but under the given and inherited circumstances with which they are directly confronted. The tradition of the dead generations weighs like a nightmare on the minds of the living. And, just when they appear to be engaged in the revolutionary transformation of themselves and their material surroundings, in the creation of something which does not yet exist, precisely in such epochs of revolutionary crisis they timidly conjure up the spirits of the past to help them; they borrow their names, slogans and costumes so as to stage the new world-historical scene in this venerable disguise and borrowed language. Luther put on the mask of the apostle Paul; the Revolution of 1789–1814 draped itself alternately as the Roman republic and the Roman empire; and the revolution of 1848 knew no better than to parody at some points 1789 and at others the revolutionary traditions of 1793–5. In the same way, the beginner who has learned a new language always translates it into his mother tongue: he can only be said to have appropriated the spirit of the new language and to be able to express himself in it freely when he can manipulate it without reference to the old, and when he forgets his original language while using the new one.[13]

The relevance of this passage to the description of the masqueraders needs no comment. The same figures of speech appear as ways of illuminating failed revolutions. No one would claim that Hawthorne is a Marxist in spite of himself. But his deep interest in the idea of revolution and his scepticism as to the possibility of this being achieved gets full play in *The Blithedale Romance*, and that interest has implications for the limited authority that is given to narrative and the narrator. Terry Eagleton, in a review of poetry translations, brings together many of these issues when he discusses theories of literature, narrative and even *The Eighteenth Brumaire* in the light of translation theory. He sees *The Eighteenth Brumaire* as a text which "eschews all myths of origin" and goes on to argue that narrative, while "a necessary mode of living our relations to history," is a necessary fiction. This political point is related to a literary one – that "every text is, in some sense, a translation ... What is being displaced ... is the mythological notion of the founding or primary text." The practice of translation "may lay bare some of the ... productive mechanisms of textuality – may figure as some kind of model or paradigm of the very secret of writing."[14]

Hawthorne's ironic deployment of the translator metaphor is less theoretical than Eagleton's and his view of history less optimistic than Marx's, but it is as penetrating in its implications. I have already suggested that mime and mimesis are criticized in *The Blithedale Romance* – except when (carefully) confined to works of art. And translation remains translation. The hope of transcendence to the level of transformation is tragically rejected as history asserts its authority. Coverdale in his last chapter states, notoriously, that he has kept one secret – that he was in love with Priscilla. It is no secret to any half-way careful reader. His attempt to constitute an ending, a conclusion from that confession is, as Coverdale knows, a failure. The translator/narrator admits this. Translation has not become transformation: "But what, after all, have I to tell? Nothing, nothing, nothing" (225).

# 7

## The American Claimant Manuscripts
### *or, the absence of an ending*

I

> [A]ny narrative of human action and adventure – whether we call it history
> or romance – is certain to be a fragile handiwork, more easily rent than
> mended. The actual experience of even the most ordinary life is full of events
> that never explain themselves, either as regards their origin or their tendency.
>
> (1,232)

This passage comes from the fiftieth chapter of *The Marble Faun* – a
novel which is profoundly concerned with many of the major historical,
theological and mythic narratives which have structured Western
culture. This radical scepticism about narrative challenges presupposi-
tions about the explanatory authority that story or plot can offer and, as
such, provides a way of initiating discussion of the concerns and
strategies of Hawthorne's last fictions. It is a passage to which I shall
return in the chapter on *The Marble Faun* when discussing more
specifically the ways in which Hawthorne presents the question of
beginnings and endings as profoundly problematic – and, in particular,
what implications the deliberate absence of an authoritative ending to
that novel has for the sense of that fiction. But it is as well to have it before
us now if only as a way of suggesting that the unfinished novels should
not be dismissed merely because they are unfinished.

Examinations of the last part of Hawthorne's career have tended to
concentrate almost exclusively on *The Marble Faun* with, occasionally, a
few kind or not so kind words about *Our Old Home*. This was
understandable when the texts of the unfinished novels were unavailable
or only available in incomplete or corrupt versions – but now that we
have well edited texts in the form of *The American Claimant Manuscripts*

and *The Elixir of Life Manuscripts* (volumes XII and XIII of the Ohio
Centenary Edition)[1] there is little excuse for looking at *The Marble Faun*
in isolation and still less for seeing it as the fourth and final item in a
sequence which began with *The Scarlet Letter*. Even if merely on the
grounds of historical propinquity, it should be clear that the unfinished
fictions not only deserve attention in their own right but are relevantly
helpful to reading *The Marble Faun*. *The Blithedale Romance* was
published in 1852 and *Tanglewood Tales* (Hawthorne's second book of
Greek myths retold for children) in August 1853, a month after the
Hawthorne family had left for England. *The Marble Faun* was not to
appear until 1860 but Hawthorne's pen was not idle in the intervening
years. Indeed, there is a case for arguing that the last decade of his life was
by far the most productive – at least as far as productivity is defined by
sheer wordage. Even if the question of quality is postponed or evaded,
the sheer bulk of the writing is evidence enough that Hawthorne had not
chosen silence, not abandoned writing – and it is not irrelevant to note
that *The Marble Faun* is easily the longest of his completed fictions. The
dates of composition of the later years are as follows:

1.  *The English Notebooks*: August 1853–January 1858.
2.  *The Ancestral Footstep*: April and May 1858. (*The American Claimant
    Mss*).
3.  *The French and Italian Notebooks*: January 1858–December 1859.
4.  *The Marble Faun*: 1858–1859.
5.  *Etherege*
    *Grimshawe* } July 1860–August 1861 (approximately)
    (*The American Claimant Mss*)
6.  *Septimius Felton*
    *Septimius Norton* } autumn 1861–1862
    (*The Elixir of Life Mss*)
7.  "Chiefly About War Matters": May 1862.
8.  *Our Old Home*: 1860–July 1863.
9.  *The Dolliver Romance*: the last half of 1863.[2]

Even if the notebooks are dismissed as tourist diaries combined with
material gathered for an English romance and for the guide-book
elements of *The Marble Faun*, enough remains to show that Hawthorne
was capable not only of sheer production but of producing excellent
work. The case for the distinction of the unfinished novels I will concede
still surprisingly needs to be argued – and it is profoundly to be regretted
that Davidson's important and pioneering work on those fictions should
have been so unnecessarily apologetic about their quality – and still more
to be regretted that subsequent critics have taken him at his word.[3] But

there stands *Our Old Home* so percipiently praised by Nina Baym, and, more importantly, there is the cool and witty balance of "Chiefly About War Matters" – evidence enough that Hawthorne's intellect and style could cope with what might have been expected to be uncongenial and recalcitrant material.

To see *The Marble Faun* in splendid (or not so splendid) isolation is to distort not only the very real non-fictional achievements of his last years but also his fictional accomplishments. I certainly do not want to deny that there is a difference between *The Marble Faun* (where Hawthorne *refuses* to provide the conventional ending) and *The American Claimant* and *Elixir of Life Manuscripts* which are patently unfinished (though not, I shall argue, inherently unfinishable). But there is, surely, a comparison to be made between the claims made for a certain type of fiction implied by that notorious postscript to the *Faun* which added insult to injury, responding to aggrieved readers by offering them another conclusion in which nothing is concluded, and the kind of novel Hawthorne aimed at in *The Ancestral Footstep*, his first attempt at the material of *The American Claimant*. There his American in England was to make "singular discoveries, all of which bring the book to an ending unexpected by everybody, and *not satisfactory to the natural yearnings of novel-readers*" (xII, II, my emphasis).[4]

Yet it is the connections between the concerns in the writings of the last phase that I want to emphasize. The fact that the materials in *The American Claimant* volume both precede and follow *The Marble Faun* and that (as I shall show) the Elixir of Life material draws on and develops ideas from *The American Claimant Manuscripts* should forcibly suggest that these works are likely to share common concerns. I shall also argue that the struggles with his themes and materials is not evidence of imaginative failure but rather of Hawthorne's intelligence, courage and ambition in facing remarkably complex issues at a time of great historical crisis which (had he lived longer) might well have produced a radically new kind of fiction. And in Hawthorne's struggles with that rough angel, art, we get a privileged look into the artist's workshop – and can see enough to see not only that a less subtle mind, a cruder intelligence could have "solved" the difficulties at the price of simplifying the situations but also that he had provided a solution to many if not all of the thematic and plot problems – and that without compromising. (The Elixir of Life problem is rather different: there we do have an outline of a whole story in *Septimius Felton* and here sheer physical exhaustion may explain the failure to provide a completed worked-up version in *Septimius Norton*.) At this stage, this probably sounds like an act of faith – but it is worth noting that Hawthorne (who was *not* normally given to praising his own work) did say of the Elixir of Life material "I have a notion that this last book would be my best; and full of wisdom about matters of life and death" (letter to Longfellow: XIII, 577).

The difficulties, then, come from the ambitiousness of Hawthorne's concerns. *The Marble Faun*, for example, not only attempts to confront all Western history but also juxtaposes art, theology and secular history as modes of representing the world and investigates whether any one of these modes can be shown to have priority over the others. These thematic concerns (which have formal implications of course) remain strikingly consistent over the period from 1858 to the sad abandonment of *The Dolliver Romance* – and they are large themes such as the Fall, immortality, inheritance, genealogy, and the meaning of home, and, perhaps most importantly, the ways in which the past and the present can or should be connected (or disrupted) – problems that all have to do with originations and destinations, beginnings and endings. In other words, narrative is presented as central – yet profoundly problematic. Even if the external pressures of public and private history on Hawthorne are ignored, it may not be surprising that the unfinished novels remain unfinished in any conventional sense. If narrative authority is being challenged or interrogated, the problems of the form of a story become immediately important. One example of the form this problem can take comes from *Septimius Felton*: a character who believes in the possibility of physical immortality is (as we shall see in the final chapter) hoping to construct a life story which has no ending (and one in which interruptions and gaps are feared). Another comes from *The Marble Faun*: it has frequently been remarked that the novel is slow-moving (and Baym has, very plausibly, suggested that Hawthorne must have been tempted to finish the novel when Kenyon brings Miriam and Donatello together by the statue of Pope Julian in Perugia). This, I suggest, is because Hawthorne, by delaying the moment of closure (and by providing moments of possible closure) wants to raise the problem for our attention. Even if the notorious question of the Fortunate Fall is looked at, the question of the presence or absence of an ending irresistibly occurs. Miriam first broaches the apparent paradox to Kenyon (who is almost as shocked as Hilda – and expresses himself in virtually identical terms). Some chapters later, Kenyon picks up Miriam's argument and appals Hilda (who, in her turn, appals many a reader). This combination of repetition and sequence (Miriam to Kenyon, Kenyon to Hilda) invites consideration of the possibility that the sequence will continue beyond the end of the novel – especially since Hilda and Kenyon in such similar language have not answered the intellectual problems that the Fortunate Fall raises – that, indeed, Donatello's story raises. It is at the least possible that after a suitable lapse of time Hilda may enunciate the same heresy – if heresy it be – in a quiet New England village . . .[5]

II

> My ancestor left England in 1635. I returned in 1853. I sometimes feel as if I
> myself had been absent these two hundred and eighteen years – leaving
> England just emerging from the feudal system, and finding it on the verge of
> Republicanism. It brings the two far separated points of time very closely
> together, to view the matter thus.     (*English Notebooks*, October 9, 1854)

> In my Romance, the original emigrant to America may have carried away
> with him a family secret, whereby it was in his power (had he so chosen) to
> have brought about the ruin of the family. This secret he transmits to his
> American progeny; by whom it is inherited throughout all the intervening
> generations. At last, the hero of the Romance comes to England, and finds
> that, by means of this secret, he still has it in his power to procure the downfall
> of the family. It would be something similar to the story of Meleager, whose
> fate depended on the firebrand that his mother had snatched out of the flames.
>                                         (*English Notebooks*, April 12, 1855)

In the preface ("To a Friend") to *Our Old Home*, Hawthorne signalled
his abandonment of the work we know now as *The American Claimant
Manuscripts*. If everything had gone to plan, *Our Old Home* would not
have existed:

> These and other sketches, with which, in a somewhat rougher form than I have
> given them here, my Journal was copiously filled, were intended for the side-
> scenes, and back-grounds, and exterior adornment, of a work of fiction, of
> which the plan had imperfectly developed itself in my mind, and into which I
> ambitiously proposed to convey more of *various modes of truth* than I could
> have grasped by a direct effort.               (v, 3–4, my emphasis)

At the same time that Hawthorne regrets that the English Romance will
never exist, he makes a specific claim for the authority that the fiction
would have possessed – and, significantly, it is a claim for truth. I believe
(and argue this at the end of this chapter) Hawthorne when he claims that
the Civil War has led to the abandonment of that English Romance – if
only because when he begins *The Elixir of Life Manuscripts* he introduces
the American Revolution and explicitly parallels this with the Civil War
(and frequently refers to the War of Independence as a civil war). As I
shall try to show, Hawthorne needs there to be a single (if complex)
entity called America not only for the structure of his Romance but also
if it is to have the authority of mimesis. If the Romance is dependent on
the idea of a representative American in Europe (and Hawthorne flirts
with the idea of making him a congressman or an ambassador), then
there is a necessity for there to be an America to represent. And if the
claimant to an English estate at least ought to want to return home to
America, then America needs to seem a place that one would want to go

to. It is no wonder that he appeals "to that grand idea of an irrevocable Union" (v, 5) – and more than understandable that he insists on a parallel between his fiction and an idea of a united America:

> The Present, the Immediate, the Actual, . . . leaves me sadly content to scatter a thousand peaceful fantasies upon the hurricane that is sweeping us all along with it, possibly, into a Limbo where our nation and its polity may be as literally the fragments of a shattered dream as my unwritten Romance. (v, 4)

The history of a fiction and the fiction of a history are brought uncomfortably close together.

Hawthorne draws attention to the "existence" of a work that history has rendered "abortive" – and draws what comfort he can from the idea that he can find room for "the abortive work on a certain ideal shelf, where are reposited many other shadowy volumes of mine, more in number, and very much superior in quality, to those which I have succeeded in rendering actual" (v, 4). It was, of course, hardly the first reference to the category of the abandoned, the unwritten, the unwritable, the unfinishable or, at least, the unfinished. I have drawn attention to this concern – even obsession – of Hawthorne's in the chapter on "Ethan Brand" and "Main-Street" so here I need do no more than repeat the point that "Passages from a Relinquished Work" carries a significant meaning in its title – as does "Ethan Brand: A Chapter from an Abortive Romance." And this passage from "A Select Party" shows that in *Our Old Home* Hawthorne was making a personal application of a common Romantic point:

> In the alcoves of another vast apartment was arranged a splendid library, the volumes of which were inestimable, because they consisted not of actual performances, but of the works which the authors only planned, without ever finding the happy season to achieve them . . . The shelves were crowded; for it would not be too much to affirm that every author has imagined, and shaped out in his thought, more and far better works than those which actually proceeded from his pen. (T&S, 955)

Though *Our Old Home* may be principally a record of Hawthorne's impressions of England, he did not repress all concern with what had concerned him in the various versions of the English Romance. I am not thinking merely of the passages in "Consular Experiences" which deal with those unbalanced Americans who feel themselves heirs of England – though Hawthorne did see such figures as a way into his Romance:

> Now, as to the arrangement of the Romance; – it begins, as an integral and essential part, with my introduction, giving a pleasant and familiar summary of my life in the Consulate at Liverpool; the strange species of Americans, with strange purposes in England, whom I used to meet there; and, especially, how

> my countrymen used to be put out of their senses by the idea of inheritances of English property. Then I shall particularly instance one gentleman who called on me, on first coming over; a description of him must be given, with touches that shall puzzle the reader to decide whether it is not an actual portrait. And then this Romance shall be offered, half seriously, as the account of the fortunes that he shall meet with in his search for his hereditary home. (XII, 87)

Rather the presence of these concerns emerges more clearly in a comment at the end of "Glimpses of English Poverty." Hawthorne sets beside the account of a mass marriage of the poor (done in Easter week because it is free then) a description of "an aristocratic wedding" – and concludes his chapter with a meditation which is his version of the Condition of England question:

> If the most favorable of earthly conditions could make them happy, they had every prospect of it. They were going to live on their abundance in one of those stately and delightful English homes, such as no other people ever created or inherited, a hall set far and safe within its own private grounds, and surrounded with venerable trees, shaven lawns, rich shrubbery, and trimmest pathways, the whole so artfully contrived and tended that summer rendered it a paradise, and even winter would hardly disrobe it of its beauty; and all this fair property seemed more exclusively and inalienably their own, because of its descent through many forefathers, each of whom had added an improvement or a charm, and thus transmitted it with a stronger stamp of rightful possession to his heir. *And it is possible, after all, that there may be a flaw in the title deeds?* Is, or is not, the system wrong that gives one married pair so immense a superfluity of luxurious home, and shuts out a million others from any home whatever? One day or another, safe as they deem themselves, and safe as the hereditary temper of the people really tends to make them, the gentlemen of England will be compelled to face this question.              (V, 308–9, my emphasis)

"Is, or is not, the system wrong . . .?" There is an unusual willingness here to confront the reader with an explicit social criticism. This questioning of aristocratic rights to a home can be seen to be the more pointed when it is remembered that it comes from the Hawthorne, "curious to see what kind of home was provided" (V, 293) for the poor, who had visited a poorhouse.[6]

Is there a flaw in the title deeds? It is a question that *The American Claimant Manuscripts* obsessively and repeatedly ask – the extent that the question becomes rephrased and generalized: is there a flaw in *any* title deed? Is the idea of property necessarily and inevitably compromised – yet an unavoidable part of history? There is a passage in *Etherege* – Hawthorne's second attempt at a narrative of the American claimant materials – in the middle of a debate about the relative values of English monarchical aristocracy and American republican democracy, where the American touches on the same question that Hawthorne had asked in his own voice in *Our Old Home*:

> "ever since I set my foot on your shores . . . I have had a feeling of coming change, among all that you look upon as so permanent, so everlasting; and though your thoughts dwell fondly on things as they are and have been, there is a deep destruction somewhere in this country, which is inevitably impelling it in the path of my own." (XII, 162)

Yet, of course, the meaning is not the same – if only because the context is different. Etherege has at the back of his mind the possibility of his inheriting an English estate and perhaps a title, and, whether or not his claim is legally or morally justified (and Hawthorne refers to the "flaw in Etherege's title" [XII, 205]), his political comments are almost necessarily compromised – and take place in the middle of a debate in which the English views of class, of hierarchy, are allowed their full persuasiveness and authority. "[I]t might change your feelings, perhaps . . . if you were one of the privileged class," (XII, 163) slyly says an Englishman of the privileged class to Etherege. It was a conflict that Hawthorne saw as central to his English Romance:

> The great gist of the story ought to be the natural hatred of men – and the particular hatred of Americans – to an Aristocracy; at the same time doing a good degree of justice to the aristocratic system by depicting its grand, beautiful, and noble characteristics. (XII, 475)

This comes from the second of seven studies that Hawthorne wrote while working on the materials of his English Romance. The sequence and dating of these studies have eluded even the scrupulous attentions of the Ohio editors – but they tentatively suggest (convincingly to my mind) that the first four relate to *The Ancestral Footstep* fragment.* These notes to himself clearly show Hawthorne's socio-political concerns provisional though they are. In the first four studies it appears that one function of the American claimant is to be (unconsciously?) subversive –

---

* Here a note on the arrangement and pagination of vol.XII, *The American Claimant Manuscripts*, may be useful. The studies occupy pages 473 to 485. The dating of these is provisional, but the editors (while giving the evidence which may work against this hypothesis) suggest that the first four relate to *The Ancestral Footstep* – while the last three clearly relate to *Etherege* and possibly *Grimshawe*. These titles refer to the three versions of the English Romance narrative. *The Ancestral Footstep* (pp. 3–89) contains the germs – though only the germs – of the narrative in all three forms it takes. *Etherege* (pp. 90 to 342) returns to this material, expands it, and provides the claimant with a childhood. *Grimshawe* (and here I shall argue that Hawthorne had solved his plot problems) goes from p. 343 to p. 470. One major change here is in the character of the father-figure of the American Claimant from an eccentrically virtuous to a far darker figure. I have already given the dates of composition insofar as they can be determined by the Ohio editors. The titles are, as the editors state, arbitrary. I shall give the page numbers for each section as it is discussed.

and to dramatize a conflict not merely between nationalities but also different political systems:

> The American's researches must bring about results unexpected by himself, and not such as he had at all aimed at – overturning whatever seemed fixed. The nobleman's title and estate, for instance.     (xii, Study 1, 474)

The relation between this and the passage I quoted earlier about an ending "not satisfactory to the natural yearnings of novel-readers" is clear enough in the implied point that novel-readers are naturally conventionally conservative. But Hawthorne even at the stage of the studies doesn't want to present merely a naive contrast between virtuous democrat and vicious aristocrat though he certainly wants to contrast two social systems. Class necessarily complicates the issue – as, for example, when Hawthorne flirts with the idea of the English as a *very* extended family. An Englishwoman "shall turn out to be one of" the American's "relatives; he shall find another in a factory person; another descendant of an old family in a groom; another in a rich merchant" (xii, Study 1, 473). It is a pity that Hawthorne dropped this potentially rich seam – but it is revealing of his fascination with the complexities of class identification. The opposition of Democrat and Aristocrat is too crudely allegorical for Hawthorne, refusing as it does any consideration of the complex historical truths and the psychological pressures on the American. He is to be "a self-made man" (xii, Study 5, 479) – but also "an American gentleman" (xii, Study 1, 473) – and very conscious he is shown to be of this in all three versions of the narrative. He is also to be a public man. Hawthorne experiments with different versions of the idea – but this is not untypical:

> The American is of course a lawyer, and might too have been a soldier in the Mexican War; yes, he shall. And since a politician, and governor of a state; and still quite a young man; therefore capable in affairs.     (xii, Study 2, 475)

The American democrat will, of course, celebrate his country's institutions – but not only is he tempted by the notion of inheriting a great estate, he is also disgusted by the price to be paid for living in a "meritocratic" democracy in which one has to be elected to rather than inherit public position:

> Still a very young man, he has been in Congress, has displayed brilliant eloquence, has been disappointed in some aspiration, and has thrown up public life in disgust with the abuse, the brutal violence with which it is carried on.
> (xii, Study 6, 482)

This disgust may be in part to account for the American's appearance in Europe but it also takes its part in Hawthorne's sophisticated presentation of his international themes. (The point about the claimant as an ambassador in *Etherege* provides a nice example of this. The office gives him social status in the eyes of the English even though it is at a minor German court – but the American has to wonder whether this honorable appointment is subtle manoeuvring on the part of a political rival who wants him safely out of the way in Europe). And in addition to the claimant, Hawthorne casts a hard look at another type of self-made man: he was also interested, however temporarily, in the figure of the amoral or immoral financial megalomaniac: "Among the personages introduced shall be an American defalcator, or other criminal, who shall be living here in England" (xii, Study 1, 474).[7] At one point, Hawthorne plays with the idea of having the speculator operate in Napoleonic times – as though he was making a black joke about "la carrière ouverte aux talents." This thematic possibility was, unfortunately, dropped in later drafts. Even in *The Ancestral Footstep*, Hawthorne, in finding a place for the character, confesses that it is only provisional. The claimant

> becomes interested in this Hospital; he finds it still going on, precisely as it did in the old days . . . Here he gets acquainted with an old man, an inmate of the establishment, who (if the uncontrollable fatality of the story will permit) must have an active influence on the ensuing events. I suppose him to have been an American, but to have fled his country and taken refuge in England; he shall have been a man of the Nicholas Biddle stamp, a mighty speculator, the ruin of whose schemes had crushed hundreds of people, and Middleton's father among the rest. (xii, 52)

But here I am moving too quickly from the studies to *The Ancestral Footstep*. Even from these studies, however, I hope readers can see that Nina Baym is likely to be wrong when she says of the *Footstep* that when Hawthorne "began to write his romance, he . . . invented . . . (or tried to invent) a purely gothic a-historical legend." And surely she trivializes the seriousness and ambition of Hawthorne's concerns when she glosses my second epigraph to this section like this:

> This entry . . . expresses a wish for revenge that will be familiar to any person who has felt at the mercy of a strange and unsympathetic culture, or has been frustrated by a foreign surrounding. All inexperienced visitors to a strange country are apt to feel insignificant, ineffective, and unappreciated, and retaliatory fantasies are very common.[8]

This hardly explains why Hawthorne returned to the American claimant story when he was safely back in New England. But, to make my case for the seriousness of Hawthorne's concern with history, I need to turn to *The Ancestral Footstep* – before examining the works written in New England: *Etherege* and *Grimshawe*.

III

## The Ancestral Footstep (XII, 3–89)

The first emigrant to America (200 years ago) shall have carried with him a family secret, which shall have been retained in the American branch, though latterly it shall have been looked upon as an idle tradition. The English heir shall have lost this secret. At the time of the American's appearance in England, the family shall be at some crisis; and by means of this secret, the American shall find himself empowered to influence the result. He shall keep himself unknown to the family – at least until the denouement. Perhaps he shall let the old family go to ruin; perhaps otherwise.                              (XII, Study 1, 474)

The Ancestral Footstep not only anticipates The Marble Faun but takes another different look at issues present in The House of the Seven Gables. There there were the Maine lands – the dreamed-of "incalculable wealth to the Pyncheon blood," lands "more extensive than many a dukedom, or even a reigning prince's territory, on European soil" (N, 366). There the "ancient deed, signed with the hieroglyphics of several Indian sagamores," conveyed "to Colonel Pyncheon and his heirs, forever, a vast extent to the eastward" (N, 624). The document has, of course, no authority by 1848:

> actual settlers . . . would have laughed at the idea of any man's asserting a right – on the strength of mouldy parchments, signed with the faded autographs of governors and legislators, long dead and forgotten – to the lands which they or their fathers had wrested from the wild hand of Nature, by their own sturdy toil.                                                                          (N, 367)

Here in England in contrast to America, faded documents and family traditions do ensure that a claim can be made: English land is not virgin soil and labour does not give ownership rights. Admittedly Alice, the heroine, raises the question of the justice of such a claim:

> A succession of ages and generations might be supposed to have blotted out your claims from existence; for it is not just that there should be no term of time which can make security for lack of just a few formalities.

But she raises it at a point when (in this version of the story) the claimant, Middleton, is about to enter the house he has inherited: "At last, come in! It is your own; there is none that can forbid you" (XII, 26). This is not to accept that claims on the past are safe – Hawthorne repeatedly returns to the image of the plague pit which, when reopened, lets its disease loose again on society – but, unlike the Pyncheons and the Maine lands, Middleton can revive his claim on the English estate (whether or not this is wise). In The House of the Seven Gables (some of) the past (at whatever price) can be repudiated – and the novel establishes a narrative which (however we interpret or evaluate its conclusion) does have a beginning and an ending, where Holgrave/Maule's secret story can be revealed, and the family histories become a single narrative.

The conventional explanation for the failure of *The Ancestral Footstep* is that Hawthorne simply did not know where he was going and what he was trying to do. It is certainly true that, even in the short space it occupies, Hawthorne tells, retells and changes his story in an attempt to forward his narrative – and repeatedly muses over "the present aspect of the story." It is true too that he clearly finds certain images fascinating but does not really know what to do with them. An example is the cabinet in the form of a mansion – an image which I too find profoundly suggestive. In one of Hawthorne's meditative passages he emphasizes its importance:

> in the legend, though not in the written document, there must be an account of a certain magnificent, almost palatial residence, which Middleton shall presume to be the ancestral home; and in this palace, there shall be a certain secret chamber, or receptacle, where is reposited a document that shall complete the evidence of the genealogical descent. (XII, 51)

The importance of genealogy as a or even the authoritative narrative is clearly crucial to any story of a lost heir, but Hawthorne doesn't want to use this idea crudely as simply indicating a secret hiding-place. He had already experimented with this "palace":

> Alice drew near this stately cabinet, and threw wide the doors, which like the portal of a palace, stood between two pillars; it all seemed to be enlaced, showing within some beautiful old pictures on the pannel of the doors, and a mirror, that opened a long succession of mimic halls, reflection upon reflection, extending to an interminable nowhere . . .
>
> And this then was that palace to which tradition, so false at once, and true, had given such magnitude and magnificence in the stories of the Middleton family, around their shifting firesides in America. Looming afar through the mists of time, the little fact had become a gigantic vision. Yes, here it was in miniature, all that he had dreamed of; a palace of four feet high!

The irony of the mirrors reflecting "an interminable nowhere" and the diminishing of Middleton's dreams are reinforced by the fact that, when Alice and he open a hidden compartment, there is nothing there: "Everything had been so strangely true, and so strangely false, up to this moment, that they could not comprehend this failure at the last moment. It was the strangest, saddest jest!" (XII, 28). Later, Hawthorne shifts his ironic focus – when the English incumbent of the estate takes Middleton's interest in this apparent "representation . . . of his idea of the old family mansion" as evidence of his lower-class status: "Perhaps he is of some trade that makes this sort of manufacture particularly interesting to him" (XII, 47). If Middleton is the heir, then he must be of the same class as the squire but at the same time he wants to be recognized as a gentleman in his own right – an American gentleman – and he is extremely sensitive about that status. Indeed, after Middleton has met one version of the squire, he is invited to dine and stay the night: he "could not but perceive that Mr. Eldredge must have been making some inquiries as to his social status, in order to feel himself justified in putting him on this footing of equality" (XII, 73). It is this invitation which leaves Middleton alone with the cabinet as Hawthorne returns yet again to that suggestive piece of furniture (XII, 77–9). The terms of this obsessive concern make it clear that Hawthorne is fascinated by how tradition changes the proportions while preserving the germ of a kind of historical truth. It is also a nice way of questioning whether the American as a result of accepting the traditional tales has overvalued English richness, overestimated his possible heritage. But at this stage Hawthorne seems unable to make up his mind about his valuation of England and about the symbolic weight that cabinet could or should carry. As we've seen, on its first appearance, the cupboard is bare – giving Middleton a profound psychological shock:

> It had been magnified to a palace; it had dwindled down to Lilliputian size; and yet, up to now, it had seemed to contain, in its diminutiveness, all the riches which he had attributed to its magnitude. This last moment had utterly subverted it; the whole great structure seemed to vanish.     (XII, 28–9)

This suggestion of subversion is not followed up – perhaps understandably – for if the secret of England is to be that there is no secret, this would have to be a very short story. When Hawthorne returns to allow Middleton to open the cabinet in the solitude of his bedroom, he leaves us with a different but equally enigmatic result. Out of a combination of good manners (a desire perhaps to act up to the idea of the gentleman) and fear of what he may find, Middleton decides not to open the documents he discovers. Here the solution of the secret of England is postponed – never, alas, to be revealed. I have dwelt on this comparatively minor example because it shows the potential richness of this image. I have focussed on the problematic nature of tradition and the way in which class becomes an unavoidable topic – but I have only skimmed the surface.

I certainly admit – and have just provided evidence to that effect – that Hawthorne had not solved anything like all his problems in *The Ancestral Footstep* but I hope the case of the cabinet is also evidence that the problems are at once difficult and interesting – even interesting in their difficulty. And Hawthorne's problems of establishing narratives and choosing between those narratives – his problems with his themes and form – should not be seen as those of the novelist alone for the fiction is largely about those very problems. His American claimant's difficult task is itself to construct a narrative from pieces of a story (or stories) which are not all equally available to him – and to decide what to do with this history – if it is a true history.

If it *is* a "true history." It is a continuous problem for Hawthorne to decide whether the claimant shall inherit, or turn out to be mistaken in his belief that he is the heir (there may be another American heir) – or turn his back on England and confront the potentialities of America. The question of the status of this history is the more difficult for the claimant, living, as he begins by feeling, in the middle of a certain kind of fiction. Middleton's experience of England had initially been of a "dream-land," "nothing more than a romance" (XII, 35, 41). This may merely seem a conventional raw American response to fabled England. But the question of story is central to the fragments of a fiction – so crucial to *The Ancestral Footstep* that it might better be called a would-be fiction of fragmentary narratives. I have already suggested that genealogy, "a direct lineage" (XII, 7), is the rudimentary chronicle of a would-be heir who has to assemble and (convincingly) tell (and, at the same time, genealogy needs the evidence that history very properly requires: it must be a true story). But it is not simply the American who thinks in terms of fictions. Even from the English point of view, this is "a strange family-story, of which there was no denouement, such as a novel-writer would desire, and which had remained in that unfinished posture for more than two hundred years!" (XII, 15). This is a point that Hawthorne repeatedly returns to: "It would be curious, would it not, if you had come, after two hundred years, to piece out a story which may have been as much a mystery here in England as there in America" (XII, 40). It is, then, a mystery where the solution necessarily will take the form of a narrative – though this raises doubts: "Of course, it is too like a romance that you should be able to establish such a claim as could have a valid influence on this matter" (XII, 40–1). That "happy ending" would be, it seems, too fictional, too unrealistic a conclusion to the story. Yet narrative cannot be escaped: over and over again it is emphasized that characters inhabit a world where the whole story is unknown, where only knowledge of the whole would make (historical) sense of the experience. Again and again Hawthorne returns to this point: the American claimant "arrives, bringing half a story, being the only part known in America, to join it onto the other half, which is known only in England" (XII, 52).

Hawthorne is clearly fascinated with the idea of defining what might be considered as two stories, or as two halves of a single narrative – and the implications that this may have for the recognition or definition of the beginnings and endings of stories. If the American did inherit, then the ending would have been generated by joining two middles of a story together – or, rather, a middle (which the present incumbent might prefer to define differently as the middle of *his* story) – and what the American initiator of the American section of the story may well have intended to be a new beginning. If one story can be made out of two fragments, then the American story (insofar as it *is* American) has to give way to the authority – even imperialism – of the English story. It is a position full of irony: the incumbent would prefer a different story-line and will personally hardly be comforted by the notion that the Americanness of the claimant's narrative is necessarily subverted by the acceptance of the authority of the English genealogical narrative. The dominance of the English story is ironically reinforced by the suggestion that there is *another* would-be American heir. Middleton is understandably "wonder-stricken at this strange reduplication of his own position and pursuits" (XII, 17). This still further privileges the English story not only by making the life of an English gentleman seem generally desired but also by implying the dominance of the English story as a shaping authority. These two similar if not identical American stories by their very attempts to establish a longer story concede primacy to the English narrative. And here it is worth noting the way in which Hawthorne sophisticates the problem of Englishness as he writes his way into – or around – *The Ancestral Footstep*. An example is the figure of the present incumbent – chosen because Baym has directed some of her dismissive criticism at the shifts in the presentation of this figure and if her verdict is accepted, her dismissiveness seems fair. The first version of this figure is described by Baym as waving "his gun about in a wild, threatening way and accidentally" shooting "himself dead with it." As a matter of fact, he considers shooting Middleton, changes his mind, reverses his gun, and hits Middleton with the gunbut. The shock of hitting the American makes the gun go off – and fire a fatal bullet into the squire. It is tempting to see a "moral" in this: hitting an American is the equivalent of suicide – but let that pass. The next reworking results in an expansion of the squire's character: Hawthorne

> created, in Davidson's words, "a very commonplace landowner," the texture of whose life afforded no aperture for the insertion of a gothic catastrophe. In fact, his bluff heartiness casts Middleton in a morally ambiguous light.

I have no quarrel with this – as a description of the squire and as the beginnings of an explanation as to why such a figure is inadequate to the fiction – but I have serious reservations about Baym's belief that Hawthorne is aiming for the Gothic and equally serious doubts about her implication that Middleton is not intended to appear in a morally ambiguous light for I would argue that Hawthorne is highly ambivalent about Middleton and his project – indeed, some at least of his problems come from that very ambivalence. I would also quarrel with her comments on the third avatar of the squire figure:

> English squires . . . are made fanatics in a gothic scheme with great difficulty, so Hawthorne hit on the plan of making him a recently repatriated Englishman who had been raised in Italy and who brings with him a full complement of Italian characteristics. This was a solution of sorts . . .[9]

This is to miss the subtleties of Hawthorne. The shift from the beefy squire to the Italianate "villain" is not a desire for the simplistic certainties of the Gothic. Rather it raises the question of what constitutes "Englishness". Here is a "foreigner" (in really English eyes) with a "foreign" (Catholic) religion who is defined as an Englishman because of the authority of a genealogical narrative. And this then neatly balances and parallels an American's claims for a place in England. Englishness becomes a problematic category. This is not simply an act of faith on my part. Hawthorne is quite clear in the text – even if we can see (as we see writ larger in *Etherege*) a clash between what Middleton may well at some deep level want or desire – and what Hawthorne thinks he ought to want:

> Eldredge's [at this point the name given to the incumbent] own position, as a foreigner in the midst of English home life, insulated and dreary, shall represent to Middleton, in some degree, what his own would be, were he to accept the estate. But Middleton shall not come to the decision to resign it, without having to repress deep yearnings for that sense of long, long rest in an age-consecrated home, which he had felt so deeply to be the happy lot of Englishmen. But this ought to be rejected, as not belonging to his country, nor to the age, nor any longer possible.                              (XII, 85)

By the time Hawthorne gets to *Etherege*. what had been a promising germ of an idea had been developed: "There have been three descents of this man's branch in Italy, and only one English mother in all that time. Positively, I do not see an English trait in his face, and as little in his manner." (XII, 174). And yet that amateur genealogist, the Warden, has to admit that "as fate would have it, he is the inheritor of a good old English name, a fine patrimonial estate, and a very probable claim to an old English title" (XII, 173). For fate we can read genealogy – and if such a figure can have a good claim on an English estate, how much this reinforces the subjective feelings of the American claimant that he too has a right to an English estate.

But before going on to *Etherege*, it is necessary to return again to

Hawthorne's obsessive concern with broken narratives and fragmented histories. Early on Middleton muses that the early settlers of America may have carried away with them

> traditions . . . which might . . . piece out the broken relics of family history . . . I can conceive . . . that this might sometimes be of importance in settling the heirships of estates; but which now, only the two insulated parts of the story being known, remain a riddle, although the solution of it is actually in the world; if only those two parts could be united across the sea, like the wires of an electric telegraph. (XII, 5–6)

Riddles, secrets, stories and the image of a modern "instantaneous" communications device are all interrelated in Middleton's mind, coupled with the idea of the materials of history as "broken relics" – to be made whole again when or if the full story is told. "Secrets . . . are at odds with sequence" writes Kermode in an important essay.[10] It seems that Middleton would concur, though he, unlike Kermode, sees sequence as the solution of the secret: "I believe . . . that many English secrets might find their solution in America, if the two threads of a story could be brought together, disjoined as they have been by time and the ocean" (XII, 15). Hawthorne extends this idea of the importance of story by moving on from simple sequence to a notion of the narrative containing useful knowledge – useful not only to Middleton but also to the story-teller. When Hawthorne thinks about the Italianate squire making an attempt on the claimant's life, he considers making this a "reproduction of the attempt made two hundred years before; and Middleton's hereditary knowledge of that shall be the means of his salvation." No wonder Hawthorne is pleased by this idea: "The legendary murder, or attempt at it, will bring its own imaginative probability with it, when repeated by Eldredge . . .." Not only does it add verisimilitude to the traditional story, it also allows him to approach his obsession about the two stories and the historical gap from yet another perspective: "This incident is very essential towards bringing together the past time and the present, and the two ends of the story" (XII, 82). The claimant figure has a choice. Either he can accept that the two stories are one – in which case America was (for him at least) discovered in vain. Or he can abandon this olde-worlde story and accept an American "ancestor's" story – who "wished to found a new race, wholly disconnected with the past" (XII, 17). The contemporary American should choose to repeat that ambition – or so Hawthorne at one level thinks: "he and his wife become the Adam and Eve of a new epoch, and the fitting missionaries of a new social faith, of which there must be continual hints through the book" (XII, 58). Shades of Holgrave – and of *The Blithedale Romance*! But evoking those utopian dreams reminds us how hard Hawthorne seemed to think it was to live such a project. Can Hawthorne actually write such a narrative – however much he may desire to? Perhaps Middleton *should* found a utopia – but can he? Instead of locating Eden in the future there may be a virtually irresistible psychological temptation to identify England as Edenic. Middleton

> sought his ancient home in it [the English countryside] as if he had found his way into Paradise, and were there endeavoring to trace out the signs of Eve's bridal bower, the birth-place of the human race and all its glorious possibilities of happiness and high performance. (XII, 3)

There is an odd mixture here of past, present and future. He may attempt to "trace out the signs" of where Eve's bower was, but are the "possibilities" for man lost in the past or still human potentialities – and what happened to the Fall?

The giveaway clue here is, perhaps, the reference to the search for the "ancient home." Whatever may be the right thing to do, the yearning for home is extraordinarily powerful:

> He was now at home; yes, he had found his home, and was sheltered at last under the ancestral roof, after all these, long wanderings – after the little log-built hut of the early settlement, after the shingled roof of the American house, after all the many roofs of two hundred years, here he was at last under the one which he had left, on that fatal night, when the Bloody Footstep was so mysteriously impressed on the threshold. (XII, 77)

If the English home becomes at once the origin and the destination for Middleton, then the linearity of narrative, dreams of a new beginning, get displaced by circularity – and history collapses in on itself as the two hundred years of a different history are denied validity by Middleton's imagination, thinking of himself as identical to the ancestor who left the Hall so long ago. Yet even if circularity threatens to displace narrative, Hawthorne still resists the process by including the inexplicable unique event – the bloody footstep. This disjunction carries over to the Hospital – though here rather than circularity it is the sheer fact of repetition that interests him (a theme which reappears in *Etherege* in the form of the lives of the poor). Middleton, "of course, becomes interested in this Hospital; he finds it still going on, precisely as it did in the old days." But one of the pensioners within this Elizabethan time capsule is a man who has affected modern history – "a mighty speculator, the ruin of whose schemes had crushed hundreds of people, and Middleton's father among the rest" (XII, 52).

Hawthorne seems in *The Ancestral Footstep* almost overpowered by the potential richness of his materials and themes. He is almost too aware, for example, of the various forms "history" can take, and the various pressures it can impose on people. Repetition, circularity, the past shaping the present, the present (by investigating the past) making it dangerously alive again – all these and more jostle for attention. And behind these alternatives there is the problem of deciding whether it is wiser to accept that there are two (or more) narratives – or whether to work for a single authoritative story – and with that as a central and serious problem, any fiction is going to be hard to finish. Middleton "had reason, from old family traditions, to believe that he brought with him a fragment of a history that, if followed out, might lead to curious results" (XII, 39). Curious results indeed! Hawthorne is overloaded with ideas – most, potentially, extremely interesting – and at the same time has the problem of deciding on the literary mode he should choose. For example, the squire's attempt on the life of Middleton could be written in two opposing ways: "The utmost pains must be taken with this incident to give it an air of reality; *or else* it must be quite removed out of the sphere of reality by an intensified atmosphere of Romance" (XII, 81, my emphasis). It is intriguing to see that Jamesian phrase "an air of reality" in what might appear an unlikely context. Had this choice between realism and romance been a straight choice and confined to the treatment of specific scenes, Hawthorne might have had no problem. But Hawthorne wanted something more complex and difficult which would affect the whole project of the fiction:

> I do not wish it to be a picture of life; but a Romance, grim, grotesque, quaint
> . . . It might have so much of the hues of life that the reader should think it was
> intended for a picture; yet the atmosphere should be such as to excuse all
> wildness . . . The descriptions of scenery, &c, and of the Hospital might be
> correct, but there should be a tinge of the grotesque given to all the characters
> and events. The tragic, and the gentler pathetic, need not be excluded by this
> tone and treatment. If I could but write one central scene in this vein, all the rest
> of the Romance would readily arrange itself around the nucleus.     (XII, 58)

It is profoundly understandable that writing even a single scene according to this recipe should have been a difficult ambition to achieve – for Hawthorne (even if he does not recognize this) is asking for a new kind of fiction – one which fully uses and incorporates realism and also goes beyond, transcends realism. It is an ambition which readers and writers of much twentieth century fiction should recognize – and respect.

Admitting the faults, false starts, and hesitations in *The Ancestral Footstep*, I hope it can be seen that the material was interesting enough and the problems intriguing enough for it to be completely understandable that Hawthorne wanted to return to it – especially as there was one obvious omission that must have seemed easy to remedy. One problem that he hardly faced in this version was to explain why the claimant was so strongly drawn to the old home and the values it symbolizes – and this is the problem which he immediately addresses when he begins *Etherege*. His provisional solution is to provide the claimant with a childhood as a mysterious orphan and with an aged and benevolent guardian who is, among other things, a "genealogist":

> And so the boy's thoughts were led to dwell on by-gone things; on matters of birth and ancestry, and connections of one family with another; and blood running in such intricate currents; sometimes sinking into the ground and disappearing forever; sometimes, after a long hidden course, reappearing, and ascending prominently like the gush of a fountain. And probably it was such meditations as these that led him to think, occasionally, what had been his own origin; whence came that blood that circled through his own veins. I presume there are more people occasionally occupied by such speculations in a democracy, where all claims of birth are nominally annulled, than in any land of nobility and hereditary honors; because, in the former, there is an uncertainty that admits all to claim even royal blood.           (XII, 98)

IV

## Etherege (XII, 90–342)

> Almost always, in visiting such scenes as I have been attempting to describe, I had a singular sense of having been there before . . . [T]he illusion was often so powerful, that I almost doubted whether such airy remembrances might not be a sort of innate idea, the print of a recollection in some ancestral mind, transmitted with fainter and fainter impress through several descents, to my own. I felt, indeed, like the stalwart progenitor in person, returning to the hereditary haunts after more than two hundred years, and finding the church, the hall, the farmhouse, the cottage, hardly changed during his long absence . . . while his own affinities for these things, a little obscured by disuse, were reviving at every step.           (V, 63–4)

> It seemed so singular to have so many circumstances, hereabouts, affecting to him as if he had known them before; yet always occurring with an unexpected and inexplicable difference, that bewildered and thrilled him yet more more than the similarity.           (XII, 177)

Hawthorne abandoned *The Ancestral Footstep* to write *The Marble Faun* but, when he returned to America and the American claimant material, he took it up very much where he had left off. As the historical commentary to the Ohio edition states

> For all its skeletal quality, the "Ancestral Footstep" contains almost every element of the English portion of the subsequent drafts, together with hints for the yet unsketched American scenes . . . When he took up the story again after

> returning to Concord in 1860, he would alter the proportions and reconstitute the cast of characters but the central plot core would remain.     (XII, 500)

This is enough to justify proceeding to *Etherege*, leaving *The Marble Faun* to be placed between *The American Claimant* and *The Elixir of Life Manuscripts*. As I have suggested, the most immediately obvious development is that Hawthorne begins with the American childhood of the claimant (in this version named Etherege) – though it is impossible to be quite certain that *The Ancestral Footstep* lacked anything of the sort since there are a few pages missing and the beginning we have is very much *in medias res*. These introductory scenes are partly an attempt to solve in advance plot difficulties that had appeared in the first version, and partly to generate expectation in the reader. Most importantly, of course, they give the claimant a childhood which will make his adult obsession with the question of inheritance more understandable, more psychologically plausible.[11] Hawthorne is quite clear about this in his notes to himself:

> Early and forcibly – let the deep, unconquerable interest, which an American feels in England, its people and institutions, be brought strongly out. This may partly be done by the mysterious child's yearnings towards his unknown ancestry, and having his imagination set entirely free by knowing nothing about them; so that he may, in fancy, trace his origin to the king's palace, if he likes. Then the family legends which cling dimly about his memory . . . shall have an effect in the same direction. Great stress must be laid on the effect of his vague position in making him imaginative; also, on the freedom which he feels himself to possess, by being connected by blood with nobody, at the same time that he has a dreary sense of solitude.     (XII, 124)

As we shall see, Etherege is divided in many ways but there is one important split which is a consequence of his childhood and of his consciousness of his Americanness (this a product of his young manhood – a period we only know of through Etherege's references to it when in England). That is the division between what he desires (a home, an origin, the ability to place and define himself as one of a line) – and what he thinks he ought to be (an American who repudiates the past and definition by the past in the name of the future, in the name of self-definition).

The English Romance could have been so easy to write (and so dull to read) if Hawthorne had felt that the opposition between the pensioner and the claimant in this argument had been all that was necessary:

> "How can you feel a heart's love for a mere political arrangement like your union? How can you be loyal where personal attachment – the lofty and noble, and unselfish attachment of a subject to his prince is out of the question; where your sovereign is felt to be a mere man like yourselves, whose petty struggles,

whose ambition – mean, before it grew to be audacious – you have watched, and know him to be just the same now as yesterday, and that tomorrow he will be walking unhonored amongst you again? Your system is too bare and meagre for human nature to love, or to endure it long. These stately degrees of society that have so strong a hold upon us in England, are not to be done away so lightly as you think. Your experiment is not yet a success, by any means; and you, young man, will live to see it result otherwise than you think." (XII, 162)

These are pointed words for a writer of a Presidential campaign biography to produce when the storm-clouds of the Civil War were gathering – and it is understandable that Etherege begins his reply by prophesying coming revolution for England before he goes into his testament of democratic faith:

"I love my country . . . I am proud of its institutions . . . I have a feeling, unknown probably to any but a republican, but which is the proudest thing in me, that there is no man above me – for my ruler is only myself, in the person of another, whose office I impose upon him – nor any below me. If you could understand me, I would tell you of the shame I felt when I first, on setting foot in this country, heard a man speaking of his birth as giving him privileges; saw him looking down on a laboring man, as one of an inferior race; and what I can never understand, is the pride which you positively seem to feel in having men and classes of men above you, born to privileges which you can never hope to share. It may be a thing to be endured, but surely not one to be absolutely proud of. And yet an Englishman is so." (XII, 162–3)

That crowing of young America might be all very well – if Etherege and Hawthorne could hold to it. The question of class is not so easily dismissed. Etherege shows himself highly sensitive about being recognized not as any man's equal but as a gentleman. And Hawthorne writes almost a mini-essay about the differences between the English and the American gentleman (XII, 169–171) – an essay which, while showing a remarkable sensitivity to differences in manners, ends with a very strange image to point to the felt difference. Etherege "had felt, in the closest coming together, as if there were a naked sword between the Englishman and him, as between the Arabian prince in the tale and the princess whom he wedded . . ."

There is also a genuine uncertainty about how to value English life – and how to define the realities of the English cultural and historical scene. There is something strange and "thrilling" about the idea represented by a nine centuries old English graveyard. The villagers

all, the very oldest of them, bearing a resemblance of feature, the kindred, the family likeness, to those who died yesterday – to those who still went thither to worship; and that all the grassy and half-obliterated graves around had held those who bore the same traits. (XII, 178)

Thrilling it may be – temporarily – but how is it to be evaluated?

> With Etherege's Yankee feelings, there was something sad to think how the generations had succeeded one another over and over, in immemorial succession, in this little spot, being born here, living, dying, lying down among their fathers' dust, and forthwith getting up again, as it were, and recommencing the same meaningless round, and really bringing nothing to pass; for probably the generation of today, in so secluded and motionless a place as this, had few or no ideas in advance of their ancestors of five centuries ago. It seemed not worth while that more than one generation of them should have existed . . . The stirring blood of the new land – where no man thinks of dying in his father's house – awoke within him, and revolted at the thought; and, as connected with it, revolted at all the hereditary pretensions which, since his stay here, had exercised such an influence over the fanciful part of his nature. In another mood, the village might have seemed a picture of rural peace, which it would have been worth while to give up ambition to enjoy; now, as his newer impulse stirred, it was a weariness to think of. The new American was stronger in him than the hereditary Englishman. (XII, 179–80)

That bleak vision of the sheer boringness of history as redundant repetition clearly made a deep impression on Hawthorne. Versions of this response appear in *The English Notebooks*, here, and in *Our Old Home*.[12] It is not merely the short and simple annals of the poor that elicit such a response. Tamed English nature has much the same effect:

> It is very delightful to me, for the present; and yet, I think, in the course of time, I should have a madness for something genuine, as it were; something that had not the touch and breath of man upon it.                (XII, 185)

But it is not only a question as to how this English world is to be evaluated. There are also very real problems about what is there. Is English social organization a fixed caste system where the individual must remain where he is initially placed – or is it a class society where individuals and families can rise and fall within what may be set categories? And is the American claimant sensitive enough to recognize the difference? The Warden of the Hospital has told Etherege of a decayed and fallen once great family and of the rise of a Birmingham manufacturer who originated in that seemingly repetitious village and who has pulled down the family home of an equivalent of the D'Urbervilles/Turbeyfields and erected a "grand show-place in its stead" (XII, 176). Etherege seems uncertain to take this information – and it is, significantly, at this point that he muses inconclusively (in my second epigraph to this section) on difference and similarity.

At the same time, it is asked how much real history (as opposed to a vague appeal to symbolic tradition) is there embodied by that traditional symbol of English history, the graveyard – when it is opposed to an

American one. "Etherege really found less antiquity here, than in the graveyard which might also be called his natal spot" (XII, 182). The explanation may seem dully simple: climatic difference. In England, the weather wears away the inscriptions on the tombstones – but the way this is phrased makes it more than just another complaint about the English climate: it is "quite impossible to make out the record" (XII, 182). That is a resonant phrase when the question of the record of the genealogy of the Etherege family is remembered. And this leads on to the question whether English history is a record of class-consciousness – or whether the introduction of the class issue is principally the product of Etherege's perception. The upper class monuments are, as the Warden assures Etherege, mostly safe against the weather's defacement of the record inside the church. The repetitious "round" of peasant life may repel Etherege – but he responds rather differently when he sees the old family hall:

> The whole scene impressed Etherege . . . as an abode of ancient peace, where generation after generation of the same family had lived, each making the most of life, because the life of each successive dweller there was eked out with the lives of all who had hitherto lived there; and had in equally those lives which were to come afterwards; so *that this was a rare and successful contrivance for giving length, fullness, body, substance, to this thin and frail matter of human life.* And, as life was *so rich in comprehensiveness*, the dwellers there made the most of it for the present and future, each generation contriving what it could to add to the cosiness, the comfortableness, the grave, solid respectability, the sylvan beauty, of the house with which they seemed to be connected both before and after death. The family had its home there; not merely the individual. Ancient shapes, that had apparently gone to the family tomb, had yet a right by family hearth and in family hall; nor did they come thither cold and shivering, and diffusing dire ghostly terrors, and repulsive shrinkings, and death in life; but in warm, genial attributes, making this life now passing more dense as it were, by adding all the substance of their own to it. Etherege could not compare this abode, and the feelings that it aroused, to the houses of his own country; poor tents of a day, inns of a night, where nothing was certain, save that the family of him who built it would not dwell here, even if he himself should have the hap to die under the roof, which with absurdest anticipations, he had built for his posterity. Posterity! An American can have none. (XII, 186, my emphases)

This is a passage of considerable interest and I shall return to it when I deal with the Elixir of Life material because it explains why Septimius, his hopes for physical immortality dashed, should retreat to the idea of inheriting an English estate, an idea of a life far larger and longer than any individual can hope to achieve on his own. The passage provides a very persuasive vision of English cultural life as one of accumulation and conservation with the ability to transmit that inherited cultural (and material) wealth in a way which makes death seem hardly real – as long as the family remains in possession. Indeed, if isolated, it reads as one of the great defences of the conservative country-house in a tradition that stretches back at least to Jonson's "Penshurst" – and even in context it is very powerful – too powerful, perhaps, for Etherege. His response has, after such an eloquent passage, something of a hollow ring as he makes a somewhat desperate declaration of faith:

> "All this sort of thing is beautiful; the family institution was beautiful in its day," ejaculated he aloud, to himself; not to his companion; "but it is a thing in the past. It is dying out in England; and as for ourselves, we never had it. Something better will come up; but as for this, it is past.';'     (XII, 187)

This may be the reasonable position, despite its vague Micawber-like hopefulness that something will turn up in the future, but Etherege can only hold to it if he can sustain a commitment to the communal notion of "ourselves", we Americans. His individual psychology, shaped by his childhood experiences, draws him very strongly towards what England seems to offer.

As Hawthorne worked his way into the fiction, this magnetic attraction of the country-house was presented even more strongly in terms of Etherege's desire for a home which would be at one and the same time origin and destination. The Hall

> seemed the ideal of home. The thought thrilled his bosom, that this was his home; – the home of the wild western wanderer, who had gone away centuries ago, and encountered strange chances, and *almost forgotten his origin*, but still kept a clue to bring him back, and had now come back and found all the original emotions safe within him. It even seemed to him, that by his kindred with those who had gone before – by the line of sensitive blood linking him with that first emigrant, he could remember all these objects . . . He spread out his arms in a kind of rapture, and exclaimed:–
> "Oh home, my home, my forefathers' home! I have come back to thee! The wanderer has come back!"     (XII, 259–60, my emphasis)

This equation of origins with destination in the single figure of "home" might merely seem a rapturous Romantic rhetoric – were it not for Etherege's self-knowledge which explains if it cannot justify this powerful, peculiar nostalgia. He is advised to leave – to turn his back on the seductions of England:

> "Gone hence!" repeated Etherege aghast. "I tell you – what I have hitherto hardly told to myself – that all my dreams, all my wishes hitherto, have looked forward to precisely the juncture that now seems to be approaching. My dreaming childhood dreamt of this. If you know anything of me, you know how I sprang out of mystery, akin to none, a thing concocted out of the

elements, without visible agency – how, all through my boyhood, I was alone; how I grew up without a root, yet continually longing for one – longing to be connected with somebody – and never feeling myself so. Yet there was ever a looking forward to this turn on which I now find myself. If my next step were death, yet while the path seemed to lead onward to a certainty of establishing me in connection with my race, I would yet take it. I have tried to keep down this yearning, to stifle it, annihilate it, with making a position for myself, with *being my own past*, but I cannot overcome this natural horror of being a creature floating in the air, attached to nothing; nor this feeling that there is no *reality* in the life and fortunes, good or bad, of a being so unconnected. There is not even a grave, not a heap of dry bones, not a pinch of dust, with which I can claim connection, unless I find it here.                    (XII, 57–58, my emphasis)

This is a moving and brilliant passage in its confession that there is a powerful truth of private desire as well as a reasonable public truth, in its account of the attempts to repress that private desire, those "dreams," and in its confession that Etherege sees himself as a manufactured man ("concocted" almost suggests Frankenstein's laboratory), rather than organically grown (so to speak), a man who fears that to float free may be to make oneself too much the victim of random forces. It is a bitter irony that this private desire is not a wish to assert the validity of the claims of the subjective self for self-definition but rather a desire to be publicly, historically placed in a genealogical line which will confer an identity on the too isolated, too fragile self. A sense of one's own reality (as so often in Hawthorne) is here felt to be dependent on thinking that one has a place in a history larger than the history of a single isolated self. To be one's own ancestor ("being my own past") may be a magnificent ambition but (for Etherege) it is harder to live than to respect. The irony that Etherege fears that he cannot "create" (so to speak) a past but is deterministically defined by the past that he has experienced is another formulation of the problem with which Hawthorne is so often concerned – the desirability of a revolutionary rupture with the past and the impossibility of such a break. (It is, surely, no accident that the man who proudly announced "Moi, je suis mon ancêtre" was Junot, one of Napoleon's Marshals, and thus a beneficiary of the French Revolution.)

That task of being self-historicizing connects with the difficulties of being an American. At some points Etherege's position might be expressed like this: I think I (ought to) want to be an American – but can I? To be an American is certainly shown as a complex fate here – and Etherege's fate suggests that it may be harder than Henry James imagined to fight against a superstitious valuation of Europe:

> "But what do I mean to do?" said he to himself, stopping short and still looking at the old house. "Am I ready to give up all the actual life before me for the sake of taking up with what I feel to be a less developed state of human life?

"Would it not be better for me to depart now, to turn my back on this flattering prospect? I am not fit to be here – I so strongly susceptible of a newer, more stirring life than these men lead; I, who feel, that whatever the thought and cultivation of England may be, my own countrymen have gone forward a long, long march beyond them, not intellectually, but in a way that gives them a further start. If I come back hither, with the purpose to make myself an Englishman – especially an Englishman of rank and hereditary estate – then for me America has been discovered in vain, and the great spirit that has been breached into us is in vain; and I am false to it all!"                    (XII, 281)

Here, the claims of time and space conflict: Etherege's American life may be potentially before him but actually he confronts, is before, (and is drawn towards) the physical embodiment of the best that England has to offer in the material form of the old house. And here he seems to be conscious of the danger of splitting the "I" of himself off from the "we" of America yet to be nearly powerless in the face of the mansion. It is a nice if unkind irony to make Etherege officially an American ambassador (even if it is to a minor German court) when he is considering whether he is spiritually an American, or a traitor to that last best hope of mankind. The passage just quoted continues with first a very long sentence of which I give less than half – and which begins with a very important word:

> But again came silently swelling over him like a flood all that ancient peace, and quietude, and dignity, which looked so stately and beautiful as brooding round this old house; all that blessed order of ranks, that sweet superiority, and yet with no disclaimer of common brotherhood, that existed between the English gentleman and his inferiors . . . What could there be in the wild, harsh, ill-concocted American approach to civilization which could compare with this? What to compare with this juiciness and richness? What other men had ever got so much out of life as the polished and wealthy Englishmen of to-day? What higher part was to be acted, than seemed to lie before him, if he willed to accept it?                    (XII, 281–2)

The point about America being discovered in vain is to be taken very seriously – the more seriously because Etherege here is taking the English gentry at their own valuation far too easily. He is questioning the whole project of America as he opposes the apparent peace of England, that ideological unity among the gentry, "that seeming taking in of all that was desirable in life" to American life, marked by "the fierce conflict of our embittered parties." (This English charm, incidentally, makes the pensioner figure a *very* enigmatic figure. If he is the true heir – and knows it – what is he doing subsisting on English charity and not claiming the estate? I wish I knew – and suspect that at this stage Hawthorne felt the same).

There is a further turn of the screw applied by Hawthorne – in addition to the possibility or probability that Etherege may not be the heir he so deeply at one level of his being desires to be. Cruelly, Hawthorne suggests that what Etherege mistakes for his innate Englishness may (to an objective observer) be rather a proof of his Americanness:

> He fancied himself strangely wonted, already, to the house; as if his every part and peculiarity had at once fitted into its nooks, and corners, and crannies; but, indeed, his mobile nature and active fancy were not entirely to be trusted in this matter; it was perhaps his American faculty of making himself at home anywhere, that he mistook for the feeling of being particularly at home here.
>
> (XII, 285)

Whether "the new American" is "stronger in him than the hereditary Englishman" may make little practical difference if Etherege cannot tell which is which.[13] It may be not only more difficult to define and evaluate "home" than the claimant realizes but also it may be hard if not impossible to recognize it – and, if Hawthorne's argument is extended, there may be no such place. Yet this idea is obviously dangerous for Hawthorne: if he entirely subverts and dissolves the idea of "home" as something locatable, then he comes dangerously close to destroying an important part of his subject.

Etherege, poor fellow, is himself highly ambivalent about his situation when he is actually staying in the Hall. It is one thing to make a free choice between two ways of life or even to be divided between what one desires and what one knows one ought to desire. It is another to feel freedom slipping away:

> he was frightened to perceive what a hold the place was getting upon him . . . and how, in no place that he had known, had he had such a home-like feeling. To be sure, poor fellow, he had no earliest home except the almshouse. (XII, 298)

He fears that he will find the "fettering honour" of the life of the Hall will (if accepted) "bind him hand and foot." Perhaps the comforts of continuity have a darker side. Yet the Hall cannot quickly be dismissed in the name of liberty for it is possible that it embodies that crucial if problematic quality that so concerned Hawthorne – reality: "the mansion itself was like dark-colored experience, the reality; the point of view where things were seen in their true lights." This is, it is true, only a possible version but if it is "the true world, all outside of which was delusion" (XII, 299) then Etherege may feel that morally he should not leave. As we shall see, this anticipates a passage in the Elixir of Life material where Hawthorne speculates on the problem of the perception of reality – and also a passage where Septimius Felton states that is is "the snake-like doubt that thrusts out its head that gives us a glimpse of reality" though he is more confident and wants to privilege such glimpses: "Surely such moments are a hundred times as real as the dull quiet moments of faith" (XIII, 11). Etherege considers that, "dreamlike" as the experience of the house is, here may be "the absolute truth" – whatever that is. If Hawthorne had held to his plans, Etherege would have had a rude awakening. He would turn out not to be the heir "and Etherege finds himself at once deprived of all kindred and left in a truly American condition" (XII, 233). Getting the heroine out of this would be small comfort for this picture of the existential loneliness of modernity. Unless that relationship was greatly developed (and I don't see much evidence that Hawthorne intended this), the girl would have been clearly and cruelly a consolation prize. Indeed, the juvenile female lead plays virtually no part in *Etherege* easy though such a figure would be to produce.

Here to be deprived of all kindred is to be displaced from history but the problem of situating the self in a wider history is not confined to that moment of disenchantment. After the Italianate squire (with the good English name of Brathwaite) has drugged the claimant to get him either permanently or temporarily out of the way, he is taken to a secret chamber. This seems not so much a Gothic moment but rather an opportunity to get Etherege to ask himself not so much the conventional question of "Where am I?" nor even "Who am I?" – but the more interesting "When am I?" It is clearly a question that matters a great deal to Hawthorne. In *Grimshawe*, he advances the moment when the claimant can ask the question – and complicates his sense of his place (or rather places) in history. There he turns up in the Hospital – an unchanged three-hundred-year-old charity – after being shot. There Hawthorne makes great play with the idea of repetition and doubling. The claimant in his semi-delirium thinks himself at one and the same "time" back in the English historical past *and* back in his own childhood in an institution. In *Etherege*, Hawthorne had not developed that concern with repetition and a virtually simultaneous sense of experiencing the two pasts so far. He merely remarks that had "the scene of the story been laid three hundred years ago" he need not have changed a particle in the scene that confronts Etherege's idea of a part of Europe. But when Brathwaite drugs Etherege, the claimant feels as though he had broken free from his temporal and historical setting – at first "willing . . . to keep it uncertain whether he were not back in America, and in his boyhood, and all other subsequent impressions a dream or a prophetic vision." But along with this "phantasmagoria" of his past, he subsequently wonders if he has not been (like a sensitive and intelligent Rip van Winkle) cast forward into the historical future:

> What if all things, that were extant when he went to sleep, had passed away, and he were waking now in another epoch of time! Where was America, and the republic in which he hoped for such great things? Where England? had she stood it better than the republic? (XII, 309)

Significantly even in his drugged state Etherege's initial concern is with a public future. Though he does wonder about the estate, that is dismissed: "Poor, petty interests of a single day, how slight!" But Hawthorne is more interested in the English past rather than an international future for Etherege sees an old man (immured for reasons I will discuss later), who appears to the still dazed claimant as "the old family personified" (XII, 311), and we get a long speculative paragraph which ranges through English history. This scene reads very much as an experiment at an ending. It is obviously intended as a parallel and contrast with the scene that, so to speak, introduced Etherege to one kind of English history – his experience of an ancient, unchanged Elizabethan charity to which he has been brought unconscious after having been mysteriously subjected to "intentional" "great bodily harm" (XII, 131). In both cases the dazed Etherege initially feels himself temporally disorientated. In the first case, he felt "that he had somehow gone astray into the past." In the second, he is uncertain whether he is in the past or the future – "put out of time, as it were" (XII, 134, 310). In both cases he confronts a figure who does not seem to belong to the modern world:

> It was an elderly, and venerable looking man, with a skull cap on his head, beneath which descended some silvery curls and fell upon his shoulders, and this, with a beard long and white, made him resemble an ancient palmer. His dress had a singular correspondence with the antique walls and furniture of the room. (XII, 133)

> [H]e seemed to be sensible, that, in a high-backed chair, . . . sat a figure in a long robe; a figure of a man with snow-white hair and a long beard, who seemed to be gazing at him, quietly, as if he had been gazing a hundred years.

> [T]here was an influence as if this old man belonged to some other age and category of man than he was now amongst.

> His garb might have been of any time, that long, loose robe that enveloped him. (XII, 310, 311)

Though Etherege does not know it when he encounters them, both are, in a sense, "heirs." The pensioner in the Hospital is (probably) the true heir: the aged gentleman in the secret chamber is the "heir" on the English side, kept here partly out of his sense of guilty danger, partly so that the Italianate squire can guiltily enjoy the fruits of the estate, and partly as the revenge of the Doctor who had brought up Etherege. He dies when Etherege speaks his name and the name of someone he feared (probably the Doctor) "in the most violent emotion of terror and rage . . . as if he saw before him that stern face that had . . . so fearfully avenged the crime that he had committed" (xii, 314). Etherege is rescued from the chamber by the pensioner who knows its secret:

> "And who are you who know it?" asked Etherege, surprised.
> "He whose ancestors taught him the secret – who has had it handed down to him these two centuries, and now only with regret yields to the necessity of making it known."
> "You are then the heir!" said Etherege.
> In that gloomy room, beside the dead old man, they looked at him, and saw a dignity beaming on him, covering his whole figure, that broke out like a lustre at the close of day.                    (xii, 323)

But this is, of course, not the end of this draft of the American claimant material – even though it may well have been an experiment at a conclusion. There are another twenty pages to come and Hawthorne immediately continues beyond this "ending":

> Try back again; – Raise the curtain as before, and discover the Doctor's study at the corner of the Charter-street Burial ground; the Doctor is there, with two children.                    (xii, 323)

We then get thirteen pages of Hawthorne discussing plot possibilities, followed by half a dozen or so pages of meditative narrative in which Hawthorne imagines various stages of the earlier life of the man in the secret chamber – an experience which "seems to me like entering a deep recess of my own consciousness, a deep cave of my own nature; so much have I thought of it" (xii, 336). *Etherege*, then, remains very obviously unfinished and Hawthorne breaks off at a point where there seems very little pointing to a conclusion. However, the question remains whether he stopped because he had written himself into a corner or whether he broke off to begin *Grimshawe* because he at least thought he had solved the plot problems. The common critical consensus has been that the whole project was doomed. I cannot share that confidence in Hawthorne's lack of ability, and think it is worth looking at what the problems were and what Hawthorne worried about.

Of course it may be that Hawthorne was so ambivalent about the issues he attempted to confront that he could not generate a narrative nor establish the meaningful structure a plot necessarily implies – and some of the refinements on ambivalences and ambiguities to which I have tried to draw attention may appear to support this idea. It may also be that Hawthorne knew what he wanted to say all right but could not find adequate (narrative) symbols in a way that could be embodied in the sort

of fiction he thought he ought to write. There is some evidence which
supports this. Here, for example:

> When Etherege appears, he should set some old business in motion . . . What
> can that be? how can it appear as if dead men's business, that had been buried
> with them, come to life again, and had to be finished now? Truly this is hard;
> here's the rub; and yet without it, the story is meagre and barren. (XII, 197–8)

There is no need to show that Hawthorne believed in the power of the
past to irrupt into and shape the present – even if one can argue as to how
far he regretted or celebrated that power. In any case, he feels the
omnipresence of this idea that he donates one of its clearest expressions to
the Italian/English villain:

> "We cannot tell when a thing is really dead; it comes to life, perhaps in its old
> shape, perhaps in a new and unexpected one; so that nothing really vanishes
> out of the world. I wish it did."                                              (XII, 284)

The problem is to find something that embodies this idea in narrative
form – a problem that has carried over from *The Ancestral Footstep*. The
plague pit which, when reopened, lets loose its fatal disease again may be
a very adequate image for the possibly dangerous consequences of the
claimant's actions – but it is only an image. One cannot imagine him
with a spade.

It was not a problem confined to this strand of the narrative – nor
Hawthorne's only difficulty. Postponing for the moment consideration
of some of the other problems that he had with the pensioner/real heir
figure, there was the question of how what he stands for is to be
embodied in a story:

> [T]he character needs an exponent – something to represent and symbolize it
> . . . [T]here must be something in this old man, that shall put to shame
> hereditary distinctions, and make the reader feel that he must have stooped
> from a position of higher dignity, had he taken up the rank he had inherited. It
> is not possible to work this out; the idea does not take to itself representative
> form.                                                                          (XII, 219)

Here too Hawthorne is in no doubt about what he wants to say, nor does
he abandon this idea about the role of the pensioner within the web of the
plot, but the terms he uses are revealing about his consciousness of what
the difficulties were and what kind of story he wished to tell.
"Exponent" is a surprisingly technical word – and unusual in this sense.
The significant phrase, however, is the almost Jamesian "representative
form." The idea he wishes to convey is clear enough but the problem
seems to be how to make it part of a narrative without too crudely
thrusting the meaning on the reader. It is a problem that confronts him

repeatedly and from different angles – and shows how uninterested he was in merely moralizing and how conscious he was of the technical questions involved in writing fictions:

> The old Doctor's spider's web must of course have a signification; it signifies a plot in which his art has involved the story and every individual actor; he has caught them all, like so many flies; nor are they set at liberty by the death of the magician who originally enthralled them. This is good, as an unshaped idea; but how is it to be particularized & put in action?                    (XII, 287)

Here, the process is partially reversed: first, there is the (fictional) fact of the Doctor's pet spider and its web, then secondly the web as symbol – and then the hard part. How is it to take its proper place in the narrative? The idea has to become an action. (The whole problem of what to do with the Bloody Footstep is related to these difficulties: it is such a tempting and promising looking symbol – but how is Hawthorne to put it into action, make it take "representative form" – especially as there are so many possibilities?)[14] Later, when discussing a plot problem (which arises because he had changed the character of the Doctor from good to bad and has to do with his desire for revenge and his means of achieving that revenge), Hawthorne writes "Then he turns all the resources of art and ingenuity to avenge himself and this man and his whole race. How easy to say such things!" (XII, 325) Yet again Hawthorne is quite clear about what he wants to say, and unclear how to construct a story which will satisfactorily "narrativize" such sayings, such meanings.

Hawthorne, however, did not give up, and the criticism that he could not find adequate story-shaped symbols is too easy. No doubt he did find it extremely difficult, partly due to his high standards and sophisticated consciousness of the demands of a story: he appears to want his meanings to be absorbed into the narrative as fully as they are in a parable like that of "The Good Samaritan" and also to make *The American Claimant* a fiction of debated ideas. And while he did not succeed for reasons outside his control, his experimental investigations of what will satisfy his demand on his narrative are revealing not only about his ideas about the art of fiction but also his ideas about history. For instance, the passage about the Doctor, the web and the plot continues

> Thus, for instance. It must be an ancient story, certainly; something coming down from the days of the Bloody Footstep; some business which was left unsettled by the sudden disappearance of the original emigrant to America. It must relate to property; because nothing else survives in this world. Love grows cold and dies; hatred is pacified by annihilation.                    (XII, 287)

It is a chilling statement in its acknowledgement of the historical power of materialism – and it reads, perhaps, as though it was going to be a nugget of sad wisdom which could take its place in the narrative. Yet it is more: Hawthorne works on and around the idea – and solves part of his problem as he investigates and rejects alternatives. "Could there be," he continues, "a document or record" containing a clue to some valuable object "which each succeeding heir reads; and is immediately smitten with insane desire . . . to obtain?" This will not do, he decides – buried treasure or anything of that sort is boring and inappropriate. "It awakens an unhallowed ambition . . . for something that ought not to be – cannot be possessed." That is better – and Hawthorne then sees another connection which has to be made: "The Doctor must then have an agent in England . . . who has been taken possession of by the subtlety and force of the Doctor's character, and continues to do his will even after he has been dead twenty years" (XII, 287). The idea of the agent is not a complete solution for Hawthorne has to work out, for example, a way the Doctor can exercise remote control on his loyal puppet from across the sea, and, indeed, beyond the grave but it is an important step in the process that he had been musing over.

As the historical commentary tells us, there are nine meditative passages in *Etherege* (XII, 98–9, 114–5, 122–8, 195–208, 218–34, 262–9, 285–93, 323–5). There is nothing like this in bulk or tone in *Grimshawe* (which helps support my case that the problems had been very largely solved). The one passage in *Grimshawe* is short (440–1) and is mainly composed of fairly trivial notes of the aide-memoire kind. Even though this last version breaks off shortly after the claimant had arrived in the alms-house, by the time this stage had been reached in *Etherege*, there had already been three passages of more or less serious meditation. And Hawthorne had made in *Grimshawe* a crucial change in the Doctor's character (from a benevolent to a malevolent figure) – a change which helps with many if not most of the difficulties. I shall try to follow Hawthorne's thinking through, beginning with the Doctor – though it is, of course, impossible to focus exclusively on one character, as when the conception of one character changes, the whole fictional world necessarily has to take on a new shape.

As we have seen, the introduction of Etherege's childhood with the Doctor had the substantial advantage of making Etherege's intense desire for a lineage and a home understandable. But Hawthorne was not satisfied with this: "A deeper life should be given to the Doctor, who has no real connection with the story." At this point, Hawthorne considered giving him a brother in England, a man with a past, a speculator, but now a pensioner in the Elizabethan Hospital: "It shall have been one of his schemes to transfer the heirdom of this old English to the American descendant" (XII, 116), perhaps because he feels remorse for having defrauded Etherege's father. At this stage, the claimant was obviously to be the true heir who should do the decent thing and renounce the English estate in the name of American independence. But as Hawthorne worked on, the pensioner as brother came to seem less attractive – especially as Hawthorne was more and more drawn to the idea that Etherege should not be the heir. One consequence of this was that the pensioner then would need to be virtuous rather than a man with a past:

> Here, then, is a meek, patient, unpretending, wise old man, who develops peculiarities which draw the attention of profound observers upon him; though others see little that is remarkable in him. This is a better aspect than what I at first thought of. Follow out this clue, stubbornly, stubbornly.
>
> (XII, 199)

As the clue is pursued, the idea grows: perhaps the pensioner should be the true heir – though this gives the writer possible difficulties: it is one thing to have one person fly to America and much harder to think of a scenario in which two brothers flee at the same time. Still, "Not yet, 'Eureka'; but it will be so. The old man is conscious of being the heir, but chooses quietly, and without eclat, to give up his claim. He too knows of the flaw in Etherege's title" (XII, 205).

If the pensioner is to be the true heir, then "I have not sufficiently provided for him" (XII, 218). If "I cannot consent to such a degradation as is implied in his seeking the estate" (XII, 223), then motives must be contrived for rejecting the estate and for being a pensioner of an English charity. If he discovered his lineage through the agency of the doctor, the Doctor then "must have a great agency in these doings, both of the Pensioner and Etherege, making tissues of cobweb out of men's life threads; he must have the air, in the Romance, of a sort of magician, without being called so; and even after his death, his influence must still be felt. Hold on to this" (XII, 224). Hawthorne must have been pleased to be able to weave his web imagery together with the threads image that had so obsessed him in *The Ancestral Footstep*. More importantly, if this idea of the Doctor's pervasive influence is to be held to, then, maybe, he must be darkened: "Perhaps the Doctor himself might be an English misanthrope, who had spite against the family" (XII, 224). This is to be a crucial shift in emphasis – though Hawthorne only gradually realizes how useful an idea it will prove. Initially, it makes it logical to have Etherege "an American son of nobody." This has a nice moral with it too: "we are to give up all those prejudices of birth and blood which have been so powerful in past ages." If "there shall be but vague reason to believe that Etherege is of" the true descent, then he is to be rebuked "for giving up the noble principle that a man ought to depend on his own individuality, instead of deriving anything from his ancestors" (XII, 225). Of course, there is a small difficulty here: how far can Etherege (or anyone) be said to be in a position to construct his independent individuality? But that is a question with which Hawthorne struggles throughout his fiction. In the immediate context there is another problem: what then is to be done with the idea that the pensioner learnt of his right to the estate from the Doctor – and why should he have encouraged Etherege to believe himself the rightful heir? Here Hawthorne rather weakly suggests that the Doctor merely informed the pensioner of the possibility of the relationship and did not know just how good his claim was "due to his lack of acquaintance with the traditions of this pauper' (XII, 225). He admits that "It is a snarled skein, truly," but cheers himself up: "I half fancy there is a way to unravel the threads, by dint of breaking one or two" (XII, 225).

The answer to Etherege's ill-fated belief in a noble lineage can easily come – if the Doctor is further darkened: he "shall have been at deadly enmity with the holder" (XII, 225) of the English estate when a young man. If he hates the family as well as the individual, then "it will be yet sweeter revenge to substitute some nameless child for their long descended heir." Yet sweeter, because he knows of the family legend that the senior branch of the family is in America. Failing to find one of those, "(being an unscrupulous man) he finds this boy . . . in the alms-house, . . . of untraceable origin" (XII, 226). This and more (especially about the matter of "discrepant traditions" [XII, 228]) seems to have given Hawthorne confidence: "To-morrow, arrange chain of events" (XII, 229).

And so he does. He harks back to the beginning again and sketches the principal characters. The doctor is not to be merely a villain: "Something high and noble must be put into the man, together with morbidness and poison" (XII, 229). The introduction of a girl, a distant relation adopted by the Doctor, helps – as well as preparing the story for the later love interest if that should be needed. The reader "must see reason to doubt, very early, or to be puzzled, whether or not the boy is the heir" (XII, 230). The death of the Doctor will play its part in keeping the reader off balance: "His death-scene shall make it appear that he had something on his mind, which he had half a mind to reveal, but yet he could not bear to give up a revengeful purpose; neither at the moment of death, can he do what remains needful towards carrying it into execution." This is not "a portentous struggle and uncertainty" merely to add to "the mystification of the plot" (XII, 231). His failure to do "what remains needful" is crucial as otherwise there is a danger that Etherege will immediately rush off to England instead of making his own way in the world. But all is not yet clear sailing – even though he has connected the Italo-English incumbent to a wider English history by having him come from a branch of the family which emigrated with the

Stuarts – a nice development given the importance of the English Civil War in explaining why another branch (or branches) had come to America.

After a narrative passage, Hawthorne returns to the problem of the Doctor's connections with England, and, in a passage already referred to, to the question of the English agent. He is crucial if the Doctor is to enjoy his revenge while he is alive and while Etherege is too young to go to England, while he is still experimenting with ways of being American. But Hawthorne then has to think of something for him to do. What can this revenge be? After some extravagant and confessedly absurd notions, Hawthorne has the barest flicker of an idea: "Could there be, through all these times, some person hidden in the old house?" (XII, 288). At first sight, this presents more problems than it solves. What can he have done and how can he have been persuaded to immure himself? And why is the agent so loyal to the Doctor as it is hardly enough to make him evil? That last question is easily (if absurdly) answered: the Doctor has brought him back to life after being hanged. But the other questions are not so easy to solve – even if Hawthorne is willing to risk absurdities. A tentative explanation of the Doctor's hatred of the English squire he knew in his youth is advanced:

> One great point must be the power of the old Doctor's character, operating long years after his death, just as when he was alive. The prisoner should have been very wicked, and worthy of his doom; seducing the Doctor's young wife, and taking her home into his mansion.                    (XII, 289)

That, coupled with class resentment may be enough – and *Grimshawe* stands in evidence that he expanded on the class theme that is merely hinted at here: "He is a man in humble life, resenting the wrongs done by those hereditarily above him" (XII, 292).

The attraction for the Doctor of having the hated squire locked up is clear – especially as his hate has extended to the whole family. Through his agent he can let incumbents know that they hold the estate at his pleasure – while holding Etherege in reserve, as it were. But this must mean that the incumbents must not be men of integrity as, if they were, they would hardly be willing to remain in possession. And so it proves:

> There is the house, with its hidden tenant in it, who throws a gloom all over it, and imbues it with horrors . . . A change has taken place in the characters of the two persons who have inherited it; both have been in great pecuniary distress; so that it required superhuman virtue to make the disclosure that would have deprived them of their property. One has hitherto been a retired man; he becomes madly dissipated, a drunkard, and dies in delirious fever occasioned by drink. Another was an idle gambler, a man of pleasure, a vaurien, a blackguard; this is the Italian, and he adopts recluse habits.          (XII, 292)

This has an additional advantage in explaining the psychological pressures on the Italian/English incumbent which predisposes him to treat Etherege violently. No wonder, when he sees himself in danger of being dispossessed from an unexpected quarter, that he should wish Etherege out of the way and placed in the secret chamber along with the other "heir". But Hawthorne is still troubled by the problem of how to get the Doctor's enemy into the chamber – a problem that is related to problems of style and tone:

> Now, if this great bleakness and horror is to be underneath the story, there must be a frolic and dance of bacchanals all over the surface; else the effect will be utterly miserable. There may be a steam of horror escaping through safety-valves; but generally the tone must be joyous. (XII, 292)

The image of the bacchanals on the surface of the story is reminiscent of Hawthorne's interest in *The Marble Faun* in the carvings on Roman sarcophagi – and it is striking that he should at one and the same time hark back to the antique world and use the image of steam. Just how this would have been achieved given the story he had to tell is unclear if this was the form the story was to take:

> Introduce a chapter, early in the book – without saying where the scene is laid – in which the prisoner is represented in his secret room; make it as mysterious as possible. Then, before the close of the American part, another chapter; then after the arrival in England, another chapter; all developing the progressive state of the prisoner. The excellence of the execution must redeem all absurdities of the narrative – and it may. If we can once establish the prisoner in his dungeon, and keep him there a year, it would all be a matter of course that he should stay there; for the thought of going out would become a horror to him. (XII, 292–3)

No wonder that, in the final meditative passage, Hawthorne saw an important part for the female juvenile lead to play: "This girl must be cheerful, natural, reasonable, beautiful, spirited, to make up for the deficiencies of almost everybody else" (XII, 333). But in that final section, after having sketched out what is very clearly a draft of the beginning of *Grimshawe*, Hawthorne turned back to the difficulty of getting the Doctor's victim into the secret room.

That final section begins with what is pretty clearly a sketchy version of the opening of *Grimshawe*. But he quickly moves on to his great problem:

> Now what has been the motive for this man's leaving England and coming hither? He had saved an imperfectly hanged person and made him morally a slave; so far good; and he thus has an instrument ready to assist him in perpetrating any monstrosity. But what? Then he has been deeply wronged by a gentleman in his neighborhood; a man of wealth and rank, against whom he

> vows and executes a dire revenge. How? He must somehow subjugate that
> man, and make him a prisoner and a slave in spite of his rank, and in spite of
> being himself an inhabitant of another country. In what way?     (XII, 324)

He circles round and round the problem, depressing and amusing
himself with ludicrous notions, knowing what he wants but not how to
get it. Eventually he gets a "glimmering" not from the wildest Gothic
extravagances but from his own work: "One of the family to disappear,
of his own will, and to remain in seclusion; the story of Wakefield might
afford some hint of it" (XII, 327). Interestingly, Hawthorne is quite
convinced that there is no need to explain why the prisoner would
remain hidden – once he can be lured or forced into the chamber (and
this conviction may help us with "Wakefield"):

> There must be a motive, in the first place, strong enough to keep him secluded
> a week; then let him get out if he can. The fact should show that a strange
> repulsion – as well as a strong attraction – exists among human beings . . . It is a
> very common thing – this fact of a man's being caught and made prisoner by
> himself.                                                   (XII, 328)

He works on – and it is fascinating to see him gradually moving towards
his solution, experimenting extravagantly, rejecting inadequate notions,
laughing at his material and himself, giving mock-serious cries of
anguish, – until he finally gets close to what he wants:

> He might have seduced or broken the heart (which would be better) of the
> Doctor's sister. A quarrel ensues, in which he had reason to suppose that he has
> killed the Doctor, and that the law will be wreaked on him. He takes refuge in
> the secret chamber of the mansion, confiding himself to the care of this half-
> hanged man; who, being a devoted adherent of the Doctor, acts according to
> his instructions, and so makes him disgraced, his affections outraged, chooses
> to vanish from life, and departs for America, leaving no record behind him –
> no knowledge of where he is, except with this servant. He goes abroad, with
> the purpose of pursuing his revenge upon the whole race of his enemy; with
> this view, knowing the family history, he determines to raise up a false heir,
> who shall oust the present possessor.                         (XII, 329)

This does not give Hawthorne everything he wanted. Ideally, the
Doctor's revenge should have depended on "a knowledge of the history
of the family, and the character of its successive representatives" (XII,
325). But still we can't have everything and the real plot problem has
been solved – even if that solution doesn't carry as much thematic weight
as Hawthorne would have liked.

It seems quite clear to me that, when Hawthorne had found a way of
getting the Doctor's hated victim into the secret chamber, he felt that he
had now solved all the principal plot problems. Gone is the agonizing
over alternatives to be replaced by the tone of a writer tidying up before

getting down to writing the real story. In the next paragraphs, he goes straight to technical matters about the arrangement of the narrative. He plans a structure where he would cut between the American narrative and descriptions of the self-imprisoned victim – and, even after Etherege comes to England, that inter-cutting was to be preserved. And I would think that Hawthorne intended to parallel Etherege and the Doctor's victim: both were to be prisoners of illusion – illusions which rob them of any real direction in their lives: "Throughout life, still a purpose to emerge. This runs through the Romance like the vertebrae of the back-bone" (xii, 331). This is explicitly directed to the English character – but it is equally applicable to Etherege as it has to be if Hawthorne is to make it a structuring principle of the narrative, the skeleton of the story.

The tidying-up process continues. First Hawthorne deals with the juvenile female lead. Hawthorne has to work out an explanation for her to be in England, and after a few false starts has the beginning of a solution: "Well, she can be received in England by an old maiden relative, where she may live in a narrow way, sketching, and otherwise idly employing herself, and longing for the wide sphere that America opens to women." (xii, 332). He has to be careful: the heroine must not sink too low socially if Etherege is to marry her and she has to know the Pensioner. The first is taken care of by the aged female relative, the second requires very little agility. The problem that is more difficult is to find a way of declaring her Americanness:

> She has some peculiar little handiwork, which enables her to get a living; something that she had learnt in America. Indian manufactures, with beads? No. She sells Indian meal, done up in neat packages, for washing hands. Oh, the devil! (xii, 332)

Still, the tone of Hawthorne's prose suggests that this is a minor difficulty which can await the inspiration of the moment: "Something of wildness in her, intimating an origin not exactly normal, but yet nothing extravagant or unwomanly. The Indian beadwork may do" (xii, 333).

After having dealt with the heroine, Hawthorne very confidently turns to the pensioner, wrapping up the problems this character had earlier given him – and dismissing them: "Now for the old pensioner – his origin, pursuit, biography." He provides the pensioner with a family history, going back to the original American forebear who had been repudiated by the English side of the family who were then Catholics and who is equally disliked by American Puritans because of his religious position as "a preacher of a reformed doctrine, very like those of George Fox" (xii, 333). Obviously he needs to encounter the Doctor, the claimant as a child, and the heroine to be. Hawthorne finds a way of doing this (more fully spelt out in *Grimshawe*) and of accounting for his knowledge of his English heritage. Hawthorne ends this section by implying a connection between seventeenth century radicalism and nineteenth century transcendentalism:

> He might be a Fifth Monarchy man; that is to say, obedient to the higher law within himself, and rejecting human law when it interfered. In figure, Mr. Alcott.                                                    (XII, 335)

With the pensioner provided for, Hawthorne could afford to finish this final meditative passage – and he uses the last few pages of the *Etherege* fragment confidently anticipating a complete version of the American claimant story by writing two scenes of the figure of the isolated prisoner. He had earned the right to anticipate, for he had thought and fought his way through to a beginning, provided himself with the material and the structure of the middle of the story, and had at least sketched out the shape of an ending – an ending which bears every sign of being "not satisfactory to the natural yearnings of" nineteenth-century "novel-readers" (XII, 11) with its refusal of the plots of reconciliation and accommodation.

v

## Grimshawe (XII, 343–471)

> There is no remoteness of life and thought, no hermetically sealed seclusion, except, possibly, that of the grave, into which the disturbing influences of this war do not penetrate. Of course, the general heart-quake of the country long ago knocked at my cottage-door, and compelled me, reluctantly, to suspend the contemplation of certain fantasies, to which, according to my harmless custom I was endeavoring to give a sufficiently life-like aspect to admit of their figuring in a romance.[15]

This detailed commentary on some of the twists and turns of Hawthorne's struggles with his plot may have left the impression that plot complications had become so overwhelmingly important to him that thematic concerns had gone out of the window. Yet if the notes Hawthorne made to himself about the change in the character of the Doctor in *Etherege* are set beside the presentation of him in *Grimshawe*, it can be seen that the interlocking demands of narrative and theme have come together to provide a fairly coherent story. To recall the moment when Hawthorne began thinking about the crucial shift that would enable the American claimant story to take significant form, and to set the following passage beside the beginnings of *Grimshawe*, is to see how carefully he had absorbed his own meditations on the plot:

> Perhaps the Doctor himself might be an English misanthrope who had a spite
> against this family . . . He shall have meant Etherege as his tool, certainly; but in
> the end, he shall prove to have no ancestry, an American son of nobody . . .
> (XII, 224–5)

It was towards the end of *Etherege* that he saw his way more clearly:

> Try back again; – Raise the curtain, as before, and discover the Doctor's study
> in the old house at the corner of the Charter-street Burial ground . . . He . . .
> appears to be an Englishman . . . (XII, 323)

Hawthorne, in this last version of the claimant theme, begins by fleshing
out these instructions to himself. Here, Dr. Grimshawe brings up the
revised version of Etherege (now Edward Redclyffe) to be a gentleman
for very similar motives to those of Magwitch when he does the same for
Pip in *Great Expectations* – as a kind of revenge not so much on an
individual but on a class system which has victimized him:

> in the manner and matter of his talk, [there was] a certain hereditary reverence
> and awe, the growth of ages, mixed up with a newer hatred that impelled him
> to deface and destroy what, at the same time, his deepest impulse was to bow
> before. It was the feeling of a man lowly born when he contracts a hostility to
> his hereditary superior; in one way, being of a powerful, passionate nature,
> gifted with forces and ability far superior to that of the aristocrat, he might
> scorn him and feel able to trample upon him; in another, he had the same awe
> as a simple country boy feels of the magnate who flings him a sixpence, or
> shakes his horsewhip at him. Had the grim Doctor been an American, he
> might have had the vast antipathy to rank, without the sense of awe that made
> it so much more malignant; it required a low-born Englishman to feel the two
> together. (XII, 368)[16]

Passages like this indicate Hawthorne's remarkably sensitive intelligence
about the question of class. It is, significantly, not a radical or
revolutionary response: Grimshawe, even though he has come to
America, does not seem to conceive of a classless democracy. His
response is to manufacture an heir – and here the consciousness that
motivates such an action surely comes very close to what Nietzsche
identified as *ressentiment*. This shift in the doctor's character not only has
the advantage of giving him sound (if not good) motives for acting as he
does but also strengthens the psychological plausibility of the "heir's"
feelings and reactions – reinforced, it is worth noting, by his initial
dramatic experiences of England.

When little Ned asks "Dr. Grim" where he came from, he gets more
than he bargained for as an answer:

> "Out of the darkness and mystery, out of nothingness, out of a kingdom of
> shadows; out of dust, clay, impure mud, I think, and to return to it again. Out

> of a former state of being, whence we have brought a good many shadowy
> reflections, purporting that it was no very pleasant one. Out of a former life, of
> which this present one is the hell!"                                      (XII, 356)

After these pessimistic metaphysics comes the cruel stroke. Ned is a
foundling from the alms-house "and if ever hereafter you desire to know
your kindred, you may take your choice of the first man you meet" (XII,
357). Amends are made – but in a way which reinforces the power of the
grim doctor over the child's ideas of his identity:

> "If you must go on dreaming about your race, dream that you come of the
> blood of this being; for mean as his station looks, he comes of an ancient and
> noble race, and was the noblest of them all. Let me alone, Ned; and I shall spin
> out the web that must link you with that race."                          (XII, 359)

Again class complications occur, for the portrait that the Doctor shows
Ned is that of a bond servant with a noose round his neck: "it seemed the
representation of a man of no mark" but "the face of the portrait,
nevertheless, was beautiful, noble, though sad" (XII, 359). The effect of
the Doctor's words on Ned is to dislocate him from any secure sense of
an American identity:

> After what the Doctor had told him of his origin he had never felt any home
> feeling there; it seemed to him that he was wandering web [sic], which the
> wind had blown from afar.                                                (XII, 422)

Blown from England, he dreams and hopes. He felt that England and
only England could give him a firm sense of his own identity – and in this
he is contrasted to his play-mate Elsie, who identifies home as the house
of the grave-yard. Female "delusion" though Hawthorne insinuates it
may be, it is one she firmly holds to – and that key-word is repeated half a
dozen times in the short paragraph that describes her feelings about it
(XII, 431–2).

When Grimshawe dies, Ned tries to search for information about his
origins – but finds nothing:

> he was left with no trace of [his birth] except just so far as the alms-house
> whence the Doctor had taken him. There all traces of his name and descent
> vanished, just as if he had been made out of the air, as an aerolite seems to be,
> before it tumbles on the earth with its mysterious iron.                 (XII, 438)

It is a nice combination of the immaterial and the only too material.
Redclyffe's self has to be constructed around what the Doctor has told
him – and we do not need case histories to tell us that those who fear they
may be illegitimate give themselves distinguished genealogies. As an
adult (and I am confident that Hawthorne would have drawn upon this

passage from *Etherege* since it comes after his speculations about the consequences and advantages of darkening the Doctor's character), the would-be claimant still feels himself under that figure's power:

> He looked back through the vanished years to the time which he had spent with the old Doctor, and he felt unaccountably as if the mysterious old man were yet ruling him, as he did in his boyhood; as if his inscrutable, inevitable eye were upon him in all his movements; nay, as if he had guided every step that he took in coming hither, and were stalking mistily before him, leading him onward. (XII, 296)

It is, of course, not "unaccountable" to the reader of *Grimshawe*. The character muses about escape from the house of his "forefathers" – but, as Hawthorne insists, he would have to lose his desires, his "dreams" and the "recollections" that generate those desires before that could be possible. The "witchcraft" of the doctor may have been evaded by Redclyffe when a young man making his way in America – but it has infected him deeply "like an influenza that remains latent for years, and then breaks out in active disease" (XII, 296).

In *Grimshawe*, the American section is clearly dated. It is shortly after the American revolution – a revolution that signifies the coming of modernity as the gravedigger (an appropriate speaker) tells us:[17]

> since we are under the republic, we have given up remembering these old-world legends, as we used to. The newspapers keep us from talking in the chimney-corner; and so things go out of our minds. An old man, with his stories of what he has seen, and what his grandfather saw before him, is of little account since newspapers came up. (XII, 419)

It is not a romanticized revolution – except, perhaps, in so far as the young stranger, the Alcott figure (the pensioner to be), can be said to represent one strand in American life.[18] He makes the acquaintance of the Doctor in an anti-Tory riot, saving him from a beating-up if nothing worse by taking a blow by accident that was aimed at Grimshawe. It is the crowd that apparently represents America at this historical moment: "Had they been created for the moment; or were they fiends, sent by Satan in the likeness of a blackguard population?" Nothing so metaphysical – they are merely Americans: "There you might see the off-scourings of the recently finished war, old soldiers, rusty, wooden-legged; these sailors, ripe for any kind of mischief" (XII, 384). The stranger has been a schoolmaster but unable to control the children who are equally the products of history, "an unruly set, born of parents who have lived rough lives – born in war-time too, with the spirit of battle in them" (XII, 391). It is tempting to speculate that it was Hawthorne's fear of the civil war and its possible consequences which helped to cause this rather less than rapturous presentation of the first fruits of a fight for independence. Whatever the cause, it leaves Hawthorne with a problem that would have caused him considerable difficulty – if Redclyffe had been supposed finally to choose America over England. It looks as though Hawthorne meant either to return to *The Ancestral Footstep* and expand on the figure of the hero as a fitting missionary "of a new social faith" or (and I suspect this is much more likely) to leave him as an entirely isolated figure, developing a hint from *Etherege* – "a son of nobody, with all the world for his ancestry" (XII, 58, 229).

In any case, it is clear that the revolution has not solved the anxieties of how to locate oneself (and be placed) in a class society – especially for a Redclyffe with all his insecurities about his identity. Even when Redclyffe is still recovering from his injuries which have brought him to the Elizabethan Hospital, and meets the Warden for the first time, he "felt that the new-comer had not precisely the right idea as to his own position in life; he was addressing him most kindly, indeed, but as an inferior" (XII, 462). Fortunately, "his finely modulated voice" and a letter of credit for a substantial amount in the name of the Honorable Edward Redclyffe mean that he need not worry: the Warden (clever man) realizes that "it showed no ordinary ability and energy, for so young a man to have held such a position as this title denoted in fiercely contested struggles of the new democracy." Redclyffe has been perceived as distinct from other Americans ("the men branded sons of equality") – and the Warden gives him the significant title of "gentleman" (XII, 465, 6).

But what does the American gentleman encounter when he comes to England? There is nothing quite so menacing on his initial appearance in the English landscape as the passage in *Etherege*, where "there is a foreboding, a sense within us that this traveller is not going the right way" (XII, 131). However, like his predecessors in *The Ancestral Footstep* and *Etherege*, the claimant discovers that the apparent dreamy peace of the English countryside contains a violent surprise. In *Ancestral Footstep*, the squire, "mad with rage" (XII, 19), points a gun at him then decides to hit him with the butt – and, as I noted earlier, commits involuntary suicide, so to speak, when the gun goes off by accident. (This notion that the incumbent will do away with himself accidentally is never followed up – understandably. Satisfying though such a death might well be, it could only work in a narrative if the American was to inherit and if it was to be a short story). Etherege is, of course, the victim of a mystery assault. In *Grimshawe* it is the English spring-gun which gets Redclyffe – the sign of a social system which is willing to maim or kill at random to preserve the sacred life of English game from those Englishmen of too low a social status:

> "You had almost fallen a sacrifice . . . to the old preference which our English
> gentry have inherited from their Norman ancestors, of game to man."
>
> (XII, 463)

Pheasants before peasants, it seems – but that is not the only irony.
Redclyffe had been dreamily admiring the tameness and peacefulness of
English nature, and considering that here is a "Paradise for the birds"
(XII, 442). Perhaps it is – but each generation of pheasants gets an annual
rude dismissal from Paradise. However, the most significant point is
that, in each of the three versions of the claimant's tale, Hawthorne seems
to feel that "England" must do some violence to the claimant – and in
*Grimshawe* it is made very clear it is the social system which does the
violence.

As in *Etherege*, the violence is also a plot device to get the claimant into
the Hospital where his desire for passivity and his tendency to dream can
be given free rein – in a place where the past seems to have survived
unchanged into the present. The image of the electric wires, so prevalent
in *The Ancestral Footstep* here takes on a different significance (and I
would argue that its reappearance suggests that Hawthorne had carefully
re-read and rethought his earlier versions of this story):

> the electric wires, that had connected him with the battery of life, were broken
> for the time, and he did not feel the unquiet influence that kept everybody else
> in galvanic action. (XII, 458)

With the freedom of the sick-bed Redclyffe can escape, however
temporarily, from the pressures of the present into a "strange
illusiveness" (XII, 452), a double "consciousness" of two pasts, and, more
strongly, back in the historical past of England. His psychology in so far
as it has been structured by Dr. Grimshawe (which is very far)
predisposes him to see England *as* history – and we know from *The
English Notebooks* that Hawthorne saw the Hospital as "a kind of model
of [a] long past age," which has come "down into the midst of ours"
(July 1, 1855). Redclyffe has a multiplicity of roles to experiment with –
and he has, in a sense, to experiment to discover where, when and what
he is – important questions since he is "strongly tenacious of the actual"
with "a natural horror . . . of being seriously at odds . . . with the real
world about him" (XII, 450). In one way, he is a child again – only he is
wrapped in his sense of the past rather than a mother's arms: "I never
knew a mother's care . . . And since my boyhood, I have lived among
harsh men – a life of struggle and hard rivalry. It is good to find myself
here in the long past" (XII, 455). The pensioner, his nurse, has advised to
him to be "again a child" so that he can "be born anew." The question is
what is to be this new self? While in the Hospital, his self-treatment has
been to lie in the womb of time – an experience of the past which he half

knows to be an illusion, one where he is at once a spectator and an actor in
a work of fiction:

> He . . . would willingly accept the idea, that some spell had transported him out
> of an epoch, in which he had led a brief [life of] trouble, of battle, of mental
> strife, success, failure, all equally feverish and unsatisfactory, into some past
> century, where the business was to rest; to drag on dreamy days, looking at
> things through half-shut eyes; into a limbo where things were put away; shows
> of what had once been, now somehow parted, and still maintaining a sort of
> half-existence, a serious mockery; a state likely enough to exist just a little apart
> from the actual world, if we only know how to find our way into it. Scenes
> and events that have once stained themselves, in deep colours, on the curtain
> that Time hangs around us, to shut us in from eternity, cannot be quite effaced
> by the succeeding phantasmagoria, and sometimes, by a palimpsest, show
> more strongly than they.                                    (XII, 452–3)

This is, surely, an important passage. Redclyffe gives his assent to this
role which is strikingly reminiscent of the kind of assent Hawthorne
wanted the reader to give his Romances. And is not the past here very
like "the neutral territory" of "The Custom-House" – "where the
Actual and the Imaginary may meet, and each imbue itself with the
nature of the other"? The second sentence is almost a classic statement of
the power of the past in an individual consciousness to penetrate the
"phantasmagoria" of the present, where the script of the past, the
"palimpsest", insists on being read in the present, and exerting an
authority on the present.

The kind of rebirth which Redclyffe experiences is only too likely to
confirm him in his desire for the estate and the ancestry that possession
would give him. Despite his achievements, he seems to have no desire to
be his own ancestor: "The unknown boy has come to be no
undistinguished man! His ancestry, should he ever reveal himself to
them, need not blush for the poor foundling" (XII, 457). It is not only a
result of what the doctor has made of him. He also has recognised in the
figure of the pensioner the mysterious transcendental stranger of his
youth- and his virtue, coupled with his ability to show enough of a tie
with England to live off a three hundred year old charity with a clear
conscience, suggests indirectly but strongly to Redclyffe that his claim
on the estate is a morally valid as well as a deeply psychologically
attractive project – the project that has brought him, "a republican,
hither as to an ancestral centre" (XII, 461).

*Grimshawe* breaks off with Redclyffe feeling that his America may
have nothing so "enticing" to offer him as the Warden's library, and
musing on how much trouble would be saved by taking his former
public career "not as dealing with things yet malleable, but with fossils,
things that had had their life, and were now unchangeable and recorded

here" (xii, 469). If only American political history would become fixed
and safely dead, its memory preserved in an English gentleman's library!
And there, unfortunately, Hawthorne leaves him – with the claimant
entertaining himself by translating "Yankee Doodle" into a dead
language he had learnt from the grim Doctor. It does not bode well for
the young American – especially when Hawthorne has told us that the
Warden of the Hospital, that representative of old England, has
previously amused himself by translating "Mother Goose" into Latin
and Greek.

If I am correct in my hypothesis that the central plot problems of *The
American Claimant Manuscripts* had been solved, then it is Hawthorne's
will rather than his literary ability that fails him at this point in the
narrative – that will sapped, as I have tried to argue, by the Civil War.
This is not so much a matter of the psychological pressures he may have
felt, painful though these probably were, but rather that the fiction's
relationship to the actual historical world became necessarily unstable as
that world itself became unstable. For example, Hawthorne repeatedly
tried to use the English Civil War to explain the departure of the English
heir (or heirs) to America, employing a family who were ideologically
divided to explore the ways in which a split in political loyalties could be
paralleled by a split in a private family. The strength of the contrast is lost
if he went to a country which, whatever its history may have been, at the
very moment that Hawthorne is writing, is suffering the biggest,
bloodiest civil war in history – where, indeed, it looks as though there
may be not one United States for the claimant to represent. (At one point
in *Etherege*, Hawthorne breaks off to doodle, so to speak, with various
names. He ends by writing "President Buchanan of dis United States"
[xii, 220]). No doubt there is a black comedy to be written with this
material – but that would not and could not be the novel Hawthorne had
been wrestling with since 1858. And if, as Turner tells us in his
biography, Hawthorne was disappointed in English reaction to the Civil
War, then England too may no longer be what Hawthorne needed it to
be for his fiction to work, to take a purchase on reality. Turner quotes
from a letter to Harriet Beecher Stowe: John Bull was "a hardened and
villainous hypocrite," caring "nothing for or against slavery, except as it
gave him a vantage-ground on which to parade his own virtue and sneer
at our iniquity."[19] The England of the fiction was a more complex and
multi-valued entity. Such reasons are, no doubt, not the only ones. Such
concerns as appear in *The American Claimant Manuscripts* and are
developed in *The Elixir of Life Manuscripts* show that there were
temptations which, when taken with the felt pressures of history, made
the move on virtually irresistible. Still, that passage from the introduction to *Our Old Home* seems to me to be profoundly revealing in the

parallels it suggests between fiction and history and Hawthorne's fears of "a Limbo where our nation and its polity may be as literally the fragments of a shattered dream as my unwritten Romance" (v, 4).

If this line of argument about the pressures of contemporary history is anything like correct, then "Chiefly About War Matters, By A Peaceable Man" should be able to be read as a conclusion or, perhaps, as an obituary to the American Claimant materials. It frequently has the tone of an ironic black comedy. Take, for example, the intriguing story that Hawthorne had heard from Monckton Milnes: "He said . . . that in the next voyage of the Mayflower, after she carried the pilgrims, she was employed in transporting a cargo of slaves from Africa – to the West Indies, I suppose. This is a queer fact, and would be nuts for the Southern people" (*English Notebooks*, September 22, 1854). He does more with it in "War Matters":

> There is an historical circumstance, known to few, that connects the children of the Puritans with these Africans of Virginia, in a very singular way. They are our brethren, as being lineal descendants from the Mayflower, the fated womb of which, in her first voyage, sent forth a brood of Pilgrims on Plymouth Rock, and, in a subsequent one spawned slaves upon the Southern soil, – a monstrous birth, but with which we have an instinctive sense of kindred, and so are stirred by an irresistible impulse to attempt their rescue, even at the cost of blood and ruin. The character of our sacred ship, I fear, may suffer a little by this revelation; but we must let her white progeny offset her dark one, – and two such portents never sprang from an identical source before.
> (12, 319)

"War Matters" is, of course, as this little fable suggests, a fascinating piece of prose in its own right. Product of a tour taken in March 1862, like many another war report throughout history, it was liable to be censored. Here the censorship is the product of editorial sensitivity rather than governmental activity – but Hawthorne turned this "editing" into something of an ironic triumph by anticipating (in most cases) that sensitivity, writing his own footnotes which subversively draw attention to the gaps and silences in his text – as well as rebuking himself very firmly for his failures in maintaining the correct ideological positions. It is a deliberately double-voiced performance – at once the voice of the "peaceable man" (who would have been known to be Hawthorne) and an ironic parody of the official editorial voice – though the wit does not mask the seriousness of the question as to how a writer is to find a role, or, indeed, a voice at such a moment of historical crisis. It would be interesting to know how Fields read Hawthorne's adoption of the editorial role as the question is one that Hawthorne can only be asking himself and (possibly) Fields – for the first readers would not all have realized that Hawthorne was in part acting as a ventriloquist. He manages to catch to perfection the obtuse tone of a bemused but loyal censorship. After Hawthorne has asked whether it is possible to be loyal to such a vague entity as the United States which claims devotion "only to an airy mode of law," where the only symbol "is a flag," after he has suggested that if a man loves his own State, "and is content to be ruined with her, let us shoot him, if we can, but allow him an honorable burial in the soil he fights for," the censorious "editor" is, very properly no doubt, suspicious:

> We do not thoroughly comprehend the author's drift in the foregoing paragraph, but are inclined to think its tone reprehensible, and its tendency impolitic in the present stage of our national difficulties. (12, 315)

When Lathrop came to republish the piece in his edition of Hawthorne's works, the passage on Lincoln was re-inserted. Fields as editor had explicitly asked for that to be changed or cut (though it seems harmless enough now). Hawthorne removed it while claiming that he thought it the only part of the article worth publishing – but replaced it with a footnote which he must have thoroughly enjoyed writing as it invites the readers to imagine what they are missing and also suggests that Hawthorne can be placed politically among somewhat surprising company:

> We are compelled to omit two or three pages, in which the author describes the interview [with Lincoln], and gives his idea of the personal appearance of the President. The sketch appears to have been written in a benign spirit, and perhaps conveys a not inaccurate impression of its august subject; but it lacks *reverence*, and it pains us to see a gentleman of ripe age, and who has spent years under the corrective influence of foreign institutions, falling into the characteristic and most ominous fault of young America. (12, 312–3)

There is the voice of Brahmin Boston! Hawthorne risked the wrath of the fiercely abolitionist section of Northern opinion with his judgement of John Brown:

> Nobody was ever more justly hanged. He won his martyrdom fairly, and took it firmly . . . [A]ny common-sensible man, looking at the matter unsentimentally, must have felt a certain intellectual satisfaction in seeing him hanged, if it were only in requital of his preposterous miscalculation of possibilities.

Hawthorne added a footnote – which, while showing what the party-line was on the issue, ironically ensures that the reader will notice, remember and place Hawthorne's verdict: "Can it be a son of old Massachusetts who utters this abominable sentiment? for shame!" (12,

327, 8). Just in case the reader does not remember this, Hawthorne returns to it at the end. The last paragraph speculates about the future. There is a choice:

> Since the matter had gone so far, there seems to be no way but to go on winning victories, and establishing peace and a truer union in another generation, at the expense, probably, of greater trouble, in the present one, than any other people ever voluntarily suffered . . . Or, if we stop short of that blessed consummation, heaven was heaven still, as Milton sings, after Lucifer and a third part of the angels had seceded from its golden palaces, – and perhaps all the more heavenly because so many gloomy brows, and soured, vindictive hearts, had gone to plot ineffectual schemes of mischief elsewhere.

But the "editor" will not allow the peaceable man the last word:

> We regret the innuendo in the concluding sentence. The war can never be allowed to terminate, except in the complete triumph of Northern principles . . .
>
> We should be sorry to cast a doubt on the Peaceable Man's loyalty, but he will allow us to say that we consider him premature in his kindly feelings towards traitors and sympathizers with treason. As the author himself says of John Brown (and, so applied, we thought it an atrociously cold-blooded *dictum*), "any common-sensible man would feel an intellectual satisfaction in seeing them hanged, were it only for their preposterous miscalculation of possibilities." There are some degrees of absurdity that put Reason herself into a rage, and affect us like an intolerable crime, – which this Rebellion is, into the bargain.                                          (12, 344–5)

There is, however, a sting in the tail – and the "editorial" scorpion in his attempt to limit authorial authority wounds himself. Not only does he remind the reader of the verdict on John Brown but, by taking the argument over and re-applying it, he confers in spite of himself a certain validity on it – unintentionally inviting the reader to define the Rebels as unrealistic rather than wrong.

Whatever else a reading of "War Matters' may achieve, it does at least get rid of the idea that Hawthorne's difficulties with the unfinished novels can be explained by claiming that his intellectual powers were failing. The poise, the wit, the multi-layered irony, the excellent journalistic eye – all show a writer magnificently in control of his materials. As well as demonstrating that Hawthorne's hand had lost none of its cunning, the article has a particular relevance for the American claimant materials. Hawthorne begins by telling his readers that he has been forced by the political situation to give up his fiction-writing, "to suspend the contemplation of certain fantasies, to which . . . I was endeavoring to give a sufficiently life-like aspect to admit of their figuring in a romance" (12, 299). It is interesting to see him claiming that he was aiming at a certain level of realism in this fiction – given the prefaces to the earlier novels. Hawthorne does not exclude himself from his irony as he attempts to make a virtue out of a necessity, and gives a mock-heroic touch to his abandonment of his work: "I magnanimously considered that there is a kind of treason in insulating one's self from the universal fear and sorrow" (12, 299–300).

And so he proceeds to the capital:

> It is natural enough to suppose that the centre and heart of Washington is the Capitol; and certainly, in its outward aspect, the world has not many statelier or more beautiful edifices, nor any, I should suppose, more skilfully adapted to legislative purposes, and to all accompanying needs. But, etc. etc.
>
> .    .    .    .    .    .    .    .    .    .    .    .
>
> We found one man, however, at the Capitol, who was satisfactorily adequate to the business which brought them thither.

The effect of the break in the text is to suggest that Hawthorne has only found one man at the Capitol who is adequate. The footnote appended to "etc." supports the idea that this is precisely what was intended – and the attention drawn to the omission may make the case more forcefully than pages of invective:

> We omit several paragraphs here, in which the author speaks of some prominent Members of Congress with a freedom that seems to have been not unkindly meant, but might be liable to misconstruction.          (12, 305)

The irony intensifies when we discover that this adequate man is an artist rather than a politician – engaged on cartoons in preparation for a great fresco in the Capitol. Artist he may be, but Hawthorne reads his work politically. It will be "emphatically original and American," producing "new forms of beauty" from the far West. Hawthorne finds this "most cheering." The work looked "full of energy, hope, progress, irrepressible movement onward, all represented in a momentary pause of triumph" (12, 306). But despite the cheering effect of seeing the artist fulfilling his task, "beautifying and idealizing our rude, material life, and thus manifesting that we have an indefeasible claim to a more enduring national life," Hawthorne's historical sense makes him keep an ironic distance from this artist of the beautiful. It is one thing to have an enduring claim and quite another to be able to exercise it. The possibility that the capital will have to be moved "far to the northward and westward" is a very real one. It may not be only the course of Empire which forces a move to the West. (Apparently the mural took its title from Berkeley: "Westward the Course of Empire Takes Its Way." I am unsure whether Hawthorne did not know this – or whether he suppressed the information in order to enjoy a hidden, private irony.)

Hawthorne ends this section of his article with a reference to a "sinister omen" that was pointed out to him in the Capitol:

> The freestone walls of the central edifice are pervaded with great cracks, and threaten to come thundering down, under the immense weight of the iron dome, – an appropriate catastrophe enough, if it should occur on the day when we drop the Southern stars out of our flag.          (12, 307)

It is hard to believe – given not only this sentence but the subtlety of the prose throughout the essay – that Hawthorne did not intend the irony in "*free*stone." It is certainly left open for the readers to speculate that, despite the powers of the artist, he may be both literally and symbolically merely papering and painting over the cracks.

With the America Hawthorne had known all his life in such dire straits, it is no wonder that he could not continue with the American claimant material – for that was, as I have argued, crucially dependent on stable if complex ideas of America and England and on their interrelationships. Nor should it be surprising that, by the time Hawthorne wrote "War Matters," he had turned to the Elixir of Life materials. There he could begin from a nation in crisis, struggling to be born – and it is a conflict frequently described by Hawthorne as a civil war. There, in Septimius, he had a figure who attempted to take a *very* long historical view (with his search for immortality) when faced by an immediate political crisis – whether that historical crisis be called the War of Independence or the American Revolution (rather as the conflict that Hawthorne confronted was to be known as the War between the States or the Civil War). Septimius's search, I shall argue, is deliberately analogous to the project of a certain kind of artist. There, in the figure of the country-boy turned soldier, was someone who lived intensely and matured dramatically under the pressures of an historical crisis, of the experience of war. There, in Septimius, he had a figure who claimed to evade and avoid the historical situation but whose project depended for its success on his having killed (for whatever reason) an Englishman, an enemy of his emergent country. But before that work can be examined, I must turn back to another American encounter with Europe – and especially with Rome, the eternal city – "eternal" because it contains so much history – *The Marble Faun* in which Hawthorne dramatized an encounter with History and Art.

# 8

## The Marble Faun *or, the ambivalences and ambiguities*

I

Many works of the ancients have become fragments. Many works of the moderns are fragments from their inception.

(Friedrich Schlegel, *Athenaeum* fragment no. 24, 1798)

[A]s the mutilated torsoes of the perfections of antiquity are not unworthy the student's attention, neither are the most bungling modern incompletenesses; for both are torsoes; one of perished perfection in the past; the other, by anticipation, of yet unfulfilled perfections in the future.

(Herman Melville, *Pierre Or, The Ambiguities*, Book XXVI, i)

In the previous chapter I drew attention to Hawthorne's intention expressed in *The Ancestral Footstep* to write a fiction with "an ending . . . not satisfactory to the natural yearnings of novel-readers" (XII, 11), and suggested that these words were equally appropriate for *The Marble Faun*. Its critical reception certainly seems to bear this out. For example, Henry Bright (Hawthorne's friend), reviewing the novel for *The Examiner*, found in it "a want of finish. The rich tissue of crimson and gold ends in a tangle, and we know not how the closing mystery shall be unravelled. The book is, perhaps, of all good novels, the most tantalizing" (XVIII, 260, fn. 1). That review provoked Hawthorne's clearest statement of his ideas about "plottish proprieties":

> As for what you say of the plot, I do not agree that it has been left in an imperfect state. The characters of the story come out of an obscurity and vanish into it again, like the figures on the slide of a magic-lantern; but, in their transit, they have served my purpose, and shown all that it was essential for them to reveal. Anything further, if you consider it rightly, would be an impertinence towards the reader. (XVIII, 259)

185

Hawthorne's note to himself understandably reveals more of his desire to challenge the norms of novel-readers than his polite note to his English friend, yet there are clearly connections between the two statements. This attitude is, as I have argued earlier, not only a product of the last phase. Hawthorne's letter, for instance, almost irresistibly recalls "Main-Street" and especially the way in which the showman/narrator there constructed a narrative with the aid of his images – an unfinished narrative because of the breakdown of his machinery and one in which the ending is profoundly problematic. Yet the parallels must not be over-emphasized despite the tempting presence in "Main-Street" of that member of the audience who resists the authority of the narrator. The narrative of "Main-Street" is fragmented in the sense that the break in the machinery breaks off what the narrator claims would have been if not a complete then at least a much longer story – the whole history of Salem right up to the "now" of 1848. *The Marble Faun* differs in its ending – though, of course, Bright was right: in terms of a conventional nineteenth century novel it does lack finish. It offers itself not so much as a fragment (though it is often *about* fragments, profoundly concerned with the lost wholeness of the antique) but rather it has built into its very structure an incompleteness which is designed to be suggestive. And that incompleteness – in crude plot terms – is not only a matter of the story continuing on beyond the end(s) we are given but also the mystery which somehow generates so much of the narrative we have. The reader principally wants to know what has already happened (in other words, the story behind Miriam and the Model), though, as I shall argue, we are invited to use the lack of a conventional closure to speculate further about one central element of the narrative – the story of the Fortunate Fall.

An examination of the kind of formal experiment that Hawthorne designed in *The Marble Faun* can perhaps be begun by setting beside it another fiction that challenged conventional ideas of form: Melville's *Pierre Or, The Ambiguities* (1852). Obviously an extended comparison of the two novels could easily be made – whether it began from the use the two writers make of that old nineteenth-century chestnut, dark and blonde heroines, or the fascination with the kinds of information carried by visual works of art, or the concern with Beatrice Cenci and the implied interest in incest, or the Fall (fortunate in Donatello's case – hardly clearly so in Pierre's loss of his country innocence). Indeed, given the shared obsession with ambiguity, it is worth asking whether *Pierre* was an influence on *The Marble Faun*.[1] Here, however, I want merely to note Melville's overt concern with the form of his fiction – and the possible implications this may have for that fiction's form and meaning. While no doubt Melville's comment in my epigraph is partially at least his alibi for *Pierre* and also a declaration of his ambition, its closeness to Schlegel's famous comment is notable – and may suggest connections between German and American Romanticism (a point to which I shall return). It also can be related to and casts light on Hawthorne's fascination with fragments and the unfinished and with the interpretative problems such objects necessarily present. Of course, form and content cannot be simplistically separated. Pierre meditates on Isabel's story thus:

> In her life there was an unraveled [sic] plot; and he felt that unraveled it would eternally remain to him. No slightest hope or dream had he, that what was dark and mournful in her would ever be cleared up into some coming atmosphere of light and mirth.

A parallel with Hawthorne's dark heroine, Miriam, immediately suggests itself – with the difference that Hawthorne revels in generating alternative explanatory stories of Miriam's mystery as a way of intensifying that mystery. And Melville goes on to contrast what can be known of Isabel's story to the neatly shaped stories offered by conventional novels and to criticize the ideology implied by those fictions:

> Like all youths, Pierre had conned his novel-lessons . . . but their false, inverted attempts at systematizing eternally unsystematizable elements; their audacious, intermeddling impotency, in trying to unravel, and spread out, and classify, the more thin than gossamer threads which make up the complex web of life; these things over Pierre had no power now . . . [H]e saw, that not always doth life's beginning gloom conclude in gladness; that wedding-bells peal not ever in the last scene of life's fifth act; that while the countless tribes of common novels laboriously spin veils of mystery, only to complacently clear them up at last; and while the countless tribe of common dramas do but repeat the same; yet the profounder emanations of the human mind, intended to illustrate all that can be humanly known of human life; these never unravel their own intricacies, and have no proper endings; but in imperfect, unanticipated, and disappointing sequels (as mutilated stumps), hurry to abrupt intermergings with the eternal tides of time and fate.  (Book VII, viii)

This is very close to Hawthorne's questioning of the explanatory authority of narrative in chapter L of *The Marble Faun*. The "gossamer threads" of Melville's "complex web" parallel Hawthorne's hope that his kindly reader will not look on "the wrong side of the tapestry," will refrain from "tearing the web apart," while Melville's belief that "the profounder emanations of the human mind . . . never unravel their own intricacies, and have no proper endings" is echoed by this:

> any narrative of human action and adventure – whether we call it history or romance – is certain to be a fragile handiwork, more easily rent than mended.

> The actual experience of even the most ordinary life is full of events that never explain themselves, either as regards their origin or their tendency.   (1,232)

Hawthorne is probably more radically sceptical than Melville for Melville (by implication at least) opposes the authority of the historiographical narrative to the shaped sugary stories of popular romantic fictions. See, for example, the first paragraph of Book XVII where he discusses ways of writing history but does not question that it can be written satisfactorily without undue strain.

Isabel's last words on the last page of *Pierre* ("All's o'er, and ye know him not!"), addressed to the readers as well as to the fictional characters, announce a mystery, and recall part of the last paragraph of *The Marble Faun* as Hilda muses over Miriam's wedding present of the bracelet with its Etruscan gems which "brought tears into her eyes, as being, in its entire circle, the symbol of as sad a mystery as any that Miriam had attached to the separate gems." Yet at just this point it becomes clear that the parallels cannot be pursued too far. *Pierre* ends with a pile of bodies like a Jacobean tragedy and with Isabel adding to it. Dying, she "fell upon Pierre's heart, and her long hair ran over him, and arbored him in ebon vines." Hawthorne leaves us with Hilda's "hopeful soul" and the claim that she saw "sunlight on the mountain-tops." While this vision demands interrogation (which I will attempt later), there is nevertheless a mixture of the sweet and sour with the sweet apparently dominating that last paragraph. More importantly at least in terms of form is the contrast between Melville's basic narrative linearity and Hawthorne's subtle opposition between linearity (connected with the unfinished) and the image of the circle (however ambiguously and ambivalently presented) with at least an implied idea of completion or improvement – even if the circle still leaves the question of beginnings and endings as profoundly problematic. I shall return to this, but here I want to note the way in which Hawthorne insists on the image of the circle as he concludes his fiction. Most famous are Miriam's words to Kenyon about Donatello in chapter XLVII: "He has travelled in a circle, as all things heavenly and earthly do . . ." (1,214). But it is the final chapter (chapter L) which repeatedly emphasizes the circle. I have already mentioned the symbolic bracelet, which, by incorporating the Etruscan gems, links an "immemorial" past with the present. The very title of the chapter suggests circularity as it repeats that of Chapter I: "Miriam, Hilda, Kenyon, Donatello." Were it not for these instances, the fact that the last scene is set in the Pantheon might appear Hawthorne's last attempt to get his sightseeing into his fiction but clearly more is intended. It is there that Hilda and Kenyon have their last sight of Miriam – the Pantheon which Byron had celebrated in *Childe Harold's Pilgrimage*:

Relic of nobler days, and noblest arts!
Despoil'd yet perfect, with thy circle spreads
A holiness appealing to all hearts –
To art a model . . . (Canto IV, stanza cxlvii)

Obviously Hawthorne hardly needed Byron to notice the shape of the Pantheon – though the suggestion that it offers itself as a model for art is interesting as is the notion of something despoiled yet still perfect. Whether inspired by Byron or not, he presents the building as significant in both its situation and its form, seeing it as a "huge, black rotundity . . . almost at the central point of the labyrinthine intricacies of the modern city," and situates Hilda and Kenyon "in the free space of that great circle" (I,233). It is here that we last see Kenyon and Hilda – at the centre of a building which is itself at the centre of a maze-like Rome.

It is, however, not enough merely to assert the presence of images of circularity: the fascination with fragments needs to be connected to the concern with circles. And here a critic concerned with the form of the unfinished is very helpful:

> The crucial facts about the ruin are that it was once finished and that contemplation of it is instigated by the discrepancy between the whole that was and the fragment that is. It is important not as itself, but by virtue of its position in the restorative effort which its vestigial existence appeals to the viewer to undertake. The relation of the part to the whole, the consciousness of loss, and the endeavour of retrieval which characterize our contemplation of survivals are thus singularly prominent in the way the ruin is viewed. It therefore needs to be emphasized that they are not singular to the nature of the ruin itself. In fact their foundation lies in a more inclusive form of circular seeking in which the aspiration is the union of *telos* and origin.

This is, of course, in one sense too simple for it ignores the problem of the artificial (the fictional) ruin – a problem that Hawthorne briefly toys with in chapter VIII: "The Suburban Villa." However, the passage does usefully relate the response to the ruin or fragment to an "inclusive form of circular seeking" – a phrase which is relevant to the story of Donatello. And Rajan's general point stands: we need to distinguish between the ruin or fragment and an unfinished work – and also between the responses proper to both. Both the torso and the ruin, he claims, invite (imaginative) completion or reconstruction, while the unfinished work should not:

> If [the unfinished work] falls short of finality (as *The Faerie Queen* and *The Cantos* do) or resists it (as *The Triumph of Life* does), it should do so because of forces that have been demonstrated to be grounded in its nature and that forbid arrival at a closure even when (as in *The Faerie Queen*) the gestures accompanying closure are richly invoked.

> The inquiry narrows when we recognize that the form of the unfinished is the form of the poem as it is and not some larger form in which the poem participates and to which we are persuaded to annex it. A poem that is properly unfinished should be less satisfactory if we were to pursue any of the conceivable ways of finishing it. Instead of speaking of its failure to achieve closure we should regard any prospective closure of it as an imminent admission of its failure.[2]

Is this not (and especially the second paragraph) remarkably close to what Hawthorne is saying in that nicely named "Postscript," that conclusion in which nothing is concluded, where closure is obstinately rejected? With the perspective provided by Rajan, it becomes clearer why Hawthorne should claim that his narrative was generated by the sight of an unfinished sculpture – one which presented an interpretative problem. And, since beginnings and endings, origins and destinations, are being put in question, it should not be entirely surprising that Hawthorne chooses to withhold this information until the conclusion of chapter XLI.

II

> And accordingly, Donatello's bust (like that rude, rough mass of the head of Brutus, by Michel Angelo, at Florence) has ever since remained in an unfinished state. Most spectators mistake it for an unsuccessful attempt towards copying the features of the Faun of Praxiteles. One observer in a thousand is conscious of something more, and lingers long over this mysterious face, departing from it, reluctantly, and with many a glance thrown backward. What perplexes him is the riddle that he sees propounded there; the riddle of the Soul's growth, taking its first impulse amid remorse and pain, and struggling through the incrustations of the senses. It was the contemplation of this imperfect portrait of Donatello that originally interested us in his history, and impelled us to elicit from Kenyon what he knew of his friend's adventures.                                   (1,170)

Rather as Hawthorne claims in "The Custom-House" that the discovery of the letter helped to originate his narrative, so, he says, the sight of an unfinished sculpture was the beginning of the writing of *The Marble Faun*. Both letter and sculpture are works of art; both are difficult to interpret and both demand interpretation. But they are not equally hard to interpret. While Hawthorne says of the letter that "there was some deep meaning in it, most worthy of interpretation, and which, as it were, streamed forth from the mystic symbol, subtly communicating itself to my sensibilities, but evading the analysis of my mind" (145–6), this resistance to the claims of the intellect is only momentary. Mr. Surveyor Pue's text accompanies the "mystic" letter, and enables the author to discover its meaning – or at the least one of its meanings – its original one. The letter can gain (or regain) its meaning by being restored to an historical context: it has a place in Hawthorne's fiction of history. The bust is equally complex and rather more difficult to place – and the fact that Hawthorne saves this clue to his story until so late in the narrative further complicates the issue. It is too a fictional clue and, even if we did not know from *The French and Italian Notebooks* that it was the sight of the Faun of Praxiteles that was the origin of his fiction, we would realize that the bust must be a fictive object if only because the story of Donatello is so clearly a parable – a parable, I shall be arguing, of "The Conjectural Beginning of Human History," to use the title of a relevant essay by Kant. In this it differs from the scarlet letter. We read Hawthorne's discovery of it as a fiction no doubt, but, if evidence were to turn up that he found both letter and document, it would not, I would argue, change the way we read *The Scarlet Letter* – if only because we know that such letters were worn in New England, had a real historical existence. In any case, it comes before the beginning of the story proper and can be considered independently of Hester's narrative. The passage about the bust, however, disrupts our reading. We know that the beginning of the fiction starts with and from a resemblance between Donatello and the Faun of Praxiteles perceived by the fictional characters, and we have been told that this resemblance "forms the key-note of our narrative" (869). At the least the introduction of Hawthorne's account of the origin of his story introduces a dissonance in the text as this fictional account forces into the foreground the question of the difference between beginnings and origins.

While the bust (and Hawthorne's "response" to it) is offered as a crucially important clue, it has to be said that it is remarkably problem-laden, raising a wide range of questions about the production and reception of (aesthetic) meaning. To begin with production: Hawthorne raises the question as to how far the meaning of the sculpture is the product of the design of the artist – and thus complicates questions of intention's relation to meaning. Hilda (not entirely politely) suggests that the strange success of the bust is not the result of purpose:

> "I question whether this striking effect has been brought up about by any skill or purpose on the sculptor's part. Is it not, perhaps, the chance-result of the bust being just so far shaped out, in the marble, as the process of moral growth had advanced, in the original?"                                                                (1,169)

This inevitably recalls Kenyon's first attempt to mould Donatello's head – and, just in case we had forgotten that holiday work, Hawthorne reminds us of it by having Kenyon say that the expression on the bust is the very one he had unsuccessfully tried to achieve in the clay. But this adds another layer of difficulty for, while neither Kenyon nor Donatello were aware of it, Kenyon's last "accidental touches" resulted in a success that he never realizes he has achieved: "here were still the features of the antique Faun, but now illuminated with a higher meaning, such as the old marble never wore" (1,079, 1,080). Here, then, we have two versions of Donatello both produced by chance or Kenyon's unconscious. It seems as though this is another version of that statement of Sophia's which Hawthorne so liked: Man's Accidents: God's Purposes – and thus is another perspective on the Fortunate Fall. Hilda's interpretation goes some way to confirm this:

> "It gives the impression of a growing intellectual power and moral sense. Donatello's face used to evince little more than a genial, pleasurable sort of vivacity, and capability of enjoyment. But, here, a soul is being breathed into him; it is the Faun, but advancing towards a state of higher development."
>
> (1,169)

Hawthorne confirms her reading (in the epigraph to this section) and thus exposes Hilda to a charge of inconsistency if nothing worse. She notoriously denies the doctrine of the Fortunate Fall when it is put before her as a proposition by Kenyon – but, when it comes to decoding his work of art, her interpretation does quite clearly (however unconsciously) confirm that doctrine. Since she makes the connection between the bust and Donatello and thus accepts the mimetic status of the work of art, since Kenyon has admitted that her interpretation and his intention are the same, she cannot claim that her judgement is only a verdict on the work of art. It is a very satisfying irony for those readers who find Hilda emotionally and intellectually dishonest – and suggests that her shocked response to Kenyon's formulation of the Fortunate Fall "paradox" should be ironically placed.

Hilda reads a moral meaning out of the bust's lack of finish – and is undoubtedly right to do so. For example, when Hawthorne speaks of the sculpture revealing the Soul struggling through "the incrustations of the senses," he surely means the reader to recall what he had written two pages earlier, where he presented the bust as "incrusted all round with the white, shapeless substance of the block" (1,170, 1,168). Thus the unworked stone becomes a concrete symbol of moral meaning, is incorporated into the work of art – a sophisticated idea and, I think, a modern one and certainly not one that a Praxiteles or a medieval sculptor would have understood. But there is more than mere morality here: the material facts that declare the bust's lack of finish also go to compose historical and cultural meanings. It is this area of concern which, I suspect, caused Hawthorne to compare the bust to Michelangelo's Brutus since Brutus is a figure who can be seen as either murderer or would-be saviour of the state, and Michelangelo a sculptor notorious for his unfinished works.[3] Hawthorne had mused over Michelangelo in *The French and Italian Notebooks*:

> The conceptions of this great sculptor were so godlike, that he appears to have been discontented at not likewise possessing the godlike attribute of creating and embodying them with an instantaneous thought; and therefore we often find sculpture from his hand, left at the critical point of their struggle to get out of the marble. This statue of Saint Matthew looks like the antediluvian fossil of a human being, of an epoch when humanity was mightier and more majestic than now, long ago imprisoned in stone, and half-uncovered again.
>
> (XIV, 372–3)

This concern with the fossil and with the idea that history may well involve loss as well as gain bear directly on what Hawthorne has to say about Kenyon's Cleopatra and his bust of Donatello. There is too a wider relevance as can be seen when it is seen what a modern art-historian makes of the idea of the unfinished. Wittkower, when discussing Michelangelo and Leonardo, writes of the unfinished, the *"non-finito"*, as being born "from the new self-awareness and self-analysis of Renaissance man," having explored the idea in ways that are directly relevant for both the form and content of *The Marble Faun*:

> So far as we can see, never before had a tension existed between the conception and execution of a work. But now doubt in the validity of worldly art, self-criticism, dissatisfaction with the imperfect realization of the inner image, the gulf between mind and matter and – in Michelangelo's case – between the purity of the Platonic idea and the baseness of its material realization prevented these masters from finishing their works.

The language of Hawthorne, the nineteenth-century amateur of art, is not so very far from that of the twentieth-century professional art-historian. This certainly provides a way of placing the debate between Hilda and Kenyon about his Cleopatra. Kenyon speaks of finding it "a mere lump of senseless stone, into which I have not really succeeded in moulding the spiritual part of my idea." Hilda, attempting to encourage him, goes still further towards a neo-Platonism:

> "It only proves you have been able to imagine things too high for mortal faculties to execute. The idea leaves you an imperfect image of itself, which you at first mistake for an ethereal reality, but soon find that the latter has escaped out of your closest embrace."

Ever the little optimist, she even attempts to make the proper audience for art-works into neo-Platonists: "there is a class of spectators whose sympathy will help them to see the Perfect through a mist of imperfection" (1,167, 1,168). As Kenyon and Hilda put the case, this is of course as much a Romantic as a Renaissance response – and Wittkower emphasizes that it is necessary in the case of the *non finito* to differentiate between two stages of modernity. He opposes the self-analysis of the Renaissance to the impressionist *non finito* of the nineteenth century:

> In contrast to Michelangelo, whose unfinished works were unfinished, Rodin created partial figures which are the finished product. This requires a new (we might call it, modern) form of self-analysis and introspection, for the artist had to develop a sophisticated control of the act of creation.[4]

This provides a very suggestive way of looking at *The Marble Faun*, which may, I hope, go some ways towards killing off the idea that Hawthorne was always naive about the aesthetics of the visual arts and their relations to the written. He has written a fiction which is, in Wittkower's terms, a partial figure but, *at the same time*, a finished product. It is deliberately structurally analogous to the bust – only Hawthorne has a more purposeful control over his fiction than he donates to Kenyon. It is an analogical rather than a metaphoric relationship that Hawthorne aims to establish between sculpture and text for Kenyon's bust, to use Wittkower's terms, is closer to a Michelangelo work while the novel is, so to speak, Rodinesque.

If I am right about the relationship between bust and fiction (and Hawthorne does seem to indicate that there is a significant relationship), then this may help to explain why Hawthorne wanted to attach something of the ancient world to Kenyon's very modern sculpture. It is clear from the first couple of pages of *The Marble Faun* that he wanted the pressure of the past to be felt as one of the defining elements of the experience of Rome *and* of reading the book – Hawthorne writes of his "hope of putting the reader into that state of feeling which is experienced oftenest at Rome" (858). So, given the bust's importance as a – however fictive – origin of the story, he needs it to suggest the past as well as the present:

> In the midst [of the marble], appeared the features, lacking sharpness, and very much resembling a fossil countenance, (but we already used this simile with regard to Cleopatra), with the accumulations of long-past ages clinging to it.
>
> (1,168)

Thus, while the sculpture appears very much as work in progress ("not nearly finished, but with fine white dust and small chips of marble scattered about it" [1,168]), it is also associated with the past – an instant antique which anticipates the discovery of the Venus in chapter XLVI where the "shapeless fragment[s]" can, however temporarily, be reassembled, and the "beautiful idea" assert "its immortality" (1,205–6). A seeming confession of linguistic clumsiness calls attention to

Hawthorne's fascination with ambiguities as he further complicates his complex of ideas by reminding the reader of what he had said a couple of pages earlier about Kenyon's modern sculpture of a heroine from the ancient world. There "fossil" meant something rather different, for the Cleopatra is a highly finished work rich in naturalistic detail:

> The fierce Egyptian queen had now struggled almost out of the imprisoning stone; or, rather, the workmen had found her within the mass of marble . . ., the fossil woman of an age that produced statelier, stronger and more passionate creatures than our own.   (1,166)

It is in this chapter that Hawthorne picks up Thorwaldsen's "threefold analogy" – that little narrative of the process of a sculpture towards completion – claiming that it is applicable to the bust of Donatello: "the Clay-model, the Life; the Plaister-cast, the Death; and the sculptured Marble, the Resurrection." Kenyon's Cleopatra is not so much a resurrection (with the clearly spiritual implication) but rather an historical re-creation of a kind of temperament which, it seems, the modern world has lost. While no doubt these losses are to be set against the gains implied by Donatello's progress, still there is the clear suggestion that any simplistic idea of history as progress is not to be endorsed.

Among the oppositions between the two works are the modes of their production. The bust of Donatello is, it seems, all Kenyon's own work.[5] Cleopatra, however, is a product of the modern division of labour: "as it is not quite satisfactory to think," she has been transferred from the cast to the marble by "some nameless machine[s] in human shape" (948, 949). The way a conventional sculpture like the Cleopatra has been made can only be known by seeing the work in the processes of its production; the finished work bears no overt traces of the labour that has gone into making it. The unfinished work (in either the Michelangelo or the Rodin sense) does – if only in the sense that the most naive spectators can see that more work could have been put into the production of the work of art. In that sense the *non finito* offers itself as demanding a narrative, an explanation, not necessarily of what it represents but of the reason its representation takes a particular, even a peculiar, form – bearing as it does the signs that it has been laboured over, and that the labour (in conventional terms) has been abandoned. Any response must be more than pure aesthetic contemplation as the spectator is forced to ask why the work remains in what seems patently to be an incomplete state. I have suggested that the authority of narrative is repeatedly interrogated in *The Marble Faun*. However, it is presented as nearly always a central component (in one form or another) of responses to works of art.[6] With the Cleopatra it is clear that spectators are unlikely to ask for a narrative of its making when they view the completed object, but they do want to know "who" they are looking at. Thus Miriam asks Kenyon to give her the title of his sculpture, trusting that she has the right cultural baggage to make sense of the response. He answers her question but insists that "The special *epoch of her history*, you must make out for yourself" (957, my emphasis). The sculpture takes much of its meaning from its place in a culturally available narrative. Very early on in the novel Miriam and Kenyon discuss the competing claims of painting and sculpture in terms of their relations to time and story. Kenyon (at this stage) is quite clear:

> "Flitting moments – imminent emergencies – imperceptible intervals between two breaths – ought not to be incrusted with the eternal repose of marble; in any sculptural subject, there should be a moral standstill, since there must be of necessity a physical one."

Here is another use of the term "incrusted" – and Miriam in her mischievous response defines sculpture in terms of the fossil:

> "You think that sculpture should be a sort of fossilizing process. But, in truth, your frozen art has nothing like the scope and freedom of Hilda's and mine. In painting, there is no similar objection to the representation of brief snatches of time; perhaps because a story can be so much more fully told, in picture, and buttressed about with circumstances that give it an epoch."

She continues "For instance, a painter would never have sent down yonder Faun out of his far antiquity, lonely and desolate, with no companion to keep his simple heart warm" (865–6). The sentimentality of the way she puts her point should not mask the fact that Miriam seems to see narrative as necessarily involving something like a dialogue. However, hers may be too strong a polemic, for Hilda's art in so far as it is constituted by her career as copyist is hardly full of "scope and freedom" – except for her freedom to omit parts of the paintings, to fragment the works of the old masters in her representations. And the inadequacies of the copyist's craft is another form of art to set against the achievement of Kenyon's willed abandonment of the bust. Hilda is, of course, a marvellous copyist – up to a point. Hawthorne dismisses most copyists in terms that inevitably recall his distaste for the mechanical production of Cleopatra: the copyists "convert themselves into Guido machines, or Raphaelic machines" (901). But, in the previous paragraph, despite Hawthorne's admiration for her achievements, doubts creep in. It is not only her tendency to ignore the demands of formal composition as she selects only portions for reproduction, but also the terms in which the paintings are transmitted to the wider world. She is not so far from Kenyon's assistants or the conventional copyists: "the girl was but a finer instrument, a more exquisitely effective piece of mechanism" (900).

The decision not to finish the bust of Donatello solves an aesthetic and moral problem for Kenyon. The conventionally finished sculpture must, according to his early principles, deal with a moral and physical moment of rest and repose. The bust is a mid-point between a traditional, finished sculpture with its inevitable stasis and the entirely fragile and momentary work which Kenyon worked on at the beginning of chapter XLI, "Snowdrops and Maidenly Delights." He had modelled "a beautiful little statue of Maidenhood gathering a flower," which is "one of those fragile creations which are true only to the moment that produces them" (1,164). Again, the sentimentality here should not blind the reader to the radical idea of a disposable art only available to the artist himself.[7] At the moment of Kenyon's greatest gloom after Hilda's disappearance, he had still managed to admire the Laocoon, looking upon "the group as the one triumph of Sculpture, creating the repose, which is essential to it, in the very acme of turbulent effort' (1,179). The bust is at once a modern equivalent and a development from the Laocoon, unfinished while the Laocoon has become a fragment. By abandoning the sculpture Kenyon has managed to produce an art-work which embodies a narrative of the soul's development, which is dynamic and open-ended ("It gives the impression of a growing intellectual power and moral sense" [1,169]) – and thus, as I have tried to argue, analogous to the structure of the fiction that contains it and claims to spring from it.

At the same time, the sculpture is to be interpreted in terms of Hawthorne's approval of the Romantic aesthetic of the sketch:

> The charm lay partly in [the sketches'] very imperfection; for this is suggestive, and sets the imagination at work; whereas, the finished picture, if a good one, leaves the spectator nothing to do, and, if bad, stupefies, disenchants, and disheartens him.                                                      (968)

And this formulation is, I think, clearly to be related to what Hawthorne wants the reader to do. Writing to Motley, thanking him for a congratulatory letter about The Marble Faun, Hawthorne put it like this: "You work out my imperfect efforts, and half make the book with your own imagination, and see what I myself saw, but could only hint at" (XVIII, 256).[8] If the letter had stopped after "imagination," this might sound like an invitation to the most unbridled subjectivism, but Hawthorne makes it clear that, in his version of reader-response theory, the ideal reader completes or expands on the design rather than embarking on a series of irresponsible improvisations. Given the complexity and subtlety of this remarkably rich novel, this does not mean that the reader's role is an easy one. But what Hawthorne's letter does legitimate is a reading which develops hints rather than relying on overt statements. The example where the need for such a reading seems most necessary and clearest is, I think, the case of Hilda. Almost without exception, critical judgement has, very understandably, agreed that we are meant to take her at her own (and Kenyon's) valuation:

> "Has any misfortune befallen you?" asked Hilda with earnestness. Pray tell me; and you shall have my sympathy, though I must still be very happy. Now, I know how it is, that the Saints above are touched by the sorrows of distressed people on earth, and yet are never made wretched by them. Not that I profess to be a Saint, you know," she added, smiling radiantly. "But the heart grows so large, and so rich, and so variously endowed, when it has a great sense of bliss, that it can give smiles to some and tears to others, with equal sincerity, and enjoy its own peace throughout all."
>
> "Do not say you are no Saint!" answered Kenyon, with a smile, though he felt that the tears stood in his eyes. "You will still be Saint Hilda, whatever church may canonize you."                                                    (1,155)

Almost without exception, too, critical opinion has found her insufferable – only too understandably in the light of such passages as the above – and criticized Hawthorne for giving us such a repulsively smug heroine who badly flaws the fiction she inhabits. However, I want to argue that Hawthorne by no means uncritically celebrates her or what she seems to stand for. On the contrary: he has intensely ambivalent feelings about her and he presents Hilda with sufficient ambiguity for the reader to see that the very form of the fiction (and especially its open-endedness) enables the fiction to undercut, to subvert the apparently immaculate heroine. To examine this proposition – given the importance of her repudiation of the idea of the Fortunate Fall as formulated by Kenyon – is necessarily to look at Hawthorne's treatment of the Fortunate Fall. And since he presents it as *the* central narrative of origin in and of Western culture (both Pagan and Christian), it is necessary to recognize that it is the backbone, so to speak, of this brilliantly encyclopedic fiction with its attempts to include or refer to all history, all religion, all myth, all art – with its extraordinarily ambitious push towards totalization. If the principal direction of the fiction is to approve the idea of the Fortunate Fall as exemplified by the story of Donatello, then (even without any other evidence) this would suggest that there is an inadequacy (at the very least) about Hilda's repudiation of the idea. If her negative judgement is accepted, then the whole project of the novel would have to be denied.

### III

> What is the front the world always shows to the young spirit? Strange to say, The Fall of Man. The Fall of Man is the first word of history and the last fact of experience. In the written annals or in the older tradition of every nation this

dark legend is told of the depravation of a once pure and happy society. And in the experience of every individual somewhat analogous is recognised.

"Did Adam fall, that we might ultimately rise to a far loftier Paradise than his?" (1,236)

Emerson's formulation here is considerably richer than his better known statement on the Fall (that the Fall is the discovery we exist, in "Experience"), with its emphasis that the Fall is at once the fall of humanity into history and a recurrent element in individual histories.[9] History is, of course, a central presence in *The Marble Faun*, a necessary condition of the text's production: "the very dust of Rome is historic, and inevitably settles on our page, and mingles with it." But it is a problematic past, one where the very importance of the history makes it difficult to apprehend, "crowded so full with memorable events that one obliterates another; as if Time had crossed and re-crossed his own records till they grew illegible" (937). Decodable or not, its burden is unavoidable:

> It is a vague sense of ponderous remembrances; a perception of such weight and density in a by-gone life, . . . that the present moment is pressed down or crowded out, and our individual affairs and interest are but half as real, here, as elsewhere. Viewed through this medium, our narrative . . . may seem not widely different from the texture of all our lives. Side by side with the massiveness of the Roman Past, all matters, that we handle or dream of, now-a-days, look evanescent and visionary alike.[10] (858)

One structuring principle for this history (if only to prevent the sheer chaotic bulk of the past becoming overwhelming) is the idea of the Fall which is, at the least, a way of thinking about the origins of history. What is noticeable and important about Hawthorne's treatment of this narrative is that he goes beyond the conventional Christian terms for the story (as expressed, for example, by Kenyon's questions above), that (as I shall try to argue) he has secularized and generalized the seeming paradox in a way that strikingly parallels the German Romantic secularization of the Biblical story. And the very form that Hawthorne's development of the Fortunate Fall story takes necessarily commits him to a positive valuation of it. This is to argue against what seem to have been common critical attitudes. Thus, Hyatt H. Waggoner in 1963 wrote "The question as posed by Miriam and Kenyon is never resolved in the novel," and Graham Clarke some twenty years later virtually echoes him: "The question, of course, cannot be answered." And Male was confident that Hilda was right:

> The point is that Hawthorne and Hilda reject Kenyon's argument precisely because it is a line of reasoning. Take the narrative element out of the Christian

story; make a logical formula (the Fortunate Fall) of it; remove the temporal
lag between Adam's sin and Christ's redemption and it becomes a frozen creed
that is at best a paradox, at worst a mockery of true morality.[11]

But (leaving aside the question of what happens to those unfortunate
souls who lived between Adam's fall and Christ's coming) the point
about the Fortunate Fall in the narrative form it takes in *The Marble Faun*
(the story of Donatello) is that it lacks the temporal lag that Male
demands. Seconds after the murder of the Model we are told, in a chapter
entitled unambiguously "The Faun's Transformation", that "the fierce
energy . . . had kindled him into a man; it had developed within him an
intelligence which was no native characteristic" (996). Admittedly that
change has to be legitimated and refined into morality by suffering over
time, but Hawthorne could hardly be more emphatic about the rapidity
of the change (and that very rapidity should suggest that he is not simply
recycling the Christian version of the narrative). If Male thinks that the
temporal lag is crucial, he has no alternative but to accuse Hawthorne of
mocking true morality, for it seems to me to be crystal clear that the
fiction as a whole entirely endorses the idea of the Fortunateness of the
Fall, containing, indeed negating, the apparent opposition to it.

The classic English Protestant statement of the apparent paradox is, of
course, Milton's in *Paradise Lost*, and the fact that Kenyon has produced a
bust of the poet based on "long perusal and deep love" (951) of the poet's
works should remind the reader of that famous passage (though one may
well wonder why Kenyon seems to have forgotten it). When Christ
comes again, according to the archangel Michael, He will reward

> "His faithful, and receive them into bliss,
> Whether in heaven or earth, for then the earth
> Shall all be paradise, far happier place
> Than this of Eden, and far happier days,"        (Book XII, 462–5)

Adam, understandably replete with joy and wonder, replies

> "O goodness infinite, goodness immense!
> That all this good of evil shall produce,
> And evil turn to good; more wonderful
> Than that which by creation first brought forth
> Light out of darkness! Full of doubt I stand,
> Whether I should repent me now of sin
> By me done and occasioned, or rejoice
> Much more, that much more good thereof shall spring,
> To God more glory, more good will to men
> From God, and over wrath grace shall abound."        (Book XII, 469–78)

We leave Adam "Full of doubt," hypothesizing rather than asserting, and he goes on to change the subject quite neatly. But still this may appear quite close to the way Kenyon presents the problem to Hilda:

> "Here comes my perplexity . . . Sin has educated Donatello, and elevated him. Is Sin, then - which we deem such a dreadful blackness in the Universe – is it, like Sorrow, merely an element of human education, through which we struggle to a higher and purer state than we could otherwise have attained. Did Adam fall, that we might ultimately rise to a far loftier Paradise than his?"
>
> (1,236)

He may seem to be merely repeating Miriam's argument, and, very importantly, he is – up to a point. This is Miriam:

> "The story of the Fall of Man! *Is it not repeated in our Romance of Monte Beni?* And may we follow the analogy yet farther? Was that very sin – into which Adam precipitated himself and all his race – was it the destined means by which, over a long path-way of toil and sorrow, we are to attain a higher, brighter, and profounder happiness, than our lost birthright gave?"
>
> (1,215, my emphasis)

But Miriam has a wider range – and the fact that the subtitle of the novel is *The Romance of Monte Beni* indicates the centrality of her formulation of the topic for the whole novel. Equally importantly, the way in which she introduces the dangerous question shows a radical break with Milton's treatment of the issue:

> "Is he not beautiful?" said Miriam, watching the sculptor's eye as it dwelt admiringly on Donatello. "So changed, yet still, in a deeper sense, so much the same! He has travelled in a circle, as all things heavenly and earthly do, and now comes back to his original self, with an inestimable treasure of improvement won from an experience of pain . . . Was the crime – in which he and I were wedded – was it a blessing in that strange disguise? Was it a means of education, bringing a simple and imperfect nature to a point of feeling and intelligence, which it could have reached under no other discipline?" (1,214)

Milton never suggested – never would have dared to suggest – that it was to *Adam's* advantage to have sinned, and, as far as Milton is concerned, Male's argument is perfectly correct. But it cannot be applied to Hawthorne, who is here very firmly in a Romantic tradition which is interested in the Adamic but shows little concern with Christ. Whatever else has been found in *The Marble Faun*, no one has had the nerve to propose a Christ figure. Miriam's emphasis on Donatello's beauty, on an aesthetic placing, would be enough to mark her statement as Romantic even without the introduction of the figure of the circle (or spiral).

Here I must gratefully confess a debt to M.H. Abrams' *Natural*

*Supernaturalism* and especially section 4: "The Circuitous Journey: Through Alienation to Reintegration" which draws particularly on Kant and Schiller. I can find no evidence whatever that this is a case of straightforward intellectual influence yet the parallels between the ideas of the Germans about the Fall narrative as presented by Abrams and Hawthorne's treatment of that story are so remarkably striking that I can only presume that it is the result of Hawthorne musing over the same problems as the Germans.[12] Abrams quotes much of the passage from *Paradise Lost* but it is the German Romantic variations and developments of this story-shaped theme which seem so relevant and to illuminate Miriam's statement and, indeed, much else in the novel:

> in the most representative Romantic version of emanation and return, when the process reverts to its beginnings the recovered unity is not, as in the school of Plotinus, the simple undifferentiated unity of its origin, but a unity which is higher because it incorporates the intervening differentiations. "We have now returned," as Hegel said in a comment which was added to the conclusion of his shorter Logic, "to the notion of the Idea with which we began," but "this return to the beginning is also an advance." The self-moving circle, in other words, rotates along a third, a vertical dimension, to close where it had begun, but on a higher plane of value. It thus fuses the idea of the circular return with the idea of linear progress, to describe a distinctive figure of Romantic thought and imagination – the ascending circle or spiral. Hugo von Hoffmannsthal's later description of this design is terse and complete: "Every development moves in a spiral line, and leaves everything behind, reverts to the same point on a higher turning."[13]

An American may patriotically feel that Clifford Pyncheon (fl. c. 1848) had pre-empted von Hoffmannsthal (1874–1929): "all human progress is in a circle; or, to use a more accurate and beautiful figure, in an ascending spiral curve" (574). And an unfriendly critic may feel that, while this passage might just conceivably be useful for *The House of the Seven Gables* (if too Germanically abstract), it has little relevance to Donatello's Adamic role. But, as Abrams subtly and richly traces the variations in this cluster of ideas, a crucial development occurs:

> A number of [German] thinkers adapted the Christian fable of a lost and future paradise into a theory which neatly fused the alternative views of human history as either decline or progress. This they accomplished by representing man's fall from happy unity into the evil of increasing division and suffering as an indispensable stage on his route back toward the lost unity and happiness of his origin, but along an ascending plane that will leave him immeasurably better off at the end than he was in the beginning.                    (A.201)

> After Kant and Schiller it became a standard procedure for the major German philosophers to show that the secular history and destiny of mankind is

congruent with the Biblical story of the loss and future recovery of paradise; to interpret that story as a mythical representation of man's departure from the happiness of ignorance and self-unity into the multiple self-divisions and conflicts attendant upon the emergence of self-consciousness, free decision, and the analytic intellect; . . . and to evaluate the fall as a fortunate self-division, because it was the necessary first step upon the educational journey by which thinking and striving man wins his way back towards his lost integrity, along a road which looks like a reversion but is in fact a progression.          (A.217)

The way in which this parallels the story of Donatello (up to a point) is, I think, both clear and striking. I shall expand on the parallels when I set Donatello's story beside an essay of Kant's. Here I simply want to set beside Abrams' words this comment: "Nature . . . is what it was of old; but sin, care, and self-consciousness have set the human portion of the world askew" (1,050). The recognition of the continual burden of self-consciousness at one and the same time marks Hawthorne's closeness to the Germans and also indicates his difference. Abrams draws attention to the way in which, in the German version, the artist's or philosopher's vision was presented as both privileged and prophetic of an ending: they, as "the avant-garde of the general human consciousness," possess "the vision of an imminent culmination of history which will be equivalent to a recovered paradise or golden age" (A. 255). Now in *The Marble Faun* the contemporary artist's vision may be privileged but it hardly prophesies any new golden age – whether it is the vision of the characters or that of Hawthorne. The most the artist in the fiction can achieve is, as I have suggested, Kenyon's unfinished bust of Donatello – unfinished partly because it indicates an unending story. Hawthorne refuses even to point towards a Utopia. The fiction ends with Donatello in prison and Miriam suffering. And, while the linking of Hilda and Kenyon could with forcing be assimilated to the pattern Abrams describes, I would argue that it is hard to see this as anything but a retreat and defeat (if, perhaps, a temporary one) – especially as that union and the flight home are explicitly related to Kenyon's and Hilda's hysterical rejection of the Fortunate Fall.[14]

Hawthorne's view of the modern world, while providing an implied reason for valuing the truthtelling, playfulness, and inventiveness of art, is hardly optimistic:

> The entire system of Man's affairs, as at present established, is built up purposely to exclude the careless and happy soul. The very children would upbraid the wretched individual who should endeavour to take life and the world as (what we might naturally suppose them meant for) a place and opportunity for enjoyment.
>
> It is the iron rule in our days, to require an object and a purpose in life. It

> makes us all parts of a complicated scheme of purpose, which can only result in
> our arrival at a colder and drearier region than we were born in . . . We go all
> wrong, by too strenuous a resolution to go all right.          (1,049–50)

This is clearly an authorial voice – and the judgement applies at least as much to America as to Europe. Indeed, playfulness may be – in the abstract – desirable in art and life but the works of art of the past that console and impress Hilda and Kenyon at their lowest moments are those that have suffering as their subject, that cope with contradiction or embody a kind of dynamic tension (to borrow a phrase from Charles Atlas). Thus Hilda (and her author) get comfort from Sodoma's picture of Christ bound to a pillar: "Sodoma . . . has done more towards reconciling the incongruity of Divine Omnipotence and outraged, suffering Humanity, combined in one person, than the theologians ever did" (1,134). Even here, though, one is forced to wonder why the theologians have failed with such a crucial problem – and incongruity is a surprisingly weak term. I have already referred to Kenyon's admiration of the Laocoon. He saw it "as a type of the long, fierce struggle of Man, involved in the knotted entanglements of Errour and Evil, those two snakes, which (if no Divine help intervene) will be sure to strangle him and his children in the end." Kenyon may admire this "as the one triumph of Sculpture" – but Hawthorne may well bracket off the statement about Divine help: knowledge of mythology, available to both Kenyon and the reader, tells us that no intervention occurred – which suggests that this sentence should be read pessimistically: "Thus, in the Laocoon, the horrour of a moment grew to be the Fate of interminable ages" (1,179). In other words, Hawthorne writes the story of the Fortunate Fall as a tragedy and not as a comedy – a comedy, that is, in the sense that Lovejoy uses the word in his classic essay on the *felix culpa*:

> for writers whose purpose, like Milton's, was a religious interpretation of the
> entire history of man, the paradox [of the Fortunate Fall] served, even better
> than the simple belief in a future millenium or celestial bliss, to give to that
> history as a whole the character, not of tragedy, but of a divine comedy. Not
> only should the drama have . . . a happy ending, but the happy ending had been
> implicit in the beginning and been made possible by it.[15]

Perhaps Hawthorne wrote the story as a tragedy because, while he can conceive of a beginning to the narrative of the Fortunate Fall, he is too secular and/or sceptical to project an up-beat ending or, indeed, any conclusion or closure at all. But even with this scepticism, he does, in *The Marble Faun*, offer a model of a "Conjectural Beginning to Human History" – and something of a middle too.

IV

> The history of nature . . . begins with good, for it is the work of God, while the
> history of freedom begins with wickedness, for it is the work of man.[16]

Kant begins his conjectural history by confessing the closeness of such a
project to fiction, but claims that reason and a map provided by Genesis
2–6 may enable him to hypothesize almost playfully about origins of
human freedom. I shall try to use Kant as my principal map to see how
far Hawthorne follows the sign-posts established by the German
intellectual tradition located by Abrams. Hawthorne begins *his* conjectural history by presenting us with a work of art and a handsome but
almost pre-human youth who "might have figured perfectly as the
marble Faun" (859). Reversing the normal process of mimesis, the
sculpture comes before the "model." This is not only a forceful way of
suggesting that, in the modern world, culture, human history inevitably
shapes our perceptions, but also, by presenting Donatello in the light cast
by the pagan sculpture, Hawthorne assimilates the Christian myth of
origins to other narratives of beginnings in Western culture. It is a
remarkably bold and ambitious move. That the sculpture of the Faun
points to origins is clear – but Hawthorne leaves it open as to whether
this is a Greek speculation, a fiction of "a being in whom both races" of
man and animals meet, or something like a real memory, "a poet's
reminiscence of a period when man's affinity with Nature was more
strict" (8,561). Donatello himself, Hawthorne suggests, may be some
kind of bridge between the animal and human worlds:

> And into what regions of rich mystery would it extend Donatello's
> sympathies, to be . . . linked . . . with what we call the inferiour [sic] tribes of
> being, whose simplicity mingled with his human intelligence, might partly
> restore what man has lost of the divine.                                    (910)

The syntax here is not entirely clear: given that Donatello is hardly
notorious in his pre-fallen state for his intellectual powers, presumably
"his human intelligence" refers forward to "man" rather than back to
Donatello – in which case Hawthorne is hinting at the desirability of the
reintegration of man at a higher level. What is clear, however, is that
Hawthorne points to a lost wholeness, a point reinforced by Miriam's
idea of Donatello as "a being not precisely man, nor yet a child, but in a
higher and beautiful sense, an animal; a creature in a state of development
less than what mankind has attained, yet the more perfect within itself
for that very deficiency" (916). Almost exactly like Abrams's Germans,
Hawthorne offers Donatello as being in a state of primitive wholeness – a
wholeness that is nevertheless inadequate.

Kant places his original fictive couple in "a place richly endowed by nature with all means of nourishment and blessed with a perpetually mild climate, hence a garden, as it were" (K.54). Hawthorne cannot offer Donatello and Miriam a genuine garden of Eden – as always in this fiction culture and art shape not only virtually every perception but almost everything that there is to be perceived. But for an Eden before Donatello's fall he can provide the grounds of the Villa Borghese – a place where even the ruins are artificial. This is, it seems, almost a camp Eden, given Hawthorne's sophisticated appreciation of the place:

> The final charm is bestowed by the Malaria. There is a piercing, thrilling, delicious kind of regret in the idea of so much beauty thrown away . . . For if you come hither in summer, and stray through these glades in the golden sunset, Fever walks arm in arm with you and Death awaits you at the end of the dim vista. Thus the scene is like Eden in its loveliness; like Eden, too, in the fatal spell that removes it beyond the scope of man's actual possessions.     (912–3)

The melancholy of the place is, predictably, not felt by Donatello – and for a moment Miriam can, with him beside her, live a fiction of an Arcadian Eden: "It was a glimpse far backward into Arcadian life, or, farther still, into the Golden Age, before mankind was burdened with sin and sorrow, and before pleasure had been darkened with those shadows that bring it into high relief, and make it Happiness" (921–2). But it is only for a moment that this illusion of an a-temporal paradise can be sustained. With the appearance of Miriam's model, her fiction of an escape from temporality collapses under the weight of history back to the fallen actuality as does her fiction of herself as an (artful) nymph:

> Just an instant before, it was Arcadia and the Golden Age. The spell being broken, it was now only that old tract of pleasure-ground, close by the people's gate of Rome: a tract where the crimes and calamities of ages, the many battles, blood recklessly poured out, and deaths of myriads, have corrupted all the soil, creating an influence that makes the air deadly to human lungs.     (927)

The history of fallen man is, it appears, so dominant, so pervasive that it even has dominance over the natural world.

Kant sticks so closely to his Genetic map that he wants his semi-secular version of the fall story to depend on an expansion of the human diet – and thus gets himself into difficulties:

> So long as inexperienced man obeyed this call of nature all was well with him. But soon reason began to stir. A sense different from that to which instinct was tied – the sense, say, of sight – presented other food than that normally consumed as similar to it; and reason, instituting a comparison, sought to enlarge its knowledge of foodstuffs beyond the bounds of instinctual knowledge.     (K.55)

It is hard to see why such a basic human sense as sight should ever conflict with instinct but this is not Kant's only problem. It is all very well to have a symbolic tree of the knowledge of good and evil as that which is to be avoided, but when it is simply a question of just another fruit – a raspberry, say – his argument sounds rather weak as Kant is forced to admit:

> The original occasion for deserting natural instinct may have been trifling. But this was man's first attempt to become conscious of his reason as a power which can extend itself beyond the limits to which all animals are confined. As such its effect was very important and indeed decisive for his future way of life. Thus the occasion may have been merely the external appearance of a fruit which tempted because of its similarity to tasty fruits of which man had already partaken . . . Even so, this was a sufficient occasion for reason to do violence to the voice of nature.                                                      (K.56)

Kant does not even try to strengthen his position by suggesting a more radical dietary change – from, say, vegetarianism to meat-eating. Nor does he put the blame on Eve – even if a greatly changed sexual consciousness is, for him, one crucial consequence of the Fall. Hawthorne avoids these problems by eliding the Biblical story when it comes to the moment of Donatello's Fall. An "Eve" can certainly be said to tempt an "Adam" but the sin is Cain's sin even if the result is as if Donatello had eaten of the tree of knowledge of good and evil. The serpent is understandably absent from the cast since Miriam is already fallen (to appear, however, rather forcefully in her image of the unity between Donatello and herself: "The deed knots us together for time and eternity, like the coil of a serpent!" [997]).

Kant claims that, as an immediate consequence of the Fall, man "discovered in himself a way of life, of not being bound without alternative to a single way, like the animals. Perhaps the discovery of this advantage created a moment of delight" (K.56). Hawthorne's novelistic imagination with its stress on exhilaration and freedom is strikingly close to the conjectures of the philosopher. He tells the reader that "guilt has its moment of rapture, too. The foremost result of a broken law is ever an ecstatic sense of freedom" (999). The two continue to concur as they muse on the further consequences of this fall into freedom. The exhilaration is only momentary. Kant continues "But of necessity, anxiety and alarm as to how he was to deal with this newly discovered power quickly followed" (K.56). Hawthorne offers the sight of the paralyzed Donatello in the Medici Gardens on the day after the night of murder and passion – and Kenyon's gloss on his behaviour: a "calamity . . . threw Donatello into a stupour of misery. Connected with the first shock, there was an intolerable pain and shuddering repugnance"

(1,086).[17] But, despite the misery involved, Kant is in no doubt that the Fall should be seen as Fortunate:

> From this account of orginal human history we may conclude: man's departure from that paradise which his reason represents as the first abode of his species was nothing but the transition from an uncultured, merely animal condition to the state of humanity, from bondage to instinct to rational control – in a word, from the tutelage of nature to the state of freedom.   (K.59–60)

Nor is Hawthorne's fiction as a whole in any doubt about the issue. He is careful to tell us what would have been the consequence had Donatello remained untouched by sin and sorrow. As age crept on, "as the animal spirits settled down upon a lower level, the representative of the Monte Benis was apt to become sensual, addicted to gross pleasures, heavy, unsympathizing, and insulated within the narrow limits of a surly selfishness" (1,046). And when Miriam and Donatello meet in Perugia to receive the blessing of the art-work, the statue of Pope Julius, the authorial voice insists on the beneficial effect on Donatello of the Fall:

> That tone [of voice] . . . bespoke an altered and deepened character; it told of a vivified intellect, and of spiritual instruction that had come through sorrow and remorse; so that – instead of the wild boy, the thing of sportive, animal nature, the sylvan Faun – here was now the man of feeling and intelligence.
>
> (1,119)

Hawthorne could hardly be clearer.[18] The only serious opposition to this idea comes in Kenyon's timid response to Miriam's hypothesis and in Hilda's hysterical refusal to consider Kenyon's formulation of the idea of the Fortunate Fall – and that opposition is compromised for, as we have seen, both Kenyon and Hilda have in effect committed themselves to the validity of the Fortunateness of the Fall, Kenyon in the form his bust takes and Hilda in her interpretation.

The closeness of Donatello's story to the narrative structure identified by Abrams and exemplified by Kant's essay may have its implications for a reading of the ending of *The Marble Faun* – especially if Schiller is also brought into play. The parallels could have been extended had I used his *Something Concerning the First Human Society, According to the Guidance of the Mosaic Records* especially when discussing Miriam's figure of the circle or spiral. Abrams's comment shows Schiller's relevance:

> In Schiller . . . the concept of a fall, or historical decline, has been fused with the idea of progress so as to give history a spiral form; for the unity with himself to which man will return is not only as good as the unity he has forfeited; it is far better.
>
> (A.207)

And Schiller's *On Naive and Sentimental Poetry* (as well as his *Aesthetic Education*) also illuminate *The Marble Faun*.[19] Take, for example, this passage from *On Naive and Sentimental Poetry* which Abrams quotes. In understandable moods of oppression and depression, Schiller says

> we see in non-rational nature only a more fortunate sister who remained at home in her mother's house, out of which we stormed into an alien land in the arrogance of our freedom. The moment we begin to feel the oppression of culture, we desire with painful longing to go back home, and hear, far-off in the alien country of art, the moving voice of the mother. So long as we were mere children of nature, we were both happy and perfect; we have become free, and have lost both.                                                   (A.214)

Thus far Abrams – but it is worth continuing with Schiller:

> Thence arises a dual and very unequal longing for nature, a longing for her *happiness*, a longing for her *perfection*. The sensuous man bemoans the loss of the first; only the moral man can grieve at the loss of the other.[20]

"A longing for her *happiness*" – is this not very close indeed to Donatello's attempt to recover his lost unity with nature when he returns to Monte Beni, and particularly his attempt to re-establish his contact with the animal world with what "might have been the original voice and utterance of the natural man, before the sophistication of the human intellect formed what we now call language"? (1,058). And does not Hilda feel very precisely "the oppression of culture . . . in the alien land of art" in chapter XXXVII, "The Emptiness of Picture Galleries" – and desire to go home? –

> And now, . . . she began to be acquainted with the exile's pain. Her pictorial imagination brought up vivid scenes of her native village, with its great, old-elm trees . . . and her mother's very door, and the stream of gold-brown water . . . Oh, dreary streets, palaces, churches, and imperial sepulchres . . . of Rome, with the muddy Tiber eddying through the midst, instead of the gold-brown rivulet! . . . The peculiar fragrance of a flower-bed . . . came freshly to her memory across the windy sea, and through the long years since the flowers had withered.                                                                          (1,136)

And the parallels continue. Kenyon offers comfort to Donatello – cold though it is: "We all of us, as we grow older . . . lose something of our proximity to Nature. It is the price we pay for experience" (1,059). Schiller is more brusque: "That nature which you envy in the non-rational is worthy of no respect, no longing. It lies behind you, and must lie eternally behind you" (S.188).

If Hawthorne is using much the same narrative form as that identified by Abrams (always remembering that Hawthorne refuses the comedic structure that Abrams's Germans propose), then Abrams' account of the typical conclusion to such stories may help to place Hawthorne's conclusion to *The Marble Faun*:

> The dynamic of the process is the tension toward closure of the divisions, contraries, or "contradictions" themselves. The beginning and end of the journey is man's ancestral home, which is often linked with a female contrary from whom he has, upon setting out, been disparted. The goal of this long inner quest is to be reached by a gradual ascent, or else by a sudden breakthrough of imagination or cognition; in either case, however, the achievement of the goal is pictured as a scene of recognition and reconciliation, and is often signalized by a loving union with the feminine other, upon which man finds himself thoroughly at home with himself, his milieu, and his family of fellow men.                                      (A.255)

This is at once so close to and so different from the form Hawthorne's narrative takes that it reads as though he is self-consciously offering a parodic criticism of that facile optimism. The most apparent contradiction – the paradox of the Fortunate Fall – is (as far as Kenyon and Hilda are concerned) still a contradiction – and one they wish to evade. And while Kenyon returns to his ancestral home with his feminine other, the tone is one of defeat and retreat:

> "Forgive me, Hilda! . . . I never did believe it! . . . I have neither pole-star above, nor light of cottage-windows here below to guide me home. . . . Oh, Hilda, guide me home!"
> "We are both lonely; both far from home!" said Hilda, her eyes filling with tears. "I am a poor, weak girl, and have no such wisdom as you fancy in me."
>                                                                    (1,236)

This is the last piece of dialogue in the novel – and it forms a radical contrast with what Abrams names as lying at the end of the circular voyage: "the attainment of self-knowledge, wisdom and power" (A.255). Hawthorne's gloss on the decision to go home is strikingly half-hearted:

> We defer the reality of life . . . until a future moment, when we shall again breathe our native air; but, by-the-by, there are no future moments; or, if we do return, we find that the native air has lost its invigorating quality, and that life has shifted its reality to the spot where we deemed ourselves only temporary residents. Thus, between two countries, we have none at all, or only that little space of either, in which we finally lay down our discontented bones.                                      (1,237)

These is no sense here of any achievement but rather the tone is that of a sceptic who considers that exile may be man's permanent condition.

V

> "Take heed; for you love one another, and yet your bond is twined with such black threads, that you must never look upon it as identical with the ties that

unite other loving souls. It is for mutual support; it is for one another's final good; it is for effort, for sacrifice, but not for earthly happiness!" (1,121)

If Hawthorne presents the Fortunate Fall as a tragedy rather than a (divine) comedy, then part of the tragedy lies in the fact that there can, according to Hawthorne, at this historical moment be no prediction or vision of a fully redeemed future. There can only be the tragic knowledge which the various characters have more or less absorbed in their various ways – or not absorbed, as in the case of Hilda (and that is *her* tragedy). David Howard offers the carnival scene as what it undoubtedly is – a great achievement of Hawthorne's but also as a positive to set against a lot of negatives:

> It becomes a magnificent image of a revolutionary condition, of a licence drawing on all the forms of the past, and of present society, to make a kind of dance of the dead . . . It is not merely "a sympathy of nonsense" but commands the attention of the whole apparatus of church and state and real power. There seems the possibility of a revolution in earnest . . . The carnival reaches out to encompass everything: "The sport of mankind, like its deepest earnest, is a battle."[21]

But unfortunately the carnival opens up possibilities only to close them off again. All that the characters get from the carnival is the arrest of Donatello and the related return of Hilda. The arrest involves corrupt state power, "an inscrutable tyranny" (1,232), and the most that could possibly be claimed for that arrest is that Donatello has by insisting on his guilt forced that State to act ethically by arresting a private murderer whom otherwise it would be happy enough to ignore. The return of Hilda is not so much the return of the repressed but rather the return of the repressor. The circle, then, when we go beyond Miriam's version of the tale of Donatello, may be, so to speak, a vicious one. It is here that Hawthorne breaks with the narrative structure identified by Abrams and we can now see that in the last chapter Hawthorne has set up the image of a different kind of circle to set against the positive image deployed by Miriam. That final chapter may have the same title as the first ("Miriam, Hilda, Kenyon, Donatello") but Donatello is absent – and Miriam is silent while her "extended hands, even while they blessed, seemed to repel" (1,237). We have an absence in the text and, with Miriam, a moment of stasis – a stasis that is reached by the pressure of opposites.

That ambivalence about the figure of the circle/spiral can best be shown by putting a famous passage from Coleridge's letters in evidence – a letter which unambiguously celebrates circularity:

> The common end of all *narrative*, nay, of *all*, Poems is to convert a *series* into a *Whole*: to make those events, which in real or imagined History move on in a

> *strait* Line, assume to our *Understandings* a *circular* motion – the snake with its
> Tail in its Mouth.

Coleridge goes on to make it quite clear that the narrative or poem
should mimic in miniature God's creation. Thus, by implication, the
achieving of a circular structure is, so to speak, a happy ending or at the
least a satisfying culmination to the artist's work:

> Doubtless, to *his* [God's] eye, which alone comprehends all Past and Future in
> one eternal Present, what to our short sight appears strait is but part of the great
> Cycle . . . Now what the Globe is in Geography, *miniaturing* in order to *manifest*
> the Truth, such is a poem to that Image of God which we were created into.

Hawthorne is, as I tried to show earlier, hardly coy about emphasizing
the figure of the circle in his final chapter but he lacks Coleridge's neo-
Platonic optimism. Miriam's description of Donatello's career can be
assimilated to Coleridge's idea without much difficulty:

> tho' in order to be an individual Being it must go forth *from* God, yet as the
> receding from *him* is to *proceed* towards Nothingness and Privation, it must
> still at every step turn back toward him to *be* at all – Now a straight Line,
> continuously retracted, forms of necessity a circular orbit.[22]

But her judgement not only comes before the final chapter, it also has to
be set beside what may be Kenyon's scepticism – though it sounds very
like that of the author:

> the ways of Providence are utterly inscrutable; and many a murder has been
> done, and many an innocent virgin has lifted her white arms, beseeching its aid
> in her extremity, and all in vain; so that, though Providence is infinitely good
> and wise, (and perhaps for that very reason,) it may be half an eternity before
> the great circle of its scheme shall bring us the superabundant recompense for
> all these sorrows! But what the lover asked, was such prompt consolation as
> might consist with the brief span of mortal life . . .            (1,198)

No wonder Hawthorne wrote in *The English Notebooks* that God himself
could not compensate him for life being anything short of eternity – and
no wonder he turned to *The Elixir of Life* theme.

According to Kenyon, the circular Pantheon is the "noblest edifice"
which the "barbarism" of the past has spared to us. He sees its
significance as lying in yet another circle, in "the aperture in the Dome –
that great Eye, gazing heavenward – . . . It is so heathenish, as it were; – so
unlike all the snugness of our modern civilization!" (1,233). Rather
surprisingly Hilda does not rebuke him for this – but she offers her own
gloss on its meaning: "Would it be any wonder if we were to see angels
hovering there, . . . not intercepting the light, but only transmuting it
into beautiful colours?" (1,234). Here the circle contains two radically

opposed meanings rather than any higher unity. And here I want to circle back to that bridal gift of Miriam's to Hilda of the bracelet. It was "composed of seven ancient Etruscan gems, dug out of seven sepulchres, and each one of them the signet of some princely personage who had lived an immemorial time ago" (1,237). The Etruscan reference points us back towards a mythical golden age about which we can only speculate while the bracelet is a modern work, which incorporates within it tokens of an irrecoverable past, containing within itself signs of a past whose meanings have to be speculated about, which are, indeed, spaces for free invention: "once, with the exuberance of fancy that distinguished her," Miriam "had amused herself with telling a mythical and magic legend for each gem, comprising the imaginary adventures and catastrophe of its former wearer" (1,237). But her "historical" fictions are "characterized by a sevenfold sepulchral gloom" – a subjective vision shaped by "her own misfortunes" (1,238). There is no suggestion that the modern bracelet by incorporating these mysterious fragments of the past in any way transcends them. Gone, in the final paragraph of the fiction, is anything like Miriam's optimism as well as any Coleridgean sense that a circular structure somehow mirrors relevantly God's vision. That circular bracelet tragically signifies a "sad mystery." After all this, it is hard to feel much confidence in Hilda's sunny vision: "a hopeful soul" is, at this late stage in the novel, scarcely firm ground to build on.

I suggested earlier that Hawthorne takes a profoundly ambivalent attitude to Hilda and what she stands for. I do not mean just that it is hard to believe that someone usually so piercingly intelligent about moral matters could miss the moral, emotional and intellectual dishonesty of Hilda's use or misuse of the confessional, for, while I do find this hard to take, I do not see that here at least Hawthorne intends any criticism of his virginal heroine. It can be claimed in Hilda's defense that Hilda has made a pardonable mistake for one of her naivety – and Hawthorne does say that Catholicism would be an excellent religion were the priests superhuman. But I think that the beginnings of evidence for taking a somewhat critical look can be found elsewhere in the novel – in, indeed, the first chapter. There Miriam says "Our friend Donatello is the very Faun of Praxiteles. Is it not true, Hilda?" Hilda replies in a surprisingly dithering way for someone "whose perceptions of form and expression" are supposed to be "wonderfully clear and delicate": "Not quite – almost – yes, I really think so" (858–9). Her response to a question about Donatello's age equally lacks Napoleonic decisiveness: "Twenty years perhaps . . . But, indeed, I cannot tell; hardly so old on second thoughts, or possibly older. He has nothing to do with time, but has a look of eternal youth in his face" (864).[23] Those are minor points, of course. But, given that Donatello's "wonderful resemblance" to the Faun of

Praxiteles forms the key-note of our narrative" (869), it is hard to forgive or even understand Hilda's response to another of Miriam's questions. She, meditating on the Faun in the second chapter, claims that "He is not supernatural, but just on the verge of Nature, and yet within it," and goes on to ask our heroine "What is the nameless charm of this idea, Hilda? You can feel it more delicately than I." Hilda's response is more than a trifle weak: "It perplexes me," said Hilda, thoughtfully and shrinking a little; "neither do I quite like to think about it" (862). If she is, as she repeatedly claims, a daughter of the Puritans, then it has to be said that their tradition has become if not decadent then dangerously attenuated. Milton should indeed be living at this hour.

These examples of Hilda's inadequacies may be dismissed as too trivial to convince. I would agree that the case against her must confront her explicit denunciation of the Fortunate Fall if it is to have any chance of succeeding:

> "Oh, hush!" cried Hilda, shrinking from him with an expression of horrour which wounded the poor speculator sculptor to the soul. "This is terrible; and I could weep for you if indeed you believe it. Do not you perceive what a mockery your creed makes, not only of all religious sentiment, but of moral law, and how it annuls and obliterates whatever precepts of Heaven are written deepest within us? You have shocked me beyond words." (1,236)

Well, one has to note that she has not – alas – been shocked beyond words. And is there any evidence from the narrative that Hilda's verdict is correct? It can hardly be said of Donatello and Miriam, the two most directly implicated in the sin, that there are any signs that moral law or the precepts of Heaven have been annulled or obliterated within them. The very opposite is closer to the story we have been following. Nor has Hilda evaded involvement in that story for she has firmly committed herself to the Fortunate Fall as narrative if not as logical proposition in her appreciation of the bust of Donatello. The most subtle way that Hawthorne subverts Hilda's hysterical repudiation of the Fortunate Fall is related to the manner in which he situates the Fall as a formula in his narrative. Male fails to notice that the repetition of that formula makes it one element in Hawthorne's narrative structure. Miriam first puts the proposition to Kenyon who, almost exactly like Hilda, is shocked. Kenyon, when discussing Donatello's progress, puts an hypothesis to Hilda: "Life has grown so sadly serious, that such men must change their nature, or else perish, like the antediluvian creatures that required, as the condition of their existence, a more summer-like atmosphere than ours" (1,235–6). When that historical hypothesis is rejected by our immaculate virgin, he retreats to another: the Fortunate Fall. We have seen how that was received. Given that Kenyon virtually repeats Miriam word for word (with the exception of her celebration of the circle), given that we have ample evidence of Hilda's (unconscious?) commitment to the Fortunate Fall in its narrative form, given that the form of *The Marble Faun* resists closure, then (as I suggested in the last chapter) does not the fiction as a whole invite a reader to consider very seriously the possibility that, in some quiet New England village, Hilda may very well do as Kenyon has done – and enunciate the apparent heresy, the seeming paradox, of the Fortunate Fall? Otherwise, what has she got out of Europe that is not available to the most simple-minded tourist – though, admittedly, few tourists get to see a genuine olde worlde murder?

If her rebuttal is accepted, then Hilda must be seen to have been used by Hawthorne to subvert, even destroy, Donatello's story, the central strand of the narrative. *The Marble Faun* would then come dangerously close to being a self-consuming artefact. Myra Jehlen has this to say of Hilda's refusal to listen to Miriam's account of the night of sin and passion:

> The problem is that her refusal to listen to Miriam's story effectively stops not only Miriam but also the development of the novel's story, at least in that direction. Indeed, Hilda's determination not to alter her divinely deeded robe would require her to reject any story, even one with a pious ending. *It amounts to a rejection of story as such.*                                    (her emphasis)

If this is true of that comparatively minor incident, how much truer and more important it is when applied to Hilda's horror of the idea of the Fortunate Fall. Jehlen seems to think that Hilda's position is perfectly valid: "As moral philosophy . . . Hilda's reasoning works perfectly well. Nor does it seem to me problematical in her own character."[24] However, I am not sure that Jehlen has realized just how high the stakes are. The rejection of one story in the middle of a larger narrative is easily bearable, of course, but the implications of the final rejection of the Fortunate Fall story if accepted would mean that Hawthorne had allowed Hilda to repudiate, to cancel almost all of his narrative. In other words, if we swallow Hilda's rejection of that story whole, then Hawthorne as much as Kenyon is to be rebuked: he should not have written Donatello's story, he should not have written *The Marble Faun*. Indeed, if Jehlen's point is taken just a little further, he should not be a novelist, for the original sin looks, from Hilda's and Jehlen's position, very like writing or even reading a story.

If my hypothesis about the New England village is legitimate – and it does seem that the logic of the narrative permits the possibility – then it would appear that Hawthorne intends and even needs the last lines of the novel to be read with at least a pinch of irony not only at Hilda's expense but also at that of readers who demand conventional happy endings:

"But Hilda had a hopeful soul, and saw sunlight on the mountain-tops." Hill-tops are, after all, sunny in the light of a setting as well as a rising sun – and we should remember that the bottled sunshine, the wine of Monte Beni, does not travel. More importantly, there is a moment when sunshine on mountain-tops is described – and it is not a reassuring one:

> Far into this misty cloud-region, however – within the domain of Chaos, as it were – hill-tops were seen brightening in the sunshine; they looked like fragments of the world, broken adrift and based on nothingness, or like portions of a sphere destined to exist, but not yet finally compacted. (1,072)

Even if the gaze shifts heavenward, "it looked airy and insubstantial, like the dreams of an alchemist" (1,073). Perhaps some comfort could be gleaned from what Kenyon "fancied" as he looks out on the natural world: "the scene represented the process of the Creator, when He held the new, imperfect Earth in His hand, and modelled it" (1,072). But surely this has to be cold comfort: not only is this merely a fancy of Kenyon's, a metaphor arising from his profession as sculptor, but Hawthorne introduces in that fancy the possibility of another and potentially more dangerous heresy than the Fortunate Fall could ever be. Can the Creator's work at any stage before the Fall be seen as imperfect? Unfinished it may be – but hardly imperfect. A vision of "Chaos," of "fragments . . . based on nothingness" is hardly one that solid hopes can be built on. The most that can be offered, apparently, is an act of faith – that here are "portions of a sphere" (a circle to end all circles?) which resembles something destined to exist at some point in an unknowable future.

The Fortunate Fall story, though clearly it could be and indeed has been treated in terms of a Puritan world-view, is here to be seen not in terms of that tradition, but rather in terms of the Romantic transformation of the Genesis story as identified by Abrams – that is, it is to be seen in those terms up to the point at which the Romantic version of the Fall narrative offers or predicts a semi-secular happy ending while Hawthorne proffers instead a tragic structure which sceptically interrogates the positive valuation of that circular story. I suppose it might just be possible to argue that the tragic direction that Hawthorne gives to the narrative could be read as the return by the back-door of a disillusioned semi-Calvinistic Puritanism. However, the entire absence of any reference to the figure or even the role of a Christ would need some explaining away given its crucial importance in the Miltonic version.[25] And, if I am right that Hawthorne provides material for an ironic subversion of Hilda, then the novel cannot permit the return of even a decadent Puritanism. This is to suggest that *The Marble Faun* is, if not a proto-modernist work – a nineteenth century *Ulysses* or *Waste-Land*, say

– then it is one that is self-consciously post-Romantic in its meditations on a modern art and its difficulties. I have argued that Hawthorne offers Kenyon's bust of Donatello as a type of a modern art. But it must be remembered that, however much of an achievement it may be, it has to be read as a very fragile project, and also one, perhaps, that is in danger of making other works almost redundant. On the one hand, it can hardly be expected that a career can be made out of modelling Donatellos for, at this stage of the world's history, however representative his story may be, Donatellos are rare. On the other hand, if this is the central narrative of humanity, then one sculpture telling the tale may be enough – though one justification for the fiction's existence is the need to supplement the sculpture with a narrative that situates the sculpture and what it symbolizes in a variety of histories. And the process of creating such sculptures is pretty chancy – given Kenyon's lack of control over his creation.

The last of Kenyon's artistic activities is his attempt to gather the limbs of Venus ("one of the few works of antique sculpture in which we recognize Womanhood, and that, moreover, without prejudice to its divinity" [1,207]) – an attempt to re-create a fragmented antiquity. (It has, significantly, been discovered by Donatello – "his keen eyes detected the fallen goddess" (1,209) – and at this late stage in the narrative "fallen" is a word that resonates. Kenyon, having abandoned his bust of Donatello, does much the same by Venus, when he remembers Hilda, "by the greater strength of a human affection, the divine statue seemed to fall asunder again, and became only a heap of fragments" (1,207). With these contrasting kinds of art, Kenyon spans the historical alternatives available to one kind of modern man: the recovery and re-creation of the antique world and the production of an image of dynamic, open-ended growth. But he abandons both as well as fleeing from the intellectual and moral challenge of the Fortunate Fall. Kenyon is, then, so to speak, a failed Hawthorne. From a world composed of fragments, of the unfinished, Hawthorne constructs a fiction which is a critical anthology of examples of such issues and self-conscious enough about such issues not only to include a chapter entitled "Fragmentary Sentences" but also where the very form of the fiction as a whole is mimetic of these concerns. It offers itself as a confrontation with the problems and difficulties of being modern in a world overladen with history – history, that is, almost exclusively defined in this fiction as the past and historical problems equally almost exclusively defined in terms of the proper attitude to take to the past – or pasts.

*The Marble Faun* is so ambitious that it is tempting to explain that the unfinished novels remain unfinished not merely in the terms of the death of the author but also by an only too understandable feeling on the author's part: how am I going to top *that*? How am I to go beyond what I have achieved here? *The Elixir of Life Manuscripts*, however, suggests that Hawthorne had recognized one omission in *The Marble Faun*. What *The Marble Faun* does lack is, oddly, any real notion of the future. When earlier I discussed the encyclopedic tendency of the fiction, I mentioned the ambition of trying to include all history. That would have been better phrased as – all *past* history. Despite the fact that the action takes place in the very recent past, there is virtually no consideration of a future history – and when it does appear it tends to be referred to in semi-religious terms:

> you behold the obelisks, with their unintelligible inscriptions, hinting at a Past infinitely more remote than history can define. Your own life is as nothing, when compared with that immeasurable distance; but still you demand, none the less earnestly, a gleam of sunshine, instead of a speck of shadow, on the step or two that will bring you to your quiet rest . . .
>
> How wonderful, that this our narrow foothold of the Present should hold its own so constantly, and, while every moment changing, should still be like a rock betwixt the encountering tides of the long Past and the infinite To-come! (1,196)

What does fascinate Hawthorne both here and throughout the fiction is that fictive construct we are often so committed to – the idea of the now. Perhaps the most explicit statement of its fictive nature comes when Miriam and Donatello have disguised themselves as peasant and contadina and have attempted in this fancy-dress to escape (however momentarily) from the burden of history both past and future into the Paradise of a Present:

> The fancy impressed him [Kenyon], that she, too, like Donatello, had reached a wayside Paradise, in their mysterious life-journey, where they both threw down the burthen of the Before and After, and, except for this interview with himself, were happy in the flitting moment. To-day, Donatello was the sylvan Faun; to-day Miriam was his fit companion, a Nymph of grove or fountain; tomorrow – a remorseful Man and Woman, linked by a marriage-bond of crime – they would set forth towards an inevitable goal. (1,215)

Miriam and Donatello may attempt to play out a mythic version of the pastoral – but just as the idea of the now is a fiction, so myth is a fiction. It is with *The Elixir of Life Manuscripts* that we get another and (at least potentially) profounder meditation on the nature of history. It is set at a time of revolution, the consequences of which, as Hawthorne tells us, are still reverberating in his time, and it concerns a character who, while drawing immensely on the heritage of the ages, does so in the name of a claim on the future.

# 9

## The Elixir of Life Manuscripts: *"Had we but world enough and time . . ."*

I

God himself cannot compensate us for being born, in any period short of eternity.     *(English Notebooks*, Jan. 20, 1855)

Express strongly the idea that the shortness &c of life shows that human action is a humbug.     (XIII, 507)

As for Septimius, let him alone a moment or two, and then you would see him, with his head bent down, brooding, brooding, with his eyes fixed on some chip, some stone, some common plant, any commonest thing, as if it were the clue and index to some mystery; and when, by chance startled out of these meditations, he lifted his eyes, there would be a kind of perplexity, a dissatisfied, wild look in them, as if, of his speculations, he found no end.
    (XIII, 6)

"May it not be possible," asked Septimius, "to have too profound a sense of the marvellous contrivance and adaptation of this material world, to require or believe in anything spiritual? How wonderful it is, to see it all alive on this spring day, all growing, gushing! Do we exhaust it all in our little life? Not so; not in a hundred or thousand lives. The whole race of man, living from the beginning of time, have not, in all their number and multiplicity and in all their duration, come in the least to know the world they live in! And how is this rich world thrown away upon us, because we live in it such a moment. What mortal work has ever been done since the world began! Because we have no time. No lesson is taught. We are snatched away from our study, before we have learned the alphabet. As the world now exists – I confess it to you, frankly, my dear pastor and instructor – it seems to me all a failure, because we do not live long enough."     (XIII, 11–12)

The Elixir of Life material develops out of the differing concerns of *The American Claimant Manuscripts* and *The Marble Faun* while attempting to go beyond them. The relation of Septimius's search for immortality to the claimant's fascination with what the English estate symbolizes for him is clear enough as I will try to show: Septimius's project is, so to speak, a mirror image of the claimant's – as an attitude towards the future reflects an attitude to the past. In the way this material self-consciously raises questions about the nature and function of the artist's work, in its encyclopedic ambitions and in its sceptical questioning of conventional theological positions, it is also close to *The Marble Faun* (though a Faustian attempt to replace supernaturalism by natural supernaturalism – in the sense of Goethe's rather than Marlowe's Faust – replaces the Fortunate Fall as a central concern).

Perhaps the most striking formal difference between this volume of unfinished work and *The American Claimant* is that there are few or none of the signs of struggle with a recalcitrant plot that so mark *Etherege* in particular – except for *The Dolliver Romance* but in that case there is so little material – and exhaustion, illness and the consciousness of approaching death are, sadly, probably sufficient explanation. This difference presents problems in discussing the material. It is necessary to treat *The American Claimant Manuscripts* as three separate (if closely related) pieces of work. Here, leaving *The Dolliver Romance* on one side, we have, along with a number of studies and a detailed scenario (XIII, 498–530), a completed draft (*Septimius Felton*, XIII, 3–194), and a revised and expanded but incomplete version of the story (*Septimius Norton*, XIII, 195–497). The scenario appears to have been written between the completion of *Felton* and the beginning of *Norton*, and *Norton* was, as the editors show, written with *Felton* in front of Hawthorne. *Norton* is basically an expansion of *Felton*, though there are differences – for example there are changes in the ordering of the material and in the weight given to Septimius's genealogy. Hawthorne also had to tidy up his story after he had changed his mind half-way through *Felton* about making one of the young heroines Septimius's half-sister rather than his fiancée. Given the amount of repetition and the extent to which the second version is often little more than an expanded version of the first, it is hard to justify treating the two pieces separately, but it is equally impossible to concentrate exclusively on either the first or second version. I have chosen to focus on *Norton* for the first part of the story and to revert to *Felton* when Hawthorne's abandonment of *Norton* means that the story only exists in the scenario and in *Felton*. I have, however, drawn on the earlier part of *Felton* where the differences between the two versions seem relevant.

*Norton* is abandoned for no apparent reason half way through the ninth of the fifteen scenes that Hawthorne had projected in his scenario. *Felton* and the scenario suggest that Hawthorne knew where he was going – and why he failed to continue Septimius's story can only be a matter for speculation. If nothing had followed *Norton*, then it might be easier to understand, but Hawthorne turned instead in the last half of 1863 to *The Dolliver Romance*, where, instead of following the spiritual and intellectual adventures of a young man who wishes for and works towards immortality for (mostly) the best of reasons, he projected an old man who would become younger and who might already be in possession of the elixir of immortality. Again there are sketches in which we can see Hawthorne speculating about his story but, oddly, there is no overt reference back to the story of Septimius. All that we have of this last brave effort are bits and pieces – "I see nothing better than to call the series of articles 'Fragments of a Romance'" – and Hawthorne's recognition that he would never finish:

> I hardly know what to say to the Public about this abortive Romance, though I know pretty well what the case will be. I shall never finish it. Yet it is not quite pleasant for an author to announce himself, or to be announced, as finally broken down as to his literary faculty . . . I cannot finish it, unless a great change comes over me; and if I make too great an effort to do so it will be my death.
>
> (XVIII, 612, 640–1)

This is poignant enough as it stands – what makes it so very painful is that Hawthorne had high ambitions for this work: "I have a notion that this last book would be my best; and full of wisdom about matters of life and death" (XVIII, 626). This is sadly reminiscent of "Fragments of the Journal of a Solitary Man," where the young Hawthorne had speculated about the death of his alter ego, the youthful writer, Oberon: "He had evidently cherished a secret hope that some impulse would at length be given him . . . But life never called the dreamer forth; it was Death that whispered him" (T&S, 488). Hawthorne died on the night of May 16, 1864, leaving behind him, like Oberon, fragments for an editor to bring before the public. In the case of Septimius's story at least, the writing is so fascinating that we must congratulate those editors who, like the fictive editor of "Fragments," have strung "together in a semblance of order my Oberon's 'random pearls'" (T&S, 487).

If my hypothesis about the effect of the Civil War on the writing of the American claimant fictions is correct, it is not hard to see why and how Hawthorne, while carrying over many of the concerns of the claimant material, turned to the themes of *The Elixir of Life Manuscripts* – and why, particularly, he chose to set *Felton* and *Norton* at the time of the American Revolution – a time of disturbance and divided loyalties very like the civil conflict surrounding Hawthorne and, ironically, the beginning event of the American story of the United States which Hawthorne fears he may see concluded if the Union is fragmented. And the problems that concern Septimius are, up to a point, strikingly analogous to those of an artist like Hawthorne – at one and the same time feeling distanced from the conflict and also (perhaps unconsciously in Septimius's case) a product of that conflict. At the same time that *Felton* and *Norton* dramatize problems analogous to Hawthorne's very situation as a writer, these fictions continue from and build on the earlier work – and not merely in such details as the Bloody Footstep which obsessively stuck in his memory. The American claimant wanted to hook himself on to an old English family to provide himself with a continuous history, so that he might acquire a sense of his identity as something stable and real – and that desire is strikingly analogous to Septimius's project. (Incidentally, it also takes us back to Oberon, who once "fancied that my sleep would not be quiet in the grave unless I should return, as it were, to my home of past ages" [T&S, 489].) A passage I have already drawn on from *Etherege* will indicate the parallels between the searcher for a past and the quester for a future history. The old family home "was a device for giving length, fullness, body, substance, to this thin and frail matter of human life" (xii, 186). If "the family home" is replaced by "immortality," the sentence would speak directly to Septimius's condition and desire, his sense of the profound inadequacy of the conventional three score years and ten:

> "I doubt, if it had been left to my choice, whether I should have taken existence on these terms; so much trouble of preparation to live, and then no life at all; a ponderous beginning, and nothing more."

> "[W]e find [man], just opening his eyes, crawling about a little, and then dying, without really so much as one moment enjoying the earth, for which he was made, and was made for him, when the elaborateness of the make of each, and the relations between each, would seem to indicate thousands of years for the existence of that relation; if indeed the individual man should not be as permanent as the earth on which he lives."        (xiii, 7, 201)

This ingenious perversion (if perversion it be) of the argument from design gains a certain piquancy from the fact that Septimius is expected to become a minister – and, as I hope to show, suggests that one theme that Hawthorne is playing with is to consider Septimius as enacting a secular version of the Puritan way of life (and death).

Despite the difference in means, there is something very similar about the ends the claimant and Septimius have in mind. The claimant looks to the past for a way of establishing himself as a link in a great chain, while Septimius (who has, as we shall see, the longest possible American genealogy) hopes to project himself into an unending future. Yet, while his desire for immortality may have more noble and certainly has more energetic motives than those of the claimant, Septimius, like the claimant, feels that he needs to protect and sustain his identity – even though he wants to experiment with a multiplicity of selves. As he says to the significantly named Sybil, "I would fain, if I might, live everybody's life at once – or since that may not be, each in succession." He envisages the acquiring of immortality as analogous to becoming an heir, "as a man newly coming into possession of an estate" (XIII, 170). But special precautions are necessary even if he is, unlike the claimant, willing to become his own ancestor. When he muses about the advantages and risks of immortality, he considers that it must not be a solitary success, that identity is necessarily dependent on society – even if it is to be a society of two:

> unless he strung the pearls and diamonds of life upon one unbroken affection, he sometimes thought that his life would have nothing to give it unity and identity; and so the longest life would be but an aggregate of insulated fragments, which would have no relation to one another, and so it would not be one life, but many unconnected ones. Unless . . . some sympathy of a life side by side with his could melt two into one; looking back upon the same things, looking forward to the same; the long, thin thread of an individual life, stretching onward and onward, would cease to be visible, cease to be felt, cease by and by to have any real bigness in proportion to its breadth, and so be virtually non-existent except in the mere inconsiderable now.   (XIII, 150–1)

When Sybil, as the two fantasize about their future, pleads for a few centuries of sleep, Septimius is horrified partly because his spirit rejoices "in the thought of an infinite activity" but also for *self* preservation:

> "I fear . . . our identity would change in that repose; it would be a Lethe between the two parts of our being, and with such disconnection, a continued life would be equivalent to a new one, and therefore valueless."   (XIII, 177)

His attempt at a revolutionary break with the past habits of humanity is to be a once and for all rupture. Thereafter the continuity of *his* consciousness at least must be of paramount importance – and that continuity is, for him, crucially dependent on the existence of another consciousness. At the end of the scenario, Hawthorne insisted on Septimius's radical dreams for social transformation as one of the most important motives for desiring immortality – thus, incidentally, not only making another link between Septimius's projects and the American Revolution but also showing that his ministerial ambitions have not totally disappeared, heretical though they may be:

> One of Septimius's grand objects is to reform the world, which he thinks he can do; if he can only live long to study and understand the nature of men, and get at the proper methods of acting on them. The reason why the world has remained dark, ignorant, and miserable is, because the benefactors of the race have been cut off before they more than partially understood their task, and the

> methods of it. This must be broached in his first conversation with the
> minister; perhaps in reference to the troubles of the country, and the war, then
> about to begin. When he shall have completed the reformation of the world,
> seen war, intemperance, slavery, all manner of crime, brought to an end; then
> he will die. (XIII, 529)

Yet he immediately goes on to say that the likely result would probably
be an increasing selfishness – not surprising perhaps given the
megalomania implied by this one man's attempt to create a heaven on
earth. But Hawthorne throughout the two narratives extends his
criticism. There are repeated ironic hints that, whatever the radical hopes
of the seeker for immortality, possession of immortality may make the
would-be revolutionary a conservative of conservatives in spite of
himself – a point of view that carried over to *The Dolliver Romance*
where Hawthorne makes the point explicitly when the old man is
described as "so conservative" (XIII, 544). Septimius's attempt may not
only be doomed to failure in the sense that he makes a poison instead of
the elixir of life – but the very pursuit of the goal of immortality may be
self-imprisonment rather than freedom to change the world.

It should, then, come as no surprise that, when his dream of the elixir's
potency is shattered by Sybil's sacrificial proof that he had made a
poison, Septimius might retreat to an English estate – and not only
because the plot has prepared the reader for such a choice (with the
references to documents and the Doctor's enquiries about his family tree)
but because it makes perfect thematic sense and sense too in terms of
Septimius's psychology. Inherited possession of such a property is the
nearest equivalent to physical immortality that Septimius can get. That it
is a claim on the past principally rather than on the future is Hawthorne's
ironic criticism:

> I . . . should be rather sorry to believe, that, after such magnificent schemes as
> he had entertained, he should have been content to settle down into the fat
> substance and reality of an English life. (XIII, 193)

This is to argue against what seems to have been a general judgement
on Septimius's project – that Hawthorne intended the search for an elixir
to be seen as silly. Thus Baym complains

> Perhaps Hawthorne meant to associate a foolish search for the elixir of life with
> the foolish search for an English connection, but the identification of these two
> motifs is farfetched and requires excessive rhetorical elaboration for its
> basically minor place in the story.

And the editors of the Elixir material are quite clear in their minds when
they comment on the revisions that went to make up *Norton*:
"Hawthorne's own judgement emerges transparently in his report of

Septimius's reveries which leave no doubt that he considered them misguided" (XIII, 570). I hope I have said enough to show that there is a significant and clear analogy between the two searches. And Hawthorne went to considerable length to emphasize that Septimius's project should not be dismissed as foolish or irrational. Immoral it may be – or the moral end initially in view may necessarily but not obviously involve immoral means – but that is another matter. Given his genealogy, given the revolutionary situation which disrupts conventional ideas about reality, and given the state of scientific knowledge at the time, "it would be difficult, from the incidents of this narrative, to show that Septimius did anything that a wise man, on similar grounds, and with the same phenomena before him, would not have felt impelled to do; and it is a point which we are not aware human science has yet attained, if his idea can be said, on absolute proof, to be an absurdity" (XIII, 254). To complain, as Baym does, that "an emigrated ancestor, a bloody footstep, an American claim on an English estate" were not "germane"[1] is to fail to notice that there is a sense in which Septimius is intended to be an heir of all the ages, and that thus Hawthorne had very good reasons for wanting to get the middle ages or at least the Renaissance into his fiction – and Sybil's tale of the Bloody Footstep is a nicely economical way of doing this. Not only does it raise the topic of traditional legends and their relation to history, not only does it have its part to play in the complex question of Septimius's genealogy, it also should remind us that the text with which Septimius struggles is an alchemical one. I shall be returning to many of these topics – and especially genealogy and revolution for they resonate through the whole of *Felton* and *Norton* – but what should be emphasized here is Hawthorne's explicit statement that, scientifically at least, Septimius's plans are not unreasonable:

> electricity had been discovered, and at a comparatively recent date, by an American. It had seemed to open a new epoch, from which no one could tell how much might be expected, or what effect this mysterious agency was destined to have; so subtle as it was, so like spirit, so pervading; and there were many who deemed themselves philosophers, at that day, who had projects at least as absurd as that of our poor Septimius, who, after all, was not so very absurd in so far as he supposed that human life had been shortened, by men's own neglect of natural laws, to a period very far briefer than his Creator originally intended. The difference might be ten years, or ten centuries – still he was right as to his fact. (XIII, 269)

That is not to say that irony does not from time to time play over Septimius – but "still he was right as to his fact."

Perhaps the most important index of the radical differences between *The American Claimant* and *The Elixir of Life Manuscripts* is the choice of historical moment for *Felton* and *Norton* and the continued insistence on the importance of that moment – as, for example, Septimius's plans are repeatedly contrasted with those of his soldier friend as ways of responding to revolutionary upheaval. *Grimshawe* may have begun with a period just after the American Revolution, but that is only the beginning of the claimant's tale, and, in coming to England, he flees from the agitating world of American history to the sinister security of an England apparently safely locked in the past – while the Revolution right up to the collapse of Septimius's hopes is the crucially important frame for this actions. The historical moment is the more important because of its parallels with Hawthorne's present – and the more noticeable given the paucity of Hawthorne's fiction which deals *directly* with the Revolution. He can now take emotional and imaginative possession of that time of the birth of a nation because his emotional experience in the present has taken possession of him:

> Every ordinary man . . . was today a nobler creature, and drew heroic breath . . . while besmeared and bemuddled with the toil and petty thoughts of daily life; so that he felt himself another man, and beheld his familiar neighbor transfigured since yesterday . . . Oh high, heroic, tremulous crisis; when standing on the verge of a struggle that weeded out whatever was feeble in his nature, man felt himself almost an angel, from his set purpose to thrust, to smite, to slay, to take on himself the responsibility of man's life-blood and the tears wrung out of woman's heart. We know something of that time, now; we that have seen the muster of the village company, . . . beheld the familiar faces, that we hardly knew, because a moment had transformed them into the faces of heroes; . . . felt how a great impulse lifts up a whole people, and every cold, indifferent spectator, making him religious whether he will or no, and compelling him, however reluctantly, to join in that great act of devotion which we recognize when so many myriads of hearts conspire together for something beyond their own selfish ends.                (XIII, 217–8)

Hawthorne carefully makes it clear that it is analogy he is aiming for rather than identity. His model of history would collapse if it were to be dependent on repetition – for example, if the idea of identity was pursued too far, the South would have to be the equivalent to the thirteen states and the North would have to be seen as the equivalent to England. And within the fiction repetition is presented as a terrifying possibility. Septimius is Romantic enough to be shocked by the notion that he may have no genuine individuality but is merely one in a long family line: "he was depressed and appalled by the idea that he had really been extant, nobody knows how long; repeated identically from generation to generation" (XIII, 295). This fear that he may be only the product of history's assembly-line is transferred to a fear that, if he achieves his ambition, the future may come in the form of drearily predictable cycles:

"Perhaps . . . we shall discover that the same old scenery serves the world's stage in all ages, and that the story is always the same, yes, and the actors always the same, though none but we may be aware of it; and that the actors and spectators would grow weary of it, were they not bathed in forgetful sleep, and so think themselves new made in each successive lifetime." (XIII, 176)

It would indeed be a cruel irony if immortality was to give Septimius and Sybil unique access to the sheer boringness of world history.

For all that Hawthorne may have called *Felton* an "internal" story, he had to admit when revising the passage for *Norton* that "the course of the narrative running along like a vine sometimes leads us amid historic events," and he chose to begin the action by reference to "a great historical event" (XIII, 15, 210) – the battle of Lexington. The revolutionary atmosphere affects the way in which Septimius conceives his project: "he deceived himself, when he imagined that the feverish excitement, which was throbbing through the veins of all his countrymen, had no effect upon his own dreamy composure" (XIII, 225). The spirit of the times may take freedom from the would-be ironic spectator and make him a revolutionary, in spite of himself the prisoner of a history he thinks irrelevant to him. It is that fever which stimulates Septimius to take his gun out on to the hill, and to kill the Englishman from whom he obtains the document which seems to contain the recipe for immortality, and his investigation continues in parallel with the historical ferment. Septimius

> drained the cup that was offered to everybody's lips, but was intoxicated in his own peculiar mode . . . In times of Revolution, . . . even the calmest person is, to some degree, in an exaggerated and unnatural state, . . . there is enthusiasm, there is madness in the atmosphere. The decorous rule of common life is suspended; absurdities come in, and stalk unnoticed, madmen walk abroad unrecognized. Heroic virtue marches among us, . . . vices too, and great crimes, creep darkly or stalk abroad. Woman, likewise, catches the wild influence, and sometimes, flinging aside her fireside values as of little worth, is capable of crimes that man shudders at, of virtues and valor that he can never imitate, of deeds and thoughts that she would, a little time ago, have died to anticipate; the disenfranchised soul exults at losing its standpoint; old laws are annulled; anything may come to pass; miracles are on the same ground as the commonest occurrence . . . [T]here were the throes attending the birth of a new epoch in the world; and among seething opinions and systems, and overturned and deposed principles, Septimius had nothing fixed and recognized with which to compare his own pursuit. (XIII, 317–18)

Hawthorne is patently profoundly ambivalent about this ferment, and it is the very intensity of that ambivalence which makes the prose so powerful. Revolutionary "transfiguration" may make man feel himself "almost an angel", but he may turn out to be a destroying angel, ready "to thrust, to smite, to slay." The earlier version of the passage (XIII, 67) emphasizes more the insanity that may result. Here he is at once appalled *and* exhilarated by the creative and destructive energies released by Revolution. And when he describes the strange figures thrown up from the depths of society, apparently "without any hold upon the community anywhere," he gives a marvellous lengthy list of such figures as "religion crazed preachers, missionaries, jugglers, outlaws of themselves, wildly running away from the recollection of murder, mind readers, sharpers . . ." All these and more, it would seem, have "broken the chain" that links them to the community – but the sentence turns back on itself in Hawthorne's recognition of the complexity of social bonds as he goes on to say that these isolatoes serve, "in their wild airy way, to tie together by slender ligaments distant parts of the world, and places that have no other connection" (XIII, 309). This concern with revolutionary turmoil extends everywhere. For example, Hawthorne's generalization about the transformation of conventional female roles had already been exemplified in *Norton* by his account of the courtship between the young soldier, Robert Hagburn/Garfield, himself transformed by the experience of war, and Rose, Septimius's half-sister:

> There is an influence in revolution [such that] rules of decorum are obliterated, maiden chariness is shaken from its proprieties, the great restraining orderliness of human life being done away with, for the time, by the interposition of critical circumstances, all the ordinary rules are suspended along with it.
>
> (XIII, 212–3)

The centrality of this theme in *Felton* and *Norton*, this fascination with an historical moment when "all the ordinary rules are suspended," suggests that *The Elixir of Life Manuscripts*, far from being peripheral texts for an understanding of Hawthorne, should rather be read as attempts at a summation of life's work, a direct confrontation with issues that Hawthorne had repeatedly, if often obliquely, approached. David Howard, in his excellent essay on *The Marble Faun*, pointed, it will be remembered, to a defining characteristic of Hawthorne's best work. He argued that Hawthorne's major fictions, long and short, all centre on "moments of transition" and deal, directly or indirectly, with "a revolutionary condition, a condition where life's possibilities are freed momentarily from time and presented for human choice." As he stated in "*The Blithedale Romance* and a Sense of Revolution," this fascination with the revolutionary moment is very obviously not necessarily optimistic but rather "a sense of the liberated possibilities and the liberated negations of a certain kind of life; a free-running hope and despair."[2] Howard's words speak directly to Septimius's condition – and here it is not a metaphoric revolution, like the Roman carnival in *The Marble Faun*, nor the compromised utopian experiment of *Blithedale*, but a very real and a very modern one where Septimius's act of (revolutionary) violence, killing the young Englishman, initiates and enables his decision if not to escape from time and history at least to attempt to transcend their tyranny, to postpone (if nothing more) the closure to his story:

> By the bloody hand – as all great possessions in this world have been gained and inherited – he had succeeded to this inheritance, the richest that mortal man could receive.                                    (XIII, 49)

II

> I mused and meditated, and thought within myself, and tried to make out what manner of man this might be, that deemed it within his power to subvert the usual conditions of humanity.                      (XIII, 500)

> [H]ere was a sort of wildness in the look of many of the inhabitants, and elderly citizens, in powder, and ruffles at their sleeves, walked along as men in a dream, unable to realize what great change it was, that had put them into a new, uncomfortable world, since they were young.                  (XIII, 131)

> In everybody and everything the uncertainty of a transitive state. (XIII, 132)

The American Revolution can be seen in both *Felton* and *Norton* as representing the dawn of the modern world, the initiator of the age of revolutions, where "revolution" signifies a rupture with the past rather than another turn in fortune's wheel. Septimius stands in the middle, as it were, at once pulled back to the past by his absorption in an ancient manuscript and at the same time anticipating the future – by which I mean not so much the unending story of immortality that he projects for himself – but rather that the terms in which he expresses his ambitions as how to fill that future are (Romantically) modern. There are, however, a number of other narratives which bear on Septimius's situation, and play their differing parts in explaining why he should desire "to subvert the usual conditions of humanity" – principally those of genealogy, tradition and secularization. *Norton* begins with an emphasis on these three themes in its first two pages. Thus attention is drawn to Septimius's "wild genealogy," to "certain strange traditions that suggested to each generation" of his family "the exceptional character and fortunes of its ancestors" and to "the influence of puritanism," for he was originally to be a minister, "which state, as it had been ever since the Pilgrims came, was deemed the highest object of earthly ambition, as well as Christian duty" (XIII, 196, 195).

While one reason for the long passage on Septimius's genealogy (XIII, 256–69) is to provide "some natural causes why . . . Septimius . . . should still be liable to devote himself to the pursuant [sic] of an object which we choose to pronounce impossible" (XIII, 269), another (though related) reason is, by emphasizing his minister great-grandfather, to place him in the Puritan tradition. Thus his approach to the ancient manuscript that may contain the secret of the elixir is, not surprisingly for someone booked for the manse, not unlike that of a clergyman approaching a Biblical text: "He meditated long upon them, making each the theme of . . . interpretation, enlargement, symbolical reading, and practical development" (XIII, 322–3). Septimius's meditation on how to decide what level of interpretation is appropriate is explained in terms of his intellectual heritage: "Perhaps it was the spirit of mysticism, which he inherited from his great grandfather, . . . that led him to this idea" (of reading the manuscript as a parable or as a "symbolic mystery"), "for it certainly did not belong to the time in which he lived, nor had the present dynasty of New England mystics then begun to be" (XIII, 400). While this situates him between Puritanism and Transcendentalism, it may seem to imply that Septimius's tendency is to look backward rather than forwards. But the opening pages of Norton have already placed Septimius as a proto-Romantic:

> "what if I find that what I took for Belief, is but a slothful mental habit, an early prejudiced impression never faithfully examined, a formality, a surface, a fossil, a dead root that was alive in some other person's mind, but has no principle of life in mine! If the true life is in my Doubt, then let that be my Belief."
>
> (XIII, 199–200)

That claim of the validity of subjective feeling and the implied rejection of theology's claim to universal truth seems very close to Emerson, and particularly to the notorious passage from "Self-Reliance":

> Nothing is at last sacred but the integrity of your own mind . . . I remember an answer which when quite young I was prompted to make to a valued adviser who was wont to importune me with the dear old doctrine of the church. On my saying, "What have I to do with the sacredness of traditions, if I live wholly from within?" my friend suggested, – "But these impulses may be from below, not from above." I replied, "They do not seem to me to be such; but if I am the Devil's child, I will live then from the Devil."[3]

In effect what Septimius is doing as he responds to his adviser, who is importuning him with "the dear old doctrine of the church," is to provide a blasphemously secular version of the clergyman's role. The conversion of the idea of spiritual immortality to that of physical immortality is straightforwardly to secularize theology, to aim for a natural supernaturalism, and one task he conceives for himself is to be "the minister of Providence" (XIII, 164). Septimius may, indeed, be more dangerous to ordinary religion than a straightforward atheist in that he doesn't seem to doubt the existence of God, but rather redefines conventional theological ideas about man's place in the world. The idea of a long life seems to him "the soundest sense and the truest piety, because it does some degree of justice to the wisdom of the Creator, in making such a world. Else why did he make it? Can a man exhaust it in a little lifetime such as ours? No; nor in a thousand and such." With his image of the world as a text that it is man's task to interpret, Septimius is undoubtedly heretical in that he is overtly repudiating the consequences of the Fall:

> "We find the world propounded to us as a great riddle; and we are to suppose that only seventy years at most – a great proportion of which is infancy and decrepit age – was given to us to expound it in. Never! It is my belief, that according to the original scheme of the Creator, each individual man was to inhabit the world until he guessed its riddle; else it is but a mockery to him . . . The effect of Man's Fall, it seems to me, has been to deprive him of all the benefit of his earthly existence by the shortening of his stay here, so his coming here at all is made ridiculous."                                    (XIII, 201, 202)

But because Septimius is willing to accept what is the foundation of the clergyman's beliefs (the existence of God), it is harder for the minister to distance himself from him – and harder still because he no longer feels himself to have the authority to denounce Septimius as a blasphemer. He would need to take a hard-line Calvinist position, unimpressed by the beauty and complexity of the physical world, convinced of Nature's fallenness. That "Tomahawk of Righteousness," Septimius's great-grandfather, is rumoured to have made "the very leaves wither on the trees . . . with the fierce blast of his denunciations against the wicked," but the minister of the 1770s has to say "I dare not talk with you any further; for . . . you disturb and discompose what it is better should remain fixed in my mind" (XIII, 207, 202). He can only mildly rebuke Septimius for being "wild" and "impious," and recommend him to join the revolution – advice which resembles that of a muscular Christian telling an aesthete to take up football to resolve his doubts (XIII, 201).

While Puritanism is the intellectual tradition to which Septimius is disloyal heir, it is not the only influence on him. There is, as I mentioned earlier, the genealogy that Hawthorne provides for him, which traces his family tree back to "the very earliest Englishman that settled on these shores" (XIII, 257) – to him and (necessarily) an Indian bride – and Hawthorne follows the family history through the subsequent half-breeds, the Puritan great-grandfather and his sister, the witch, down to the 1770s. Despite some exceedingly commonplace reflections about the vices of half-breeds, one thing that makes this history so interesting is that Hawthorne hints at the possibility of an alternative path for

American history – potentially a more subtle version of "The Maypole of Merrymount" where "Jollity and gloom were contending for an empire" (T&S, 360). Here was an Englishman who apparently had no desire to export and impose European civilization:

> This remarkable chief appeared to have no desire to civilize his people, . . . but only to improve what we call savage life on its own plane, and make it, if a civilization, still a civilization of the woods, of hunters and fishers, . . . owning individually no land, . . . children of Nature, but all this made sweet and soft, made beautiful, idealized, by improving such life within its laws. (XIII, 257)

To redefine the meaning of civilization, to avoid the concept of property, to aestheticize social life – these are radical aims indeed. And these aims may be related to some of Septimius's ambitions. This presumed forefather, "this great Prophet – for so . . . might his Indian character be translated," may play his part in influencing Septimius's ambition to "be a prophet, a greater than Mahomet," and his desire to preside over the withering away of the state, "to fit the people to govern itself, to do with little government, to do with none" (XIII, 259, 174, 173). (Is Hawthorne here remembering Thoreau who told him the legend of the man who believed he would not die – and particularly the first sentences of "On the Duty of Civil Disobedience": "I heartily accept the motto, – 'That government is best which governs least;' and I should like to see it acted up to more rapidly and systematically. Carried out, it finally amounts to this, which also I believe, – 'That government is best which governs not at all;' and when men are prepared for it, that will be the kind of government which they will have".)

The coming of the Puritans destroys this Utopian possibility. They are willing enough to accept this Sagamore's status as a "direct messenger from the great Spirit" – as long as they can attach their moral categories to him and define the Spirit as Satan – and with "their usual energy . . . exterminate" what they have defined as evil (XIII, 260). That reference to Puritan energy inevitably recalls "the Anglo-Saxon energy – as the phrase now goes" on which Hawthorne had cast such an ironic eye in "Main-Street," and as in "Main-Street" that energy seems irresistible (T&S, 1,030). Here Hawthorne speaks of the conflict between the Puritans and the Indians as having "such a character of fate, that it almost precludes the ideas of wrong and pity" (XIII, 260). Almost – but not quite. Hawthorne with his fictive introduction of a white who saw things differently has opened up for consideration the question as to whether history could – or should – have taken a different path. Perhaps Hawthorne at one time in his composition of this story meant to suggest that an alternative valuation of official Puritan history had not been entirely suppressed even though it had to fight against a white, male definition and valuation. Septimius's aunt is presented as more Indian than her genealogy could technically justify. Her death-bed scene in *Felton* is full of complaints about the status of women in her world, about how limiting it is to be a respectable white woman: "But a white woman's life is so dull! Oh, Seppy, how I hate the dull life that women lead. I'm glad I'm going from it . . . If I'm ever to live again, may I be whole Indian, please my maker!" (XIII, 122). And she speculates about what sheer fun it must be if one is a witch away on one's broomstick: "You . . . in such an ecstasy; and all below you the dull, innocent, sober humankind, . . . all so innocent, all so stupid, with their dull days just alike, one after another." It is not just more interesting to be a witch. There may be a kind of social justice obtainable there, a kind of democracy which it is hard to encounter in decent daylight society: "There's an Indian; there's a nigger: they all have equal right [sic] and privileges at a witch meeting" (XIII, 121). This explanation of the appeal of witchcraft would be shocking enough at any time in the nineteenth century: it is particularly remarkable when it is remembered that Hawthorne was writing in the middle of the Civil War when the equal rights of niggers were very much on the agenda. The proto-feminist theme reappears when Sybil and Septimius are speculating as to how they will fill their time in the future. She "will find out what is the matter that woman gets so large a share of human misery laid on her weak shoulders' (XIII, 171). Regrettably, if understandably, Hawthorne seems to have backed away from most of Aunt Nashoba's fascinating subversive suggestions when he revised this passage for *Norton*. Though he still allows auntie to hope that she may escape the decent and boring Christian heaven, the full radicalism of the implied feminism and anti-racialism is moved into a more decorous background.

But even with this editing of his first, more radical ideas, there is enough evidence from *Norton* alone to show that Hawthorne was even at this late stage still meditating over the problematic processes of history, and especially the question of the authority that stories of the past possess. There are repeated hints within this genealogy that the (mythical?) founder of the Norton family may have had access to the elixir of life. The difficulty is to know what status we should attach to such claims. Aunt Nashoba is in possession of a drink that she believes lengthens life – but she also believes that it lacks the one ingredient that her forefather had. But her belief is but boggy ground to build on – and, to make matters worse, when she tells her version of the family story, it is hard to know what assent she gives it, or what degree of assent she expects from her audience – and, nicely, Hawthorne attributes this difficulty to her very Americanness:

> Now, touching the legend, it may be pertinent to remark that Aunt Nashoba was of Yankee blood (one of the Yankees, extant indeed, considering how long before the epoch of the pilgrims she dated her New England ancestry,)

> and it is a characteristic of theirs, to tell very strange stories with a grim face, and yet, as I think, without the purpose or expectation of being seriously believed.                                                     (XIII, 354–5)

And, giving another dimension to the problem, while the family story as told directly by Hawthorne has (more or less) the status of history especially as it approaches Septimius's present, Hawthorne begins the story with a series of qualifications:

> It may contribute to the better understanding of our story, if we give some slight sketch of Septimius's ancestry; although it must be done with a large intermixture of legendary matter, such gossip as clusters round old truths, like gray lichens, or moss; having their roots and nourishment in what is true; and if ruthlessly separated, there remains only something very unpicturesque, sapless; and indeed it is these fanciful things, these lichens, and natural growth over dull truth, that after all constitute its value, as springing from whatever is rich and racy in it, and being a distillation from its heart, oozing out, & clustering in a sort of beauty on the outside.            (XIII, 256–7)

Despite that very odd assertion that historical truth is usually boring, this is no simple opposition of truth *versus* fiction. Hawthorne seems to be suggesting that the value of history lies in the fictions that are built on factual foundations – and that fiction and history must remain organically connected if fiction itself is to continue to have value and life. This has, as I shall be arguing, clear implications for the way in which Hawthorne uses Septimius's quest as an analogy for his art and also for the confessional moments in which he shows the importance that he attaches to serious fiction. More immediately, part of the fascination of this is that it seems deliberately to be the exact reverse of what makes Septimius value old legends. He welcomes the story that Sybil tells thus:

> "I, too, shall like to hear the legend . . . if it is a genuine one that has come down in chimney corners from time immemorial, . . . and so, by passing from one homely mind to another, has gained a truth it did not begin with. No single man can make a fireside legend; it takes a century at least, of successive narrators to make it, and it is only good when its originator is long dead buried." [Sic]                                          (XIII, 333)

Here the value and truth of legends are the products of a collaborative – even democratic – process of telling and retelling a story, of the development of a narrative over time, a movement from a fiction or a fantasy into a kind of truth. The fact that it survives must, presumably, mean that it not so much retains as acquires relevance, that it is true to something, if only the psychological truth of a general desire for a certain kind of story, and, more especially, the desire that it be true – or, perhaps, the gradual recognition that it has somehow acquired a truth. Hawthorne seems to have decided to emphasize the contrast between the two attitudes in *Norton*. In *Felton* Septimius's words might well have allowed the two to be assimilated each to the other:

> "such stories get to be true, in a certain sense; and indeed, in that sense may be called true, throughout; for the very nucleus, the fiction in them, seems to have come out of the heart of men, in a way that cannot be imitated of malice aforethought. Nobody can make a tradition; it takes a century to make it."
>
> (XIII. 92)

If this had simply been carried over to *Norton*, then the two views could have come together – if only under such a handy umbrella as "the heart has its reasons . . ." Since the editors of the Centenary Edition have shown quite clearly that Hawthorne had *Felton* in front of him as he wrote *Norton*, we can be sure that the changes are deliberate.

What makes the revision so intriguing is that we can see Hawthorne thinking and thinking again about this problematic area where different kinds of fiction and history come together. There is, in the rethinking, a direct contrast between Hawthorne's own views of the relations between history and fiction and the position he attributes to Septimius. The first offers a base of truth with fiction organically growing from it, while the second begins from a fictive core, which, over the centuries, somehow accretes a kind of truth around it – perhaps in part as a creative or interpretative input from the audience (some of whom will necessarily be the retellers of the tale). There is no simple resolution to this contrast, but rather it provides terms for a debate about kinds of fiction. It would seem that Hawthorne is (very ambitiously) trying to establish – or reach for – a way of differentiating between fiction and myth. If this is correct (and I realize it is a large claim), then Hawthorne could be seen as attempting to write a fiction about a very old and traditional mythic story – the search for and acquiring of physical immortality. His fiction maintains its relation to history in that (unlike almost all the stories that deal with this theme) Septimius never reaches his goal of immortality, realistic in that its story never goes beyond the possible, or, perhaps more accurately, beyond what is agreed to be considered possible. It does, however, contain two legends, told by the mysterious Sybil and Aunt Nashoba, which turn on this impossibility and which may be either parts of a single story or different versions of the same myth. That overarching fiction can, then, be seen as a kind of meta-fiction which contains and examines mythical fictions which ask for another kind of assent from that demanded by either history or (historical) fiction – examines those fictions to see in what ways they carry their meanings and assert their relevance.

The question of interpretation is foregrounded in Sybil's telling of the legend of the English Baron who kills an innocent young girl to obtain the necessary plant for the elixir of life. It is only too easy to dismiss this as merely another version of the Bloody Footstep. It is that, of course, but it is much more. In this, its last appearance, it is clear why it so obsessed him. It is because a mark which rationally has to be claimed for the domain of nature is claimed for that of culture or history. Hawthorne is fascinated – had always been fascinated – by the idea that history leaves behind traces and signs which it is felt must have meaning – even if that meaning is not clear. (Think, for example, of that famous example – the scarlet letter – though that is apparently easier to decode in that it is clearly from the realm of culture and Hawthorne claims to have an explanatory text accompanying it. But even here there are the multiple meanings it accretes within the text, that readers have imposed or discovered – to say nothing of the fact that the primary meaning of A for adultery (but how do I know that this is the primary meaning?) is never overtly stated in the text). Those traces, while they are offered as signs that signify something, do not declare their meanings, may even contain an essential ambiguity (is, for example, the Bloody Footstep left by a victim or a victimizer – a sign of innocence violated or guilt?) and so are open to have meanings imposed on them – though Hawthorne also leaves it open for readers to debate what meanings either inhere in the objects or can (legitimately?) be imposed on them. Those signs may, Hawthorne wants us to remember, fall victim to the psychological or cultural needs of the present to impose significance on the past, while claiming to discover it there.

The central point of interest in Sybil's tale is that she insists on interpreting it as a moral allegory. As far as a reader can tell, she does not change the story to fit it to what she wants it to mean, but she does, so to speak, provide oral footnotes. Thus a part of the story, as she transmits it to her audience of Septimius and Nashoba, goes like this: "It was the object . . . of the lord of Smithills Hall to wrest from the control of Nature his own life, and as Nature . . . did not choose to be utterly defrauded, it was necessary to pay with another life for his own, since he would not let Nature have his body, to turn to grass and flowers, which she holds it her right to do." Sybil runs through various versions of what has been understood by this. Some believe that the sacrifice must be repeated every thirty years or so. Others believe that one death is all that is needed. A gruesome old woman to whom Sybil has spoken, claims that "some drops of the heart's blood of a pure young boy or girl . . . was to be mingled with a certain potent drink that the Baron had taught himself how to brew from potent herbs" (XIII, 339–40). She, having transmitted the story in sufficient detail for other interpretations to be possible, refuses to accept it literally:

> "I think the fiction must have been framed symbolically, purporting that the person who seeks to engross to himself more of life, its advantages, comforts, pleasures, than rightly belong to an individual, can only do so by depriving some other human being, with the same rights as himself, of his due share, and, so, in fine, immolating that victim to his selfishness." (XIII, 340)

For her the story has to be a symbolic fiction with a democratic meaning (and it is worth noting that when Septimius has radical doubts about the level of interpretation appropriate to the mysterious text, when he considers that it possibly should be read purely morally or politically, he thinks of "all the talk of herbs, of processes, alchymic or other," as "but a symbolic mystery, purporting what were the virtues, and how to enrich the human nature, or the national character with them, by which this great result was to be claimed") (XIII, 400). Sybil refuses to accept the possibility that this could be the (historical) tale of a man who, for apparently the best of moral reasons, seduces himself into making a tragic mistake. Nor is this an isolated example of her insistence on interpretation. The Baron, she tells her audience, had decided that "He might kill twenty others without effect; but mixing Sybil's pure and fragrant life with the other ingredients of the medicine, it would be the draught of immortality." By naming the victim Sybil she opens up the question as to how far she tells the story as masked autobiography – but that is less important than the interpretation she insists on:

> "I have meditated deeply on this ugliest feature of my story, and am very loath to take it in its most obvious sense; and looking for a spiritual meaning (every fact, you know, has its spiritual truth, which, to the outer one, is what the soul is to the body) I am resolved to believe, that spiritually, the interpretation of the legend is, that the scholar to earnestly seek knowledge, must give up to it the warm joy of life – that no man can be great, or do great things without sacrificing to Death and Nothingness inconceivable things that other men enjoy, and especially the one thing that his heart craves; for the Mind and the Heart struggle together, and one must triumph. In this sense I interpret this demand for a victim. But the earthly old tradition, which I endeavor faithfully to recount to you, strenuously insists that the lord of Smithills Hall did actually resolve to murder this loving and beloved maiden." (XIII, 341–2)

While her interpretations are the product of her own sensibility and are also to be seen as being addressed indirectly to Septimius, there is as well a sub-text in which Hawthorne allows Sybil to address himself as scholar/artist. I merely mention this now, as an indication of how deeply the autobiographical element penetrates the whole text.

In some ways Sybil's is a very poor story on its own. For example, it has no proper ending either in purely formal terms or in any nice neat moral provided by its teller when she has finished. The Baron, if he has acquired immortality, does nothing with it (which is rather boring of him) and merely plods about, leaving a bloody footstep behind him, and finally plods out of the story, leaving behind him merely the question of who shall succeed to his estate – a secular and rather dull ending, which may acquire more significance if the European and American legends are parts of the same story, and if Hawthorne had followed through his plan to have Septimius retire, defeated, to England as the ending of *Norton*. But then the significance of the ending of Sybil's story would have only been imposed retrospectively: Septimius would have retreated back, centuries afterwards, to where his ancestor had started off from – and history would have sadly come full circle. But if/until either the American dimension (in the form of Nashoba's legend) is connected up, and/or Septimius's story is added, it may seem that we are left with little more (apart from Sybil's interpretations) than an open-ended story which may seem boringly lacking in meaning. This, I should emphasize, is not clumsiness. Hawthorne had considered this point in one sketch: "Sybil's story must not refer to the alchymist having emigrated to America; this the reader is to infer from Aunt K's story. Perhaps Septimius may make that inference, and follow it out in his thoughts, but without speaking of it to Sybil" (XIII, 517). And the readers, along with Septimius, are provided with more help. Portsoaken with his enquiries about the Norton family tree provides material for that traditional old plot, the inheritance narrative which Septimius could construct into a real history with himself as hero, if he would provide his family papers, and thus establish a solid bourgeois narrative. But that lost heir plot he finds uninteresting as opposed to the riches he believes inhere in the mysterious manuscript.

Aunt Nashoba finds Sybil's tale of mystery and murder "a real pleasant story" but claims that "it shows . . . that there must be some kind of truth in this notion of a drink that makes people live forever." Her reason for finding it pleasant is obscure – her reason for believing it true is that it parallels what she has to tell: "because my story hangs on it too" (XIII, 351, 352). Her story is, in the main, a fabulous retelling of the semi-historical genealogy story Hawthorne has already given us with particular reference to the section on the white sagamore, and thus differs from Sybil's which has nothing with which it can be compared. Crucially the story is a criticism of the results of possessing immortality (though it is unclear how far Aunt Nashoba sees this as its message) as necessarily entailing an authoritarian conservatism which cripples mortals. And once this is clear, it can be seen that one message of Sybil's story is that an appalling if unconscious immorality is necessarily entailed in obtaining immortality, while Nashoba's story shows that ends as well as means are equally compromised. Hawthorne writes a very firm note to himself in *Felton* which makes his intention quite clear:

> Make this legend grotesque, and express the weariness of the tribe at the intolerable control the Undying One had of them, his always bringing up precepts from his own experience, never consenting to anything new, so impeding progress, his habits hardening into him, his assuming to himself all wisdom, – his intolerable wisdom – and depriving everybody of his rights to successive command; his endless talk, and dwelling on the past; so that the world could not bear him.                                              (XIII, 85)

This, in a way, subverts the semi-authorized version as told by Hawthorne: the white benevolent dictator may (quite unintentionally) have made it easier for the Puritans to conquer the Indians by sapping their individual and social independence and aggression – yet another of the democratic points that pepper the text. But, more importantly, it should undercut Septimius with his radical dreams of transforming the world. As seen by the eyes of popular legend, the possessor of immortality quite unintentionally becomes a Tories' Tory, a tyrant – not that Septimius understands this strand of the tale. If Sybil's tale is weakly open-ended when read in isolation, Aunt Nashoba's allows history to move back to centre stage with the coming of the Puritans – and she gives a horrific thumb-nail sketch of what happens to a descendant of the Sagamore handed over to the Puritans to be educated: "they taught him to drink rum, and set him in the stocks for being drunk" (XIII, 363). The mythic, legendary element remains, however, but in a remarkably material form: "the only really valuable inheritance the great Sagamore left to his posterity was the recipe for my herb-drink, which I verily believe was the drink that made him live such a tedious while, only he left out just one herb, for fear that any that came after him should be tempted to do the same thing" (XIII, 363). That materiality problematizes the question as to how mythic her story really has been. The drink and the tale are her only legacies to Septimius.

The drink tastes nauseating – even if later Septimius is to discover that the product of tradition, the recipe, parallels very closely the written lore of the complex text that he has spent so much time and intellectual energy in learning to decode. But the immediate effect of listening to the two stories is mixed. Sybil's gives him a moment – but only a moment – of really radical metaphysical doubt about the actuality of anything called reality. The effect of Aunt Nashoba's, however, is, we must infer, to send him back to his alchemical manuscript.

III

If our analysis and interpretation are well founded, alchemy prolongs and consummates a very old dream of *homo faber*: collaboration in the perfecting of matter while at the same time securing perfection for himself . . . One common factor emerges from all these tentative probings: in taking upon himself the responsibility of changing Nature, man put himself in the place of Time.[4]

Septimius unfolded the parchment cover, and found inside some fold of manuscript, closely written in a crabbed hand; so crabbed, indeed, that Septimius could not at first read a word of it, nor satisfy himself, indeed, in what language it was written. There seemed to be Latin words, and some interspersed ones in Greek characters, and here and there he could doubtfully read an English sentence; but on the whole it was an unintelligible mass, conveying somehow an idea that it was the fruit of vast labor and erudition, emanating from a mind very full of books, and grinding and pressing down the great accumulation of grapes that it had gathered from so many vineyards, and squeezing out rich, viscid juices, potent wine, with which the reader might get drunk. (Take Burton's Anatomy as the thing to be described here.) Some of it, moreover, seemed, for the further mystification of the affair, to be written in cypher.                                          (XIII, 49)

Ernest Burgravius, a disciple of Paracelsus, hath . . . another tract of Mumia . . . by which he will cure most diseases, and transfer them from a man to a beast, by drawing blood from one, and applying it to the other, *vel in plantam derivare*, and an *alexipharmacum* (of which Roger Bacon of old, in his *Tract. de retardanda senectute*) to make a man young again, live three or four hundred years; besides panaceas, martial amulets, *unguentum armarium*, balsomes, strange extracts, elixars, and such like magico-magnetical cures.

    (Robert Burton, *The Anatomy of Melancholy*, Part 2, Sect. 2, Memb. 4).

"My thoughts," said Septimius, "are of a kind that can have no help from any one; if from any, it could only be from some wise, long-studied and experienced scientific man, who could enlighten me as to the bases and foundation of things, as to cryptic writings, as to chymical elements, as to the mysteries of language; as to the principles and system on which we were created."                                          (XIII, 64–5)

I have argued elsewhere that one reason for the change of name from Felton to Norton was to signal that the text that Septimius struggles to interpret is an alchemical one – for Norton is the name of one of the best known of English alchemists – and it is clear that one function of Sybil's story is to alert us to the way Septimius's search for the elixir connects to alchemical theory and practice.[5] It was a brilliant stroke of Hawthorne's to connect alchemy with revolution, for both speak to similar feelings. As a percipient reviewer wrote of a recent production of Jonson's *The Alchemist*, "alchemy signifies the deep imaginative desire for sudden, radical transformations and liberation."[6] For "alchemy," we can read "revolution." There is too the irony that, as in the political realm, long patient hard work (both moral and scientific in the case of the alchemist) is precisely what the searcher for the elixir of life must involve himself with: there may be a radical disjunction – even contradiction – between the desire and the means necessary to satisfy that desire (and this neatly parallels the radical aims of Septimius which motivate his search for immortality *versus* the folk-wisdom of Aunt Nashoba's tale which suggests that possession of immortality may lead inevitably to a sterile conservatism). Nor is Septimius's project to be seen as outdated – if, that is, we accept the conclusions that Eliade draws from his deep learning in *The Forge and the Crucible*:

> We must not believe that the triumph of experimental science reduced to nought the dreams and ideals of the alchemist. On the contrary, the ideology of the new epoch, crystallized around the myth of infinite progress and boosted by the experimental sciences and the progress of industrialization which dominated and inspired the whole of the nineteenth century, takes up and carries forward – despite its radical secularization – the millenary dream of the alchemist.[7]

Here again we can see the connection between the modern desire for revolutionary change and what motivates the alchemical project.

But at this point, a difference between Septimius and most traditional alchemy becomes apparent. While he patently is in possession of an alchemical text, it is an unusual one in that no interest whatever is taken in the transmutation of metals. Nor does Septimius ever show any interest in this area, confining himself to botany and the problem of interpretation. In this he is very unlike the Aylmer of "The Birth-Mark" (with whom he otherwise has much in common) who is profoundly conscious of belonging to a tradition.[8] Septimius, in contrast to Aylmer, begins as anything but a scientist but rather as a trainee clergyman with the traditional metaphysical concerns and the equally traditional respect for the authority of the written. He becomes a special kind of alchemist by wrestling with a text which is designed to resist decoding – and thus Hawthorne brilliantly puts the question of interpretation at the very centre of his fiction. That move from theological student to alchemist is not an unnatural one for Septimius to make. As Abrams says in *Natural Supernaturalism*, "though the one mode of wisdom undertakes to explicate the secret of Scriptures, and the other to expound a secret practice, they share certain principles." Admittedly Abrams is talking about the Kabbalists rather than Christian interpreters of Holy Writ and opposing their methods to "the metaphysical foundation of the science of alchemy" (A, 157). But what he says of Kabbalists is equally appropriate to interpreters of the Bible, and he can be used to supplement and reinforce the grand sweep of Eliade's argument as he shows how interest in such esoteric areas as alchemy was a central concern for many Romantics:

> Certain major poets of the Romantic Age . . . incorporated into their writings myths and images which are recognizably esoteric in origin. They used such elements, however, as "metaphors for poetry." The older view of the world helped them to define the malaise of their own time, and they sometimes adopted its mythology to project and dramatize their feeling that they did not belong in the intellectual, social, and political milieu of their oppressive and crisis-ridden age.     (A, 171–2)

And elsewhere, commenting on the links between mystical theology and alchemy (Boehme being an obviously relevant name), he writes: "the inherent tendency to return to the one origin is expedited by the Philosopher's Stone, the principle of transformation and unification which it is the task of the alchemist to disengage and purify. In the ultimate transformation, man will be transfigured and will circle back to his point of departure" (A, 159). Of course Septimius, who aims to take literally that which Abrams's Romantics thought of as "metaphors for poetry," has so far secularized the alchemical project that he plans an almost infinite linearity rather than the traditional circular voyage. (Indeed, we have seen that he is appalled by the possibility of what can be called a vicious circle: repetition).[9] And here it can be seen that Hawthorne has gone beyond that concern with the problematic of the circle that, I have tried to argue, so preoccupied him in *The Marble Faun*. As in *The Marble Faun*, but with a different if related set of emphases, Hawthorne looks back at the dawn of the great time of (Romantic) ferment, attempting to preserve an ironic but informed placing distance from his central character, who certainly feels (if mistakenly) alienated from his "oppressive and crisis-ridden age" and who chooses an apparently esoteric activity as a way of escaping from – or transcending – that history.

Hawthorne presents Septimius's alchemical project not so much as a metaphor for his art but as a simile – and it is the parallels between the psychological states of the would-be alchemist and the creative writer that (at least initially) he emphasizes. I shall expand on this later – but here Hawthorne's *aide-memoire* to himself in the scenario can be noted:

> All through, represent Septimius as visited by frequent fits of despondency as to the pursuit he is engaged in, perception of its utter folly and impracticability; but after an interval, without any apparent reason why, he finds himself in full faith again – just as in writing a poem or romance.     (XIII, 530)

While the psychological states may be similar, and while much of the same ground may be covered by both interpreter and creative artist, it is crucial to differentiate between the two projects. Otherwise, one may fall into the same error as James D. Wallace does in his extremely interesting article on *Septimius Felton* (and only, alas, *Felton*). He argues (very temptingly) that we are to see in Septimius the reader as author, basing his argument on this passage from *Felton*:

> [H]is mind seemed to grow clearer; his perceptions most acute; his sense of the reality of things grew to be such, that he felt as if he could touch and handle all thoughts, feel round about all their outline and circumference, and know them with a certainty as if they were material things. Not that all this was in the document itself; but by studying it so earnestly and as it were creating its meaning anew for himself out of such illegible material, he caught the temper of the old writer's mind, after so many ages as that tract had lain in the mouldy and musty manuscript . . . (XIII, 103)

> At issue here is the problem of *origin*. Traditional texts present themselves as "authority," as a prescribed set of information and instructions which the reader, whether cherishing and obeying or disregarding and violating encounters as reified law. No matter how flexibly encoded and lovingly meant, the wisdom of the past, to the extent that it obviates the trials and errors of the living, is finally oppressive and intolerable rather than liberating; it fixes the reader in the life-and-death cycle of human time and represents a *memento mori*. The manuscript by virtue of its incompleteness, its ciphers, its mysterious obscurity, transforms the reader into an *author* – that is, the authority of the text has its origin in the creative efforts of the reader. Rather than oppressing the life force of the present generation, this "mouldy and musty" text stimulates a creative vivification of it and, at least temporarily, frees Septimius's spirit from its thanatophobia.

> This description of Septimius trying to read is also the most circumstantial of all Hawthorne's many descriptions of the artist at work. If Septimius's long labors with the manuscript, his alternating depression and exhilaration, his search for an elusive meaning, and his struggles with language all combine to make him author rather than reader, they also make him seem, specifically, Hawthorne himself in his protracted and painful struggles with the manuscript of *Septimius Felton*.[10]

This celebratory account is heavily dependent on selective quotation: Hawthorne goes on to refuse to reproduce the text because it is so dangerous, so powerful and plausible.[11] An alchemical text like this can hardly be a way to "creative vivification," for it is to result in a practice and the authority it claims is so great that translation might be a more appropriate term than interpretation. Indeed, rather than the reader having power over the text, the text (if it is to do its work) must have extraordinary authority over the reader. The reader must, if he is to understand the text, be converted – converted into an alchemist (and that is more than a matter of applying a cookery recipe, involving as it does moral principles – a whole life-style).

Just as in a cookery recipe (but with rather more serious results), there is an objective test as to whether the text has been correctly interpreted or not. It is – quite literally – a matter of life and death to get the meaning right. Septimius must not create or originate meanings: his task is to *re-*create. And he may only be able to do that if he is reformed by the text:

> Invariably . . . when the author seemed on the verge of some utterance that would illuminate his whole subject, . . . there came in an interval of cryptic writing, a tract of dense, impenetrable darkness, on the other side of which appeared a disconnected radiance, which could not be brought into relation with what had gone before. Yet, so far as Septimius could judge, this secret cipher was intended not so much ultimately to conceal the mystic meaning from a genuine and persevering search, as to be the test of earnestness in the seeker, in a sort of coffer, of which diligence, natural insight, and practical sense, should be the keys, and the keen intelligence, with which the meaning should be sought, should be the test of the seeker's title to possess the inestimable treasure.    (XIII, 315–6)

It was a point that Hawthorne thought important enough to return to and to expand it to include the notion of historical change (or even progress):

> It was a whimsical . . . way of writing . . . to give the reader the shells and husks of his real thought, and to keep free the golden grains, to communicate which was the only rational object of writing at all; but perhaps the author considered, that when the world arose to that stage of improvement that it could advantageously read his hidden meanings, the cryptic characters would shine out in legible light, potent to a comprehension that would embrace all particulars in its universal lore; or that if, before that epoch came, the earnest desire of an individual for knowledge made him worthy to possess it, the test of his worthiness would be shown by his being able to find the cryptic key, and turn it, in the mysterious lock.    (XIII, 369)

That idea that the ancient writer expected a time when the world would be ready for his message, coupled with the idea that to decode the text is to prove the interpreter's worthiness, suggests that Hawthorne had in mind the writings of the alchemists but also that he remembered Delia Bacon's book – and, indeed, when (in *Felton*) Septimius thinks he has cracked the code, Hawthorne explicitly refers to her: "here was part of that secret writing for which, as my poor friend Miss Bacon discovered to her cost, the age of Elizabeth was so famous and so dexterous" (XIII, 163). His preface to her book makes the connection clear:

[T]he author's researches led her to a point where she found the plays claimed for Lord Bacon and his associates, – not in a way that was meant to be intelligible in their own perilous times, – but in characters that only became legible, and illuminated, as it were, in the light of a subsequent period.

The reader will soon perceive that the new philosophy, as here demonstrated, was a kind that no professor could have ventured openly to teach in the days of Elizabeth and James. The concluding chapter of the present work . . . shows . . . how familiar the age was with all methods of secret communication, and of hiding thought beneath a masque of conceit or folly. Applicably to this subject, I quote a paragraph from a manuscript of the author's, not intended for present publication:–

"It was a time when authors, who treated of a scientific politics and of a scientific ethic internally connected with it, naturally preferred this more philosophic, symbolic method of indicating their connection with their writings, which would limit the indication to those who could pierce within the veil of a philosophic symbolism. It was the time when the cipher, in which one could write *"omnia per omnia"*, was in such request, and when "wheel ciphers" and "doubles" were thought not unworthy of philosophic notice . . . It was a time when . . . enigmas, and anagrams, and monograms, and ciphers, and puzzles, were not good for sport and child's play merely; when they had need be close; when they had need be solvable, at least, only to those who *should* solve them . . .

The great secret of the Elizabethan Age was inextricably reserved by the founders of a new learning, the prophetic and more nobly gifted minds of a new and nobler race of men, for a research that should test the mind of the discoverer, and frame and subordinate it to that so sleepless and indomitable purpose of the prophetic aspiration. It was "the device" by which they undertook to live again in the ages in which their achievements and triumphs were forecast, and to come forth and rule again, not in one mind, not in the few, not in the man, but in all."[12]

To "test . . . frame and subordinate" the mind of the discoverer – this is precisely what the text does to Septimius.

But the fact that Septimius is aiming for immortality puts him and his text firmly in the alchemical camp, where deliberate and overt obscurity is almost the defining characteristic. Norton, in his famous *Ordinal*, says that his work will have to be read at least twenty times before it becomes comprehensible, and warns that changing one syllable may ruin his message. Thomas Fuller, commenting on Ripley's *Compound of Alchemy* which "presenteth the reader with the twelve gates leading to the making of the philosopher's stone," speaks for the ordinary man: "Oh for a key, saith the common reader, to open these gates, and expound the meaning of these words" (words such as cibation, exaltation and projection), "which are familiar to the knowing in the mystery!"[13] But the author of an alchemical text did not rejoice to concur with the common reader. Such a text is always potentially elitist and it is no surprise that Septimius, once he believes himself in possession of the elixir, should refer to the mass of humanity as "the foolish, short-lived multitude and mob of mortals," an attitude that compromises what might otherwise have been noble ambitions (XIII, 162). Perhaps it is partly because they perceived dangers in a conscienceless powerful elite that the alchemists constantly stressed that moral preparation was a crucial qualification for success. Sir Isaac Newton told an acquaintance that "They who search after the Philosopher's Stone by their own rules [are] obliged to a strict and religious life" – and his was not a lone voice: Waite is quite correct when he says "The first point which strikes the alchemical student is the unanimous conviction of all the philosophers that certain initiatory exercises of a moral and spiritual kind are an indispensable preliminary to operations which are commonly supposed to be physical."[14] Hawthorne follows this pattern, distinguishing between the "rules" and the "recipe" (XIII, 163). The process of learning to begin to interpret the text is long and hard – almost an apprenticeship in itself – before Septimius manages to decode the "rules," his first substantial achievement.

The first thing Septimius gets from his manuscript is the sense that a sentence may have a sense – and Hawthorne neatly reminds us of his hero's Biblical background in his ironic deployment of key epistemological terms in a religious vocabulary: "I know not whether it was by faith or revelation that Septimius . . . read, or fancied he read, a single sentence . . . To say the truth, he was by no means certain whether he read that one sentence" (XIII, 287–8). But it was enough for him to decide that it was worth looking for a meaning – however eccentrically presented that meaning may be. Second, he manages to pick out a sentence of (mystifying) instruction with the aid of a peculiarly unreliable light source, a "flaming, bickering, smoking, brilliant, yet obscure" series of pitch pine torches:

> he caught a glimpse of the same sentence, which he now saw, did not follow in regular succession of words, but was sprinkled about, as it were, over one of the pages, so as only to be legible, like a constellation in the sky, when you chanced to bring those words into the proper relation with each other. It was to this effect. "Plant the seed in a grave, and wait patiently for what shall spring up"; and then again – "wondrous rich, and full of juice." (XIII, 304)

Septimius is, of course, predisposed to see some sort of significance in this, given that he has his own private grave, inhabited by the man he killed, and from whom he obtained the manuscript. Even so, if we did not know about the deliberate obscurity of the alchemical text, it might look like the most irresponsible (Romantic?) subjectivism on Septimius's part, but compared, say, to Ashmole's comments on Norton's *Ordinal*, Septimius's methods look fairly traditional ways of interpreting, and he one in the long line of "the searching *Sons* of *Arte*":

> From the *first word* of this *Proeme*, and the *Initiall letters* of the *six* following *Chapters* (discovered by *Acromonosyllabiques* and *Sillabique Acrostiques*) we may collect the *Authors* Name and place of *Residence*: For those *letters* (together with the *first line* of the seventh *Chapter*) speak thus,
>
> > Tomas Norton *of Briseto*
> >
> > *A parfet Master ye maie him trowe.*
>
> Such like *Fancies* were the results of the *wisdome* and *humility* of the Auncient *Philosophers*, (who when they intended not an absolute concealement of *Persons, Names, Misteries, &c*) were wont to hide them by *Transpositions, Acrostikques, Isogrammatiques, Symphoniaques*, and the lyke, (which the searching *Sons* of *Arte* might possibly unridle, but) with designe to continue them to *others*, as concealed things; And that upon the Question no other Answer should be returned, then the like of the . . . *Angell's* to Manoah. [*His name was Peli*, to wit, *admirable* and *secret*].
>
> In imitation of whome, tis probable our *Author* (not so much affecting the *vanity* of a *Name* as to *assist* the lovers of *Wisdome*) thus *modestly* and *ingenuously* unvailes himselfe; Although to the generality of the word he meant to pass *unknowne*, as appears by his own words.[15]

Actually, as has been pointed out, what one gets from the text as published by Ashmole is something slightly different: "Tomais Norton of Briseto / A parfet Master ye maie him call trowe." But, of course, our ability to correct Ashmole merely proves that he was right as to the way to approach such a text – and thus Septimius's approach is, at least up to a point, validated.

Given Newton's and Waite's testimony, it comes as no surprise to the reader (though it does somewhat puzzle Septimius), that, after his first arduous approaches, the first substantial passage that he manages to translate is a set of moral rules – though we may well be taken aback since the morality they adumbrate takes the form of a prudential egotism. Septimius is faced by four pages of advice like this:

> Interweave some decent and moderate degree of human kindness and benevolent acts in thy daily life; for the result, there is reason to believe, will be a slightly pleasurable titillation of thine own heart, and thy nature will be wholesomely warmed and delectated with felicitous self-laudation; and most beneficial is an admixture of such; but all that concentrates thy thoughts cheerfully upon thyself tends to invigorate that central principle, by the growth and nourishment whereof thou art to attain indefinite life. (XIII, 320–1)

These rules, if practiced, would run entirely counter not only to Septimius's desire to experience all but also to the ethical part of his reasons for seeking immortality – and Hawthorne chooses to remind us of that motive just as his hero finishes translating the anonymous sage's immoral/moral rules:

> The young man had made such the conditions, in all his aspirations of his living long; the attainment of wisdom, and the use of it for benign, majestic, unselfish purposes; and he deemed, too, that these would come inevitably from the removal of the miserable fear and low and grovelling necessity of death.
>
> (XIII, 323)

Septimius at one point seems to see that this contradiction between means and ends may make it impossible for him to live out his desires – ethical or otherwise:

> might it not be, that, for the attainment of permanence in earthly life, it was necessary to sacrifice whatever in life was most precious, burning its standards in potent fire, melting its precious things, doing what was equivalent to his fossilizing a green tree, with its tender leaves, and flexible boughs, its capacities for enjoying shower and sunshine, in order to make it indestructible, and no longer responsive to any impulse of delight. . . . Was he not already conscious of such a process within him! Did not his heart, even while it throbbed, strike cold and hard against the very breast that held it!          (XIII, 416)

However, this is only a momentary perception: he is so committed to pursuit of his goal that he is forced, when faced by these rules which are a perversion of true morality, into making what is at best a shifty interpretative move:

> He saw, however, or thought he saw that . . . the real meaning was, to keep one's self in an awful and holy reserve from the passion of life, its violent struggle, its dust, its heat, as the angels do, who live long, and do good, and probably are stronger and livelier with all the good they do. When once he had gained the rare secret, which was as yet concealed in the cryptic writing, this should be his course.          (XIII, 323)

Here there is another twist in the hermeneutic tale, where it seems as though interpretation as translation has to be distinguished from interpretation as judgement. Septimius has managed to translate/ interpret: he now has to decide on the significant meaning of what he has decoded – and we can see him wilfully (if understandably) misreading as he illegitimately extracts what he insists on as "the real meaning." The reader or critic, spared the hard work of decoding the cryptic text, and in no doubt that what he is reading is fiction, can afford to see that Septimius deceives himself by comparing himself to a selfless angel, that he remains a prisoner of his text. Which may be to suggest that Hawthorne sees one task of his fiction as enabling us to be free, in contrast to the authoritarian text which imprisons Septimius.

There are moments when Septimius seems almost aware of that

danger, when he thinks of the manuscript as "possessing a bewildering *power* of making whosoever should read it a dreamer" (XIII, 399, my emphasis). And he makes an almost unconscious attempt to repudiate its authority by considering whether he is interpreting it correctly, whether he has decided on the appropriate level of meaning:

> Once, . . . he took an entirely different view of the whole thing, and was inclined to believe that some mystic, under the guise of inventing a drink of immortality, had been prescribing the methods (in the language of parables and symbol, under which the wise hid their wisdom, in days of darkness) by which a nation, not an individual being, might attain enduring existence on earth; and perhaps the mystic writing had still another purport, teaching how the soul might attain a better immortality; and all the talk of herbs, of processes, alchymic or other, were but a symbolic mystery, purporting what were the virtues, and how to enrich the human nature, or the national character with them, by which this great result was to be claimed.
>
> (XIII, 399–400)

If Septimius had maintained this interpretative strategy, it would have allowed him to make and maintain a connection with his historical and political circumstances. But he (though ingenious) is, finally, insistent on remaining a comparatively simple-minded reader. As a theology student, he should know of the traditional fourfold levels of reading a text, the anagogical, moral, allegorical and literal. His insistence on returning to a "literal interpretation of what he read" (XIII, 400) sends him back to the prison-house of the text's language. And Hawthorne's suspicion here of literal, single readings may explain in part his fondness for what Winters called "the formula of alternative possibilities."[16]

It looks as though the only way out for Septimius would be for him to refuse to read the manuscript as a text with a private meaning for him alone, but to interpret it as having a social, a public application – as, indeed, a documentary equivalent of a Hawthorne novel, of the very text we are reading. Or, if that is too extreme, then at least he should refuse to accept the idea that the fact he can interpret the document is a satisfactory proof that it is true and worth interpreting, or that he is worthy of the message. But he is unable to repudiate the work that has gone into his decoding, and, to be fair to him, this is not just slavery to the power of the written word. Not only does alchemy involve a practice which makes it harder to repudiate what hermeneutic hard work has achieved, but also circumstances conspire against him. With, presumably, a little help with Sybil, the grave sprouts peculiar plants seemingly just as it should, and there is the strange coincidence between Aunt Nashoba's oral folk version of the recipe and that of the ancient document. That text may help him to become a cold-blooded egotist who experiments on his dying aunt, but it is understandable that he should at least give assent to the recipe part of the manuscript – even if he shouldn't have been taken in by the (im)moral rules:

> There must be a potent virtue in it, stronger than death; else why should it have survived? Why else should Providence, or fate, have provided for its transmission; on one hand, in the hereditary hall, and among the archives of an ancient and noble family, by a leap, as it were, from a far generation to the present; on the other, by transmission from one old woman's hand to another, in a humble chimney corner – in two separate methods.          (XIII, 408)

Aristocratic and democratic histories seem to have combined to deliver the recipe to Septimius in a remarkably persuasive fashion (even the implied egotism is pardonable in this context) – but as he goes on, he is shown not so much now as the prisoner of the text but as the prisoner of a method of interpretation, who, when thinking of the story of Medea, wants to read that too as history:

> Who could tell what far antiquity it came down from? With some changes, losing ingredients of power by the way, here might be the spell, the concoction of natural drugs, which Medea brewed into her cauldron, and so renewed her from age to rosy youth. Myths have their truth, and why not this, since the heart of man (ever dying just as he begins to live) so imperatively demands that it should be true.          (XIII, 408–9)

It is not so much the appeal to the heart that is significant here but rather Septimius's insistence on reading the truth that may inhere in myth not as the truth of desire but instead as a literal, an historical truth. He seems to define history as a story of loss and even goes so far as to define one consequence of the Fall as the loss of the crucial element:

> Ah, but one ingredient – the precious one, that had the spell in it, the mighty herb of Paradise, that married all the rest, and made it possible for their varying virtues to combine, this condition of efficacy – that, alas! had vanished forever.          (XIII, 409)

Of course this is only a temporary doubt, if one that Hawthorne seems to have intended to confirm, judging by the scenario, where he refers to the plant being "an extinct flower now" (XIII, 528). But, even though that would leave alchemy as a scientific theory untouched, this may involve a peculiarly modern position, relating centrally to the question of why Septimius fails. He is misled by Sybil, of course, but that is the comparatively uninteresting reason. The idea of a botanical species becoming extinct appears to be a comparatively modern one. The OED gives one meaning of extinct as that which has died out, such as, among other examples, "a race or species of animals or plants": it fails to give any quotation illustrating this meaning, and the closest it comes to it is a quotation about the end of a family line such as the Tudors – a very different thing from the disappearance of a species. And Jefferson, in his *Notes on the State of Virginia*, denies the possibility of the extinction of a species – and one rather more noticeable than an obscure plant:

> It may be asked, why I insert the Mammoth as if it still existed? I ask in return, why I should omit it, as if it did not exist? Such is the economy of nature, that no instance can be produced of her having permitted any one race of her animals to become extinct; of her having formed any link in her great work so weak as to be broken.[17]

As that mention of the work "link" suggests, Jefferson is here committing himself to that traditional idea, the great chain of being, a theory that, as Herbert Leventhal shows in his *In the Shadow of the Enlightenment*, was also crucial for alchemical theory. As well he makes it clear not only that Jefferson was committed to the idea of the chain of being but why this was so necessary for him:

> A decade later [Jefferson] reaffirmed his belief in the chain of being, and showed why it was so necessary for him to believe it eternal, when he argued that the "megalonyx," the fossil remains of a great sloth which Jefferson incorrectly identified as a large carnivore, could not be extinct. "For if one link in nature's chain might be lost, another and another might be lost, till this whole system of things should evanish by piece-meal . . ."[18]

What we can see here, I suggest, is Hawthorne breaking with the traditional idea of the chain of being and self-consciously raising the possibility that the modern world may be emptier, may have lost something of its original plenitude.

If the idea of modernity enters with the idea of an extinct botanical species, then it also makes an appearance when Septimius fantasizes about what he will do when he is an immortal, where he is in part revolting against the sterile discipline imposed upon him by the (im)moral rules, and partly displaying the egotism which those rules inculcate, displaying the megalomania and the desire for the totality of experience which mark him as a modern Faust who wants to experience both good and evil, to go, perhaps, beyond good and evil:

> "I have learned, Sybil, that it is a weary toil for a man to be always good, holy, and upright. In my life as a Saint and Prophet, I shall have somewhat too much of this; it will be enervating and sickening, and I shall need another kind of diet. So – in the next hundred years, Sybil – in that one little century – methinks I should fain be what men called wicked. How can I know my brethren, unless I do that once? I would experience all. Imagination is only a dream; I can imagine myself a murderer, and all other modes of crime; but it leaves no real impression on the heart. I must live these things. The rampant unrestraint, which is the joy of wickedness." (XIII, 174)

"Imagination is only a dream" – there is that cursed commitment to the literal again. This desire for a totality of experience is mirrored by the demand for a totality of knowledge which interpretation of the manuscript apparently involves – and that very demand for all knowledge seems to validate the project – the more so for a man who has, like Septimius, "an insatiable desire to know – especially for hidden knowledge" (XIII, 273):

> He began to think . . . that it would require all science, all learning, fully to comprehend what was written in this little space; so impossible was it to grasp this flower, and pull it up out of the remainder of human knowledge, its roots being so deep in the soil, and so intertwined with the heart-strings of the Universe.

It is at this point that Hawthorne generalizes the point immediately before giving it a particularly personal application:

> It is, I presume, in this way that a man's peculiar branch of study often seems to him of such paramount importance to all others; because when he gives a tug at it, hoping to pull it up, he feels the whole soil quake around him, and so convinces himself (and with a certain correctness) to have grappled with the whole universe in that one thing.                    (XIII, 368)

It is here that we can see Hawthorne make a particularly naked confession about the felt importance of his subject – a confession that would, no doubt, have been lost had he lived to complete this fragmentary masterpiece.

I V

> So it is ever with what seems an idle tale that, too, slight as it is, wreathes its tendrils about human knowledge, belief, superstitions, hopes, efforts, and, being taken only for a flower growing wild on a hill-side, with a fragrance of its own, we find that we have life and death, and burdens, and all the questions that men have ever argued about, twining with its tendrils, so that here too we have hold of the moral universe. ⟨I find myself dealing with solemn and awful subjects, which I but partly succeed in putting aside.⟩        (XIII, 368–9)

> Thoreau first told me about this predecessor of mine; though, I think he knew nothing of his character and history, nor anything but the singular fact, that here, in this simple old house, at the foot of the hill, and so close to the Lexington road that I call it the Wayside (partly for that, and partly because I never feel as if I were more permanently located than the traveller who sits down to rest by the road which he is plodding along) here dwelt, in some long-past time, this man who was resolved never to die.            (XIII, 499)

That first epigraph to this section is, surely, a unique passage in Hawthorne's work in its overt confession of the importance he attached to his art. I find that sentence in angle brackets (an intercalary note according to the Ohio editors) very moving in its undisguised seriousness (to say nothing of the moments when, as critic, I have felt that I have rather more in common with Septimius than it is entirely comfortable to admit). It is, however, from this parallelism of the seriousness and Septimius's and Hawthorne's projects that a discussion of the autobiographical elements of the fiction can be begun.

There may be a legitimate doubt about which (if any) one house in Salem was the house of the seven gables. There can be no such doubt about the roof over Septimius's head. Hawthorne begins by donating his house and his habits to Septimius in so much detail that both the house in the fiction and the historical residence not only have a field on the other side of the road from the house, but also a hill behind the house on which both Septimius and Hawthorne walk and meditate. In October 1861, Hawthorne wrote to Fields: "In compliance with your exhortations I have begun to think of that story [*Felton*], not as yet with a pen in my hand, but trudging to-and-fro on my hill-top" (xviii, 408). When he did get round to using his pen, he wrote of Septimius pacing up and down on the hill-top as he meditated "upon the still insurmountable difficulties," making a path for himself which is also a text, "this track and exemplification of his own secret thoughts, and plans, and emotions, this writing of his body" (xiii, 68, 61). This autobiographical parallelism would almost certainly have had to remain in any final version, though, presumably, it would have had mainly a semi-private meaning available principally to Hawthorne and his friends and acquaintances. (Acquaintances such as Bronson Alcott, who wrote about Hawthorne in his journal of February 17, 1861, "I get glimpses of Hawthorne as I walk up the sledpaths, he dodging about amongst the trees on his hilltop as if he feared his neighbor's eyes would catch him as he walked" [xviii, 363, fn. 1].) The closeness of these semi-private parallels is evidence of one kind of importance that Hawthorne attached to this tale. But, of course, he sets up his analogies to offer also a wider cultural and political significance — most obviously the analogy Hawthorne made between the dawn of the Republic, the beginning of the Union, and the start of the Civil War, the possible end of the story of the Union. That example exemplifies the point that it is a series of analogies rather than any simple question of identity — a series of analogies that goes something like this: young man/aging man; decoding/creation; physical immortality/hoped-for immortal works; scientific experiments/fiction as a field for research.

That last perhaps demands comment. It is easy enough to see what is meant by experimental research when we think of Septimius and his study with "its implements of science, crucibles, retorts," and its modern "electrical machine" (XIII, 185–6). It is less obvious to see how the term can be applied to a writer. What I am trying to get at can best be shown by Hawthorne's meditations over one of Septimius's morally dubious experiments – his willingness to use his aunt as a guinea-pig when he uses the mysterious plant that has grown from the grave as an ingredient in her herb-drink. Hawthorne muses over the morality of this. Septimius (now called Hilliard Veren)[19]

> had administered it . . . with no deadly purpose, but the contrary; and I have observed that men may seldom burden their consciences with remorse for results, however calamitous, which they did not directly and absolutely intend . . . And, moreover, if any man could trace, and not very remotely, the consequences of his own actions, as he passes carelessly along the narrow bridge of life, he would see that the mere swing of his arms, as it were, and sway of his body, had thrust people into the black gulf on either side. Not only soldiers (who have a dispensation for drinking blood) but statesmen, quiet, elderly people, who have never hurt a fly, bring about the deaths of myriads, by blunders, mistakes, or even of fell purpose, and never dream of immorality. Even the child unborn, so innocent as it proverbially is, is often a fratricide. We are all linked together in a chain of Death, and feel no remorse for those we cause, nor enmity for that we suffer.                                             (XIII, 432)

This is chilling and challenging as it stands – with that metaphor of the bridge of life and Hawthorne's insistence on interrogating that cliché of the innocence of the unborn babe. But this can be seen as returning to questions that Hawthorne had already discussed in, for example, "Fancy's Show Box" – and Hawthorne presses on to write himself further into another set of problems: "And the Purpose? what is Purpose? Who can tell when he has actually formed one? Or how little it may have to do with the very deeds that follow upon and seem entirely in accordance with it?" Radical though the scepticism is here, it is not really threatening. It can be assimilated to that statement of Sophia's that Hawthorne seemed so fond of and quoted in "Chiefly About War Matters": "Man's accidents are God's purposes" (12, 332). And it can also be related to what Hawthorne saw, in his scenario, as a possible moral of the story: "Perhaps the moral will turn out to be, the folly of man in thinking . . . that any settled plan of his, to be carried on through a length of time, could be successful. God wants short lives, because such carry on his purpose inevitably and involuntarily; while longer ones would thwart and interfere with his purpose, by carrying on their own" (XIII, 529–30). The very formulation here shows the way the fiction is an experiment. But it is after this questioning of the nature of purpose, of will, that Hawthorne really does begin to voyage into chartless waters:

> And speaking of remorse, it has sometimes occurred to me to doubt whether there really is such an emotion, independently existent in the criminal's own

breast, or whether it be not – as men are generally constituted – a pang and agony caused by the world or some influential part of it, an arrow shot by alien opinion, and rankling in the guilty breast, that otherwise would well enough have digested its secret guilt.

This is, of course, to doubt whether there is such a thing as conscience – whether ethics is other than a social construct. God's purposes begin to look not merely obscure but positively dubious. But Hawthorne does not step back – he rather writes himself more deeply into the problem, writes himself into a confessed doubt: "People have so often been known to live comfortably and even fat under great hidden crimes, and all at once to wither away and die, in unmistakeable agony, when exposed to the public eye. I known not what to make of this" (XIII, 432–3). Starting from Septimius's experiment on his aunt, Hawthorne in less than the space of a page, has moved on to this subversive idea – subversive, that is, of all conventional idea about conscience and morality. Still, he is tough enough to write on: "While Hilliard Veren sat by the bedside, possibly perplexing his mind with questions and dark surmises like these here suggested," he finds himself holding the dead hand of Aunt Nashoba. That willingness to experiment and explore – what is it but a fine example of what Keats meant when, in his letter of December 22, 1817 to George and Thomas Keats, he speculated about "what quality went to form a Man of Achievement especially in Literature and which Shakespeare possessed so enormously"? "I mean *Negative Capability*, that is when man is capable of being in uncertainties, Mysteries, doubts, without any irritable reaching after fact and reason."

The analogy between the would-be interpreter and the artist is made explicit when Hawthorne compares Septimius's state of mind when he leaves his study to travel to Boston to that of the artist when he steps aside from his creative work: "it seemed as if he were coming . . . out of an enchanted land . . . where impossibilities looked like things of everyday occurrence." It can be seen, however, that it is not simply a question of psychologies alone but also of the political circumstances that surround Septimius and, by implication, Hawthorne, for this passage irresistibly recalls what Hawthorne had to say about revolution: "In times of Revolution, . . . old laws are annulled; anything may come to pass; miracles are on the same ground as the commonest occurrence" (XIII, 317–18). Despite Septimius feeling as though he had "dreamed a life-like dream, most life-like in its force and vividness, most unlife-like in its inconsistency with all that really is," this is not to be read as a simple confidence in the existence of a common-sense reality for, as we shall see, "what really is" is anything but an unproblematic category in this fiction. And the confession of fellow-feeling is not to be read as a hostile value-judgement on either endeavour:

> I know well what his feeling was! I have had it oftentimes myself, when long
> brooding and busying myself on some idle tale, and keeping my faith in it by
> estrangement from all intercourse besides, I have chanced to be drawn out of
> the precincts enchanted by my poor magic; and the[n] look back upon what I
> have thought, how faded, how monstrous, how apart from all truth it looks,
> being now seen apart from its own atmosphere, which is entirely essential to its
> effect.                                                        (XIII, 129–30)

The first epigraph to this section is evidence enough that Hawthorne,
despite the apparent modesty of the reference to an "idle tale" and the
tone of a self-consciously down-market Prospero ("enchanted by my
poor magic"), does not mean to diminish the value of the art-work any
more than he means to devalue Septimius's quest. "Put the above in the
third person" he advised himself in *Felton*, and when he did rewrite the
passage for *Norton* he opened it up to make it applicable to a very wide
range of human endeavour, though the Romance writer remains as a
key figure:

> Inevitably, sometimes, the airy architect steps out of this magnificent edifice
> by some side-portal, and sees what a vaporous material he has builded with.
> Every man, however prosaic his pursuit, however plodding himself, knows
> something of this despair; the merchant sees heaps of gold as unreal as the
> yellow of sunset; empires, that were to be, and based on the wisest calculations
> of statesmen, . . . would vanish into nothing, beneath the feet of those who
> plowed, leaving statesmen, homes, people, that were to be, to sink into
> perdition, if once they could slip out of the magic influence and see the sober
> truth. Perhaps none are more subject to it than Romance writers; they make
> themselves at home among their characters and scenery, and know them better
> than they know anything actual, and feel a blessed warmth that the air of this
> world does not supply, and discern a fitness of events that the course of human
> life has not elsewhere; so that all seems a truer world than that they were born
> in; but sometimes, if they step beyond the limits of the spell, ah! the sad
> destruction, disturbance, incongruity that meets the eye; distortion, impossibi-
> lity, everything that seemed so true and beautiful in its proper atmosphere, and
> nicely adjusted relations, now a hideous absurdity. Thus he that writes the
> strange story of Hilliard Veren may well sympathize with the emotion of that
> moment.                                                       (XIII, 446–7)

Hawthorne abandoned *Norton* a page after writing this – in a way that is
reminiscent of the end of Marvell's *Coy Mistress*.[20] But in *Felton*
Septimius went on into revolutionary Boston, on into "the uncertainty
of a transitive state" (XIII, 132). It is hardly an environment that would
make Septimius decide that here there was a clear and definite reality – to
say nothing of the fact that he had only left his study to consult Dr.
Portsoaken about his alchemical recipe. And, of course, someone like
Septimius can hardly think of reality that is something unquestionably

out there, for he plans a redefinition of reality by living if not for ever then for as long as he wants. More importantly, he begins from a mistrust of conventional ideas of the real:

> "It has seemed to me, . . . that it is not the prevailing mood, the most common one, that is to be trusted; this is habit, formality, the shallow covering which we draw over what is real, and seldom suffer it to be blown aside. But it is the snake-like doubt that thrusts out its head, that gives us a glimpse of reality. Surely such moments are a hundred times as real as the dull moments of faith — or what you call such." (XIII, 11)

Though religious faith is the principal point at issue here (and I have already suggested its connections with Emerson's position, using the *Norton* version of these ideas), these comments lay a foundation for subsequent and more extensive statements about the very nature of reality and the question whether we can ever feel fully confident that we have apprehended it.

Against Septimius's feeling that "he would require all science, all learning, fully to comprehend" his manuscript, must be opposed his radical epistemological doubt — an equally "solemn and awful" question and one that is related to the Revolutionary disturbance of conventional ideas of norms and reality. But Hawthorne goes beyond that disruption of social reality to a more general questioning of our access to any stable reality — and here Hawthorne firmly allies himself with Septimius's meditations on the problematic nature of the real:

> All unreal; all illusion. Was Rose Garfield a deception too, with her daily beauty, and daily cheerfulness, and daily worth? In short it was a moment, such as I suppose all men feel (at least I can answer for one) when the real scene and picture of life swims, jars, shakes, seems about to be broken up and dispersed, like the picture in a smooth pond, when we disturb its smooth mirror by throwing a stone; and though the scene soon settles itself, and looks as real as before, a haunting doubt keeps close at hand, asking — "Is it stable? Am I sure of it? Am I certainly not dreaming? See; it trembles again, ready to dissolve." (XIII, 101)

These musings begin from Septimius's response to Sybil's legend but becomes so totalized that even the reality of the commonsensical Rose becomes a matter for doubt. This was rewritten in *Norton* — but not in a way that defuses its force:

> If part of his life, and that which seemed as solid as any other, was an illusion, then why not all. It was, in short, a moment with Septimius such as many men have experienced, when something they deemed true and permanent appearing suddenly questionable, the whole scenery of life shakes, jars, grows tremulous, almost disappears in mingled and confused colors, as when a stone is thrown into the smooth mirror of Walden Lake, and seems to put in

> jeopardy the surrounding hills, woods, and the sky itself. True; the scene soon
> settles itself again, and looks as substantial as before; but a haunting doubt is apt
> to keep close at hand, persecuting us forever with that troublesome query – "Is
> it real! Can I be sure of it? Did I not once behold it on the point of dissolving?"
> And he is either a very wise man, or a very dull one, who can answer one way
> or the other for the reality of the very breath he draws, and steadfastly say
> "Yes!" or "No!"                                                     (XIII, 354)

The omission of the personal confession results in a more radical, a
deeper generalization, where Hawthorne seems to be suggesting that we
never have direct access to the real – that it is always mediated through
"reflection." The "very breath he draws" – this internalization involves
a very radical scepticism not only about the nature of our recognition of
the real but also our own reality. But even if we remain with the
apparently easier question of the status of reflection and its relationship to
the real, rather more is at stake for Hawthorne than may at first appear –
for he seems, by the time of *The Elixir of Life Manuscripts*, to have lost an
earlier confidence about the truth that inheres in reflection. "Monsieur
du Miroir" is one obvious point of reference, where, for all the "mystical
depth of meaning" that Melville rightly claimed for it, reflection
remains comparatively unproblematic.[21] More relevant still is a very
interesting passage from *The American Notebooks*:

> I have never . . . had such an opportunity to observe how much more beautiful
> reflection is than what we call reality. The sky, and the clustering foliage on
> either hand, and the effect of sunlight as it found its way through the shade . . . –
> all these seemed unsurpassably beautiful, when beheld in the upper air. But, on
> gazing down, there they were, the same even to the minutest particular, yet
> arrayed in ideal beauty, which satisfied the spirit incomparably more than the
> actual scene. I am half convinced that the reflection is indeed the reality – the
> real thing which Nature imperfectly images to our grosser sense. At all events,
> the disembodied shadow is nearest to the soul.                     (VIII, 360)

This is a fascinating passage which deserves more analysis than it gets
here with its musings over such questions as whether mimesis can be an
idealization and whether actuality should be differentiated from reality.
But at this stage (1842), Hawthorne could take over the traditional
metaphor of the mirror and Romanticize it into a kind of neo-Platonism
very like Shelley's but more extreme in that Hawthorne appears willing
to equate beauty and truth as Keats does in "Ode on a Grecian Urn":

> Why is the reflection in that canal more beautiful than the objects it reflects?
> The colours are more vivid, and yet blended with more harmony; the
> openings from within into the soft and tender colours of the distant wood, and
> the intersection of the mountain lines, surpass and misrepresent truth.[22]

What Marjorie Levinson has to say of this fragment of Shelley's seems
even more applicable to the Hawthorne of 1842 for, in this passage from

the *Notebooks*, he lacked Shelley's feeling that reflection misrepresents –
indeed, he saw the reflection as truer than the truth. She suggests that, for
Shelley, "the reflection represents the original . . . by expressing its
essential (ideal, formal) nature in a materially uncompromised fashion."[23] But, by the 1860s, that confidence in the realities or truths of
world or reflection and in the stability of the relations between world
and reflection has, it seems, been replaced by the large question whether
one can have access to the real – and the even larger question of whether
there is a stable reality to which we can have access. The inevitable
consequences of such a question are either an abandonment of history
and art under the pressure of a paralyzing scepticism or (and it is
considerably to Hawthorne's credit that he took this path) a fiction
which is as ambitious, as inclusive, as supra-realistic as Septimius's
project – and, alas, as hard to bring to a satisfactory conclusion.
Ambitious as *The Marble Faun* was, Hawthorne has gone beyond that.
While we may only have fragments, they are fragments of a masterpiece.
In "Hawthorne and his Mosses," Melville discusses what makes
Shakespeare, Shakespeare. In his list he includes "those short, quick
probings at the very axis of reality."[24] For Shakespeare, read
Hawthorne.

# Notes

## I TRADITION AND REVOLUTION

1. Richard Chase, *The American Novel and Its Tradition* (New York: Doubleday, 1957).
2. Michael J. Colacurcio, *The Province of Piety: Moral History in Hawthorne's Early Tales* (Cambridge, Mass. and London: Harvard University Press, 1984), pp. 3–4.
3. E.H. Davidson, *Hawthorne's Last Phase* (New Haven and London, 1949). I have found only two really interesting articles on the unfinished novels. The first: Kristin Brady, "Continuity and Indeterminacy in Hawthorne's Unfinished Romances," *English Studies in Canada*, 11 (1985), 311–33. The second: James D. Wallace, "Immortality in Hawthorne's *Septimius Felton*," *Studies in American Fiction*, 14, no. 1 (1986), 19–33.
4. F.O. Matthiessen, *The American Renaissance: Art and Expression in the Age of Emerson and Whitman* (London, Oxford, New York: Oxford University Press, 1941), pp. 318–19.
5. Quoted by Marvin Meyers, *The Jacksonian Persuasion* (Stanford, California: Stanford University Press, 1960), p. 58. Jonathan Arac has suggested that there is another and discreditable way in which Hawthorne can be a conservative and a democrat: "The *Life of Pierce* early identifies Hawthorne and Pierce with the 'progressive or democratic' political stance, as opposed to the 'respectable conservative' (12,357). But on slavery, Hawthorne judges that 'the statesman of practical sagacity – who lives his country as it is, and evolves good from things as they exist . . . will be likely . . . to stand in the attitude of a conservative' (12,416). So the Democrats become progressive conservatives" ("The Politics of *The Scarlet Letter*," in S. Bercovitch and M. Jehlen [eds.], *Ideology and Classic American Literature* [Cambridge and New York: Cambridge University Press, 1986], p. 257).
6. G.P. Lathrop, *A Study of Hawthorne* (Boston: James R. Osgood and Co., 1876), p. 330.
7. Frederick Newberry, *Hawthorne's Divided Loyalties: England and America in His Works* (London and Ontario: Associated University Press, 1987), pp. 19, 207. Sacvan Bercovitch, "The A-Politics of Ambiguity in *The Scarlet Letter*," *New Literary History*, 19, no. 3 (Spring 1988), 634. Jonathan Arac, "The Politics," pp. 253, 251. He draws back from "the extremity of this . . . suggestion. *The Scarlet Letter* aims to

produce an invisible change, an internal deepening, like that which transforms the letter even as its form remains identical" (p. 251).

8. The George Eliot quotation comes from an October 1856 review in *The Westminster Review* and is quoted by G.S. Haight, *George Eliot: A Biography* (Oxford: Oxford University Press, 1968), p. 185. The Higginson quotation comes from an *Atlantic Monthly* article of 1860, "The Maroons of Surinam," and is quoted by T.G. Edelstein, *Strange Enthusiasm: A Life of Thomas Wentworth Higginson* (New Haven and London: Yale University Press, 1968), p. 238.

9. A not untypical voice is that of Myra Jehlen in the already cited *Ideology and Classic American Literature* in "The Novel and the American Middle Class." She sees Hester at the end of the book as pledging "her exceptional creativity to legitimacy and order" and says that Hester "comes to understand" that "no one who has ever placed herself in radical opposition to her society can hope to assist in its transformation" (pp. 138. 132). I fail to understand how she can read this out of the fiction's conclusion. Hester's very insistence that the relationships between the sexes is radically inadequate hardly suggests that she has any commitment to the *status quo*, to legitimacy and order.

10. John Ashworth, *"Agrarians" and "Aristocrats"* (Cambridge and New York: Cambridge University Press, 1987). See also F.J. Blue, *The Free Soilers: Third Party Politics 1848–54* (Urbana, Chicago and London: Illinois University Press, 1973) for an account of the sheer complexity of political alliances in the early 1850s – and especially the chapter "The Massachusetts Coalition" (pp. 207–31).

11. "[W]e all agree; and weeping, all but echo hard-hearted Nulli [Calhoun]." That is, all the characters refuse to choose the path of violence – so all that is left is "Time – all-healing Time – Time; great Philanthropist! Time must befriend these thralls!" For all Melville's moral hatred of slavery – this is the best he can come up with. (Herman Melville, *Typee, Omoo, Mardi*, Library of America, edited by G. Thomas Tanselle, 1982, p. 1,191, 1,192, ch. 162).

12. George Dekker, *The American Historical Romance* (Cambridge and New York: Cambridge University Press, 1987), p. 153.

13. Dekker, *American Historical Romance*, p. 143.

14. G.L. Burr (ed.), *Narratives of the Witchcraft Cases: 1684–1706* (1914; New York: Barnes and Noble, 1959), p. 387.

15. Dekker, *American Historical Romance*, p. 153.

16. Dekker, *American Historical Romance*, p. 153.

17. Raymond Williams, *Modern Tragedy* (London: Chatto and Windus, 1966), p. 64.

18. Nina Baym, in "Thwarted Nature: Nathaniel Hawthorne as Feminist" in Fritz Fleischmann, *American Novelists Revisited: Essays in Feminist Criticism* (Boston: G.K. Hall & Co., 1982), understandably picks up on Matthew Maule's resentment of Alice Pyncheon's appreciative gaze in Holgrave's tale, "Alice Pyncheon," in chapter XIII of *The House of the Seven Gables*. But what her hostile criticism of Matthew misses is that his is surely if unpardonably a *class* resentment – that he feels himself looked at and labelled as a member of the proletariat: "Does the girl look at me as if I were a brute beast! . . . She shall know whether I have a human spirit; and the worse for her, if it prove stronger than her own!" (N, 525). It is class as much as sex that motivates Maule's revenge.

19. Williams, *Modern Tragedy*, p. 66.

20. Williams, *Modern Tragedy*, p. 77.

21. Williams, *Modern Tragedy*, p. 64.

22. R.W. Emerson, *Emerson in His Journals*, ed. J. Porte (Cambridge, Mass. and London: Harvard University Press, 1982), pp. 356, 326.

## 2 AN EXPERIMENTAL FICTION

1. S.L. Gross, "Hawthorne's 'Alice Doane's Appeal,'" *Nineteenth Century Fiction* 10 (1955), 236. H.H. Waggoner (ed.), *Nathaniel Hawthorne: Selected Tales and Sketches* (New York: Holt, Rheinhart, 1964), p. xii. F.C. Crews, *The Sins of the Fathers: Hawthorne's Psychological Themes* (New York: Oxford University Press, 1966).

2. I cannot resist quoting the end of his chapter on "Alice Doane's Appeal" – entitled (unsurprisingly) "Brotherly Love": "For Hawthorne . . . the sense of the past is nothing other than the sense of symbolic family conflict writ large" (p. 60).

3. R.H. Pearce, "Hawthorne and the Sense of the Past, Or the Immortality of Major Molineux," in *Historicism Once More: Problems and Occasions for the American Scholar* (Princeton, New Jersey: Princeton University Press, 1969), pp. 150, 152. H.H. Henderson III, *Versions of the Past: The Historical Imagination in American Literature* (New York: Oxford University Press, 1974), pp. 73, 74.

4. Henderson III, *Versions of the Past*, p. 91. R.H. Pearce, "Hawthorne," p. 151.

5. M.J. Colacurcio, *The Province of Piety: Moral History in Hawthorne's Early Tales* (Cambridge, Mass, & London: Harvard University Press, 1984), pp. 83, 85, 87.

6. Arlin Turner, *Nathaniel Hawthorne: A Biography* (New York & Oxford: Oxford University Press, 1980), p. 72. I do not know where Turner got the information about Goodrich keeping a couple of pieces for the *Token*.

7. The argument about the dates of the stages in the composition of "Alice Doane's Appeal" will probably never be resolved. But this part of the story can surely be dated with some accuracy. "Till a year or two since, this portion of our history had been very imperfectly written . . . Recently, indeed, an historian had treated the subject in a manner that will keep his name alive" (T&S, 206). I agree with Colacurcio that this seems almost certainly a reference to C.W. Upham's *Lectures on Witchcraft, Comprising a History of the Delusion in Salem in 1692* (Boston, 1831) – though it could possibly refer to James Thacher's *An Essay on Demonology, Ghosts and Apparitions, and Popular Superstitions. Also, An Account of the Witchcraft Delusion at Salem* also published in Boston in 1831.

8. In 1819 and 1820 alone, Hawthorne read *The Mysteries of Udolpho, Ferdinand, Count Fathom*, several of Godwin's novels, Hogg's *Tales*, and "Monk" Lewis's *Romantic Tales*. Hawthorne's interest in Brockden Brown and John Neal is too well known to need documenting.

9. Crews, *Sins of the Fathers*, p. 55.

10. Grandfather does not seem to have any Romantic illusions about children: "here Grandfather gave his auditors such details of this melancholy affair, as he thought it fit for them to know." This sounds like decorous censorship – but the first thing the children are told is that "a frenzy, which led to the death of many innocent persons, had originated in the wicked arts of a few children" (VI, 77).

11. Crews, *Sins of the Father*, p. 54. Colacurcio, *Province of Piety*, p. 82.

12. To take what is perhaps the classic example – "Young Goodman Brown": "Had Goodman Brown fallen asleep in the forest, and only dreamed a wild dream of a witch-meeting? Be it so if you will" (T&S, 288). The sense of being cheated in this story might usefully be compared with the end of *The Monk*, when it is revealed that Mathilda is not a woman, but a demon in Satan's service – though there it is, I think, clearly a blunder by Lewis.

13. This connection between incest and a too fertile sterile nature irresistibly reminds me of the amaranth of *Pierre* which is explicitly connected by Melville to Pierre's dreams of the battles of the incestuous Gods and particularly the figure of Enceladus – himself the product of an incestuous union of Terra and Titan. See Book xxv (entitled "Lucy, Isabel, and Pierre. Pierre at his Book. Enceladus"), iii.

14. Cotton Mather to Judge John Richards, May 31, 1692. Quoted by D. Levin (ed.), *What Happened in Salem?* (New York: Harcourt, Brace & World, 1960), p. 107.
15. Quoted by Devendra P. Varma in the introduction to *The Necromancer Or The Tale of the Black Forest Founded on Facts Translated from the German of Lawrence Flammenberg by Peter Teuthold* (London: The Folio Press, 1968), p. xv–xvi.
16. D. Levin, "Historical Fact in Fiction and Drama: The Salem Witchcraft Tales," in *In Defense of Historical Literature* (New York: Hill & Wang, 1967), p. 81. Everyone interested in Hawthorne and his historical knowledge must be greatly indebted to Levin. His pages are essential reading for anyone interested in "Alice Doane's Appeal" or "Young Goodman Brown."
17. Robert Pike, a magistrate of Salisbury, to Judge Corwin, quoted by Chadwick Hansen in *Witchcraft at Salem* (London: Hutchinson, 1970), p. 139.
18. I. Mather, *Remarkable Providences Illustrative of the Earlier Days of American Colonization* (London: John Russell Smith, 1856), p. 155. First published 1684. The book was withdrawn from the Salem Athenaeum by Hawthorne or Mary Manning in 1827, 1829, and 1834. In other words, whatever the date of the composition of "Alice Doane's Appeal," it is hard to believe that Hawthorne did not have Mather's judgements fairly near his finger-tips.
19. Crews, *Sins of the Fathers* pp. 56–7. M.D. Bell, *Hawthorne and the Historical Romance of New England* (Princeton, New Jersey: Princeton University Press, 1971), 72. Colacurcio, *Province of Piety*, p. 87.
20. R. Calef, *More Wonders of the Invisible World* (London, 1700), in G.L. Burr (ed.), *Narratives of the Witchcraft 1648–1706* (New York: Barnes & Noble, 1959), p. 361. Colacurcio argues, *à propos* the presentation of Mather, that *Grandfather's Chair* "reads off, almost everywhere, as a considerate and even 'charitable' revision of the historical tales. What it ordinarily reveals is less change or development than the simple omission of ironies that are too 'wicked' (that is, 'adult') for childish simplicity" (p. 552). At the same time he wants to distinguish between Hawthorne's picture of Mather's role and that of a Bancroft. I have already pointed out that grandfather does not shelter the children from one appalling fact about the Salem experience. And, as far as Mather is concerned, the book for children is actually rather close to a Bancroft view: "From the foundation of New England, it had been the custom of the inhabitants, in all matters of doubt and difficulty, to look to their ministers for counsel. So they did now; but, unfortunately, the minsters and wise men *were more deluded than the illiterate people.* Cotton Mather, a very learned and eminent clergyman believed that the whole country was full of witches and wizards, who had given up their hopes of heaven, and signed a covenant with the Evil One" (VI, 78, my emphasis). A decade or so later, in *The House of the Seven Gables,* Hawthorne veers between straightforwardly blaming Mather *et al.* and a more general democratic point. Matthew Maule "was one of the sufferers, when Cotton Mather, and his brother ministers, and the learned judges, and other wise men, and Sir William Phips, the sagacious Governor, made such laudable efforts to weaken the great Enemy of souls, by sending a multitude of his adherents up the rocky pathway of Gallows Hill." Straight Bancroft – and the earlier reference – while it does not exempt the community as a whole from blame, is not so very far from the Bancroftian argument even if its view of democracy is a trifle more subtle: Maule "was one of the martyrs to that terrible delusion which should teach us, among its other morals, that the influential classes, and those who take upon themselves to be leaders of the people, are fully liable to all the passionate error that has ever characterized the maddest mob." One of the charms of this passage from my point of view – in terms of what I had to say about "My Kinsman, Major Molineux" in my introductory chapter – is its insistence that there is nothing unique nor uniquely

improper about mob (*alias* democratic) activity, but Hawthorne gets more interesting: "Clergymen, judges, statesmen – the wisest, calmest, holiest persons of their day – stood in the inner circle roundabout the gallows, loudest to applaud the work of blood, latest to confess themselves miserably deceived." And here comes the uniquely Hawthorne-type ironic perception: "If any one part of their proceedings can be said to deserve less blame than another, it was the singular indiscrimination with which they persecuted, not merely the poor and aged, as in former judicial massacres, but people of all ranks; their own equals, brethren, and wives" (N, 514, 357). Now this is a democratic slant on the situation which Bancroft and nearly everybody else seems to have missed – though obviously it must be asked how many of the élite actually came to the gallows.

21. George Bancroft, *History of the United States from the Discovery of the American Continent* (Boston: Charles C. Little and James Brown, 1840), pp. 98, 88. That second passage is breath-taking in the speed in which the buck passed away from the common people of New England.

22. R. Calef, *Invisible World*, p. 374.

23. R. Williams, *The Long Revolution* (London: Chatto & Windus, 1960), p. 276.

24. I wish he had spelled out the reasons for calling the victims virtuous. The astonishing bravery of the victims who could so easily have avoided death merely by confessing/lying that they were witches is quite remarkable.

### 3 SKETCHES EXPERIMENTAL AND IDEAL

1. Only two stories ("Egotism; or the Bosom Serpent" and "The Christmas Banquet") have the subtitle of "From the Unpublished 'Allegories of the Heart.'" But it is not hard to think of other stories from the Old Manse period which could come under such a rubric – such as "The Birthmark," "Rappaccini's Daughter," and "Earth's Holocaust."

2. Even Nelson F. Adkins is no help here – in his "The Early Projected Works of Nathaniel Hawthorne," *Papers of the Bibliographical Society of America*, (1945), 119–55.

3. Michael J. Colacurcio, *The Province of Piety: Moral History in Hawthorne's Early Tales* (Cambridge, Mass. & London: Harvard University Press, 1984), p. 32.

4. Though the decision to issue *The Scarlet Letter* accompanied only by "The Custom-House" was taken early in 1850, the volume as we have it still oddly contains traces of Hawthorne's earlier ideas about its form and content. This can – at least in the case of the first edition – be explained by the facts of composition. "The Custom-House" was completed and sent to Fields along with all of *The Scarlet Letter* except three chapters on January 15, 1850. Those last chapters were completed by February 4, 1850, the book itself appearing on March 16th, 1850. But it is still a matter for wonder that Hawthorne failed to notice such a passage as this: "A portion of his facts, by the by, did me good service in the preparation of the article entitled "MAIN STREET," included in the present volume" – as it is that very near the end of "The Custom-House" he chose to add a footnote rather than deleting a sentence (N, 145, 156). The very fact that the text reads "MAIN STREET" rather than "Main-Street" would, it might be thought, have attracted the eye of the laziest proof-reader. And – if, as seems to be the case, the type of the first edition had been distributed – why in the second edition did neither author not publisher make the obvious changes? It is difficult to know what to make of this. If it was pure carelessness or indifference, why any footnote – presumably added at the proof-reading stage of the first edition? If one thinks (as I do) that Hawthorne intended "The Custom-House" as a crucial part of the experience of reading *The Scarlet Letter* why then did he not suppress the traces

of his earlier intention to publish a collection? Given the way that "Ethan Brand" and "Main-Street" – works which so obviously prepare for *The Scarlet Letter* – offer themselves as works which can or should be other than they are, it is hard to believe that accident or sheer indifference provide an adequate explanation. But it is equally hard to come up with a neat solution.

5. D.F. Rauber, "The Fragment as Romantic Form," *Modern Language Quarterly*, 30 (1969), 217. The Shelley quotation comes from his *Defence of Poetry, Works*, ed. R. Ingpen and W.E. Peck (London & New York: E. Benn & Gordian Press, 1965), VII, p. 135.

6. D. Reiman (ed.), *The Romantics Reviewed: Contemporary Reviews of British Romantic Poetry* (London & New York: Garland Publishing Inc., 1972), Part B, II, p. 572.

7. S.T. Coleridge, Headnote to "Kubla Khan: Or a Vision in a Dream. A Fragment." In view of the debate about the nature of the Romantic fragment, I wonder what we should do with a *very* minor piece of his – the "Epilogue to a Rash Conjuror" – which he calls "An Uncomposed Poem"!

8. T. Moore (ed.), *The Works of Lord Byron* (London: John Murray, 1832), IX, p. 141.

9. Samuel Rogers, *Poems* (London: Cadell & Moxon, 1834), pp. 217, 236, 278.

10. Lord Byron, *Works*, IX, pp. 145, 200.

11. J.J. McGann, *Fiery Dust: Byron's Poetic Development* (London & Chicago: Chicago University Press, 1968), p. 143.

12. W.H. Marshall, "The Accretive Structure of Byron's 'The Giaour,'" *Modern Language Notes*, 76 (June 1961), 502.

13. Reiman (ed.), *Romantics Reviewed*, p. 842.

14. M. Levinson, *The Romantic Fragment Poem: A Critique of a Form* (Chapel Hill & London: University of North Carolina Press, 1986), p. 236.

15. Reiman (ed.), *Romantics Reviewed*, p. 842–3.

16. Levinson, *Romantic Fragment Poem*, pp. 49–50.

17. R.M. Rilke, *Rodin*, translated by J. Lamont and H. Trausil with an Introduction by Padraic Colum (London: Grey Walls Press, 1946), p. 24.

18. John Bunyan, *The Doctrine of the Law and Grace Unfolded, Works*, ed. G. Offor (Glasgow, Edinburgh & London: Blackie and Son, 1860), I, p. 586. I am greatly indebted to Roger Pooley of Keele University for his help here.

19. P.E. More, "Hawthorne: Looking Before and After," in *Paul Elmer More's Shelburne Essays on American Literature*, edited and with an introduction by Daniel Aaron (New York: Harcourt, Brace & World, 1963), pp. 129, 128.

20. John Winthrop, *History of New England: 1630–1649*, edited by J.K. Hosmer (New York: Barnes and Noble, 1959), I, p. 230; II, pp. 60–1.

21. Quoted in the Introduction to Nathaniel Woodes' *Conflict of Conscience* (1581), edited by Herbert Davis and F.P. Wilson (Oxford: The Malone Society, 1952), p. vi.

22. Bunyan, *Works*, III, pp. 101, 145.

23. Bunyan, *Works*, I, p. 566.

24. Bunyan, *Works*, III, pp. 582, 583.

25. Colacurcio, *Province of Piety*, p. 542.

26. R.W. Emerson, "An Address Delivered before the Senior Class in Divinity College, Cambridge, Sunday Evening, July 15, 1838," in *Works* (Riverside Edition) (London: George Routledge & Sons, 1903), I, p. 123.

27. H. Shelton Smith, R.T. Handy, Lefferts A. Loetscher (eds.), *American Christianity: An Historical Interpretation with Representative Documents* (New York: Charles Scribners' Sons, 1963), II, p. 30.

28. P. Rahv, "The Cult of Experience in American Writing," in *Literature and the Sixth Sense* (London: Faber and Faber, 1970), pp. 32, 33.

29. Hawthorne must have really wanted to make his feminist point here as he suppresses

some of the less attractive details of Dorothy Talby's life. Felt in his *Annals of Salem* makes it clear that he thinks she was criminally insane – presumably drawing on Winthrop: "Dorothy Talbye was hanged at Boston for murdering her own daughter, a child of three years old. She had been a member of the church of Salem, and of good esteem for godliness, etc.; but, falling at difference with her husband, through melancholy or spiritual delusions, she sometimes attempted to kill him, and her children, and herself, by refusing meat, saying it was so revealed to her, etc. After much patience, and divers admonitions not prevailing, the church cast her out. Whereupon she grew worse; so as the magistrate caused her to be whipped. Whereupon she was reformed for a time, and carried herself more dutifully to her husband, etc.; but soon after she was so possessed by Satan, that he persuaded her (by his delusions, which she listened to as revelations from God) to break the neck of her own child, that she might free it from future misery" (Winthrop, *History of New England*, pp. 282–3).

30. G. Bancroft, *History of the United States, from the Discovery of the American Continent*, II (Boston: Charles C. Little & James Brown, 1837), p. 454. D. Levin, *History as Romantic Art: Bancroft, Prescott, Motley and Parkman* (New York & Burlingame: Harcourt, Brace & World, 1959).

31. Quoted by John P. McWilliams Jr., *Hawthorne, Melville, and the American Character: A Looking-glass Business* (Cambridge, London, New York: Cambridge University Press, 1984), p. 15.

32. McWilliams Jr, *Hawthorne, Melville and American Character*, p. 14.

### 4 THE SCARLET LETTER

1. Cotton Mather, *Magnalia Christi Americana*, Books I and II, edited by K.B. Murdock, (Cambridge, Mass.: Harvard University Press, 1977), p. 295. Peter Farb, *Man's Rise to Civilization as Shown by the Indians of North American from Primeval Times to the Coming of the Industrial State* (London: Secker and Warburg, 1969), pp. 60–1.

2. R.R. Male, *Hawthorne's Tragic Vision* (New York, W.W. Norton, 1964), p. 114.

3. Michael Colacurcio, "Footsteps of Ann Hutchinson: The Context of *The Scarlet Letter*," *English Literary History*, 39 (1972), 459–94.

4. Austin Warren, "*The Scarlet Letter*: A Literary Exercise in Moral Theology," *The Southern Review*, 1, new series (Jan. 1965), 22–45.

5. Perry Miller, (ed.), *Margaret Fuller: American Romantic* (New York: Anchor Books, 1963), p. 162.

6. "Shaker adventism was shown to be spiritual and not physical. 'As the substance of the first woman was taken from the body of the first man: so that Divine Spirit with which the second woman was endowed . . . was taken from the Spirit of Christ.' Mother Ann thus became the 'Second pillar of the Church of God,' but the Shakers were careful to state they did not mean the 'human tabernacle' of Ann Lee. That was but the instrument for the expression of divine truth, which could not complete its work until all men had become spiritual." Alice Felt Tyler, *Freedom's Ferment: Phases of American Social History from the Colonial Period to the Outbreak of the Civil War* (New York: Harper and Row, 1962), pp. 146–7.

7. Jane Tompkins, however, draws attention to Isabella Beecher Hooker, Harriet Beecher Stowe's half sister: "This woman at one time in her life had believed that the millenium was at hand and that she was destined to be the leader of a new matriarchy." *Sensational Designs: The Cultural Work of American Fiction, 1790–1860* (New York: Oxford University Press, 1985), p. 122.

8. Nina Baym, *The Shape of Hawthorne's Career* (Ithaca and London: Cornell University Press, 1976), pp. 130, 134.

9. Sacvan Bercovitch, "Hawthorne's A-Morality of Compromise," *Representations*, 24 (Fall 1988), 1, 2, 10.

10. See John Ashworth, *'Agrarians' and 'Aristocrats': Party Political Ideology in the United States, 1837–1846* (Cambridge: Cambridge University Press, 1987), *passim* for democratic Democrats.

### 5 THE HOUSE OF THE SEVEN GABLES

1. *The House of the Seven Gables* was completed early in 1851 – the preface is dated January 27, 1851.

2. It is, of course, one of the ironies of history that Hawthorne was shortly to write a campaign biography of that rather less than distinguished President, his old college chum Franklin Pierce in which he had both to inform his readers that Pierce had won his candidacy only on the forty-ninth ballot and give the impression that here was the people's choice.

3. Oliver W. Larkin, *Samuel F.B. Morse and American Democratic Art* (Boston & Toronto: Little, Brown & Co., 1954), p. 164.

4. Howard Kerr, *Mediums, and Spirit-Rappers and Roaring Radicals: Spiritualism in American Literature 1850–1900* (Urbana, Chicago, London: University of Illinois Press, 1972), pp. 4, 7.

5. A.L. Temane (trans. R. Routledge), *The Telegraph* (London: George Routledge and Sons, 1895), p. 90.

6. Quoted by Clive Bush, *The Dream of Reason: American Consciousness and Cultural Achievement from Independence to the Civil War* (London: Edward Arnold, 1977), pp. 93–4.

7. R.B. Sewall, in *The Life of Emily Dickinson* (London: Faber and Faber, 1976) gives an account of his importance. See especially pp. 342–351.

8. Edward Hitchcock, *The Religion of Geology and its Connected Sciences* (Glasgow & London: William Collins, 1851), pp. 331, 353, 332. It is worth quoting more of the implications to be drawn from the fact that "the sentence I am now uttering shall alter the whole atmosphere through all future time." He goes on to say that "In view of these facts, we cannot regard the glowing language of Babbage as an exaggeration, when he says, 'The soul of the negro, whose fettered body, surviving the living charnel-house of his infected prison, was thrown into the sea to lighten the ship, that his Christian master might escape the limited justice at length assigned by civilized man to crimes whose profit had long gilded their atrocity, will need, at the last great day of human accounts, no living witness of his earthly agony: when man and all his race shall have disappeared from the face of our planet, ask every particle of air still floating over the unpeopled earth, and it will record the cruel mandate of the tyrant. Interrogate every wave which breaks unimpeded on ten thousand desolate shores, and it will give evidence of the last gurgle of the waters which closed over the head of his dying victim'" (p. 332).

9. Oliver Wendell Holmes, "Sun-Painting and Sun-Sculpture," *Atlantic Monthly*, 8 (July 1861), p. 18. It is worth setting another passage from Hitchcock beside Holmes: "It seems, then, that this photographic influence pervades all nature; nor can we say where it stops. We do not know but it may imprint upon the world about us our features, as they are modified by various passions, and thus fill nature with daguerreotype impressions of all our actions that are performed in daylight. It may be, too, that there are tests by which nature, more skilfully than any human photographist, can bring out and fix those portraits, so that acuter senses than ours shall see them, as on a great canvas, spread over the entire universe. Perhaps, too, they may never fade from that canvas, but become specimens in the great picture gallery

of eternity" (p. 426).

10. R. Taft, *Photography and the American Scene: A Social History* (New York: Macmillan, 1938), p. 48.

11. Joel Porte (ed.), *Emerson in His Journals* (Cambridge, Mass. & London: Harvard University Press, 1982), p. 271.

12. "Daguerreotypy," *Littel's Living Age*, 9 (June 20, 1846), 552. This was reprinted from the *Christian Watchman*, but I have given this reference as the *Dictionary of American Biography* assures me that Littel's publications were in every cultivated home in New England.

13. Holmes, "Sun Painting," p. 15.

14. Holmes, "Sun Painting," p. 14.

15. Marius Bewley, *The Eccentric Design* (New York & London: Columbia University Press, 1963), p. 176. In a letter to William Buchanan and James Hay (Paris, January 26, 1786), Jefferson wrote as follows about public buildings for the capital of Virginia: "[T]wo methods of proceeding presented themselves to my mind. The one was, to leave to some architect to draw an external according to his fancy, in which way, experience shews, that, about once in a thousand times, a pleasing form is hit upon; the other was, to take some model already devised, and approved by the general suffrage of the world. I had no hesitation in deciding the latter was best, nor after the decision, was there any doubt what model to take. There is at Nismes, in the south of France, a building called the Maison quarrée, erected in the time of the Caesars, and which is allowed, without contradiction, to be the most perfect and precious remain of antiquity in existence. Its superiority over anything at Rome, in Greece, at Balbec or Palmyra is allowed on all hands . . . I determined therefore to adopt this model." (Thomas Jefferson, *Writings*, Library of America, 1984, pp. 845–6).

16. Oliver Wendell Holmes, "The Stereoscope and the Stereograph," *Atlantic Monthly*, 3 (June, 1859), 747–8.

17. John Ruskin, *Praeterita*, II, para. 141. Harold I. Shapiro (ed.), *Ruskin in Italy: Letters to His Parents 1845* (Oxford: The Clarendon Press, 1972), pp. 220, 225.

18. Quoted in translation by Beaumont Newhall and Robert Doty in *Image: The Bulletin of the George Eastman House of Photography*, XI, 1962, no. 6, p. 25.

19. See note 9 above.

20. Bush, *Dream of Reason*, p. 186.

21. Roland Barthes, *Camera Lucida* (London: Flamingo, 1984), pp. 93–4. Translated by Richard Howard, from *La Chambre Claire* (Paris, 1980).

## 6: THE BLITHEDALE ROMANCE

1. J.C. Reid, *Bucks and Bruisers: Pierce Egan and Regency England* (London: Routledge and Kegan Paul, 1971), p. 123. George Parsons Lathrop, in his introductory note to the Riverside edition of the novel writes "The name Fauntleroy . . . was probably borrowed from that banker, whose forgeries, prosecuted by the Bank of England and leading to his execution, made him a distinguished character in criminal history, about the year 1824, while Hawthorne was still a Bowdoin undergraduate" (5, 317). I want to emphasize that Coverdale stresses that he *chooses* this very unusual name for "a man of wealth, and magnificent tastes, and prodigal expenditure," and that Fauntleroy's case was very widely reported – it was, for example, written up in *The Gentleman's Magazine* which we know Hawthorne read. Though knowledge of the historical Fauntleroy makes it certain that forgery is the crime of the fictional Fauntleroy, I would argue that this can be gathered from a careful reading of the text.

2. The relation of *The Blithedale Romance* to the historical world is difficult and complex

(and I do not mean simply the relationship to Brook Farm). Take, for example, the tactless – even tasteless – "fact" that Coverdale receives a letter from Margaret Fuller. She had died only in 1850 and her autobiography with memoirs by Emerson and others appeared in 1852 – the same year as the publication of *The Blithedale Romance*. And Coverdale reinforces the impression that he can be considered as an historical personage by mentioning in the last chapter that Rufus Griswold (1815–57), the compiler of *The Poets and Poetry of America* (1842), had placed him at a "fair elevation among our minor minstrelsy" (847). Such an appearance of real historical personages is common enough in conventional historical fiction produced in the nineteenth century but it is surely decidedly odd in a novel which (as the preface makes clear) comes from and is partly addressed to a small, even provincial society and where the action takes place only a dozen or so years before the time of writing.

3. That rock, Eliot's pulpit, was "so named from a tradition that the venerable Apostle Eliot had preached there . . . to an Indian auditory" (736). He was known as "Apostle" because he preached to the Indians in their own language and also translated the Bible. It is hard to believe that Hawthorne chose the site lightly.

4. R.R. Male, *Hawthorne's Tragic Vision* (New York: W.W. Norton and Company, 1964, first published by the University of Texas Press, 1957), p. 154; Joan Magretta, "The Coverdale Translation: *Blithedale* and the Bible" (*Nathaniel Hawthorne Journal*, 1974), p. 242.

5. T.R. Steiner, *English Translation Theory 1650–1800* (Amsterdam: Van Gorcum, 1975).

6. Susan Basnett–McGuire, *Translation Studies* (London and New York: Methuen, 1980), pp. 39, 65.

7. Ralph Waldo Emerson, "Books", *The Works*, Riverside Edition (London: George Routledge and Sons, 1903), VII, pp. 194–5.

8. Kelly, paraphrasing George Steiner in *After Babel*, notes that the hermeneutic process of translation has four stages: trust, aggression, incorporation and restitution. However coincidentally, this is not a bad description of Coverdale's narrative. L.G. Kelly, *The True Interpreter: A History of Translation Theory and Practice in the West* (Oxford: Basil Blackwell, 1978), p. 56.

9. James Boswell, *The Life of Samuel Johnson*, 2 vols. (London: Oxford University Press, 1903), II, 106. Even closer to Coverdale's words is a sentence from John Holliday's *Life of Lord Mansfield* (1797), quoted in *Albion's Fatal Tree* (p. 19, Peregrine edition): "Forgery is a stab to commerce, and only to be tolerated in a commercial nation when the foul crime of murder is pardoned."

10. Richard Francis, "The Ideology of Brook Farm," in *Studies in the American Renaissance*, ed. Joel Myerson (Boston: Twayne, 1977), pp. 14, 15.

11. F. Jameson, *The Political Unconscious: Narrative as a Socially Symbolic Act* (London: Methuen, 1981), *passim*.

12. A.W. Schlegel, *A Course of Lectures on Dramatic Art and Literature*, trans. by John Black (1811; London: Henry G. Bohn, 1846), pp. 54, 70.

13. Karl Marx, *The Eighteenth Brumaire of Louis Bonaparte*, in *Surveys from Exile* edited and introduced by David Fernbach (Harmondsworth: Penguin Books, 1973), pp. 146–47.

14. T.F. Eagleton, "Translation and Transformation," *Stand*, 19 (1978), 73.

## 7 THE AMERICAN CLAIMANT

1. N. Hawthorne, *The American Claimant Manuscripts, The Elixir of Life Manuscripts*, vols. XII and XIII of the Centenary Edition of Hawthorne's Works, edited by Edward H. Davidson, Claude M. Simpson, and L. Neal Smith (Ohio State University Press,

1977). Any reader of Hawthorne must be very grateful to the editors of these volumes in particular for their scrupulous and helpful work. All subsequent references will be placed parenthetically in the text.

2. I have taken the information about dates from the material provided by the Ohio editors.

3. Edward Hutchins Davidson, *Hawthorne's Last Phase* (New Haven: Yale University Press, 1949). Nearly forty years later Brodhead gives different reasons for Hawthorne's "failure" but is, regrettably, equally confident in his dismissive judgement: "I want to argue that the impairment of his authorial powers has less to do with political or physiological changes than with the change he experienced in the cultural status of the writer's work." (Richard H. Brodhead, *The School of Hawthorne* [New York, Oxford: Oxford University Press, 1986], p. 70).

4. Arlin Turner, *Nathaniel Hawthorne: A Biography* (New York, Oxford: Oxford University Press, 1980), p. 347.

5. A.O. Lovejoy's excellent article, "Milton and the Paradox of the Fortunate Fall," shows what a long and respectable theological history lay behind the idea. (*ELH*, 4, no. 3 (September 1937), 161–79).

6. There is at least one point where we read *Our Old Home* very differently if we remember *The English Notebooks* – and that is the description of the disgustingly diseased little boy who attaches himself to Hawthorne who is too modest to tell the story in the first person in *Our Old Home*.

7. The dating of the studies has always been provisional: "Hitherto they have all been associated with the 1861 manuscripts, but there is nothing in Studies 1 through 4 that could not relate equally well to the "Ancestral Footstep" sketch. The fact that Studies 1 and 2 were written on paper bearing Liverpool watermarks (plus a watermark date of 1853 on one leaf) invites speculation that Hawthorne might have begun to prepare his memoranda in England. There are enough verbal similarities between the April, 1855, notebook plot outline . . . and the third paragraph of Study 1 . . . to suggest that Hawthorne almost surely wrote this study with the journal open before him . . . This supports its possible composition in England and rules out its composition in Italy when the English notebooks were in Henry Bright's custody" (XII, 496). I would suggest that internal evidence makes it quite clear that Study 1 was written in England: one only writes "here in England" if one is in England – and thus Study 1 must precede the writing of *The Ancestral Footstep*.

8. Nina Baym, *The Shape of Hawthorne's Career* (Ithaca and London: Cornell University Press, 1976), pp. 221, 220–1. I have one considerable advantage over Baym: the texts of the Ohio edition were not available to her – and it is not too much to say that, without those texts, criticism of the unfinished novels is impossible unless one has access to the manuscripts.

9. Baym, *Hawthorne's Career*, pp. 225, 225–6.

10. Frank Kermode, "Secrets and Narrative Sequence," in *Essays on Fiction 1971–1982* (London, Melbourne and Henley: Routledge and Kegan Paul, 1983), p. 138.

11. It is striking that in both *Etherege* and *Grimshawe* Hawthorne planned to begin with childhood and then have a break during which the central character tries to make himself a career and an American identity in his young manhood – a period of his life which remains a deliberate gap in his story. It is, however, understandable that there are no equivalents for parents but only "grandfather figures" in the American claimant material. But the Elixir of Life material equally is noticeable for its absence of parents: Septimius is an "orphan" – and one motive for Dolliver's wish to grow younger may be to enable him to be as a parent. Indeed, nowhere in Hawthorne's longer fiction do we have what we conventionally believe to be a conventional,

normal family (of the kind that Hawthorne in his own life seemed so deeply committed to).

12.     "I never had such an impression of snugness, homeliness, neighborliness – of a place where everybody had known everybody, and forefathers and mothers had grown up together, and spent whole successions of lives, and died, and been buried under the same sods, so closely and conveniently to hand – the same family names, the same family features, repeated from generation to generation ... It is rather wearisome, to an American, to think of a place where no change came for centuries, and where a peasant does but step into his father's shoes, and lead just his father's life, going in and out over the old threshold, and finally being buried close by his father's grave, time without end; and yet it is rather pleasant to know such things are."

"It makes death strangely familiar, and brings the centuries together in a lump. But methinks it must be weary, weary, weary, this rusty, unchangeable village life, where men grow up, grow old, and die, in their father's dwellings, and are buried in their grandsires' very graves, the old skulls, and cross-bones being thrown out to make room for them, and shovelled in on the tops of their coffins."          (*English Notebooks*, June 24, 1855 and November 8, 1857).

"Tedious beyond imagination! Such, I think, is the final impression on the mind of an American visitor, when his delight at finding something permanent begins to yield to his Western love of change, and he becomes sensible of the heavy air of a spot where the forefathers and foremothers have grown up together, intermarried, and died, through a long succession of lives, without any intermixture of new elements, till family features and character are all run in the same inevitable mould. Life is there fossilized in its greenest leaf. The man who died yesterday, or ever so long ago, walks the village-street to-day, and chooses the same wife that he married a hundred years since, and must be buried again, tomorrow, under the same kindred dust that has already covered him half a score of times. The stone threshold of his cottage is worn away with his hob-nailed footsteps, shuffling over it from the reign of the first Plantagenet to that of Victoria. Better than this is the lot of our restless countrymen, whose modern instinct bids them tend always towards 'fresh woods and pastures new.' Rather than such monotony of sluggish ages, loitering on a village-green, toiling in hereditary fields, listening to the parson's drone lengthened through centuries in the gray Norman church, let us welcome whatever change may come – change of place, social customs, political institutions, modes of worship – trusting them, if all present things shall vanish, they will but make room for better systems, and for a higher type of man to clothe his life in them, and to fling them off in turn." (v, 59–60)

13.  When the phrase I've just used is set in its proper place in the text it has its own irony: Etherege is claiming that living in England would drive him mad – the life of the English villager it does not quite go without saying.

14.  There is one potentially interesting notion that Hawthorne donates to the Italian/ English incumbent:

      "I should decidedly say that the Bloody Footstep is a natural reddish stain in the stone."

"Do you so indeed?" rejoined his lordship. "It may be; but in that case, if not
the record of an actual deed – of a foot stamped down there in guilt and agony,
and oozing out with unwipeable blood – we may consider it as prophetic; – as
foreboding, from the time when the stone was squared and laid at this
threshold, that a fatal footstep was really to be impressed there."     (XII, 284)

It is, as Etherege remarks, "an ingenious supposition," – more ingenious than
Etherege realizes as "his lordship" is in a position, when he feels his hold on the estate
threatened, to make nature's prophecy come true. Perhaps Hawthorne would have
made more play with this in *Grimshawe*.

15. George Parsons Lathrop (ed.), *The Works of Hawthorne* (Boston and New York:
Houghton, Mifflin and Co.: The Riverside Edition), XII, p. 299. First published in
the *Atlantic Monthly* for July, 1862. All subsequent references will be placed
parenthetically in the text thus: L (12, 299).

16. It is tempting to argue for a direct influence of Dickens on Hawthorne. *Great
Expectations* was first published in *All the Year Round* from December 1st, 1860 to
August 3rd 1861. According to the Ohio editors, "the wisps of evidence suggest
that" *Etherege* and *Grimshawe* occupied "Hawthorne principally during the first six
or eight months of 1861" (XII, 502). The doctor, when training Edward Redclyffe to
be a gentleman, "sometimes . . . would make a low, uncouth bow, after his fashion,
saying 'Allow me to kiss your hand, my lord,' and little Ned, not quite knowing
what the grim Doctor meant, yet allowed the favor he asked, with a grave and
gracious condescension that seemed much to delight the suitor" (XII, 373).
Magwitch, of course, has to operate by remote control from Australia. Famously he
tells Pip "I've made a gentleman on you" – and goes on to say "it was a recompense
to me . . . to know in secret that I was making a gentleman" (ch. XXXIX). It is a
recompense partly because it enables him to feel that he can hold his own against the
gentleman colonists ("If I ain't a gentleman, nor yet ain't got no learning, I'm the
owner of such. All on you owns stock and land; which on you owns a brought-up
London gentleman?" [ch. XXXIX]). It is also partly a weird kind of respectful revenge
on the gentleman-like Compeyson who is so largely responsible for Magwitch's
transportation. "Had the grim Doctor been an American, he might have had the vast
antipathy to rank, without the sense of awe that made it so much more the
malignant; it required a low-born Englishman to feel the two together. What made
the hatred so fiendish was a something that, in the natural course of things, would
have been loyalty, inherited affection, devoted self-sacrifice to a superior" (XII, 368).
Malignancy and fiendishness are not really relevant terms for Magwitch – though,
however understandably, he does tell Compeyson "Once out of this court, I'll smash
that face of yourn!" Yet the desire to transform Pip into a gentleman is partly
generated by his identification that the court that tries them both concurs with: "He
set up for a gentleman, this Compeyson, and he'd been to a public boarding-school
and had learning. He was a smooth one to talk, and was a dab at the ways of
gentlefolks." It is that smooth gentleman-like appearance that lures Magwitch into
being the fall-guy. It works equally well in court: "When we was put in the dock, I
noticed first of all what a gentleman Compeyson looked, wi' his curly hair and his
black clothes and his white pocket-hankercher, and what a common sort of wretch I
looked . . . And when it come to character, warn't it Compeyson as had been to
school, and warn't it his schoolfellows as was in this position and in that, and warn't it
him as had been know'd by witnesses in such clubs and societies, and nowt to his
disadvantage?" (ch. XLII). Both Magwitch and the grim Doctor revenge themselves
on a class that has victimized them not by repudiating that class and its claims but by
the creation of a pseudo-heir.

17. He has already played his part in informing us about modern America by telling the English visitor that it is likely that "living families" may be "turned out of their homes twice or thrice in a generation (as they are likely to be in our new government" [XII, 418].) It is also worth noting that, as Davidson, has pointed out, the lawyer, Timothy Pickering, who acts as administrator for Dr. Grimshawe's estate, is an historical figure well known in the annals of Salem: "Pickering had been a Revolutionary patriot, a member of Washington's cabinet, and, after his political career was ended, had retired to spend his last years in the town of; his birth" (*Hawthorne's Last Phase*, p. 68).

18. He, like the portrait which the alert reader is supposed to see is his ancestor, is presented in an anomalous position as far as social status goes. Both the portrait and the schoolmaster have gentlemanly features but not gentlemanly clothing (XII, 386–7).

19. Turner, *Nathaniel Hawthorne*, p. 370.


## 8 THE MARBLE FAUN

1. We know that Hawthorne should have read *Pierre* since Melville inscribed a copy of the book to the Hawthornes (IV, xl).

2. B. Rajan, *The Form of the Unfinished: English Poetics from Spenser to Pound* (Princeton, New Jersey: Princeton University Press, 1985), pp. 4, 5.

3. The choice of the bust of Brutus is not an obvious one. To judge from photographs, it is not strikingly unfinished – and, unlike virtually every art-work referred to in *The Marble Faun*, Hawthorne makes no reference to it in *The French and Italian Notebooks*. I suggest that Hawthorne chose the bust of Brutus as a point of reference at this point in the novel because he either re-read or remembered a passage in Valery's *Italy* – a book that, thanks to the Ohio editors, we know he read:
   "The bust of Brutus, rough-hewn by Michael Angelo, well portrays the murderer of Caesar . . . Below is this dull distich:
   Dum Bruti effigiem sculptor de marmore ducit,
       In mentem sceleris venit, et abstinuit.
   [When the sculptor was extracting the effigy of Brutus from the marble, he came across the sinful/criminal mind and gave up]. An Englishman, the earl of Sandwich, provoked at reading this, replied impromptu:
   Brutum effecisset sculptor, sed mente recursat
       Tanta viri virtus; sistit et abstinuit.
   [The sculptor would have finished off his Brutus, but so much of the moral excellence of the man recurred to his mind that he desisted and abandoned the work]. M. Valery (Antoine Claude Pasquin), *Historical, Literary, and Artistical Travels in Italy* (Paris: Baudry, 1839), translated by C.E. Clifton, p. 323. Hilda advises Kenyon "A few strokes of the chisel might change the whole expression and so spoil it for what it is now worth" (I, 169). Is not Lord Sandwich's distich very close to Hilda's comment and Hawthorne's conclusion to ch. XLI?

4. Rudolf Wittkower, *Sculpture: Processes and Principles* (London: Allen Lane, 1977), pp. 144, 255.

5. There is a slight problem here. Is Kenyon carving the marble bust from memory or from a cast? He can hardly be supposed to have brought the clay bust back from Monte Beni and surely juggling a plaster-cast round in a saddle-bag as Kenyon escorts Donatello on his journey would not have been good for it – yet to work directly on the marble is, it would seem, highly unusual both in terms of ordinary practice and in terms of the fiction.

6. This is, of course, a classic nineteenth-century point – that every picture tells a story. But Miriam's demand for the title of the sculpture is not unreasonable even in terms of twentieth-century aesthetics. I would make a large bet that it is because of the title with its historical meanings that people praise Picasso's *Guernica* as an anti-war painting.

7. Not that there isn't something to be said for transience: this work of art is clearly related to the pleasures of courtship where pleasure comes oddly – even perversely – from the death of the flowers: "The flowers, that grow outside of those inner sanctities, have a wild, hasty charm, which it is well to prove; there may be sweeter ones within the sacred precinct, but *none that will die while you are handling them, and bequeathe you a delicious legacy*, as these do, in the perception of their evanescence and unreality" (1,164, my emphasis).

8. Motley had been very encouraging:
"I admire the book exceedingly . . . With regard to a story which has been slightly criticized – I can only say that to me it is quite satisfactory. I like those shadowy, weird, fantastic, Hawthornesque shapes flitting through the golden gloom which is the atmosphere of the book – I like the misty way in which the story is indicated rather than revealed. The outlines are quite definite enough from the beginning to the end, to those who have imagination enough to follow you in your airy flights – and to those who complain, I suppose nothing less than an illustrated edition, with a large gallows on the last page, with Donatello in the most pensile of attitudes, – his ears revealed at last thro' a white nightcap would be satisfactory . . . I don't know that I am especially in love with Miriam or Hilda, or that I care very much what is the fate of Donatello – but I do like the air of unreality with which you have clothed familiar scenes without making them less familiar – The way in which the two victims dance through the Carnival on the last day, is very striking. It is like a Greek tragedy, in its effect, without being in the least Greek" (xviii, 258–9).

9. R.W. Emerson, *The Early Lectures*, edited by Robert E. Spiller and Wallace E. Williams (Cambridge, Mass.: Harvard University Press, 1972), iii, pp. 86–7.

10. We can too easily see this as an *American* response to storied Europe. A.H. Clough and George Eliot show that the English had their problems too:
> Rome disappoints me much; I hardly as yet understand, but
> All the foolish destructions, and all the sillier savings,
> All the incongruous things of past incompatible ages,
> Seem to be treasured up here to make fools of present and future.
> Would to Heaven the old Goths had made a cleaner sweep of it!
> Would to Heaven some new ones would come and destroy these churches! . . .
> Rome disappoints me still; but I shrink and adapt myself to it.
> Somehow a tyrannous sense of a superincumbent oppression
> Still, wherever I go, accompanies ever, and makes me
> Feel like a tree (shall I say?) buried under a ruin of brickwork.
> Rome believe me, my friend, is like its own Monte Testaceo
> Merely a marvellous mass of broken and castaway wine-pots.
> Amours de Voyage (1858), Canto I lines 19–25, 35–40.

George Eliot in *Middlemarch* (1871–2) makes much the same points – and explicitly connects them to the problem a naive Protestant has in confronting such a history-filled place:
> she was beholding Rome, the city of visible history, where the past of a whole

hemisphere seems moving in funeral procession with strange ancestral images and trophies gathered from afar.

But this stupendous fragmentariness heighted the dream-like strangeness of her bridal life . . . [S]he had ended by oftenest choosing to drive out to the Campagna where she could feel alone with the earth and sky, away from the oppressive masquerade of ages, in which her own life too seemed to become a masque with enigmatical costumes . . .

[T]he gigantic broken revelations of that Imperial and Papal city [were] thrust abruptly on the notions of a girl who had been brought up in English and Swiss Puritanism.          (*Middlemarch*, Book Two, chapter 20).

11. Hyatt H. Waggoner, "The Marble Faun," (1963) in *The Recognition of Nathaniel Hawthorne*, ed. B. Bernard Cohen (Ann Arbor: Michigan University Press, 1969), p. 247. Graham Clarke, "To Transform and Transfigure: The Aesthetic Play of Hawthorne's *The Marble Faun*," in *Nathaniel Hawthorne: New Critical Essays*, ed. A. Robert Lee (London & New York: Vision & Barnes & Noble, 1982), p. 135, R.R. Male, *Hawthorne's Tragic Vision* (New York: W.W. Norton & Co., 1964), p. 176.

12. Hawthorne's command of German was poor verging on non-existent. It is possible that he could have been exposed to German ideas either through Elizabeth Peabody or the Brook Farm circle. He did know F.H. Hedge, the German scholar who produced a large anthology of German material which included the Kant essay I deal with in section IV.

13. M.H. Abrams, *Natural Supernaturalism: Tradition and Revolution in Romantic Literature* (New York: W.W. Norton & Co., 1971), pp. 183–4. All subsequent references will appear parenthetically in the text.

14. See, for example, the sylvan dance in the gardens of the Villa Borghese. Hilda and Kenyon are absent from this scene – and "The sole exception to the geniality of the moment . . . was seen in a countryman of our own, who sneered at the spectacle, and declined to compromise his dignity by making part of it" (925).

15. A.O. Lovejoy, "Milton and the Paradox of the Fortunate Fall," in his *Essays in the History of Ideas* (Baltimore: Johns Hopkins University Press, 1948), p. 279.

16. Immanuel Kant, "Conjectural Beginning of Human History," in *Kant on History* (1786), ed. L.W. Beck (Indianapolis & New York: Bobbs-Merril, 1963), p. 60. All subsequent references will be placed parenthetically in the text.

17. I am persuaded by Arnold Goldman ("The Plot of Hawthorne's *The Marble Faun*," *Journal of American Studies*, 18 [1984] 383–404), that we should read that night as one of sexual passion – the more so as the language is so close to that of the forest scene in *The Scarlet Letter* where Hester declares her sexuality.

18. If there are doubters, I refer them to pp. 1,069–70, 1,074–5, 1,079, 1,087.

19. "Is he not beautiful?" says Miriam of Donatello when she meets Kenyon in the Campagna (1,214). Donatello's earlier physical appearance had been described as possessing the "charm of grotesqueness, . . . most provocative of laughter, and yet akin to pathos" as opposed to Miriam's "artful beauty" (923). On the battlements of Monte Beni, Kenyon noted that his "original beauty, which sorrow had partly effaced, temporarily "came back elevated and spiritualized" (1,074–5). When Donatello and Miriam join hands by the statue of the Pope in Perugia, Donatello's "aspect . . . assumed a dignity" which, "elevating his former beauty, accorded with the change that had long been taking place in his interiour self" (1,121). One consequence of what has happened to Donatello is that he has acquired an aesthetic sensibility which enables him to detect the statue of Venus. All this – but especially Miriam's aesthetic judgement – seems very close to what Schiller has to say in his *Aesthetic Education* – what, indeed, is implied by his very title: "A man can please us

through his readiness to oblige; he can, through his discourse, give us food for thought; he can, through his character, fill us with respect; but finally he can also, independently of all this, and without our taking into consideration in judging him any law or purpose, please us simply as we contemplate him and by the sheer manner of his being. Under this last-named quality of being we are judging him aesthetically. Thus there is an education to health, an education to understanding, an education to morality, an education to taste and beauty. This last has as its aims the development of the whole complex of our sensual and spiritual powers in the greatest possible harmony." (Friedrich Schiller, *On the Aesthetic Education of Man*, edited and translated by E.M. Wilkinson and L.A. Willoughby [Oxford at the Clarendon Press, 1967], p. 151–3). It is tempting to take the comparisons further. For example, Schiller claims that man is most fully human when he plays – and relates this to the aesthetic realm. When Miriam begins her judgement of Donatello by praising his beauty, he has just been described in these terms: "A playfulness came out of his heart, and glimmered like firelight on his actions, alternating, or even closely intermingled with profound sympathy and serious thought" (1,214).

20. Friedrich Schiller, *On Naive and Sentimental Poetry* (1795–6), in *German Aesthetic and Literary Criticism*, ed. H.B. Nisbet (Cambridge: Cambridge University Press, 1985), p. 188.

21. D. Howard, "The Fortunate Fall and Hawthorne's *The Marble Faun*," in *Romantic Mythologies*, edited by Ian Fletcher (London: Routledge and Kegan Paul, 1967), p. 130.

22. S.T. Coleridge, *Collected Letters*, edited by E.L. Griggs (Oxford at the Clarendon Press, 1959), IV, p. 545.

23. Here, though, I have to admit that she may have a good excuse in terms of my own deployment of the German Romantics. According to Kant, pre-fall man is "wholly absorbed by the enjoyment of the present" – and one consequence of the fall is the fall into history, "the conscious *expectation* of the future" (K. 58, 57, his emphasis).

24. Myra Jehlen, *American Incarnation: The Individual, The Nation, and the Continent* (Cambridge & London: Harvard University Press, 1986), p. 174.

25. I do not mean to suggest that the Fortunate Fall is to be seen as in any way an exclusively Protestant story. Lovejoy ("Milton") makes it quite clear that the idea had a long and thus necessarily Catholic history. On the other hand, nor do I want to imply that the German version is not in many ways heavily dependent on a Protestant tradition.

## 9 THE ELIXIR OF LIFE MANUSCRIPTS

1. Nina Baym, *The Shape of Hawthorne's Career* (Ithaca and London: Cornell University Press, 1976), pp. 264, 258.

2. David Howard, "The Fortunate Fall and *The Marble Faun*," in Ian Fletcher (ed.), *Romantic Mythologies* (London: Routledge & Kegan Paul, 1967), p. 99; "*The Blithedale Romance* and a Sense of Revolution," in David Howard, J. Lucas, J. Goode, *Tradition and Tolerance in Nineteenth-Century Fiction* (London: Routledge & Kegan Paul, 1966), p. 63.

3. Ralph Waldo Emerson, "Self-Reliance," *The Works*, Riverside Edition (London: George Routledge & Sons, 1903), II, p. 52.

4. Mircea Eliade, *The Forge and the Crucible*, trans. S. Corrin (New York and Evanston: 1971), p. 169.

5. "Alchemy and Hawthorne's *Elixir of Life Manuscripts*," *Journal of American Studies*, 2, no. 3 (Autumn 1988).

6. Paul Taylor, "The Old House of Games," *The Independent*, February 15, 1988, p. 13.

7. Eliade, *Forge and Crucible*, p. 172.

8.       He gave a history of the long dynasty of the Alchemists, who spent so many
ages in quest of the universal solvent, by which the Golden Principle might be
elicited from all things vile and base. Aylmer appeared to believe, that, by the
plainest scientific logic, it was altogether within the limits of possibility to
discover this long-sought medium; but, he added, a philosopher who should
go deep enough to acquire the power, would attain too lofty a wisdom to
stoop to the exercise of it. Not less singular were his opinions in regard to the
Elixir Vitae. He more than intimated, that it was his option to concoct a liquid
that should prolong life for years – perhaps interminably – but that it would
produce a discord in nature, which all the world, and chiefly the quaffer of the
immortal nostrum, would find cause to curse.
There are a number of other parallels between "The Birth-Mark" and
Septimius's quest – most obviously the choice of the latter half of the 18th
century – in "those days, when the comparatively recent discovery of
electricity, and other kindred mysteries of nature, seemed to open into the
region of miracle.                                               (T&S, 772, 764).

9. There is, however, one point where Septimius briefly returns to the figure of the
circle – when he answers Sybil's query as to why the potion is so cold: "I know not,
unless because endless life goes round the circle and meets death, and is just the same
with it" (XIII, 186).

10. J.D. Wallace, "Immortality in Hawthorne's *Septimius Felton*," *Studies in American
Fiction*, 14, part 1 (1986), 26.

11.      It is not in our power, nor in our wish, to preserve the original form, nor yet
the spirit, of a production which is better lost to the world; because it was the
expression of a human being originally greatly gifted, and capable of high
things, but gone utterly astray, partly by its own subtility, partly by yielding to
the temptations of the lower part of its nature, by yielding the spiritual to a
keen sagacity of lower things, until it was quite fallen; and yet fallen in such a
way that it seemed, not only to itself, but to mankind, not fallen at all, but wise
and good, and fulfilling all the ends of intellect in such a life as ours, and
proving moreover that earthly life was good, and all that the development of
our nature demanded.                                               (XIII, 103–4)

12. Delia Bacon, *The Philosophy of the Plays of Shakespere Unfolded With a Preface by
Nathaniel Hawthorne* (Boston: Ticknor and Fields, 1857), pp. ix–x, xi.

13. Thomas Fuller, *The Worthies of England*, edited and with an introduction by John
Freeman (London: Allen and Unwin, 1952), pp. 506–7.

14. Quoted in Betty Jo Teeter Dobbs, *The Foundations of Newton's Alchemy or "The
Hunting of the Green Lyon"* (Cambridge: Cambridge University Press, 1975), p. 15.
Arthur Edward Waite, *Lives of the Alchemystical Philosophers* (London: George
Redway, 1888), p. 17.

15. Elias Ashmole, *Theatrum Chemicum Britannicum: Containing Severall Poeticall Piecdes
of our Famous English Philosophers, who have written the Hermetique Mysteries in their
owne Ancient Language*. A Reprint of the London Edition, 1652, with a new
Introduction by Alan G. Debus (New York and London: Johnson Reprint
Corporation, 1967), p. 437.

16. Yvor Winters, *In Defense of Reason* (London: Routledge & Kegan Paul, 1960),
p. 170.

17. Thomas Jefferson, *Writings* (Library of America, 1984), p. 176.

18. Herbert Leventhal, *In the Shadow of the Enlightenment: Occultism and Renaissance*

*Science in Eighteenth-Century America* (New York: New York University Press, 1976), p. 233. He also has a very nice quotation from Cotton Mather's *Christian Philosopher* on the concept of the chain of being:

> There is a *Scale of Nature*, wherein we pass regularly and proportionably from a *Stone* to a *Man*, the Faculties of the Creatures in their *various Classes* growing stil brighter and brighter, and more capacious, till we arrive to those noble ones which are found in the *Soul* of MAN; and yet MAN is, as one well expresses it, *but the Equator of the Universe.*
>
> It is a just View which Dr. *Grew* had of *the World*, when he came to this Determination: "As there are several Orders of *animated Body* before we come to *Intellect*, so it must needs be that there are several Orders of *imbodied Intellect* before we come to pure Mind."
>
> It is likely that the transition from *Human* to *perfect* MIND is made by a *gradual Ascent*; there may be *Angels* Faculties may be as much superior to *ours*, as ours may be to those of a *Snail* or a *Worm*.
>
> By and by we may arrive to *Minds* divested of all *Body*, excellent *Minds*, which may enjoy the Knowledge of Things by a more *immediate Intuition*, as well as without any inclination to any *moral evil.*" (p. 220)

19. Why Hawthorne should have experimented with a different name at this stage I do not know – but, since I attach some importance to the change from Felton to Norton, I feel a moral obligation to offer what I confess is a somewhat speculative explanation of the significance of the new name. The historical commentary in the Ohio edition tells us that the name was "derived from a prominent Salem court and customs official of the seventeenth century" – but, alas, no reference is given (XIII, 568). I would like to suggest that, even if there was a seventeenth-century Hilliard Veren, there are other reasons why the name seemed appropriate. Surely the first Hilliard that would come to anyone's mind is the brilliant Elizabethan miniaturist. He was the son of a goldsmith – and it is "clear that Hilliard practiced alchemy, an obvious sideline of the goldsmiths' craft in the Elizabethan age and one especially tempting to the speculative and enquiring mind of the Queen's limner" (Erna Auerbach, *Nicholas Hilliard* [London: Routledge & Kegan Paul, 1961], p. 33). "Veren" is – surely – very obviously an anagram for "Never" – implying that our hero will never succeed. Accept the anagram, and we have H.N. Transpose those letters and we have, of course, Nathaniel Hawthorne. And I think there's at least one other example that, if it does not invite, is at least available for this kind of speculation:

> Something dropt out of the envelope and fell rattling upon the floor; he picked it up, and found it to be a small antique key, curiously wrought, and with intricate words, and seeming to be of silver. In the handle of the key, there was a sort of open-work tracery, which made the cypher H.N. in old English letters. Septimius looked at this key, with great minuteness, before proceeding further, wondering where on earth could be the key-hole that suited it, and to what sort of a treasure it was the passport. (XIII, 287)

One would expect the letters to be described as a monogram rather than as a "cypher." The choice of the word "cypher" invites the reader to de-cipher (why else choose the letter "H"? – which is relevant to nothing else and nobody in the text), to transpose those letters and read Nathaniel Hawthorne (again) – as one key to unlock one small treasure of the text. Or have I been reading too much about the secret writings of the alchemists? The suspicion that I may have been seduced by Ashmole *et al.* makes me confine this to the decent obscurity of a footnote.

20. "And . . . there might be an intensity of life, into the few moment of which would be compressed all that heat, vigor, earnestness, which would have been thinly scattered over such an interminableness as he had dreamed of" (XIII, 448). That is Septimius – here is Marvell:

> Let us roll all our strength, and all
> Our Sweetness, up into one Ball,
> And tear our Pleasures with rough strife,
> Through the Iron gates of Life.
> Thus, though we cannot make our Sun
> Stand still, yet we will make him run.

But, of course, Marvell is talking about love – and Septimius is considering "how easy . . . to find a battle field to die on" and the intensity of life *might* come from "the sweet, exhilarating sense of living, with his fellow men – the free life of humanity, risking all, sacrificing all for the triumph of his country, and dying in the attainment of victory for her . . . (XIII, 448). America, the States, however metaphorically feminine, can hardly be equated with a coy mistress.

21. Herman Melville, *Pierre, Israel Potter, The Confidence-Man, Tales, etc.*, Library of America, 1984, p. 1,158.

22. P.B. Shelley, *The Complete Works*, edited by R. Ingpen and W.E. Peck (London and New York: Ernest Benn & Gordian Press, 1965), VII, p. 154.

23. Marjorie Levinson, *The Romantic Fragment Poem* (Chapel Hill and London: University of North Carolina Press, 1986), p. 31.

24. Melville, *Pierre etc.*, p. 1,159.

# Index